Bubbleheads, SEALs and Wizards: America's Scottish bastion in the Cold War

Bubbleheads, SEALs and Wizards:

America's Scottish Bastion in the Cold War

David Mackay

Whittles Publishing

Whittles Publishing Ltd.,
Dunbeath,
Caithness, KW6 6EG,
Scotland, UK

www.whittlespublishing.com

ISBN 978-184995-554-6

Printed and bound by CPI Group (UK) Ltd, Croydon, CR0 4YY

*This work is dedicated to my Mum and Dad,
and my wonderful family, especially Barbara.*

Contents

Author's note

The responses by American people in their interviews with the author have been transcribed in US English; US English is used in the extracts from US written sources, and in all the US names and titles.

In order to protect the interviewees, many of their names have been changed.

As there are inevitably numerous abbreviations, initialisms and acronyms, there is a list of them and their meanings at the end of the book.

The author has made extensive efforts to trace and acknowledge image sources but correction of any details is welcome for amendment in future printings.

PREFACE

During the Cold War, the United States had a significant military presence in Scotland.

But this has been overlooked by academics and appears to have little place in the folk memory of the nation. This narrative will reveal the crucial Cold War story of the essential work required there to maintain peace. This is its history as told by those who served at the time. This work offers a global perspective on the American military presence in Scotland during the Cold War. It deals with matters of immense international importance.

The principal Cold War threat to Scotland's security came from the Soviet Union, despite the well-meaning claims advanced by left-wing observers, many of whom were members of the Communist Party of Great Britain and other Marxist groups. But Russia was our enemy; it was not our friend. The much-lauded fraternal ties between Russia and Scotland amounted to a Russian appreciation of the poet Robert Burns and a fondness for Scotch whisky.

If the Soviet Union had taken action against the United States, Scotland would have been rapidly involved as a Soviet target of necessity. Both superpowers were fully aware of its essential military importance. Control of the vital ground of Scotland was essential for both. Geography and technological limitations had produced this perfect situation. For 30 years Scotland was the keystone in Washington's early Cold War strategy.

This account covers nitty-gritty, repetitive daily tasks, not high diplomacy. It tells the tale of the American, and the British, individuals who took part in this historic episode. They did not decide policy. They got on with making the system work. Their training was long and difficult, their working conditions were arduous. Teamwork was the key.

Scotland was a centre of US strategic operations during the Cold War. There were six significant bases in Scotland. The US stationed its first nuclear-armed submarine squadron in the Holy Loch, a short branch of the Firth of Clyde, and established large SIGINT (signals intelligence) gathering operations at three Scottish sites: Kirknewton, Thurso and Edzell. In addition, the first major American intelligence-gathering activity of the early Cold War took place in Scotland, at Evanton. The airfields at Prestwick and Machrihanish were part of the strategic reinforcement plan for Western Europe.

This American presence represented the largest peacetime number of foreign military personnel in Scotland's history. There were more American military personnel based in Scotland during the Cold War than in either the First World War or the Second. Historians have pointed out that these bases were in the UK principally for US security purposes.[1]

Scotland's importance to the United States' strategic defence plan was due solely to its geopolitical location. Because of the technological development of the Soviet Navy under Admiral Gorshkov, the UK became an 'essential factor in the home defence of the USA'.[2] The UK could gather intelligence on the Soviet fleet in northern waters. This produced a requirement to locate intelligence-gathering stations in Scotland.

As a consequence of the limited range of the U.S. Navy's submarine-launched ballistic missiles, a forward operating base much closer to Russia was essential. Such a base would be within missile range of its Russian targets, and any Soviet retaliatory nuclear strikes against it would not impact continental USA.

Scotland was the perfect fit for America's perimeter defence policy. Scotland would take the initial Soviet attack. This would give Washington additional time to increase its readiness and take steps to de-escalate tension. The Soviet missiles had a limited range but could easily reach Scotland.

And this military power was delivered by the individual American and British sailors, airmen, coast guards and others – not by high-level arm twisters deep in government circles. All military action is carried out by individuals, not governments; governments set the policy, which is then delivered by individuals.

The American military personnel in Scotland operated to a high standard of professionalism. But apart from those at Holy Loch, most of them had no idea of the perilous situation their presence had created for the local Scottish communities. From those Americans' point of view, they were defending the United States and Scotland was part of the process.

It was when the Cuban Missile Crisis arose that the destruction of the Scottish bases by Soviet missiles was seen as a realistic prospect. However, the U.S. Navy had prepared their plans for such a situation, and their submarine tender (i.e., supply depot) ship, which until then had been moored in the Holy Loch, departed for a safer mooring.[3]

This book provides an important chapter to the conventional Cold War narrative. Although the standard storyline stresses the unequal nature of this partnership, with Britain gathering a few crumbs from the mighty USA, in Scotland the United States desperately needed the assistance provided by Britain.

However, the American facilities were foreign military bases on Scottish soil. Their activities and impact on the local community need to be examined. This presence generated a series of questions which will be considered in the narrative.

- Why was it considered important to base American strategic defence facilities in Scotland during the Cold War?
- How did the US operate its critical national defensive facilities in Scotland?
- What were its principal targets? Were they Soviet military and naval activities – or did they also provide access to private, commercial and diplomatic sources?

- Was the collected intelligence information of use to the United States?
- Why did the United States close its Scottish bases if they were considered essential?
- Did the presence of these bases bring additional military threats to Scotland?

INTRODUCTION

In 1962 Scotland was at the epicentre of the Cold War's most terrifying episode – the Cuban Missile Crisis. Conventional history concentrates on the White House and Kennedy's advisers. Books have been written, films have been made – but what has never been reported until now is that Kennedy's success was greatly aided by the US military units based in Scotland. They provided him with accurate intelligence and the immense firepower of America's only SSBN fleet. This was a powerful combination.

JFK sent his closest adviser to the Holy Loch. His mission was to check the war-readiness of America's only nuclear missile submarine squadron. His report was chilling but reassuring – the submarines were ready for war. Invisible and lethal, they were a direct threat to Russia.

Kennedy was working on data from radio spy stations, two of which were in Scotland. They tracked the Russian submarines and ships moving towards Cuba. The enemy was under continuous scrutiny, and there was nowhere to hide.

Scotland's role was the game changer. Through it, nuclear mayhem was kept at bay. Cities were not incinerated, and then as the world relaxed the Scottish bases remained relentlessly alert until the end of the Cold War.

From 1952 Scotland had become an offshore military installation for the United States. But this American presence thrust Scotland into the forefront of the Cold War. The American bases (and Scottish citizens) became targets for Soviet nuclear weapons and ground force attacks. The Russians mounted a huge spying operation, and the KGB infiltrated Scotland. The CIA and MI5 countered these agents, and Scotland entered White House and Kremlin discussions.

These were exciting times. For more than 30 years, young Americans crossed the Atlantic Ocean to serve their country. They bonded themselves to Scotland in a bold fashion – they even designed their own tartans. They wore them with pride and still do. Their Cold War history is Scottish history. This is their story.

1 Early days

– Ike's tartan spy balloons

The Cold War was hardly under way when the United States made use of Evanton airfield near Inverness for the most bizarre event. There were no glistening submarines, no towering radio masts, only an empty airfield populated by a few trucks. But it was the scene of an amazing and surreal adventure …

American strategy

In the 1950s the Americans desperately needed information about the Soviet Union's military activities, and the U.S. Air Force had been developing balloon reconnaissance systems since the end of the Second World War. The Air Force collection of Russian landmass photography was out of date and incomplete. This created a large hole in the intelligence picture. Information was essential, as it would reveal any strategic military activity that the Russians were undertaking. A solution had to be found. Aircraft reconnaissance missions – ferret flights – could only observe the periphery of the target area. Russia's interior remained unseen.[4]

There were a number of possible solutions, but the favourite involved the use of balloons – with mixed success.

Project Genetrix became the code name for a top secret American airborne spy programme. Its mission was to obtain photographic and electronic information about Russia and its allies. Huge balloons would carry cameras across the Soviet Union on the winter jetstream. They would cross most of the Russian land mass, and once safely outside Soviet airspace the cameras would be cut free of the balloons by means of coded radio signals. As the cameras plunged earthwards by parachute, they would be caught in mid-air by specially equipped recovery planes.[5]

By the end of 1954 the U.S. Air Force (USAF) and the CIA had agreed on the planned use of spy balloons. The USAF had test-launched over 500 reconnaissance balloons as part of Project Moby Dick, the prototype programme. By the end of the year the USAF had drawn up an outline operational concept for all future important reconnaissance programmes. Balloons were now in the mainstream programme.[6]

But the United States could not carry out Project Genetrix from its own soil. It needed the diplomatic and military support of its NATO allies. Most of the balloons would have to be released in Western Europe to catch the jetstream winds that would carry them high over Russian territory.

The British Government was wary about the project. Prime Minister Anthony Eden was always nervous about intelligence activities. He believed Genetrix could give the Soviets a political stick to beat the Western allies. As it turned out, Eden was correct, and this was to prove the Achilles heel of the project.[7]

Eisenhower was also wary, as Secretary Dulles stated: 'the President asked me, in putting it up to Eden, to make clear that the President was not trying to pressure him. I gathered that the President has not much enthusiasm for the project'.[8]

The concept now moved into the operational development stage. By October 1954 the RAF and USAF Europe had discussed possible British bases. Potential sites were identified in Scotland at RAF Kinloss, RAF Edzell, RAF Tain and RAF Wick. Consideration was also given to the Orkney Isles and Shetland Isles.[9]

Although Project Genetrix was only finally agreed at the end of December 1955, the USAF had been on the ground in Scotland since late 1954. The military planners always carried out a range of concurrent activities, including reconnaissance, prior to operations. The Commander Third Air Force USAF proposed that a mission team should visit the UK to carry out 'an indoctrination and training visit ... to become familiar with conditions at selected launching sites'. In July 1955 this visit was carried out by the Commander First Air Division.[10]

This produced a positive report, and follow-up visits were planned. The logistics of Moby Dick shipments to RAF Edzell were discussed with the special weather officer at RAF Edzell. The concept was regarded as feasible, as the port facilities at Dundee were adequate. A back-up plan considered using the Port of Leith at Edinburgh, or Port Glasgow if larger vessels were required.[11]

Scotland's location was of strategic importance, and it was confirmed as a launch site. Initially it was proposed that all balloons should be launched from Scotland, but this was changed as 'surface weather in Scotland was expected to be unsuitable for launch activities a large part of the time'. Also, Scotland's westerly location added another day of balloon travel before photographs of interest could be captured. However, it was decided 'to retain one site in Scotland as a matter of political expediency'. This highlighted the importance of American access to British support. Scotland was the strategically vital ground required for this.[12]

Before getting permission to send American spy balloons across Russia, the USAF had to prove that this could physically be achieved. Project Grayback was launched in December 1954 to trial the various selected launch sites. Eight balloons were launched from RAF Edzell, as it was on Scotland's east coast. But none of these floated across Russia as anticipated. Instead they headed south to Africa. The trial was repeated in January 1955, but all of these balloons failed to launch. Edzell was dropped as a potential site, and attention was switched to the Royal Navy air station at Evanton, near Inverness. This was eventually chosen because of the nearby Invergordon docks, which could handle the transhipment of the large amount of equipment needed for the project.[13]

More than a year's planning had gone into the project by the time the mission was formally approved, in March 1955. The Strategic Air Command (SAC) was placed in charge. Project Genetrix was now a reality. The mission of the Genetrix programme was described as 'SAC through its 1st Air Division (Meteorological Survey) … tasked with using WS-119L to obtain photographic and electronic reconnaissance of the Soviet Socialist Republics and its satellites.'[14]

C.D. Gildenberg was a scientist who worked on the balloon programme. He described the balloons as huge, with diameters of 300 feet and a flaccid length of 430 feet. He noted that they were designed for cruising in the stratosphere, but that the balloons changed colour at high altitudes during sunrises and sunsets, while the Earth below was almost dark. These characteristics equated to a superb UFO simulator: 'They were inflated with hydrogen for additional lifting power. The flammability didn't matter, in fact it was all for the good: if a helium balloon was hit by a shell, it would simply leak and drift to ground, where it could be captured, but if a hydrogen balloon was hit, it would light up and crash, hopefully shattering the gondola into bits.'[15]

The silvery balloons were the largest ever developed, and the envelope could easily be seen in good weather. But the balloon material was hard to track with radar, and at their planned cruising altitude they were invulnerable to Russian air defences. However, if they flew beneath that altitude, they could be shot down by Soviet planes.[16]

One disadvantage was that when viewed from a distance they resembled flying saucers. Also, they carried a gondola that weighed half a ton, and its packaging harness produced a radar signal which assisted the Soviet air defence system. The Russians had liberated German Wullenweber radio masts and equipment after the Second World War as reparations. This equipment, also used by the Americans for High Frequency Direction Finding (HFDF), was able to locate the balloons and direct the air defence fighters.[17]

The Evanton balloons were forecast to take seven days to fly across Russia on their mission. The gondola would carry a radio beacon which would be picked up by American radio tracking sites which had been set up at Guam, the Philippines, Midway, Okinawa and Alaska. A timer would be set to activate the beacon after the balloon should have crossed out of Russian air space and be over the Pacific Ocean. This was the designated recovery area.

The recovery aircraft patrolled the area, and when a team spotted a balloon – the balloons would come in from a range of launch sites – they transmitted a signal to tell it to drop the gondola for retrieval. The gondola would parachute down, releasing bundles of aluminium strips, 'chaff,' to make it more visible on the recovery team's radar. Their specially modified C-119J transport plane would then snatch the payload at a height beneath 30,000 feet and reel it in until handlers could wrestle it into the cargo hold of the aircraft. During the project 40 payloads were recovered in this fashion.[18]

The cameras were carried in a package inside the gondola and could operate across distances of 50 miles from the balloon. The special, radiation-resistant, film could take 500 pictures. The cameras were operated by a timing device which did not activate until, it was forecast, the balloon would have flown a long distance from its launch site. This was to avoid photographs being taken of friendly NATO territory.[19]

The gondola was about the size of a refrigerator and was heavily insulated with Styrofoam, which protected it from the cold at high altitude. The foam also allowed the gondola to float if it came down in water. The gondola carried two reconnaissance cameras. These would take a shot every few minutes. If the balloon failed to make operating altitude within about a half-hour of launch the control system would drop the payload. The gondola was painted with international orange paint, and there were multilanguage placards, including in Russian, on its side, with a simple message for anyone who found it:

> NOTICE TO FINDER
>
> THIS EQUIPMENT IS
>
> NOT DANGEROUS

There were also return instructions – the package was to be taken to the nearest United States military location or embassy, and a monetary reward would be paid.[20]

Initially it had been proposed to use the balloons to carry nuclear weapons into Soviet territory, but this plan was abandoned as intercontinental ballistic missiles became viable. The final balloon plan had also included a SIGINT package, but this was not ready in time.

The troops required for the project were assembled. More than 3,000 USAF personnel were involved in the operational stage of the project. USAFSS 6926th Radio Squadron (Mobile) was assigned to track the balloons. USAF 28th Weather Squadron was based at RNAS Evanton for the operational period of Project Genetrix. The ground team was assembled – Detachment 4, 1110th Air Support Group (ASG), composed of 7 officers, 119 airmen and 5 civilians.[21]

To make the project a success, the ground and air crews had to be well trained. As spy balloons were a new concept, a concentrated training programme was held in late 1955. This had faced delays because of lack of approved equipment, but by the end of October that year the training was completed. The USAF did not rush the matter; they ensured that proper training and trials were held before moving to the launch phase; an example of the professional manner in which the United States military operated from Scotland.[22]

The most intriguing aspect was the recovery-phase training. The 456th Troop Carrier Wing USAF was assigned to the job. The planes were modified by the addition of a new rear door, nicknamed 'the beavertail', which was what enabled the crew to catch the camera package in mid-air while it descended by parachute.[23]

The C-119 became an aerial recovery vehicle, fitted with a grappling-hook system. Colonel Paul Worthman supervised this project: 'The Flying Boxcar had a 9 × 9-foot rear cargo bay. We fitted a clamshell device to open this, and it worked in actual operations.'

Initially, nobody knew how to launch these huge balloons. Detachment 4 at Evanton worked hard to master this skill during the second half of 1955. After trial and error, a workable system was discovered: the balloons were launched using a 2-ton, 6 × 6 heavy truck which carried a superimposed structure, the Fisher Launcher, from which the gondola was suspended and released. [24]

The launch process needed a team of 20 airmen and some basic equipment. Jack Foreman, a balloon launch team member, noted that this required the balloon envelope to be fed through a set of rollers. Brushes were then used to reduce static electricity, as it was inflated through a polyethylene tube connected to the top. The uninflated portion remained taut as it was fed through the rollers, and in this way only the inflated portion was allowed to rise as the gas was introduced. The roller method would become standard for inflating large polyethylene balloons.[25]

At the moment of launch, the gondola was driven on a truck underneath the ascending balloon to be connected to it, then the roller was released, and as the balloon swung vertically it smoothly lifted away with the gondola and its payload. The launch procedures had to be rehearsed in advance, and amendments were constantly made.

Chris Logren was a member of a balloon launch team and remembered the process: 'When a Genetrix balloon was inflated, the hydrogen lifting gas formed a small bubble at the top of the envelope. This gave the rest of the envelope a limp profile. However, as the balloon rose slowly, the gas expanded to fill the envelope. At this stage of flight, it did not resemble a balloon, and there were regular reports of UFO sightings.' [26]

There was great confidence in the ultimate success of Project Genetrix. It was expected that the balloons would drift for several days at various altitudes, moving eastward over Communist-controlled territory in Europe and descend into the planned recovery area in the Western Pacific. Preparations continued.

Everything was now ready for Project Genetrix, and the final approval to proceed came on 27 December 1955 at a White House conference involving the President and other key Administration principals.[27]

No solution had, however, been found to the concerns expressed by Britain's Prime Minister, Anthony Eden. This caused a postponement of the launch date; a short delay was agreed. But the requirement for more intelligence was urgent, and the project moved forward.[28]

A cover story was needed. This had to be credible, as huge balloons would be floating over the USSR and China. But Secretary of State Dulles warned President Eisenhower that 'This cover will probably not fool the Soviets, but it will create a situation such that they cannot take any very great offense publicly.'

The CIA, masters of misinformation, ran the story. The President agreed to how the operation was to be promulgated; the United States would claim that the operations were part of the International Geophysical Survey and would map cloud formations (which was, in fact, all that most of the photographs would show). To support this story, the suffix 'Meteorological Survey' was added to the 1st Air Division's title.[29]

It was now time for action. Official permission had been received. The cover story was released. Gildenberg noted how this was managed: 'The first step before beginning the Genetrix launches was to put the cover plan into action. Orders were issued to start, in early January, Operation White Cloud, whose objective was to launch balloons from sites in Okinawa, Hawaii and Alaska. Carrying out the two programs at the same time, SAC sought to blur the boundaries between them. The first balloon was launched from Kadena AB[1] on January 9, receiving press coverage on which USAF informed that the prototype Moby Dick program was being extended to Europe and the Far East, and the balloons would transport meteorological instruments and cameras to photograph clouds.'

Preparations in Scotland

The movement of the balloon equipment to Evanton had been a major logistics operation. When the Genetrix equipment arrived in Scotland it was a dramatic event for the local area. The USAF and RAF personnel had already arrived at the airfield. Invergordon docks, 10 miles away, were approved for handling the Genetrix cargo. Invergordon had been regularly used by the Royal Navy, so it could easily cope with the Genetrix shipments. By October 1955 more than 500 balloons had been offloaded there under the curious gaze of local inhabitants.

As the balloon components began to arrive, schoolboy Bill Grant was one of many fascinated observers. He remembered when the Americans arrived and transported material from Invergordon Pier to Evanton: 'This involved a huge number of trucks belting down the High Street for hours on end. At the height of this activity, I was in Lofty McFarlane's class, which was in the classroom that butted onto the High Street, and the building shook with the vibration of the traffic. I guess these goings-on were related to some Cold War panic about the USSR.'

Hundreds of tons of Genetrix cargo were unloaded and stored along the dockside. It covered an area larger than a football pitch, and the local people were intrigued about its destination. American military police arrived and set up traffic control points around the docks, and a fleet of military trucks appeared on the scene. Many small boys watched the proceedings.

Roy Meikle was a ten-year old growing up in Invergordon when the American 'invasion' occurred. He was a front-line witness to the exciting events in the town.[30] He can still remember the lorries coming out of the dockyard: 'At that time there were huge buildings, with the main entrance set back some 50 yards amongst them. I can remember the American military police standing at the end of an alleyway, guiding these huge lorries on to the high street and south to Evanton.' But his fondest memory was of the military police handing out gum and chocolate. For a small boy in post-war Scotland, this was amazing. He also remembered that cigarettes were being handed out to the bigger boys.

Another schoolboy was Ronald Stewart: 'I was very young at that time, still in primary school, and had little idea of what was going on, although I do remember the US ship berthing at the dockyard pier in Invergordon, the unloading and transporting of the cargo to Evanton on US military vehicles. Although interested in shipping, I failed to record the name of the ship.'

The large military trucks that moved the Genetrix equipment were highly visible, and attracted the attention of curious local boys such as Hamish Watson: 'I watched the American trucks going down the high street, and Sandy Ross and I got a lift to Alness on a couple of occasions.'

---

1 A major US air base on Okinawa.

The American descent on Evanton was keenly chronicled in eight-year-old Alan Kinghorn's diary. He lived on the Novar estate close to RNAS Evanton, and every morning he caught the bus to school from the base guardroom. He remembers that the base was guarded by Air Ministry Police.

He was precise about the men who came to Evanton: 'The Americans arrived in the summer of 1955 and were gone in the late spring of 1956, approximately 11 months. I made notes in my schoolboy diary at the time. We were told at the time it was the 28th Weather Squadron USAF, who I believe were based in Uxbridge, just outside London. I tried contacting them a few years ago but got no reply. Probably they were not involved – just another cover story.'

The Scottish media had been given an early indication of the project, and published the first UK information in the *Aberdeenshire Evening Express* on Wednesday, 10 August 1955:

Weather Research Balloon Station for Evanton … The R.A.F. and the U.S.A.F. announce that a small research station will be set up this month near Evanton. Ross-shire, for the purpose of launching high altitude meteorological balloons.

The official press release sounded reasonable, and it was accepted at face value.[31] No prying questions were asked. Scotland had recently survived the Second World War and was grateful for all defence assistance offered.

The press release contained a full description of the activities planned:

A research station from which meteorological balloons will be released to explore atmospheric conditions at altitudes above 40,000 feet is being set up near Evanton, it was announced this week. The station will be jointly manned by 150 personnel of the Royal Air Force and the United States Air Force, who will continue earlier studies into wind patterns, air turbulence, cloud formation, and the effect of cosmic radiation and other atmospheric phenomena at altitudes above 40,000 feet. Balloons used in the studies will carry meteorological and radio equipment which will transmit data to ground monitoring stations.

It sounded like a sensible scientific project. No mention was made of cameras or crossing Russia and China. These, however, were the intended target areas. Other countries such as North Korea would provide opportunity targets.[32]

The balloons had now been successfully described as part of a weather research programme. Significantly, this was a true story – but it related to another set of balloons, smaller ones, used for this purpose. At high altitudes, these balloons could resemble small red discs and had frequently initiated many flying saucer stories following their use in the United States. They would also be used at Evanton.

The Royal Navy had agreed that USAF could use their airfield, but they had been kept in the dark about Genetrix's real intentions. The Admiralty was totally unaware of the true reason for the balloon flights; the project had been presented to the navy officers as merely a meteorological study. Moreover, inside the RAF itself only high-ranking officers were aware of the true nature of the project.[33]

Many other NATO countries were also kept in the dark. Canadian airmen at Metz, France, knew nothing about its true purpose, and made innocent log-book entries noting: 'the intended release of many meteorological balloons.'

The first Project Genetrix balloons launched on 10 January 1956. While launches were under way in Turkey and West Germany, Evanton was at a standstill. The UK Air Ministry had not been given the go-ahead order. The American Embassy was puzzled at the lack of activity, and USAF officers rang their RAF counterparts.[34]

It was an internal cock-up. The MOD had failed to notify the Air Ministry that the Evanton launches could proceed, and apologies were given by embarrassed British officials. Orders were issued, and Detachment 4 swung into action. The first Evanton balloons soared skywards on 11 January 1956.

Wayne Grover was a Canadian radio operator who witnessed the balloon launches: 'I remember the balloon launches well. There were not many, but I saw a few during the daylight. It was a simple operation, using a few vehicles and a dozen or so men who helped lay out the envelope and fill it with gas. When it lifted, it was very long and silvery. As it ascended, it grew in size but was out of sight before it fully inflated, due to there being less atmospheric pressure at altitude. A truck carrying the package in its bed followed while the balloon lifted and took it from the bed at wind speed. It rose slowly and disappeared in a matter of minutes. We tracked it on radar, as it generally went east or north-easterly. The launches took place during the months of January and February 1956, and then – just as quickly as they had started – the launches stopped. I do not recall there being any special security involved with the launches.' [35]

At Evanton many local boys had eye-witness memories of the balloon launches. David Fraser was a schoolboy in Cullicudden, a tiny village 5 miles from Evanton. Whilst walking to school every day, he saw many balloons being prepared and then lifting off. He remembered being told that they were weather research balloons: 'I remember the launch sequence. For some time, they were inflated from a vehicle parked alongside. From my recall they were tethered for a while before being released. At some point, and I can't recall why, we were given some of the silky-like balloon material. It lay around for years.' [36]

A fellow pupil was Ken Munro. He was more fortunate, as he actually witnessed balloons rising into the sky: 'I was a pupil at Cullicudden primary school on the Black Isle opposite Evanton, and I have a clear memory of them rising vertically, and looking over from the school at them. I remember stories that a bounty was paid for the notification of stray balloons landing in a farmer's fields, and it was generally a hot topic of conversation at the time.' [37]

Callum McIver's father was the minister of Alness Parish. The Manse was about a mile and half from the airfield as the crow flies. It looked across Alness Bay and had a clear view of the runway: 'I had a direct view of the airfield and I saw these huge balloons being launched, and we were told that they were weather balloons. The balloons were large and went straight up. They were 60 feet anyway, and maybe more.'

One day Hamish Watson saw a large balloon in the local area. He assumed that it was probably part of a larger operation: 'This balloon we saw very visible on a clear day, hard to estimate its altitude, possibly 3–5,000 feet. It would be hazardous to aviation!'

The launches had been observed more than 50 miles from Evanton, and reports appeared in the *Aberdeenshire Evening News* on Friday, 13 January 1956:

MYSTERY BALLOONS – The mystery balloons reported at Elgin and Wick yesterday were the first of a number set off from the new meteorological station operated by the U S. Air Force at Evanton, Ross-shire. Several were seen over Alness yesterday.

After the first week, the weather stepped in to sabotage the project, and Evanton was seriously affected by winter wind and snow. The severe icing conditions meant that launches could not be made until the weather improved, so the planned schedule was not achieved. In addition, Evanton had further launch restrictions imposed by the British Government. This significantly reduced its productivity as a launch site.[38]

Week 2 brought more bad news. From a distance, the huge plastic balloons resembled flying saucers, but even worse, it had turned out that their camera package produced a radar signal. They were no longer invisible. The balloon apparatus contained a steel rod, 91 cm long. In radar terms, it lit up like a beacon. Soviet radar was able to detect balloons and track them as the altitude of the balloon sunk to lower levels at night. This meant that in the mornings they were significantly below their operational ceiling. The MiG fighters were awaiting them.[39]

The Soviet air defences improved their performance against the silvery invaders. They recovered from their initial shock and began to shoot down many of them. This drastically reduced the number of balloons which reached the recovery zone above the Pacific Ocean.

Beacons for the balloons launched from Evanton were programmed to become live after 90 hours' flight, the timespan in which the balloon should have flown across Russia. But after the early overall disappointing results, this time was increased to 108 hours and finally to 120 hours by the close of the project.[40]

Once a gondola was safely out of Soviet territory the recovery phase swung into action. As soon as the homing beacon was detected, a Flying Boxcar headed towards its location while the crew would open the clamshell doors and run out the long metal poles used for trapping the package. Once these were firmly fixed, the aircraft had to home into the target and climb above it.

As the distance decreased, the pilot would drop altitude and aim to fly 50 feet above the parachute. The aircraft would pass directly above the target, and the trailing wire would make contact. The parachute would collapse across the metal poles – success! However, the C-119L was a slow aircraft. It had to adopt a position ahead of the balloon and then attempt the recovery. The recovery process would start at 20,000 feet, and two aircraft were involved. They made continuous passes until the balloon was successfully captured. The air-to-air recovery activity was dependent on daylight and favourable flying conditions.[41]

The Flying Boxcar was not a popular aircraft. Official records show that in the 1950s sometimes a month did not pass without a C-119 crash. James Harvey Knauss was a pilot during

Project Genetrix, and rated the aircraft 'one of the world's worst airplanes. As you can tell I do not have anything good to say about the thing. But it is history.' [42]

Jim Fowler, a former member of the 456th Troop Carrier Wing, revealed the high level of security attached to the Genetrix project: 'Our unit transferred to Charleston AFB, SC, as part of a Troop Carrier Wing, and started training for a future role as an aerial recovery unit. Very few of the airmen knew about Project Genetrix.' [43]

Their aircraft were modified for the new project. This involved major changes – engine modifications, hydraulic systems to handle the recovery poles, winch reels for the recovery of parachutes and their packages; then long-range fuel tanks were added, and special rear doors to replace the old-style clamshell doors. These new doors, the beavertails, were operable during flight; the bottom door surface raised into the upper part of the door, allowing the recovery procedure to take place.

Fowler recalled the training activity: 'We had good pilots, but there were mishaps such as getting too close to a parachute and catching it with an engine and prop rather than the poles … This caused damage to the engine and the prop, not to mention a minor laundry problem for those on board!'

Pulling the package into the aircraft was a difficult process. One of the Boxcar aircrew, Chuck Dillner, was a polehandler: 'My role was to deploy the poles, ropes and hooks from a C-119J to catch the packages released from balloons that had travelled over Russia.'

Another Boxcar crew member, Ralph Gourdan, was a pilot who remembered working on Project Genetrix: 'I started flying the C-119F in 1954 at Charleston, South Carolina. They were converted to J-models, and we went overseas to catch camera parachutes. The cameras were dropped from high-altitude balloons, and we caught them coming down by intercepting the parachutes.' [44]

Braveheart

On 1 February 1956 the crew of a beavertail C-119J aircraft spotted a balloon parachute at 18,000 feet above the Pacific Ocean. This balloon was Mission 50 and had been launched from Evanton. The pilot lined up his approach to close in and snatch it. The first run was a failure, and time was running out as the parachute continued its descent towards the water. The Flying Boxcar was cumbersome and the next run was crucial.

After a wide circuit, the plane lined up again and the skipper slowed the airspeed to a near-stall. This would give him the best chance of snagging the parachute. When the plane started to wobble the pilot nursed it to avoid an Underspeed.

He held firm to his line and the beavertail wire locked onto the target. The polehandlers hauled in the parachute's rigging lines and manhandled the gondola into the aircraft. The thumbs-up signal was given to the cockpit and the plane peeled away for home. The Evanton adventure had been vindicated.

This balloon had been launched on 25 January – Robert Burns Day, the Scottish national celebration. Perhaps that was its inspiration. When it was recovered, it had travelled 158 hours and 22 minutes from Evanton, and from the camera package 900 feet of film had been exposed, providing more than 1,000 useable photographs.[45]

And that was it. This was the only successful balloon from Evanton – a success rate of one per cent. The original plan to launch all balloons from Evanton would have been disastrous. But Scotland's strategic value had been demonstrated.[46]

The Russians' reaction to Genetrix was delayed and cautious. They had initially been surprised by the appearance of so many balloons, but after two weeks the Soviet Air Force had developed a procedure to deal with them. During the final week of January 1956 they started to shoot down many balloons, facilitated by the USAF plan limiting the balloon flights to a lower altitude.[47]

C.D. Gildenberg noted how the CIA controlled the cover story. They requested that the Genetrix team should not comment on the balloon/UFO reports. The CIA's strategy was to generate a UFO outbreak over the USA that would extend to the USSR when the Genetrix balloons arrived there. Ironically, the ploy initially worked, as the Soviet Air Force, unable intercept the first wave of the balloons and equally unable to admit that Russian skies had been invaded, allowed their public to play the UFO game. The strategy ended after a few leaking balloons were shot down and the payloads were exhibited.

Although the PVO Strany[2] aircraft were capable, they lacked the range and all-weather intercept capability. The Genetrix balloons, because of their small size and very high altitude, were difficult for the IA-PVO pilots to deal with. However, they quickly learned, and as their fighter aircraft could reach an altitude of 58,000 feet, and the PVO Strany network had radios which could cover the frequencies of the balloon beacon transmissions, they quickly began to shoot the balloons down.[48]

The Russians' confidence returning, they verbally attacked the United States Government. The Soviet foreign minister, Mikoyan, declared that this action represented: 'Gross violations of Soviet air space', and demanded that the US take 'measures for the prompt cessation of the impermissible activity of the American military organs.'[49]

American embarrassment grew when 50 balloons, along with their cameras, were put on public display in Moscow during February.[50] It turned out that the wrong call had been made to reduce the operational ceiling. As a consequence, as mentioned earlier, the balloons sank to a lower altitude in the cold evening air and were therefore within range of Soviet fighters and anti-aircraft artillery.

This ill-fated decision had been taken at the presidential meeting on 27 December 1955. The optimum altitude for the balloons had been debated. USAF commander General Twining had supported the balloons flying at a higher altitude. He declared: 'It is practically impossible to pick up these by radar. It is also practically impossible to intercept them – our Air Force has made extensive attempts to do so and has never succeeded.'

But the Deputy Director of the CIA, General Cabell, USAF, wanted to avoid a 'crash' radar situation caused by the appearance of many balloons at a high altitude: 'This would have shown up on radar. The Soviets would have been alerted and could have misinterpreted it as high-flying

---

2 PVO Strany – Soviet air defence force.

nuclear bombers.' He proposed that to prevent this situation the balloons should be kept below 50,000 feet. Cabell won the argument – but the outcome was disastrous.[51]

The Russian aircraft were also assisted by the poor operational performance of the balloons; the post-mission report acknowledged that they spent most of their flight at an even lower altitude than expected.[52]

In addition to the losses from Soviet interception, other balloons simply crashed to earth. Joel Carpenter was a USAF radio operator at Gardermoen in Norway. He recalled the frenzy caused by a stray balloon: 'On 3 February, a Genetrix launched from Gardermoen overflew Oslo. For the next two hours, as the gleaming ovoid drifted overhead, people in the Norwegian capital and its suburbs sent in a bevy of UFO reports.' There were also protests from Sweden, and 'falling objects' from the Gardermoen launch site, as well as injuries to a Norwegian boy from a downed gondola. There were also problems with tracking the gondola beacons.[53]

Pressure was now mounting on the United States Government.

The USAF was very enthusiastic about the project. They had been working on it for six years. Careers had been built on it, millions of dollars had been spent on it, and they wanted to get under way. But they had been trigger-happy and jumped the gun. President Eisenhower was caught off guard by the number of balloons released. This was not what he had expected. He had anticipated problems, though, and he was right.

Within days the UK Government ordered the launches to be slowed down. This, plus bad weather, meant that Evanton launched only a few more balloons.

Protests by other countries incensed Eisenhower. He was a successful general. He knew the importance of intelligence-collecting, and he also knew when to change the plan. It was presidential election year, and a red-faced president had no option but to halt the project.[54]

He swiftly concluded that it was time to move on, and by 6 February had ordered the halt of Project Genetrix: 'The balloons give more legitimate grounds for irritation than could be matched by the good obtained from them.'[55]

On the following day, Secretary of State Dulles announced that no more balloons would be launched. He did not apologise for the overflights. Despite this, USAF were keen to commence another balloon project within weeks. Eisenhower was typically blunt: 'I am not interested in any more balloons.'[56]

Once the halt order was given, the Americans swiftly dismantled the Evanton infrastructure, packed up all the remaining equipment and sent it to Invergordon docks. The personnel were loaded onto transport and disappeared.

Alan Kinghorn was surprised at the speed of the American departure: 'The Americans disappeared as swiftly as they had arrived. When the base closed in 1956, the Americans went home, and the base went to care and maintenance. The base was cleared in 1957 and sold in 1958 to the Novar Estate in Evanton.'

However, the Genetrix photographs were priceless. Although only 40 camera packages were recovered overall they produced almost 14,000 photographs. More than one million square miles of Russia and China were revealed to the US intelligence community.[57]

The spy balloons had uncovered two significant military locations. One was a vast nuclear refining facility in Soviet Siberia. (Its existence had been revealed by a defector, but its remote location meant it could not be easily investigated.) The second was a nuclear-related site in north-western China.

Project Genetrix coincided with the start of the U-2 spy plane flights. However, it almost caused them to be postponed, as the diplomatic uproar made it difficult for the United States to obtain overflying permission from friendly nations.

Genetrix's pioneering work produced the best photography of the Soviet Union at the time and provided the baseline for the future U-2 and satellite photography missions. Another benefit was the accurate record of high-altitude wind currents – information which helped to determine optimum flight paths for future U-2 overflights.[58]

In addition, the project inadvertently revealed extensive data about Soviet radar defences. As we have seen, because of the 91-cm bar on the gondola, the Soviets had been able to detect the balloons. But in doing so, the Soviets revealed their radar station locations. So this fortuitous effect of the small steel bar also provided intelligence information on Warsaw Pact radar networks, radar sets and ground-controlled interception techniques. This data revealed the altitude capability and tracking accuracy of Soviet radars, the methods used by the Warsaw Pact nations to notify each other of the balloon's passage, known as handing off – and, most importantly, the altitude at which Soviet aircraft could attain, recorded by their interceptions of the balloons. All essential material for future U-2 flights. This was an unforeseen bonus for the Americans.[59]

But fortune also favoured the Soviets, who carried out a clever piece of scientific scavenging, courtesy of the advanced American equipment: in 1959 they used the radiation-resistant camera film from the gondolas to take photographs of the other side of the moon from their space probe Luna 3.[60]

When Genetrix was halted, Evanton had launched 103 balloons. Only 60 of them entered Soviet air space. Apart from the sole survivor, all of the 60 either were shot down or crashed into the remote Siberian countryside. The remaining 43 did not manage to leave Scotland. Some crashed to the ground at the airfield. Alan Kinghorn has clear memories of these incidents: 'The launches were not always successful, with balloons flying north and crashing into the hills. Some did not even leave the Cromarty Firth area before landing in local farmers' fields. A reward was offered for information about these crash landings.'[61]

One of the USAF personnel, Mike Brady, a Milwaukee native, confirmed the low success rate of the Evanton launches: 'The work at Evanton was straightforward. We launched balloons on a regular basis, but a great many of them failed.' Apart from failing to launch, many of them crashed down in an 80-mile arc stretching from Dornoch through Invermoriston, Blairgowrie, Inverurie and Peterhead. But this failure rate was a normal occurrence at all the other Genetrix launch sites. Only 40 of those 43 balloons were successfully recovered.[62]

After six years of research and training, and a cost of almost US$1 billion at 2020 values, Project Genetrix – which had been intended to last five months – had lasted just 27 days.[63]

Thus ended that bizarre, secretive and controversial intelligence-gathering operation. Instead of achieving stealth, it was mired in constant global headlines.

Evanton's contribution was that single successful balloon, Mission 50. However, it produced photography covering the area of the USSR which included Kiyevka, Temirtau and Astakhov

Skoye; and North Korea, including Yonpo Airfield, Hungnam, Hongwŏn, Sinpo and some coastline. Mission 50 had produced the highest number of camera frames from any of the 516 Genetrix missions. All of these targets were important. Genetrix was successful and Scotland had played its part.[64]

A mystery remains

At Evanton there were two separate USAF units: Detachment 4's specific task was to launch the Genetrix balloons; but 28th Weather Squadron was in fact a bona fide weather unit. It had probably been posted to Evanton as part of the cover story, and continued its normal work. Its aircraft would climb to 10,000 feet and release weather balloons.

Some of these were found by locals such as Hamish Watson, who had been told they were for meteorology study: 'I came across them a few times on the ground, after failure at height I presume. On inspection there did not appear to be anything sinister about them, just a balloon. I do recall seeing them in the air when at school in Ardross. I walked around Ardross with my father … I think it was in the heather somewhere. This balloon was small – possibly 2 metres long – of nylon/ silk construction … nothing attached that I can remember. Doubt this small balloon was anything other than meteorologist experiments, as per what we were told at the time, I believe there were a few of the small balloons found around at the time.'

Other weather balloons were discovered by locals. Ronald Stewart recollected one odd memory: 'The local people got their hands on translucent red polythene, which I believe was 'liberated' from the operation. We had never seen such a material before and didn't quite know what to do with it, but it was a conversation piece.'

The balloons often fell to the seashore, as David Gow recounted: 'I lived for many years, between Alness RAF camp and Evanton RAF camp, on a farm called Ballachragan, not far from the sea. They used to fly planes from Evanton. There were times when balloons came from the planes and we used to find them on the seashore; we thought they were nothing more than weather balloons, and nothing was said to tell us different.'

The true story about the spy balloons became public knowledge many years later. Ronald Stewart could not believe these details when they were eventually revealed: 'I think we were told the balloons were for weather observations, but local rumour had it that they were used for spying on the USSR. But many locals couldn't believe that anything as primitive as a camera hanging from a balloon could still be used for spying in the 1950s.'

After USAF personnel left Evanton in March 1956, the airfield was closed again, and any trace of the extravagant spy project sunk into oblivion. Memories faded, but the locals still chuckle at their recollection of the oddball events. Roy Meikle summed up popular opinion: 'Now we see the runway every time we pass along the A9. How we made up stories about these American people we had only read about in comics – if only we'd known what a daft idea the whole thing was.'

The Evanton balloons brought a splash of glamour to the local area. Genetrix was interesting and different. UFO films had started to appear in the local cinema, and there were UFO stories in the newspapers. Genetrix fed off this. Young boys were fascinated by the Evanton events. Many witnessed the activities, but few of them are still alive to tell the tale.

The UFO connection was fondly remembered by Colin Gibson: 'I was living in Inverness and waiting for the results of some Foreign Office exams, and was working on a bread van for Burnett's who delivered on a run through Bonar Bridge, Avoch, Cromarty, Muir of Ord and Invergordon, then out to Tain. One of our stops was USAF Evanton, where we delivered a large order each working day. I warmly remember being invited to have Xmas lunch with them. There was turkey, Xmas pudding, crackers etc. all served on a metal food tray. The crowning glory was that it also had a King Edward cigar, which I kept for many months. I often wondered what they were doing. Weren't the balloon flights tied up with Operation Mogul?[3] Hence a connection with Roswell.' [65]

Local historian Paul Monk researched the Genetrix events with little success: 'I'm aware that the U.S. Air Force launched high-altitude balloons in 1956 from Evanton just after the airfield was abandoned by the Fleet Air Arm. But 60 years later local memories had faded. There are no artefacts other than the redeveloped old airfield.'

Project Genetrix was a spectacular event. Its activities were attacked by the Kremlin. However, no official comments admitted the real purpose of the project. This was a deliberate policy.

The UK Government also censored all Genetrix reports. However, one finally emerged: a history of the RAF Mountain Rescue Service, by Frank Card, was published in 1993. It contained details of an incident close to Evanton. This event was mysterious because of its apparent lack of follow-up activity. The author made an intriguing comment: 'Like all good legends this was an event that by its nature has remained unknown, except to the privileged few, ever since.' [66]

The facts appeared to be straightforward. In 1962, a local shepherd, Donald McKenzie, had discovered wreckage at Ardgay, in the hills 20 miles north of Evanton. He immediately identified it as a crashed spaceship: 'The debris looked like a Sputnik.' He notified the police and they passed on the information to the military. The mountain rescue team from RAF Kinloss did not reach the site until three months later. The unusual delay in responding has never been explained.

This information came to the attention of a former rescue team leader, David Whalley, who lived in the local area. He had become interested in the local rumours regarding this long-forgotten matter. When he checked the team's historical records there was no mention of the event. This was strange, as he knew the incident had occurred.

This spurred him on to find out more about the case. He contacted former team members who had been at the crash site. 'The old team members could remember the incident clearly. They told me about finding unusual bits and pieces of debris. One of them, Jack Baines, said the team were told to keep quiet about what they had found. When he told me the story, I first thought it was an urban myth, but he convinced me, and I believe they definitely found a crashed Sputnik. The debris included a part with Russian [writing], and pictures on it explaining what to do if the satellite was found crashed, and that a reward would be given for its return.' [67]

---

3 Project Mogul was a top secret project by the USAAF involving the use of microphones attached to high-altitude balloons. Its purpose was the long-range detection of sound waves generated from Soviet atomic bomb tests during the period 1947 to 1949. The Roswell UFO incident was caused by this project.

Whalley drew the obvious conclusion from his investigation. The information must have been deliberately suppressed: 'There is no incident report, or mention in the team archives, as I checked when I became the team leader in the late eighties.'

But the story did not vanish. It resurfaced in July 2012, when a BBC News report announced: 'A former RAF Kinloss mountain rescue team leader has told how he sought evidence that a Russian satellite crashed in the Highlands 50 years ago.' [68]

Academic Dr David Clarke decided to investigate the matter. He was curious about the slow response and the suspicious sequence of follow-up actions. The mountain rescue team had seen that the debris consisted of pieces of unusual metal and strange drawings. But the wreckage disappeared, and no one knows where it is stored. All concerned were told to keep quiet about it.

Clarke discovered that what the team had found on the remote moor was a strange box-shaped object. It was large enough to have carried a human, but there were no signs of damage caused by the intense heat that would have been expected if this really had been a satellite. There were spaces for cameras, and a brass panel that explained, in pictures, what the finder should do in the event of discovery to claim a reward. Buried nearby had been 'a number of bottles of colourless fluid'. He established that some members of the team were convinced this was indeed part of a crashed Soviet spacecraft: 'But if so, why was it in such a good condition? And where was the parachute?' Although the wreckage appeared to have been a Genetrix gondola, no further answers were provided.

The matter was then taken up by Keith Bryers, a Dingwall-based amateur historian. He found mention of 'problematic wreckage' among an informal RAF list of crashes. This led him to conclude that it was the debris from a Genetrix balloon: 'The gondolas had stickers on them with cartoons showing people what to do if they found it. It was possible there was also writing in Russian, or Asian, languages on the stickers.' [69]

He was intrigued by the reaction of the mountain rescue team, who believed that this was a Sputnik: 'Their belief was boosted by the presence of a placard on the box-like object, which said that there was a reward for returning it to the military authorities. The RAF team believed that the originators of the device expected it to return to Earth within the Soviet sphere of influence.' [70]

It would appear that the Ardgay wreckage was part of Project Genetrix. Its description fits the information available about the construction of the gondola and its contents. However, there was no mention of the balloon envelope. This was made of polyethylene, a synthetic plastic that is not readily biodegradable. It accumulates in landfills. It would still have been lying on the hillside many years later but has never been recovered. This is why questions remain about Ardgay.[71]

2 The American migration to Scotland

American strategy

During the 1950s the fear of the spread of Communism intensified in the Western world. The Soviet Union successfully developed its nuclear weapons. The Korean War and the French-Indochinese War had a profound effect on the United States and its allies. The newly formed NATO alliance became an indispensable club for its members, guaranteeing them communal defence. The United States needed this as much as its allies. Washington introduced its forward defence doctrine, and its alliance partners embraced the guarantee of American assistance.[72]

Operation Mainbrace was NATO's first major naval exercise. It was held in 1952 to practise the defence of Denmark and Norway against potential Soviet aggression. Its outcome was significant to Scotland, as the conclusion drawn from the exercise was that defence of the northern waters was essential, pushing Scotland to the forefront of this activity.

Moscow's strategic position was obvious. The Soviet Northern Fleet had been moved from the Baltic to the Kola Peninsula. This would enable its submarine force to deploy into the North Atlantic, to potentially interdict NATO supply routes coming through the GIUK (Greenland–Iceland–UK) Gap. NATO needed to neutralise the Soviet fleet.[73]

The initial stages of this policy led to American requests for British bases for the US nuclear bomber aircraft fleet. United States wartime air bases reopened in the south and east of England. However, by the late 1950s the White House decided to focus on the unparalleled advantages of nuclear-powered, nuclear-armed submarines. This changed the strategic equation.[74]

The Americans' FBM (fleet ballistic missile) submarines needed a forward operating base in Europe. Without it, if they were based on continental USA, there would be a 14-day loss of patrol time. In 1958, the United States approached Britain with a request to establish an FBM refit site in the United Kingdom. President Eisenhower had suggested to the British Prime Minister, Harold Macmillan, that a site in Scottish waters would be needed. Eisenhower had reiterated that the UK was an 'indispensable partner' in this matter. The UK provided diplomatic support, and Scotland provided the location for the submarine base and other elements of the package.[75]

The Americans identified Holy Loch as suitable to provide an anchorage for a submarine tender ship, a large dry dock and supporting craft. The loch had been a British submarine base during the Second World War. Macmillan, whose family came from the nearby Isle of Arran, was cautious about this choice, and noted in his diary: 'A picture could well be drawn of some frightful accident which might devastate the whole of Scotland.'[76]

The U.S. Navy was eager to buttress its new role as America's nuclear delivery force. The Chief of Naval Operations, Admiral Arleigh Burke, wanted to base a tender in the Firth of Clyde as it was close to Prestwick Airport. But Macmillan did not want to use the Clyde, and offered Loch Linnhe, near Fort William: 'From a security point of view, a robust population of three or four thousand Highlanders at Fort William is much more to my taste than the rather mixed population in the cosmopolitan city of Glasgow.'

But Loch Linnhe was too remote.[77] Eisenhower rejected the idea for practical reasons: the submarine base needed greater shore facilities and immediate access to open seas. Largs and Bute were then suggested, but for vessels to safely moor there, the buoys would have to be moved further out into the main channel. This action would have negated the shelter provided by the location.

Macmillan vainly played his final card, claiming: 'Glasgow contains unstable elements ... and communist agitators.'

He felt, too, that it would be a mistake to site a major nuclear target so near to the third-largest city in Britain. But remorseless American pressure succeeded. On 27 October 1960 Eisenhower replied to Macmillan: 'Dear Harold, I am delighted that agreement has been reached on the project for berthing facilities for our Polaris tender in the Clyde area.'[78]

There was a political outcome for Scotland from the siting of the Holy Loch nuclear base. It gave the impression that Whitehall did not care about Scottish opinion.[79] From 1961 onwards, the Conservative vote in Scotland has declined continually. In the 1955 UK General Election, the Conservatives had won more than half of the Scottish seats. They secured 50 per cent of the popular vote. At the Hamilton by-election in 1968, Winnie Ewing won the seat for the SNP (Scottish National Party). In 2019, the SNP won 48 out of 59 seats. The Conservatives won only 6. Macmillan had also been worried about the political effect of the Polaris decision. Over time his concern was shown to be correct, except that it was the SNP who benefited and not the Labour party, who had been dominant in Scotland.

Dunoon and its neighbouring towns, meanwhile, accepted the economic benefits of the situation.[80] In turn, the American sailors and families fondly recall their tours of duty in Argyll. Scotland provided a welcoming, relaxing environment for the American sailors.

The impact of the Holy Loch facility was highlighted during the visit of Soviet premier Kosygin to Glasgow in 1967. Huge crowds greeted him. Many were friendly, many were hostile, most were curious. If he had been able to read English, he would have seen the interesting banners which proclaimed: 'Welcome to your Number One Target' and 'Welcome to Scotland – America's nuclear target magnet'.[81]

There was a definite benefit for the UK in this agreement. A senior MOD official summed up the outcome: 'The US wanted a forward submarine base, both for refit and crew turnover reasons, and asked HMG for permission. This was granted on a mutually beneficial basis. The Mutual Defence Agreement was really significant because it let the UK back into nuclear cooperation with the US. This was in the early days of the Cold War, so facilitating the US engagement in transatlantic defence would have been a good thing. The core of the UK motivation would have been to bolster NATO (and stick alongside the USA). Geography played its part. There were, of course, lots of air bases in the UK already used by the USAF. And there would have been the desire to be the reliable and indispensable ally, since we had decided after Suez to bind ourselves to the US, not strike out for independence like France.'[82]

Eisenhower acknowledged the importance of the UK's support and its strategic position in providing forward bases. He pointed out that the UK was an 'indispensable partner', and one that needed American backing in political, military and economic matters.[83]

Anti-nuclear weapons feeling was strong in Britain, and in 1960 it was measured to be at 33 per cent. The CND (Campaign for Nuclear Disarmament) organised civil disobedience. Huge rallies in London protested the Holy Loch decision. The demonstrators warned President Kennedy that CND supporters would: 'occupy non-violently the submarines, the *Proteus* depot ship, and land installations. Our aim is to immobilise the base'.[84]

Lieutenant Mike Giambattista went to Holy Loch in January 1961 as part of the U.S. Navy team which co-ordinated the arrival of USS *Proteus*, the submarine tender. On 3 March 1961 they stood ready as the tender approached Holy Loch. The team included the waterborne presence of the Chief Constable of Argyll Police aboard the frigate HMS *Blackwood*. The local police had a simple plan to contain the planned protest: a dozen constables blocked the entrance to Ardnadam Pier. In the event that this did not succeed, there were another 50 constables located inside the shelter at the foot of the pier. The plan was successful; the backup squad was not deployed and only a few protesters were hauled off to the local jail. The protests continued.[85]

CND and their allies set up a tented camp at Sandbank, Holy Loch. They sent telegrams to the Prime Minister. The pacifist left-wing of the Labour Party and Scottish trade unions supported the protests. A large demonstration was held in Glasgow. This local involvement led to an amusing situation when a group of canoeists, the Glasgow Eskimos, was formed. They intended to occupy the water with kayaks and rowing boats, and planned to 'cross the path of the *Proteus* and obstruct its entrance'. They also said, 'Specific actions of nonviolent civil disobedience to obstruct each of the submarines as they arrive will be carried out.'[86]

As it turned out, the protesters did not have enough boats to form a barrier across the loch, as only three canoes and one dinghy turned up. Nevertheless, their fame has been immortalised in a folk song, 'The Glesca Eskimos', sung to the tune of 'Marching Through Georgia':[87]

The submarine squadron commander was welcomed by the Provost of Dunoon, Mrs McPhail.[4] She invited the Americans to become part of the fabric of the town, not just visitors. This was an important statement, and the U.S. Navy adopted Dunoon in a wholehearted fashion.

Two of the anti-American demonstrators were local youths, George Robertson and Brian Wilson. In later years they became full-time politicians and members of the British Cabinet, and Robertson became NATO Secretary General.

Despite regular protests, there was also plenty of support for the Holy Loch base. The parliamentary Labour Party did not object to the establishment of the base, and only two of the local Labour-controlled burghs, Greenock and Clydebank, opposed it. The local community in Dunoon and elsewhere welcomed its economic benefits.

---

4 In Scotland a town's mayor is called the provost.

But CND did not go away. In May 1961 they staged a massive demonstration at Holy Loch. This was a twin-pronged protest: one group demonstrated on land, while the other protested by sea. The seaborne group attempted to board the tender, *Proteus*. CND had warned that all demonstrators must be able to swim, and in addition said: 'We would be most grateful if participants could either provide their own lifejackets or purchase one from us.' [88]

This time 16 canoes turned up. However, counter-protesters, supporters of the American presence, arrived too, and used the wake from their vessel to swamp the protesters. Any who reached the *Proteus* were washed off with high-powered water hoses and picked up by police boats. It was a grand day out for all involved, and there were many arrests. The U.S. Navy had previously carried out a rigorous assessment of such anticipated behaviour. Sailors had been briefed, and dealt admirably with any abuse from protesters. Months later, there was a bigger, more raucous protest at Sandbank, but like all the other demonstrations, it had no effect. Holy Loch would be home to nuclear submarines for the next 31 years.[89]

There was some opposition from locals, and letters to the editor of the *Dunoon Observer* were strident, one claiming that 'This dismal news has murdered sleep in Dunoon,' while another lamented, 'We are being subjected to the risk of contamination and total annihilation.' [90]

Others worried about Americanisation. A retired colonel was concerned about snack bars, hot dog stands, ice cream parlours, slot machines and jukeboxes. His observations were accurate, as the residents fully embraced the changes. His concern was somewhat mollified when the commanding officer of USS *Proteus*, Captain Richard B. Laning, stated that the sailors' families would join them, and their children would go to school with the children of Dunoon.

Plans were made for the housing of the ships' crews and families in the local community. There was to be no base housing, and Dunoon did not become Americanised. Instead, the visitors succumbed to the charm of Scottish life, and when the tenders returned to the United States they carried back Scottish brides. However, in Dunoon the young married American sailors had difficulty in finding suitable accommodation, as recalled by Frank Gonzales who arrived with the tender USS *Hunley* in 1965: 'I had my wife and three small children … the hotels were full and we had a difficult time looking for a room.' [91]

Captain Edward H. Mortimer commanded the submarine USS *John Adams* (SSBN-620).[5] He had a long association with Holy Loch, having served aboard USS *Abraham Lincoln* and as a (Submarine Squadron) SUBRON-14 engineer officer. In that role, he had been responsible for supporting the ships when they came in for their 28-day refit programme. He stressed the political value of all naval operations being conducted from the tender: 'This was because the Pentagon had decided that we would not build an operational base on somebody else's territory. We were afloat and flexible. This meant that the US Government could state that they did not have a base at the Holy Loch. It was an anchorage. It was very important for political purposes.'

Local resident Brian Wilson observed that the American presence in the 1960s made Dunoon a lot more interesting and diverse than would be expected of a small Scottish town: 'Having American children in school was refreshing, and created friendships and levels of awareness

---

5 SSBN: Ship Submersible Ballistic Nuclear

that would not otherwise have existed. As far as I recall, there was never any animosity towards American kids or why they were there. It was just a fact of growing up in Dunoon at that time. For a lot of local lives, it was transformational ... and gave me an early awareness that American people are often a lot better than American foreign policy!' [92]

This view was demonstrated by Tom Barbour when he arrived with *Proteus* in February 1961 and experienced the same outlook: 'On my first visit to a pub in Dunoon ... an elderly gentleman bought me the drink ... He then told me he didn't want American weapons in the Holy Loch, but "We don't object to *you*. You're here because you have a job to do. It's yer bliddy government that sent the bombs here." ' [93]

In the midst of this early excitement, the submarine USS *Patrick Henry* (SSBN-599) pulled into Holy Loch, moored alongside USS *Proteus* on 8 March 1961 and started more than 30 years of Site One's activities.

3 Boomers

– the cutting edge

Strategic changes

'The stakes were high and the world was unsafe. Our nuclear deterrent gave pause to the Soviet bear.' [94]

Captain Arthur Clark Bivens, commanding officer, USS *Sam Houston* (SSBN-609) was correct. It was the nuclear-armed submarines that kept America safe during the Cold War. Their invisibility was the major factor in deterring a Soviet first strike. The American SSBN was brutal but effective.

The world's first missile submarines had been Soviet diesel-electric boats, armed with two missiles. Although newer diesel and electric classes had been developed by 1959 and carried three missiles with a range of 350 nautical miles,[6] they had to surface to fire the missiles. So they could not remain unseen.

The United States had a significant advantage in that the US Polaris boats each carried 16 missiles which could be launched while the submarine remained fully submerged. They had a longer range, and were more accurate, than the Soviets' missiles. This American lead in military technology was also shown by the excellence of the American navigation systems. The Polaris boats were the largest, most complex and most heavily armed submarines ever developed.[95]

By the 1960s, the U.S. Navy's mission was to prevent the Soviet submarine fleet from entering the broad Atlantic. In this region the Russian nuclear missiles were within range of the continental United States. So, for the Americans, ASW (anti-submarine warfare) activities and intelligence material about the Soviet submarine fleet was essential.[96]

---

6 Nautical mile = 1.15 miles.

After the Second World War the entire concept of war at sea changed: submarines were now recognised as versatile platforms, able to gather intelligence, sink enemy surface and submerged vessels and, most significantly, to launch nuclear missiles at enemy shore targets many miles inland. The SSBNs, known as 'boomers', were very different from – and deadlier than – most submarines. Boomers[7] were invisible, could navigate to any spot under the ocean, could stay submerged for ten weeks and could carry the most awesome armoury ever devised. One SSBN could devastate a dozen Russian targets.

This change in strategic concept was driven by Admiral Hyman Rickover, whose determination built the American nuclear submarine fleet. He was known as the Father of the Nuclear Navy, and controlled the training of all the officers he selected for the nuclear submarine fleet. As a four-star admiral, he refused to retire from the U.S. Navy, but in January 1982 eventually agreed to leave before he would have been fired by President Reagan. He was 82 years old at the time, and had served under 13 presidents during his 63 years of service. Rickover's influence on the navy was immense.[97]

Captain Mortimer wryly described his service with Admiral Rickover. This had been during the selection course at Admiral Rickover's 'Charm School'. Candidates spent 13 weeks working in his office in the Old Navy Building at Washington DC: 'We studied eight hours a day and were tested by some of his henchmen in the nuclear power organisation. We had to accept his philosophy hook, line and sinker. If we knew what was good for us, we would do it the Admiral's way.'[98]

Mortimer noted that when officers were being interviewed for attendance on this course, Rickover would make them uncomfortable: 'One of his regular tricks was to offer the candidate a chair which had one leg shorter than the others. There was no way the candidate could become comfortable.'

During these 13 weeks, officers had to learn everything about the boat from the nuclear plant backwards. This meant that when they got to the ship they knew more than the engineering officer. It was a successful process and produced high-quality nuclear submarine captains, many of whom achieved flag rank.

The SSBN had a simple patrol purpose, noted Ronald P.C. Waller, PO1 aboard USS *Daniel Webster* (SSBN 626): 'The SSBN mission was to remain undetected. If the Russians thought you were around, they would throw down grenades and stuff. On patrol we went out to a 50-square mile area of ocean and sat there at 3 knots constantly, awaiting orders to fire our missiles.'[99]

The Pentagon drew up a master plan of its nuclear targets. This was approved by President Kennedy and amended by subsequent presidents. These targets had been selected because they were confirmed or suspected Soviet military locations. The Kremlin and the Pentagon both used the same targeting profiles, so the American bases in Scotland would have been on Russia's list, with Holy Loch at the top. Scotland could have been attacked, but the United States mainland was shielded by Scotland's strategic location, remote from the US.[100]

Before leaving on patrol from Holy Loch, each SSBN was allocated a specific set of targets, and this information was locked into the missile control computer. Strict rules controlled the launch of nuclear missiles.

---

7 Boomers were also known as Fleet Ballistic Missile (FBM) boats.

Captain Bivens noted the launch regulations: 'A submarine captain does not have the authority to order the use of nuclear weapons on his own. He does not have the capability to do so. Strict safety rules were rigidly applied to prevent the unauthorised or inadvertent firing of nuclear weapons. The order to fire can only come from the President via the NCA [National Command Authority]. That order must go through a complex process of verification. No single individual onboard can fire a nuclear weapon. Many people in the crew need to work together to achieve this outcome.' [101]

It was a team effort, but nuclear submarine commanders had a unique authority that could only be exercised in desperate times; should their communications to the NCA be cut, they could fire their missiles, as in this situation it was assumed that a state of war existed and the NCA was immobilised.[8] They did not need to receive the enabling codes. This placed immense responsibility on the captains, and Rickover's selection would have faced its ultimate test.[102]

During patrol, a submarine never initiated communications with headquarters; it only received incoming messages. These were received on a floating-wire antenna which snaked out 2 miles from the SSBN. Should the incoming messages cease, the submarine would attempt to use other means, and if this was unsuccessful, the commander then knew that the transmitting station had been eliminated. Fortunately, this scenario never occurred, not even during the Cuban Missile Crisis in 1962, when America's entire SSBN fleet, all from Holy Loch, was on patrol at Defcon 3 (Defence Condition) status.[103]

The use of communications was controlled, as Captain Bivens remembered: 'An FBM requires constant communication with its operational commander, and there is plenty of space and time after the operational message for the daily news and 'familygrams'. These also added 'padding' to the official traffic and hampered the Soviet cryptographers listening to the broadcasts. Official broadcasts from the headquarters of the CINCLANT [Commander in Chief, Atlantic] came via Cutler, Maine. If there was bad news for a crew member after the patrol commenced, the flotilla commander had to decide whether to inform the crew member. FBM patrols were of the highest national priority. These missions were not interrupted for personal reasons in the early days.' [104]

Communications between submarines and their headquarters were problematic, as it was difficult for the radio waves to penetrate water. The SSBN technology had outstripped communications expertise, and the submarines had to depend upon a network of radio stations to relay messages. In addition, submarines on patrol never returned calls, as this would have exposed their position. But important messages would need to be sent from the President and his advisors to the SSBNs. This was to be achieved by establishing a network of airborne radio relay stations, which enabled the signal to skip across vast distances of the ocean.[105]

So a fleet of specially rigged C-130 aircraft was formed. These aircraft trailed an antenna 6 miles long, and in times of crisis the aircraft remained constantly aloft over the Atlantic. Messages from the President passed along this network to the submarines.

The SSBNs carried out long submerged patrols, and the onboard conditions were not comfortable, recalled Giambattista: 'Their nuclear reactor needed no oxygen. All of its air was

---

8 NCA: National Command Authority.

purified. There was no noxious exhaust. The nuclear reactors lasted for several years before they needed to be refuelled. A desalination plant turned seawater into drinking water and stale air was 'scrubbed' to remove the carbon dioxide. Waste gases were burned in a catalytic converter at high temperatures so that no tell-tale bubbles were released that might give away the submarine's position.'

But artificially treated drinking water was not good for humans, as Ronald P.C. Waller recalled: 'On board an SSBN the water is distilled to the highest extent. However, on return to shore your body tended to react to natural water with its impurities.' [106]

The fleet ballistic missile submarine was completely self-sufficient. Captain Bivens emphasised this aspect: 'It carried food for 90 days and emergency supplies for longer. The crew were fully skilled in the operation of their vessel. Submarines carried 30,000 replacement parts, and crew members could repair all equipment. Craftsmen could make spare parts not carried; welders could operate safely.' [107]

Becoming a bubblehead

Surface sailors called submariners 'bubbleheads' because they were different. Submariners underwent a long training process to prepare them to function in a different environment from that of surface sailors. This training and qualification process ensured that the SSBNs operated to their maximum capability, without which the strategic benefits provided by Scotland's geographic position would have been eroded. 'Aboard a submarine, there was a very distinctive social order,' noted Bud Lewis, USS *George Bancroft* (SSBN 643): 'The crew was divided into the following sections: officers, chief petty officers, qualified enlisted men and non-qualified officers and enlisted men.' [108]

In the early days of the nuclear submarine programme, serving submariners had no nuclear experience and there was a shortage of trained crew. A large-scale training programme was launched. The candidates came from all parts of the United States to serve their country.

The first step in submarine service was sub school. A submarine is no place for claustrophobics, and as the first part of the selection process candidates were given a pressure test in a recompression chamber. [109]

John J. Roberts, ET1 SS,[9] who had served aboard USS *Theodore Roosevelt* (SSBN-600), described his sub school training: 'We learned about basic theory, construction and operation of submarines, firefighting, damage control, ship control and submarine escape. These were the essential survival matters.'

The training was thorough, recalled Mike Giambattista: 'At sub school everybody needed to learn the submarine basics/differences: buoyancy (positive, neutral and negative), submarine structure (pressure hull with its various watertight compartments) external tanks (fuel and ballast), control mechanisms (trim planes – bow and stern), angles and speed. First and foremost, we learned the first law of submarines – the number of surfacings must equal the number of dives.'

---

9 Electronics Technician Submersible Ship

The classes included diesel engine design and operation, electrical power generation, air compression, hydraulic and piping systems etc. There was also instruction in diving, trimming, surfacing operations and torpedo-firing processes.

During the six months at sub school, there was plenty of academic work. But it also included a submarine escape tower exercise, which had a degree of risk, as submarine escape is a hazardous activity.[110]

All candidates had to perform the escape drill. This test was conducted in a claustrophobic environment due to the effects created by the depth of the escape tower: a 125-foot cylinder filled with water, with several entrance chambers at varying depths: 18, 50 and 110 feet.

Mike Giambattista recalled the training: 'Each of these entrance chambers simulated an airlock in a submarine. Compressed air was bled into it to equalise the water pressure … the candidate was required to 'blow and go', i.e., expel the air from their lungs continuously. The life jacket provided the buoyancy required to reach the surface. It was not enjoyable.'

This action was dangerous. Failure to expel air fast enough would result in an embolism – 'burst lung'. Giambattista recalled his experience: 'The pain in my right ear was excruciating, but once my eardrum had burst the pain vanished. When the ascent was completed, a course of antibiotics and a day in bed helped me to recover and continue with the course. My ear damage was permanent, and I suffered constantly from ear bleeding on submerged duty.'

The course included three weeks at sea aboard various submarines, and during these stages the officer candidates crewed each station. Many hours were spent in simulators, where the operation of the ship for diving and surfacing was practised by all ranks.

Psychological parameters were also scrutinised. This was done by written exercises which probed personal attitudes and outlooks. The more sceptical sailors had fun with this activity, and many provided preposterous or colourful answers. Nevertheless, their responses were evaluated seriously, as their content provided the necessary material for an initial assessment of each candidate. Then, when an individual became an SSBN crew member, this information would be consulted again.

Because of the specific character of submarine duties, the psychological fitness of applicants had to be checked; this check alone removed 3 per cent of applicants before training. This process was continually updated. The overall conclusion in a 1979 report was 'the mental health of nuclear submarine crew members is excellent'.[111]

Sixty days underwater produced inevitable stress, and it was important to track its effects on crew members. A Navy study was undertaken by Dr Earl Ninnow in the 1970s, with USS *Sam Houston* being used as the project baseline. Captain Arthur Bivens recalled the activities: 'I remember Dr Ninnow boarding from a small boat in Firth of Clyde to begin interviews.' On occasions the results led to subtle changes in routine being introduced. The Ninnow programme reported general trends that required attention.[112]

As the SSBNs were nuclear-powered they required a new type of engineer, the 'nuke' (nuclear engineer). 'The nukes underwent a long training program before boarding their first submarine,' noted John Everson. 'The nukes already had two years' training, but once aboard they were pushed as hard as all other crew members to become submarine-qualified.'[113]

Mike Lacey, a reactor operator, petty officer 1st class aboard USS *Patrick Henry* (SSBN-599), was a nuke whose training lasted 100 weeks: 'You have a parallel qual. program for your watch-standing responsibilities – sonar, nuke, whatever. My nuke quals were substantially harder and longer than boat quals. Boat quals took me one patrol, but it took me three patrols to qualify as a reactor operator.' Lacey had spent 40 weeks at electronics technician school, followed by six months at naval nuclear power school training for shipboard nuclear power plant operation. Another six months was spent in nuclear prototype training, and then eight weeks at submarine school.[114]

Nukes were high school graduates. Aaron Amick summarised them: 'They can digest volumes of information in a short time. They are very well trained. There were three types – the reactor operator, the nuclear electrician and the nuclear workman.'

On graduation from nuclear school the enlisted personnel were advanced to the rank of petty officer 3rd class (PO3). Nukes such as Mike Lacey attended additional technical school training: 'We were sent to submarine training school and then to a diesel submarine to qualify and earn our first Dolphins. This was followed by 24 weeks of classroom study. This phase was tough, with a very high attrition rate. High standards were maintained.' [115]

The nuke students typically spent 45 hours per week in the classroom. The nuclear route placed high expectations on the candidates, and swift action was taken against those who fell behind; failure scores due to personal negligence, rather than a lack of ability, could result in charges of dereliction of duty under the Uniform Code of Military Justice. Some failing students could be held back to repeat the coursework with a new group of classmates. Others were normally released from the nuclear power programme to serve out their enlistments elsewhere.

The product of successful graduation from the course was a well-qualified submariner like Mike Lacey, ready for posting to his first nuclear submarine: 'After graduating, I received orders to pack up and join the USS *Theodore Roosevelt* (SSBN-600) in Holy Loch, Scotland. I reported on board after flying from Quonset Point via Harmon, Nova Scotia, to Prestwick, Scotland. I flew on a military transport turboprop to join the Gold Crew,[10] which was already on board alongside the tender in Holy Loch.' [116]

The quest for Dolphins

When submariners left submarine school, they had not reached the end of their qualification process. Another arduous, high-pressure episode now awaited: they had to work to obtain their Dolphins badge, the most important part of the process. Without it, they would be returned to the surface fleet. Its importance was summed up by nuclear engineer Bud Lewis: 'Without doubt, the highlight of a submariner's service is the day he gets qualified in submarines.' [117]

All new submariners had one overriding imperative – to become qualified on the boat. This brought acceptance and trust from the already-qualified crew. This point was emphasised by Captain Mortimer: 'All of this testing meant that we could keep the standard of the submarine force very high. Everyone on board was someone who knew his stuff, and we all shared mutual respect.'

---

10 Part of the two-crew system, Blue and Gold. More about this further on.

A new submariner would arrive as a 'non-qual.' He[11] would be familiar with the general principles of submarine operation, but each boat had a different layout and this knowledge had to be learned. He had to prove his worth and learn all of the ship's systems and their components, how to draw them and then show how they worked. He had to respond to fire, flooding and poison in the air on every level of the boat. Once he could do this, he could be relied upon to know what to do in case of an emergency. At this point he would be awarded the Submarine Warfare pin – Dolphins. He then became a full member of the crew.[118]

This pressure to become qualified meant that individuals did not participate in liberty trips. 'Had a crew member done so before qualifying, the qualified individuals would have looked down on them,' noted Everson. Then he added, 'You had a qual card which listed all the departments and systems. You had to go to the person in charge of that area and pass an oral exam with them. Then you would sit an oral board with two persons: one a qualified chief of the watch and one officer qualified as officer of the deck. If you passed, you would then get your Dolphins presented by the captain at quarters. And everyone would touch or punch your Dolphins for the rest of that day. It was kind of rite of passage. And acceptance. If you failed the board, you could attempt it twice more, but after a third failure you were transferred to the surface fleet.'

Aaron Amick was a sonarman: 'Living in a machine with over 100 sailors requires a person to be flexible socially and sometimes physically. I spent two decades on United States Navy submarines performing sonar duties among eccentric personalities in incredibly stressful situations. When sailors report to their first submarine, they are joining a work culture unlike any other. Surrounded by crew members busily moving about tight spaces and narrow walkways, announcements over the circuit boxes, roving watch standers, equipment humming to 400Hz fans, it can be anxiety-inducing to any sailor.'

The hierarchy of the submarine was on constant display, noted Amick: 'A NUB[12] used our limited supply of space, water, food and oxygen. They were not welcome, but BUPERS [Bureau of Personnel] kept sending them. The NUB is easily identifiable as he would be the only crewman wearing a command ball cap with the ship's name and no Dolphins symbol on the front. They always had their qualification card in their rear pocket and carried a small notebook in their hand for studying. They did not have movie privileges.'[119]

John Everson recalled his experience: 'Basically, regardless of rank, all new crew were considered a non-qual once they reported on board. The crew referred to non-quals as NUBs. There was, as with any military institution back then, a fair bit of hazing. Once you reported on board you had a year to get qualified. But your division personnel would push much harder. You were assigned someone senior to you in rank to oversee your studies. You had to have operational understanding of the entire boat to get qualified, the theory being that everybody needed to know how to surface the boat and bring it to safety. In my case, I did it in five months.'[120]

The onboard qualification process was rigorous. As indicated by Everson, it was designed so that every crew member was able to take appropriate actions in emergency conditions in any

---

11 All submariners were male.

12 Non-Useful Body

compartment of the submarine. To gain the coveted Dolphins pin an individual was required to complete a stringent qualification process. This process began when they reported to their first submarine. New arrivals were issued a qualification card that listed every system, compartment and service on the boat. A petty officer, known as a Sea Dad, was assigned for each step.[121]

Once aboard, submariners needed to trace and know how to operate each of the ship's systems (air, hydraulic, electric, saltwater and freshwater) and the emergency routines (how to rig for dive, fire, flooding etc.) This was essential knowledge. Each of the seven boat compartments had a petty officer to test the qualifying sailor. When all items had been completed, the engineering officer would spot-check the candidate's knowledge.

Giambattista explained: 'It was imperative to become qualified as soon as possible. The award of Dolphins was the only standard accepted aboard a submarine. Once qualified, a note was made in the submariner's record to signify his qualification. Submarine-qualified personnel were designated SS [submarine specialist] after their rate, such as STS1(SS) or MM2(SS).' [122]

Officer qualification was a year-long process. A notebook containing sketches of all systems, safety procedures and operating parameters had to be compiled, then reviewed by the XO (executive officer) and the captain. The officer had to qualify both as an officer of the deck and as a diving officer, which involved completing torpedo readiness preparations, controlling the ship and making a torpedo shot. The candidate was then recommended by the captain for two qualification examinations: those for in port and those for under way. These exams were conducted on two separate submarines and were certified by the captains.[123]

The Mark 14 torpedo was used in the qualification process. It had certain eccentricities such as running deeper than set, firing prematurely, failing to fire and running in a large circle, returning to hit the home ship.

Mike Giambattista had to cope with these hazards: 'My qualification shoot used a dummy warhead filled with air to make the practice torpedo float at the end of its run. This enabled it to be recovered and used again. Losing this torpedo would have cost the Navy a lot of money.[13] Once the submarine was within optimal firing range and with a good firing solution, the skipper ordered a very complicated challenge – a stern tube shot. This command required me to swing the ship through 180 degrees to bring the stern torpedo tubes to bear on the target. We also had to generate a new firing solution. Quickly ordering the course change and increasing speed to turn the ship before the target got beyond the torpedo's range, I gave the firing command. The conning tower crew gave a cheer on firing.

'The sound of the rapidly moving torpedo filled the space and everyone became quiet. The captain then changed the order, but my calculations were correct. The steam-powered practice torpedo was heard as it passed safely overhead. The captain told me, "Nice job, Mike. I'm sure the fish you made ready would have run hot, straight and normal. You're qualified!" '

Dolphins qualification was a mental and physical challenge. At sea, the submariner worked on an eighteen-hour schedule that rotated through three six-hour watches; six hours were spent on watch and the other twelve were 'off time'. Training and high standards were relentlessly maintained. Ship's drills occurred at any time of the day, designed to test crew members on their

---

13 At 2021 values, the cost of a Mark 14 was equivalent to $170,000.

ability to deal with incidents on board. There were also maintenance tasks. Although qualified crew had time for sleep, the non-quals had to fit it in around their qualification stages. All of a non-qual's free time was dedicated to qualification, and an inability to keep abreast of this schedule meant that he would be designated as delinquent, or 'dink'. Philip Giambri explained the pressure involved: 'A non-qual would muster for two hours of supervised study after completing all of his other tasks. To assist this process, his Sea Dad also had to muster at these extra periods. The Sea Dad's free time was thereby compromised. Therefore, more pressure on the NUB.' [124]

But, as Ronald P.C. Waller recounted, 'sleep was difficult in any case, as bunks were basically a 4-inch mattress fitted into a pan. They had straps to fasten to prevent sailors from falling out in rough seas. The ship could roll to 45 degrees in bad weather.'

When the non-qual was ready for the walk-through of every level of the ship, he was accompanied by a senior crew member, who tested his knowledge. The process was continuous. Dolphins holders needed to requalify every two years if serving on the same submarine. But when an individual reported to a new submarine, the qualifying journey started again. The process was relentless and delivered excellent results. The Soviets, on the other hand, staffed their submarines with poorly trained conscripts. [125]

The Dolphins certificate expressed the high level of competence achieved by the hard work done by its bearer: 'Having successfully completed the rigorous professional requirements for qualification in submarines, having gained a thorough knowledge of submarine construction and operation, having demonstrated his reliability under stress, and having my full confidence and trust, I hereby certify that he is qualified in submarines.'

A long submerged voyage was the final test for all submariners. It was not a fun experience. ' "Deterrent patrol" was the ironic euphemism used for a 60-day underwater cruise,' noted Giambattista. But even after the rigours of sub school and the escape tests, some sailors walked away while serving aboard submarines. He recalled an incident: 'I had one sailor, an electronic technician (ex-army), who passed the pressure tests, but at the end of a 68-day SSBN patrol he came to me and said that he wanted to surface permanently.' [126]

The U.S. Navy's SSBNs, too, were subjected to a rigorous process before undertaking their first patrol. Although they had been designed and constructed to the highest standards, once an SSBN had been commissioned there was a demanding qualification programme. The boat had to conduct sea trials and missile launches at Cape Kennedy. [14] The ballistic missiles were methodically tested, and practice missiles (without warheads) were fired. The firing test checked the onboard drills and navigation. This was an important time for the captain; his career depended on a good performance from the crew he had trained. A poor outcome, and he could be replaced. [127] The SSBN programme was America's strategic defence – excellence was mandatory and high standards were incessantly enforced.

Part of the sea trials before deployment to SubRon -14 was the DASO (Demonstration and Shakedown Operation). This was a series of tests to confirm the crew's ability to operate the weapons system aboard the boat. This provided a complete checkout of the launcher, guidance,

---

14 From 1963 to 1973, Cape Canaveral was renamed Cape Kennedy. Its name reverted to Cape Canaveral in 1973, but NASA's Space Mission Center retained the Kennedy name.

ship control and navigation systems. It was a full check of the SSBN's readiness for its task. Specially configured missiles were used during the Poseidon and Trident tests. The missile firing was conducted off Cape Canaveral.[128]

Early Polaris firing tests were problematic, as recalled by Captain Mortimer: 'When test-fired from my boat, it backed up and dropped into the ocean close to Cape Canaveral. Because of this fault the IRBM[15] was nicknamed 'Indian River BM'. The fault was corrected. The warheads were not fitted at this stage of training. Another Polaris A1 missile was called the Snake Chaser, as it tended to fly horizontally instead of vertically when launched; this problem, too, was resolved.'

Only one SSBN, the USS *Ethan Allen* (SSBN-608), undertook a test of an operational ballistic missile with a live warhead. This was carried out in the South Pacific, and it was successful. The report stated: 'After a 12.5-minute, 1,200-mile (1,900 km) flight, the warhead exploded in the air between 10,000 and 15,000 feet (3,000 and 4,600 m) high, with a yield of 600 kilotons.' [129]

After test firing at Cape Canaveral, the submarine would transit from Florida to the Tongue of the Ocean (TOTO) region in the Bahamas. TOTO is a U-shaped, relatively flat-bottomed sea trench, 20 miles wide by 150 miles long. Mike Giambattista recalled visiting it as navigation officer of the USS *Henry L. Stimson* (SSBN-655) in 1967: 'Located in TOTO was the U.S. Navy's AUTEC [Atlantic Undersea Test and Evaluation Center], a laboratory that performs integrated three-dimensional hydrospace/aerospace trajectory measurements covering the entire spectrum of undersea simulated warfare — calibration, classifications, detection and destruction. *Stimson* was the first ship to be evaluated in TOTO.'

It was an ideal location to accurately measure the underwater sound signature of submarines. For the sailors, though, there was little time for lounging on the sunny beaches of the Bahamas. Two weeks were spent submerged. Measurements were taken and equipment adjusted. Once the submarine had been thoroughly checked, it made its way to take up its role as a member of the Holy Loch squadron.

This process tested the submarine for noise and various other electronically measured matters. After each transit of the course, technicians would clamber aboard and adjust various pieces of equipment. However, as Mike Giambattista recalled, the trials also caused problems: 'We were required to run without air-conditioning on occasions. This had an unforeseen effect: the navigation computer was damaged.'

Submariners were subjected to non-stop testing during their patrols. Some of this was from enemy activity and navigation needs, and the remainder was part of the never-ending series of practice drills. But the most feared test came at the start of the patrol.

The Operational Reactor Safeguards Examination (ORSE) was Admiral Rickover's gold standard. It was an annual inspection of the condition of the ship's power plant and the crew's ability to operate it safely. This was the core purpose of an SSBN submarine. An SSBN was only viable if it could remain at full power for very long periods of time. Inability to do so would negate the mission, and America's strategic plan would be weakened.[130]

A special inspection team, with members hand-picked by Admiral Rickover for their persistence and doggedness, administered the ORSE. Crew members dreaded their arrival

---

15 Intermediate Range Ballistic Missile

on board; nit-picking was their strong point. The crew's readiness to handle any engineering problem or emergency was examined by observing realistic drills. It took two days and was conducted while the ship was under way and submerged. Failure meant the crew had to retrain before being allowed to operate the nuclear power plant. There were no second prizes, only the gold standard. When Admiral Rickover was notified of the results of the ORSE tests, he would personally telephone the officers involved. He knew them from their selection interviews.[131]

This ordeal was vividly recalled by Charlie Winterfeldt, who served aboard USS *Andrew Jackson* (SSBN-619). 'ORSE – these four letters struck sheer terror into the hearts of all submarine CO, XO and engineer officers.' [132]

The ORSE teams were naval officers with nuclear backgrounds. All were high-flyers. The ORSE was compared to the Spanish Inquisition for its ability to terrify the men. The team's task was simple – to examine a nuclear submarine's crew as to their ability to safely operate a naval nuclear reactor. The team stayed aboard for several days. They tested crew members, the operational drills, paperwork and equipment handling, and they closely inspected machinery. Winterfeldt recalled a typical activity: 'I personally observed a *bird* [naval aviator] captain crawl out of the bilge under the diesel generator with a white rag and a flashlight – and, luckily, no smudges. Nothing, no one, nowhere on board was exempt. These people reported directly to the Admiral.'

In the early days an SSBN would receive its ORSE while going on patrol. The ORSE team would board in the Firth of Clyde from a tug. Paul Davis was a tugman who remembered transferring these teams: 'They appeared to be focused on their task and I seldom saw any smiles.' Failure meant that the current national strategic targeting plan had to be amended. The USS *George Washington* failed its ORSE inspection twice in 1968. It missed most of its patrol through retraining. This was a most unpleasant experience for those involved, particularly the captain. However, prior to this incident another two crews had recently failed ORSE. This situation brought about a change of approach. ORSE was now rescheduled to be done on return from patrol, so if a crew failed, there would be three months available for retraining.

The Vietnam War had contributed to reducing the experience level aboard SSBNs. Understandably, fewer sailors had re-enlisted, to avoid being sent to the conflict. This lower level of expertise led to more ORSE failures. Captain Bivens recalled the solution: 'To counter this, a training officer was assigned to each SSBN squadron staff. They were predictably nicknamed 'the ORSE doctor'!'

But the SSBN faced other obstacles before facing the ORSE. Submarine sea trials were crucial to identify potential problems. Most were minor matters. But on one of USS *Francis Scott Key*'s first sea trials, a ripple launch of all 16 missile tubes was aborted after only about 7 tubes had fired. The locking pins had been left in the hydraulic control drain valves, and the boat started sinking because the compensation system couldn't blow water out of the flooded tubes. Charlie Burrow, TM 2 (torpedoman 2nd class), was aboard: 'That screw-up necessitated an additional sea trial – this time with the locking pins removed.' [133]

One of the most enjoyable sea trials activities was personal protection weapons training. Sailors loved to fire off live ammunition at the various floating targets beside the ship. All personnel were given the chance to do this.

Captain Arthur Clark Bivens and his crew enjoyed this aspect of training. A high-profile naval incident a few months earlier added urgency to these drills. In 1968 the USS *Pueblo*, an electronic-intelligence-gathering ship, had been captured by the North Koreans. One US sailor had been killed and 83 captured.

It was a major diplomatic incident. It also made a huge impression on the U.S. Navy. 'No more *Pueblos*' became a slogan, and the incident was not forgotten, as Bivens noted: 'She was sent in harm's way as an essentially unarmed spy ship with inadequate destruct capabilities. This episode would not be repeated with our SSBN. I enjoyed blasting away with a Tommy gun at boxes and bottles we had tossed overboard. This activity was closely monitored. The annual Nuclear Technical Proficiency Inspection looked closely at security readiness and compliance.' [134]

The navigation team's job was to know the submarine's exact position (Point A), so the missile team could hit its target (Point B). A key element in the navigation system was the Transit satellite system (today known as GPS). Going to periscope depth regularly and checking its actual position against what the systems were saying was vital. Getting a periodic good fix on Transit was essential to fixing Point A.

Sometimes vital equipment would cause problems on patrol. Normally these were resolved by fitting the necessary spare parts. However, on one patrol aboard USS *Francis Scott Key* there were no spares for the navigation computer, and without this the patrol would have to be aborted. But Bill Wyse and his Blue Crew navigation team came to the rescue. [135]

The Transit system had malfunctioned as its memory component heater had failed. There was no spare memory system on board and navigation was threatened.

Bill Wyse recounted the actions taken: 'The navigation team came up with a temporary solution – the use of a medical blanket to raise the temperature of the memory component. Further modification was needed to ensure that the correct temperature was achieved. We drilled a hole into the core memory. You could not believe the tension. Commander Barker, our nav officer, the CO, and the whole nav gang held their breath while we drilled into the only core memory on the boat and inserted a rectal thermometer. We hoped we were drilling in the right place. If we blew it, patrol performance would suffer.'

The solution worked for the rest of the patrol, and an extra memory system was stocked thereafter for future patrols. The benefits of thorough training were again highlighted.

Bubbleheads could be cunning, too, when required. Bob Weeks, QM2 Blue Crew, of the USS *Francis Scott Key*, was a quick thinker. The boat had set out on Christmas Eve from Holy Loch, and Weeks was on the flying bridge with the captain. As a quartermaster he was qualified in Morse code, but had seldom used this skill. The captain ordered him to send a message via signal light to one of his friends on shore. Weeks made his best effort, but then: 'Much to my dismay, someone on shore flashed a message back – I have no idea what it said, but I told the captain that it wished us a Merry Christmas and a safe journey.' [136]

Activity in Scotland

Holy Loch was the home port for SubRon -14 . The headquarters was responsible for the training, equipping and administering of the submarines and the other associated vessels.

SubRon-14 had been established in 1958, and it came to Holy Loch in 1961 as the headquarters of the United States' first operational SSBN squadron. It was Washington's front-line strategic deterrent. Captain Ron Gumbert stated its purpose: 'Its contribution to the defence of the United States was immense. Its patrolling submarines provided total strategic cover during that period.' The squadron headquarters carried out certain important tasks. When an SSBN arrived in Holy Loch from patrol the very first thing to leave the ship was 60-plus days' worth of encoded punched cards. These contained the data record of the various ship's systems. A courier would take them to the Courier Transfer Unit at USAF Prestwick. Once there, they were flown stateside and forwarded to U.S. Navy scientists for scrutiny and evaluation.[137]

The punched-card information was basically a record of every action taken by each of the ship's systems during the patrol. The data showed which systems were working correctly, which were not, and which needed replacement. It produced a list of spare parts required, and these were transhipped to Holy Loch. This meticulous analysis ensured that the SSBN should always be able to work to its full capability.

LCDR Peter Boyne, an ex-SSBN navigator, described this routine: 'Every piece of navigations and weapons data was recorded on the management data system. The IBM typewriter printed out everything, and this was part of the patrol report. During the patrols the crews were tested on their ability to launch. This was done by a series of random exercises which simulated a launch scenario on a no-notice basis. These tests were evaluated by Johns Hopkins APL after every patrol, checking the ship's performance in navigation, missile accuracy, missile readiness and communications. Every six months, a report evaluating the performance of the fleet ballistic missile submarine force went to the Joint Chiefs of Staff. They cared very deeply about that performance, because they wanted to see how effective the nation's nuclear deterrent was against the Soviet Union.'[138]

After examination, the data went to force commanders and ultimately, on a quarterly basis, to the Joint Chiefs of Staff. The special projects (SP) unit also received some information as it pertained to operational performance of ship's systems, equipment and weapons readiness states. Every deterrent patrol from Holy Loch was analysed in detail. There were many thousands of components in the ship's inventory which needed replacement or repair. The punched cards recorded this detail.[139] Also, the SSBN commanding officer would submit a patrol report. This listed the onboard activities, and contained various other pieces of information related to the ship's operation during the patrol. The squadron headquarters staff would review the report and comment accordingly. Mike Giambattista remembered this activity: 'The patrol reports were classified top secret and carried by courier for distribution to other recipients.'

Holy Loch was a vital strategic base. The Russians would have mounted an intensive espionage mission to probe its secrets. But there was a strong counter-espionage effort by the British and American intelligence agencies. Douglas H. Wise, CIA Senior Intelligence Service (Ret), explained how this operation would have been implemented: 'First of all, the CIA would not have mounted any unilateral counter-intelligence operations inside the UK. The CIA's Counterintelligence Center officers would be working closely with their UK counterparts to investigate, but they would not be running ops; they would be supporting MI5.'[16]

---

16 The United States Naval Criminal Investigative Service (NCIS) is the U.S. Navy's primary law enforcement agency. Most NCIS personnel are civilian.

However, snooping also occurred from an unexpected source, as Mike Giambattista recalled: 'A party of 50 French naval officers from their War College visited Holy Loch for an overview of the SSBN refit program. I sat in on several group discussions, and not only listened to them, but was interrogated with very detailed questions regarding SSBN operating characteristics, patrol schedules, communication capabilities, targeting and alert procedures. Sufficiently wary, I subsequently passed a detailed summary to ONI [Office of Naval Intelligence] in Washington.'

The possibility of James Bond-style activity was very real, and precautions were taken to neutralise such behaviour. The sentries at Holy Loch were fully briefed to observe the water for any suspicious activity. They were good at this, and the outcome was occasionally unexpected. On a dark and stormy winter night, Mike Giambattista was the duty officer when an emergency alert was sounded aboard the *Hunley*.

The topside watch on an SSBN alongside reported a frogman crawling out of the water onto their boat. Percussion grenades were dropped over the sides of the SSBN to impact any diver in the water.

The SSBN was illuminated by *Hunley*'s searchlights. The dive boat with its shallow-water divers arrived swiftly – the frogmen had been waiting a long time for such an incident. Hearts beating rapidly, they entered the water and started a search for explosive devices on all areas of the submerged hull. Nothing was found. The sentry who reported the incident was interviewed rigorously. He had no further information. Finally, in the early hours of morning, the answer was found … the dawn's light showed several seals swimming nearby.

The inevitable conclusion was that the mysterious figure swimming onto the boat's stern was most likely to have been one of the 25,000 harbour seals which live in Scottish waters. These seals were often sighted swimming around SSBN sterns during daylight.

Local turf war

Good communications are the central tool in all military activities, but Holy Loch had a problem in this respect. When the SSBNs were entering or leaving Holy Loch they needed to communicate with squadron headquarters. This was done by using the radio mast of the submarine. But Holy Loch did not have a squadron-specific radio mast; it used the tender's radio facilities.[140]

The base was surrounded on three sides by mountains. Radio signals are affected by intervening land. Therefore, the low radio mast height of the SSBNs on the surface was a disadvantage. This became a source of annoyance to both the headquarters and the submarines. The SSBN officers, with their urgent need for accurate information during their navigation of local waters, harshly criticised the tender's radio operators. The normal military solution was being applied – when communications do not work properly, it is the fault of the other user.

The commodore instructed Mike Giambattista to resolve the matter. His initial investigation showed that the tender radio operators were fully committed to remaining in contact with the submarines. The cause turned out to be an ongoing turf war aboard *Proteus* regarding the priority of radio usage. Both parties concerned – the submarine squadron operators and the Site One operators – claimed priority. Mike acted swiftly. He looked up the rules and found the solution.[141] He explained the situation to the captain of the *Proteus*.

It was a brief meeting: 'Captain, the tender is here to support the submarine squadron. As the 'embarked flag' [senior command], SubRon-14's needs take priority.'

'Thank you, Mike; I got the picture and will comply.'

Problem solved.

Sea trials

Before leaving on patrol, the SSBNs would undertake sea trials whose purpose was to check out all replaced equipment and familiarise the new crew members with the ship's procedures. The sea trials were busy periods. An SSBN would fire an exercise torpedo at a target ship; this was normally one of the tugs. Missile countdown exercises would be run, along with drills covering fire, flood and major steam leaks. These had to be refined, as it was essential that the crew could tackle all possible onboard incidents. These drills had to be performed perfectly. It normally took four days in the Irish Sea to reach the required standard. At the same time, this was a busy area with many other users, and other incidents could occur.[142]

Captain Bivens recalled an adventure with a prawn trawler. These boats lower two heavy metal door-shaped pieces of equipment which are then dragged along the sea floor to scoop up everything into the trailing nets: 'During *Sam Houston* sea trials we had a scrape with a trawler. The fishing boat was using its trawling gear [doors] … our sonar dome had been decapitated. This housed the underwater telephone transducer and enemy torpedo detection microphones.' Serious damage had been caused by an unexpected source. The SSBN returned to Holy Loch for repairs, and the patrol schedule was amended. The incoming boat was extended on patrol, and no strategic damage was incurred.

Saving the *Trout*

The Russians sent their intelligence-gathering submarines close to Holy Loch, and the U.S. Navy also used intelligence-gathering submarines to infiltrate the defences at the Soviet fleet near Murmansk. They carried out regular intelligence-gathering missions in this region. These were mainly carried out by Sturgeon-class nuclear attack submarines (SSNs), armed with nuclear SUBROC anti-submarine missiles. This activity led to various collisions with Soviet vessels and underwater obstacles.[143]

They would take photographs, follow Soviet submarines and listen to radio and radar traffic. Specialist intelligence staff ('riders') from the National Security Agency (NSA) would be on board.[144]

The secrecy surrounding these special missions was demonstrated by a highly sensitive rescue mission. Mike Giambattista was relaxing at home in Gourock, across the River Clyde from Holy Loch. Just before midnight he received a call from the squadron duty officer. An American submarine had reported that it had an urgent medical casualty aboard who needed to be removed to hospital. Giambattista knew the submarine must be on an intelligence mission. It was the USS *Trout* (SS-566), commanded by LCDR William Crowe. The message from the duty officer was succinct: 'I'm sending the commodore's gig to get you.'

Giambattista raced to the navy pier at Cardwell Bay, off Gourock. The men on the 2-mile trip aboard the gig had to cope with some 'sporting' conditions as it pushed at full speed across the river to Holy Loch. Within the hour, Mike was in contact with the Royal Navy to set up a rendezvous with *Trout*, near Stornoway on the Isle of Lewis, the nearest suitable location on the submarine's southward transit. *Trout* had been involved in a reconnaissance mission near the Kola Peninsula, and was on its return trip to Faslane.

The removal of the casualty was an urgent matter. Suddenly the plan was changed. The Royal Navy informed Mike that *Trout* had declined the rendezvous team's offer to take the ailing crewmember to the local hospital. Giambattista was puzzled as to why medical treatment was being delayed: 'Surely the health of the casualty was the most important matter?' It was not. In military life, the mission is paramount. Everything else takes second place.

He radioed LCDR Crowe and was told that *Trout* would continue to Holy Loch. Mike confirmed the action but was left puzzled. He made his way to the dry dock after organising the arrival of the submarine: 'On arrival, LCDR Crowe briefed Commodore Jackson and me that the individual in question was a Russian-speaking NSA agent. Crowe stated that he was unwilling to turn the agent over to the Brits, given the sensitive nature of *Trout*'s mission.'

The NSA 'rider' was there for the intelligence-gathering mission. The Americans would have preferred that the British were unaware of this, as not all missions were run jointly. On many occasions there would be a British observer aboard – but not this time.

The casualty made a good recovery aboard the tender. Giambattista had learned a lesson about the importance of intelligence-gathering missions. Crowe, meanwhile, went on to become Chairman of the Joint Chiefs of Staff.[17]

SSBN operations

An SSBN needed to stay at sea for as long as possible. It did not have to refuel, but as the crew could not cope with an endless voyage, a different approach was needed.

Captain Ron Gumbert, former Commander SubRon-14, explained the development of the SSBN fleet's most important feature, the two-crew system – Blue Crew and Gold Crew:

> 'The SSBN concept was developed to keep the submarine at sea as much as possible. The crew could not be at sea 70 per cent of a year. They had families. Life on a submarine was confining and the at-sea operating tempo (24 hours a day, 7 days a week) was exhausting. Holy Loch was selected to exploit this advantage, as it was closer to Russia than East Coast USA.'

---

17 Chairman, Joint Chiefs of Staff, is the senior military officer in the United States.

'The solution was to have two crews to man each SSBN. The two-crew concept enabled FBM submarines to spend two-thirds of their operational lifetime at sea. This minimized in-port time and allowed the FBM fleet to be one of the most operationally active in the Navy, a fact most FBM submariners were quick to point out.'[145]

Fully developed at Holy Loch, the two-crew system was replicated at all subsequent American nuclear submarine bases. The crews would alternate every three months. Ron Gumbert outlined the process:

'The incoming crew arrived at Prestwick, were bussed to Greenock and would take the boat out on a three-month patrol, then return to Holy Loch. After their handover to the relief crew, they would fly back to the USA for leave and training. This way the boat could be at sea covering its targets most of the time. The two-crew interchange was a routine matter.'

'The incoming Gold Crew would stay aboard the tender. The Blue Crew would stay aboard the submarine for three or four days before leaving for the United States. The crews would meet up and be briefed about equipment issues, supplies, and the patrol. The departing crew continued the training imperative when in the United States, and undertook more when they returned to the boat.'

The incoming crew would move on board and start stowing supplies and gear for its upcoming patrol. Every new patrol included new crew members, some of them new to subs, and some who had transferred from other subs. Every new man had to start acquainting himself with the boat and their watch stations. They had to learn every pipe, valve, tank, capacity, switch etc aboard the boat. Non-stop training continued. High standards were thereby maintained. Captain Bivens stressed this requirement: 'It was essential that the crews changed over, otherwise many individuals would have burned out. Stress aboard submarines is higher than aboard surface ships because of the confinement, long at-sea periods and limited communications with the outside world.'[146]

Each patrol could take 90 days or more, and for at least 60 days the boat would be submerged. Patrols would be extended on station for many reasons. Occasionally this was for operational reasons, but most of the time an extension was due to a mechanical problem aboard the relieving boat. One of these occurred in 1984 when the USS *Nathaniel Greene* (SSBN-636) had lost its propeller in the Irish Sea and returned to Holy Loch using its secondary propulsion system. It was moved to the Royal Navy submarine base at Faslane for repair.[147]

Another seagoing incident took place in March 1986, when the same SSBN ran aground in the Irish Sea. This caused external damage to its ballast tanks and rudder. The U.S. Navy stated: 'there was no effect on the propulsion, no injuries and no damage to the Poseidon nuclear missiles'. USS *Nathaniel Greene* returned to Site One for emergency repairs before crossing the Atlantic to Charleston, South Carolina. The extent of the damage subsequently led to the vessel being decommissioned.[148]

As these boats were constantly at sea, they required a higher degree of repair and maintenance than a regular ship. In addition, as recalled by Ronald P.C. Waller: 'Conditions onboard were uncomfortable. The patrols were carried out north of the Arctic Circle. It was very cold, and after about a month there the whole submarine cooled down to freezing point. Moisture would collect everywhere and run down the decks.' [149]

Retraining of FBM crews during the off periods was vital, as each crewman needed to know about any updated technology and equipment. The amount of training a submariner went through is astounding. A sonarman, for example, had to be well versed in the operations of an engineering space so that in a casualty situation he could operate a piece of equipment.

Everyone on a submarine had to know how to make closures or operate specific valve line-ups. Incoming crews had to be reintroduced to the submarine, as new equipment would have been installed. New crew members had to learn relevant procedures; in crew turnover face-to-face communication was the number one priority. Effective communication between the crews meant that all important facts about equipment status were exchanged. This retraining ensured that the United States SSBN fleet fully exploited the strategic advantage of its base in Scotland. [150]

The turnover period did not have a formal plan, and operated through person-to-person contacts. The crews were fully professional. The effectiveness of the system was shown when the SSBN departed on patrol; inventories of publications, test equipment and spare parts would have been accurately maintained, and the success of the mission was safeguarded by this activity. Captain Lawrence Ross noted: 'Another aspect of turnover that makes it an efficient way of running a ship is that during turnover we get two sets of eyes looking at a lot of different areas on the submarine, such as publications, materiel instructions and so on.' [151]

When an SSBN pulled into Holy Loch the nuclear propulsion plant had to be turned off. It then needed to be started up at the end of the refit and this was a dangerous activity. Nuclear engineers would watch the plant start-up activity with concern, as moisture could form in its piping and cause a serious problem: during this process, a steam pipe, 18 inches in diameter, would jump 2–3 inches until the system was fully operational. If the pipe failed, everyone in the engine room would be cooked alive. This was where the nukes, such as Mike Lacey, stood six-hour watches. He was aware of the risk: 'We only wore protective clothing when entering a contaminated area, like the reactor compartment.' [152]

Many sailors came from seafaring families. Mike Masishin was keen to follow in his father's footsteps to serve his country, and he became a submariner. As a quartermaster he completed five deterrent patrols. He recalled the main tasks: 'The quartermaster recorded various events of the watch – changes in course, speed and depth – and dealt with emergencies such as fires and flooding. One regular activity was when the pilot came aboard the boat to aid in navigating through areas that presented extra challenges to safe navigation, such as Holy Loch.' [153]

Boarding by the pilot was eagerly awaited by the captain. The pilot's presence was crucial to the safety of the boat. A formal procedure would be followed, Masishin recalled: 'The captain would always have the conn[18] and purposefully direct the quartermaster to enter into the log that the pilot was indeed aboard. Should a nasty event such as a grounding occur, that notation

---

18 Have the conn – be on the bridge and in control of the boat.

in the log would mitigate any charges that the captain did not have complete control during that evolution.'

But the SSBNs were not at sea just to carry out patrol duties; they had a specific, and spine-chilling, mission. The SSBN was a missile launch platform. This was an awesome responsibility. The missile-firing process was constantly rehearsed, and before departing on patrol all SSBN officers were briefed.

Sophisticated equipment ensured that launches were perfectly timed. This was a strong memory for Ronald P.C. Waller: 'I have been in 50-foot waves in the North Atlantic. The missile deck had upward-facing sonar. This measured the depths of the waves above. The missiles were timed to launch between the crests of the waves. Even at a depth of 400 feet we still suffered from the topside weather.' [154]

For the firing circuits to be properly armed, each of four designated officers on board would have to vote, by turning a switch. Then to fire the weapon the captain and the weapons control officer each had a key to turn, the navigation officer needed to throw a switch, and the launch control officer would then pull a large lever – the trigger. To safeguard against wrongful use, the three designated officers could officially refuse to obey the captain's order to fire. This is the only case in the United States armed forces when mutiny is sanctioned. [155]

The unreality of this situation was pointed out by Captain Mortimer: 'We were practicing all the time to be perfect at something we hoped would never happen. If the real thing came along, we knew precisely what to do. We ended up thinking that nobody could be that crazy.' [156]

On patrol, the missiles were constantly kept in an 'up' status – ready to fire at a moment's notice. The missile crews, clad in their blue poopie suits (lint-free nylon overalls), monitored each missile. [19] They checked the consoles which gave information on each missile's temperature, the stability of its guidance system, and the targets to be engaged.

They operated at a high state of readiness; for 99 per cent of the time the Poseidon crews would have 15 of their 16 missiles ready to launch. Concentration was essential and adrenalin levels were high. The targets for the missiles were initially recorded on 8-inch magnetic disks. This information was fed into the fire control computers, which converted the instructions into trajectories. The computer constantly revised the trajectory of each of the more than 100 warheads. [157]

An order to fire, whether on exercise or in earnest, came in the form of a coded Emergency Action Message (EAM), and the message was checked by comparing it against a ready-prepared twin, sitting in a special safe – the Red Box. If Main Battle Stations was then declared by the captain, the 16-step firing sequence began, and this sequence then took 15 minutes. [158] To prevent any misunderstandings the coded exercise EAM had a different layout compared with the ready-prepared twin.

American technology was used in the constant upgrading of the SSBNs. The Holy Loch submarines were regularly enhanced, and new classes were introduced. They were armed with

---

19 The standard uniform for officers and crew in a U.S. nuclear-powered submarine at sea was blue coveralls. They were made of lint-free polyester because lint could clog the air purification system. This garment, known as a 'poopie suit', was simple, easy to wear and practical. The choice of footwear was up to the individual, so long as it had a non-slip rubber sole, which also had the advantage of being quiet. Sneakers (trainers) were popular.

a series of ever-improving nuclear ballistic missiles. Captain Ron Gumbert commented on these technological advances and their ultimate effect: 'The initial Polaris missiles had a 1,200 nautical mile range. By 1982 their range had increased to 2,500 nautical miles, with multiple re-entry warheads. Poseidon, with the same capabilities, was introduced and then retired in 1985 in accordance with SALT [Strategic Arms Limitation Treaty] requirements. This was rapidly superseded by Trident which had a range of 4,000 nautical miles. Improvements were made to each class throughout their service.' [159]

Submarine communications were difficult. The radio operators had the highest security clearance, and followed strict procedures to avoid transmissions that might give away the submarine's position. A global network of communications stations relayed these messages. An airborne group of aircraft, known as Take Command and Move Out (Tacamo), flew over the oceans to relay the messages from Washington DC to the submarines.

The Soviet Union faced the same problem in communicating with submarines. It developed a similar solution with the Tu-142MR Oryol (Eagle). The R stands for *retranslyater*, which translates as 'communications relay aircraft.' However, this system did not arrive until the late 1970s. By the end of the Cold War, the Oryol squadrons consisted of seven aircraft. Oryol's mission performance was rated as inferior to the American Tacamo system.[160]

Communication was always risky, recalled Adam Scott: 'The submarine also had a floating-wire antenna; this was 1,500 feet long and would rise to the surface. They were often lost when the submarine dived, as they were cut by the propeller. These antennae were fitted with explosive bolts that would open up when the wire was cut, to sink their buoy, but sometimes they would float to shore. A couple of times they landed on beaches in Ireland. The police always believed they were some kind of bomb and would blow them up and then inform the U.S. Navy. Fishermen would occasionally report that they got caught in their nets.' [161]

As no state of war ever existed, the floating-wire antenna was put to other uses: 'It was just like an underwater cell phone, and sailors' families would be in the radio room back at base. Each sailor would get a few minutes for receiving teletype messages from home. This was a great morale booster during ten weeks of submerged silence.' The sailors were unable to reply, though, as submarine communication was one-way from headquarters until the boat surfaced on its return to Holy Loch.[162]

Essential to navigation – the Shetland outpost

The Northern Seas were the war zone for the SSBN fleet. As the boats' operational success was dependent on accurate navigation data to fix their exact firing position, a complex support system was put in place to ensure this.

During the Second World War the U.S. Navy and the Royal Navy had developed a long-range navigation system – LORAN. Its land-based radio transmitters enabled ships, or aircraft, to fix their positions when they were within range of a LORAN station.[163]

In 1957, the U.S. Navy constructed a chain of LORAN-C stations in the north-east Atlantic, the Pacific and the Mediterranean. This system was then upgraded to support the SSBN fleet.

Its impact was shown in 1958 when the nuclear-powered submarine USS *Nautilus* (SSN-571) reached the North Pole.

This sent a powerful message to the Soviet Union: the U.S. Navy could now accurately navigate to any point in the ocean, thanks to the LORAN technology. The strategic benefits for the United States were obvious, and the Soviets had no nuclear-powered submarine of their own. The U.S. Navy was even able to navigate at extreme latitudes without surfacing, because of its technological superiority. This was America's response to the shock of Sputnik. It was a highly significant achievement.[164]

By 1969 the LORAN network covered the North Atlantic, the Bering Sea and the Mediterranean, as these were the areas patrolled by the SSBNs from Holy Loch.[165]

Ballistic missile launches rely on accurate navigation. The missiles carried by the SSBNs had a powered launch but an unpowered (ballistic) flight, so no changes could be made during flight. Therefore, both the target location and the launch location had to be accurately known. A rough estimate would not suffice, as Captain Ron Gumbert explained: 'So where is the SSBN at any point in time? That is the navigation challenge. If a ship is on the surface one can use navigation systems to establish the ship's position. But an SSBN needs to remain submerged and undetected.'

Better mapping of the ocean floor was needed for improved submarine navigation, and in 1960 the U.S. Navy deployed USS *Archerfish* (SS-311) for this task. It was chosen to make a two-year geographical survey, Operation Sea Scan, to assist future SSBN operations. Its results were essential steps for the underwater launching of their missiles. This was confirmed by Commander David Ebbs: 'There is little doubt that Operation Sea Scan was part of strategic preparations for SSBN deployment.'[166]

As a result, bottom-contour navigation became easier. Satellites, star sightings and the LORAN system were also used. But satellites were not totally reliable, and star sightings were few and far between. These shortcomings increased the importance of the LORAN system, which was accessed via the SSBN's floating-wire antenna.[167]

LCDR Peter Boyne was an FBM navigator in the 1960s: 'I was responsible for the accurate location of the ship at sea at all times. If, God forbid, we had to launch nuclear missiles against the Soviet pack, the Polaris missiles had to know where they were starting from in order to reach their targets accurately. We had to know where the ship was at all times because you never knew when you might get orders to launch. If anything went wrong, I was called. Any time we went to periscope depth, I was in the Nav Center or the Control Room monitoring navigational procedures.'[168]

The Navigation Center's primary mission was to supply Fire Control with very accurate positions. It was the heart of the ship, and was manned 24/7 by specially trained submarine sailors and electronics specialists. The Nav Center continuously provided the ship's position and attitude to the missile control system for input into the Polaris missiles.[20]

LCDR Boyne explained the details: 'The Nav Center had one of the first large-scale computer systems in the Navy. When these SSBNs went to sea in the sixties, it was the first time digital

---

20 Ship's position and attitude: the ship's latitude and longitude, and its velocity, roll and pitch.

equipment was used in a weapons system. We had six or seven computers. The SSBN's position was plotted every half-hour on graph paper, and these positions were compared to fixes taken by LORAN-C.' [169]

Captain Ron Gumbert explained LORAN's purpose: 'High-technology submarines needed high-technology navigation. Without this there was no guarantee of successful missile use. The LORAN system allowed the SSBNs to position themselves with absolute precision.' [170]

The strategic necessity of LORAN was highlighted in July 1958 when the possible cancellation of a LORAN station in the Dominican Republic prompted Admiral Arleigh Burke, the head of the U.S. Navy, to write to the Under Secretary of State, stressing its importance. LORAN remained a cornerstone of US strategic detail, as it ensured that all SLBM (submarine-launched ballistic missile) targeting was accurate.[171]

LORAN in the Shetlands

There was a specific Scottish link in this complex navigation system. The signals from the individual LORAN stations were checked for accuracy by a specialist monitoring station within each group. One of these was Scatsta in the Shetland Islands, 200 miles north of Scotland.

Scatsta was a former RAF wartime airfield lying halfway between Scotland and Norway. During the Second World War, flying boats carrying sabotage teams and supplies to aid resistance groups had taken off from there for Norway. In 1944, the base had been a staging point for the RAF attack that sank the German battleship *Tirpitz*, which had been hiding in a Norwegian fjord.[172]

The wartime base had been vulnerable to attack from German planes, which could approach undetected at low level. So military engineers had laid mines under the runways. These were Canadian pipe mines spaced at 50-yard intervals, and they would enable the defenders to destroy the runway, in defence against any German invasion.

The first German bombs of the Second World War to fall on British soil were dropped on 13 November 1939, on Scatsta. Four bombs fell in a field – one rabbit perished – and at the end of the war the airfield closed.

The LORAN-C Norwegian Sea Chain was built with transmitting stations in Iceland, the Faroe Islands, Norway, Germany and the island of Jan Mayen. Initially there had been a North Sea Chain SAM (System Area Monitor) station at Tarva, in Norway. But this proved unworkable after the chain was extended in 1964. A decision was then taken to establish a new SAM station at Scatsta, which now had a new mission – to control and monitor the Norwegian LORAN-C chain.[173]

Because of Norway's veto on the presence of foreign troops on its soil, LORAN was placed under the command of the US Coast Guard (USCG). One of the Coast Guard missions is Aids to Navigation, and in earlier years this was achieved with lighthouses and buoys. The USCG manned more than 100 LORAN stations during the Second World War.[174]

LORMONSTA (LORAN monitoring station) Shetlands was a navigation aid not only to SSBNs; its information was used by other ships and aircraft. The station was an indispensable link in the anti-submarine warfare process, as it provided positional information for the ASW aircraft which were tracking Soviet submarines and other vessels.

There were two other Scottish Loran stations. They sat on the Atlantic seaboard at Mangersta, on the Isle of Lewis, and Garth's Ness in Shetland. Only Scatsta was staffed by Americans. The others had RAF and Air Ministry personnel on board, recalled Mangersta local Finlay J. McLeod: 'After 1946, when the Mangersta operation was taken over by the UK Civil Aviation Authority, it operated under a number of department titles such as CAA, Ministry of Civil Aviation, possibly Board of Trade and towards the end by NATS [National Air Traffic Services].' [175]

Cdr Fred Ver Planck, a member of the U.S. Coast Guard staff in London, explained that the United States Coast Guard HQ staff were the overseers of the Loran-C system: 'Local control was delegated to Coast Guard officers. Lormonsta Shetlands (Scatsta) was only a monitor station and did not broadcast Loran signals. But with its fixed geographic location it could detect if a particular transmitting station in the chain was broadcasting a signal that was off by a few milliseconds. This was vital information. Any deviation of the signal was immediately relayed to the station involved and it was swiftly corrected. This data ensured that the navigation information for the SSBNs was always accurate.' [176]

LORAN arrives in Scotland

The Scatsta Loran station was a small unit, built in 1968. The exploding defensive runways had added some excitement to the construction phase, and Seabees[21] gingerly removed the wartime charges. Some HF masts were erected, along with operations and accommodation buildings. John Tait, a local tradesman, worked on the base: 'This was a Loran-C station built in the mid-60s on the edge of an old Second World War airfield at Scatsta, a few miles from the village of Brae. It was completely self-contained, with its own electric generators. The building was of a high standard and had about 15 single billets.'

When the first Coast Guard personnel arrived, in May 1968, the accommodation block at Scatsta was still under construction. Several rooms were let in the nearby Sullom Voe Hotel. This had been the RAF Scatsta officers' quarters during the war. The initial crew at the Loran station consisted of two officers and fourteen enlisted personnel.

Small though it was, Scatsta would have been a front-line Russian target, as pointed out by General Sir Rupert Smith, former NATO North commander: 'Scatsta and the other radio spy stations were well within the range for a Soviet parachute assault. The flight would be low-level and use the coastline to shield the aircraft from radar. This assault would have air cover and close air support. Particularly in the case of an assault, the targets might have been bombed in advance of the drop.'

The Russians would have treated the Shetlands the same as the Orkneys. The airfields at Kirkwall and Lerwick would have been targeted, either by parachute assault or by attack from aircraft. But this was not realised by the Scatsta personnel. They did not regard themselves as a military target, as was revealed in 1981 by the commanding officer, Lt Stark: 'As far as I know

---

21 CBs, the Mobile Construction Battalion, are part of the Navy's Civil Engineering Corps. In wartime they build, maintain and repair airfields and beachheads. In peacetime they carry out projects wherever the Navy or Marine Corps require them.

Scatsta has no military significance. The system can be used by aircraft. We just make sure the signal goes out, but we have no idea what it is used for.' But in fact Scatsta had considerable military significance. The cover story about its use for civilian vessels and aircraft held sway, and Lt Stark was sticking to it.[177]

However, investigative journalist Duncan Campbell pointed out that LORAN had been modernised to support the nuclear missile submarines. He stated that it had been built to improve SSBN navigation with the sole purpose of improving the accuracy of the Polaris missile.

This was confirmed by LCDR Peter Boyne, an SSBN navigator who used LORAN-C: 'The mission of the ship was to remain undetected, so that no one knew where the boat was. Any activity at periscope depth with mast exposed could result in detection, by either friendly or unfriendly forces. So the captain wouldn't let me go up as often as I wanted, and made me rely on LORAN-C. The transmission was continuously copied on a floating-wire antenna while the SSBN remained deep. The antenna floated just below the surface, trailed behind the ship out to – I think it was – 1,500 feet.' [178]

Mike Giambattista had extensive experience with LORAN when he took part in Operation Sea Scan aboard USS *Archerfish* (SS311). He had no doubt as to the system's importance: 'Before satellite navigation arrived, LORAN-C was as good as it got for fixing position electronically. It was developed to cope with the requirements of SSBN navigation.'

Scatsta's task was described as keeping Europe's LORAN stations in correct timing and pulse shape. Former Coast Guard Edward E. Mathus recalled the routine: 'The main daily duty was to make sure the equipment was calibrated, results observed and maintenance carried out. There was a daily check of all operational activity. The swing of each chart recorder had to be registered as accurate, and each timer was checked for parameters set in the maintenance technical manual. The caesium clocks were adjusted to be in synch with the master clock and all equipment and transceivers were checked. Such detailed attention helped to maintain the standards of operation. Scatsta was an integral part of the huge American military presence in Scotland. The only acceptable standard was excellence.' [179]

Charles 'Mac' McLean was a Scatsta veteran: 'It was a distinct privilege to be a plank owner[22] on the USCG's first commissioned station in the United Kingdom.' ASW aircraft operated within its range, and they needed accurate navigation data: 'LMS Shetland was critical to maintain aerial surveillance of Soviet submarines making passage through the North Sea. The Orion P-3 aircraft would identify these Soviet boats with sonobuoys, then get a track and course from the sonobuoys. They would identify the submarine's specific location with LORAN-C. This info was sent to the fast attack NATO and US boats, who followed the Soviet boats until they returned back to base after their patrol.'

He emphasised the importance of Scatsta: 'LMS Shetland ensured the accuracy of the LORAN-C chains. This pressure on the Soviet boats, and the assistance for our boomers, gave US and NATO allies an insurmountable technology gap, which finally forced the entente and the final dissolution of the USSR.' [180]

---

22 A member of a ship's or shore station's crew from the time it had first been commissioned.

Life at Scatsta

Coast Guard historian Bill Dietz explained Scatsta's purpose: 'The Shetland SAM [System Area Monitor] station was a control station for the LORAN-C North Atlantic Chain. There would be a live watch to monitor the signal of the transmitting stations and to make corrections to keep the system in tolerance. At first it was done via radio communications or teletype. Later, with new equipment, the corrections could be done remotely.' [181]

Bill Broome served two tours at Scatsta, and remembered its equipment: 'It was the control station for part of the Norwegian Sea Chain. We continuously monitored their signals, and there was always a person on duty.' [182]

The constant routine of watches ruled life at Scatsta, as remembered by Ted Jernigan: 'Coast Guard LORAN station watches were stood by one enlisted person. One ET was on duty 24 hours a day.' Arthur Odgers recalled his service as: 'long periods of great boredom punctuated by brief moments of sheer terror.' The weather at Scatsta could be brutal.[183]

A former Scatsta XO, Larry Oliszewski, listed his tasks: 'When the commanding officer was away I was his replacement. I also was required to inspect other stations, namely those at Sylt, the Faroe Islands and Jan Mayen Island, and in Italy. I would daily check all operational activity via the log and chart recorder. The antenna transmission line and insulators were inspected as required. The final part was to note that all administrative messages had been read and signed.' [184]

As a member of the commissioning crew in 1968, Alex McMahan probably knew more about the Scatsta station than anyone else. He had arrived there as an enlisted electronic technician and was the final commanding officer in 1983.[185]

He recalled that each LORAN station had a different staffing level, depending on its location: 'Shetland was judged to have good amenities. Isolated locations had more personnel as they had no access to local resources like medical, postal, repair businesses or stores. But Scatsta had full access to such resources, and correspondingly needed fewer staff.'

The station operated in a simple fashion, and its general maintenance was undertaken by two local mechanics: 'They dealt with heating, lighting, plumbing and other household matters. Six of the Coast Guard personnel were electronics technicians, who maintained the LORAN equipment. This was housed in a large room where fans cooled the interior, and cupboards of electrical equipment hummed away 24 hours a day.'

Prior to the 1970s the United States Coast Guard had been a men-only organisation. By the 1980s it contained an increasing number of female personnel. This trend was reflected in the makeup of the crew in Shetland. The integration of the female staff was not a problem, but there were some practical difficulties which required creative management. In 1982 there were three female crew members at Scatsta, but there were no separate toilet or shower facilities in the barracks. Alex McMahan recalled the solution: 'To minimise difficulty, there was a sign at the shower/toilet entrance door. One side read *Occupied by male* and the other side *Occupied by female*. A simple system, but it worked well.'

The Coast Guard had moved with the times, and by 1990 there were women at most of the LORAN stations. Teri Sanders was a storekeeper 2nd class petty officer (E-5). When she arrived, there were 12 people assigned to the station, and she was the lone female. There were ten houses on base, and eight were occupied by families. One unit was for her as the single female, and another unit was for the two single males. About a year later another female reported, and shared a house with her.[186]

Sanders dealt with the daily administrative tasks: 'I did all the admin stuff and was a basic watch-stander, so I knew the basics of the operation. Admin included accounting, small purchasing, maintaining personnel records, handling the mail, processing invoices for medical services, stuff like that. I took care of large purchases (at that time, everything over $1,000) and most travel and assignment orders. The station had to look after itself most of the time.'

Sanders also worked with local suppliers. She procured all supplies needed from local sources such as the hardware store, other shops and U.S. Government supply stores. Most of the equipment used to operate the LORAN activity came from the Coast Guard supply depot on the East Coast of the United States.

It was a long logistical chain. LORMONSTA Scatsta was a long way from the US Coast Guard Europe Headquarters in London. It was more than 600 miles by air on two separate flights, or by a 900-mile road journey involving ferries and mountains.

But admin never stops. The Coast Guard staff in London had to visit Shetland. Chris Carlson was one of those who made the trip: 'My role at Coast Guard HQ Europe was in logistics and finance, and I visited these stations to do financial audits. My main task was to make sure all personnel were paid correctly. I also arranged the shipment of supplies to the LORSTA stations – usually from the US. Food was procured locally by Scatsta. Some American food items that were hard to find were sent from the US (peanut butter, for example). Coast Guard HQ London made sure they received all their technical gear, uniform items and personal hygiene items. The primary source for stores was the warehouse at Governor's Island, New York. My job, as logistics chief in London, was to stay abreast of each station's needs, arrange each procurement and shipment, then follow up on the progress of each shipment until everything reached the appropriate station. I spent long hours on the phone.' [187]

Carlson was the senior admin officer in London during the early 1980s: 'I was a budget, supply and money kingpin. My staff handled logistic and monetary support for the CG-manned LORAN Stations. I managed the payroll for military and civilians at these facilities, auditing, transportation of personnel and materials, civilian contracts for maintenance and construction jobs. I also set their budgets. Scatsta, although a tiny base, received top-notch support. This was necessary, as it performed an important role due to its strategically important location in Scotland.'

The CGHQ London admin inspection team regularly made the lengthy journey north to Shetland. Marvin Neylor was a contracting administrator, E-6 1st class petty officer and regular member of the team: 'The team had to inspect all money operations ... procurement of supplies and materials ... dining facilities, physical property management, maintenance of the station buildings, equipment and vehicles.'

It was an onerous activity, but further reinforced the high standards required. This inspection took about a week. Cdr Fred Ver Planck remembered his visits to Shetland. It was remote and windswept, and very far north. His first task was to familiarise himself with the base and its mission. He flew into Lerwick Airport: 'I was astonished to walk outside into daylight at 11 p.m. I settled in for a good night's sleep. I awoke to a bright sun scorching my eyes and looked at the clock. It was 2:30 a.m. Wow! What an introduction to high-latitude daylight.'

When any Coast Guard personnel at Scatsta was being discharged, one of Ver Planck's staff made the journey north. Prior to mustering out of the service and returning to civilian life, the coastie needed to be in receipt of all outstanding payments: 'We put a check in the hands of one of my staff members and put him on a plane to deliver the mustering-out pay before the member had to go home to the USA.'

The reverse was true for re-enlistment. The coastie had to travel to London to re-enlist. But there was method in this madness. The re-enlisting personnel were valuable people, and the Coast Guard administration wanted to thank them by cleverly making this morale boosting trip into a family holiday.

Any building work at Scatsta was done by local civilian contractors. The contracts were controlled by Ver Planck from his London office, and this created a different problem. The Coast Guard civil engineers were good at technical specifications and wrote proposals in a formal fashion that another engineer would understand, but then: 'I was awarding contracts to locals who were accustomed to working on a handshake and a promise, with little technical specifications from the payer.'

The Shetlands have a remote community with a wonderful lore of folk tales and myths. Scatsta naturally attracted wild stories about its activities. There were many tales, most of them tongue in cheek. Some of these even claimed that Scatsta housed missile silos.

Shetland had five military facilities: the RAF on the island of Unst, three Royal Signals stations, and the US Coast Guard LORAN monitor station. Alex McMahan chuckled at the silliness of these rumours: 'The Coast Guard station was the only facility that did not have a fenced perimeter, entrance gates and a 24-hour security guard. Anyone could come up to the station, walk on in and visit at any time. It sounds a bit lax to have been the location of missiles!'

There were no missile silos – only cattle, as the area around the station was their grazing land.

Scatsta was well loved by its crew. Their work was difficult, as recalled by former Commanding Officer Dave Orszak: 'Challenging times, but a great crew.' The Coast Guard worked well with the local community and several personnel married local people. 'The people of Shetland made it a wonderful memory,' noted Michael Ackerman, and his thoughts were echoed by fellow coastie Vern Mace: 'Some of the best days of my life were spent there. Shetland is a magical place.' [188]

But new technology brought change, and automatic equipment was installed. Bill Broome explained the advances: 'The monitoring mission of the Scatsta site was upgraded with remote monitoring equipment. There was now a receiver beacon and a data link to the station in Iceland. In short, technology made the staffing of the site redundant.' Bill Dietz explained what happened next: 'In 1983 the station was closed and the monitoring was moved to Keflavik [in Iceland], with a remote receiver at Shetland.' [189]

The closure caused a problem for local seafarers, and the *Shetland Times* highlighted it on Friday, 20 January 1995:

'Signal temporarily lost.' Most Shetland fishing boats have temporarily been left without part of their navigation equipment following changes to the operation of the LORAN-C system at the turn of last year. The chain of LORAN-C transmitting stations round the northern hemisphere has been altered and updated, changing the pattern of signals sent out. The new system means that at least 100 boats in the local fleet will have to have their wheelhouse receiving modified to accurately pick up the signals.

LORMONSTA Scatsta had operated as a vital part of the LORAN-C navigation system. It had checked the system's output for accuracy, and adjustments had been made when necessary. The U.S. Navy SSBNs had maintained their precise navigation. It had been another job well done, and the service was continued from its automated station. Scotland had provided a further building block in the United States' strategic plan.

Sonar

There were other elements in SSBN navigation. One of the most important was the operation of the boat's sonar system.

The SSBN had to keep itself clear of warships, Soviet submarines, fishing boats and other vessels. Although their mission was a taxing activity with potentially dangerous outcomes, the crew knew that they were very good at detecting other ships. This was achieved by the expert use of sonar. Sonar was a submarine's primary detection and protection system. It detected any nautical targets and fixed the distance to the target. It was also the only sensor that could be used below periscope depth. It was sophisticated equipment, but relied totally on the skills of the operator.

The sonarmen were known as 'shower techs' or 'sonar girls'. They were the most eccentric members of the submarine crew. Every other action aboard a submarine – even flushing the toilet and switching on the kettle – had a written procedure. But sonar work was a creative activity with no written procedures; a good sonarman was the product of an intensive training programme and his own talent.[190]

There was also follow-up training on return from patrols, and sonarmen listened to tapes of different types of ships and marine animals. This enabled them to train their ears and brain to identify these sounds.

Philip Giambri served aboard USS *Patrick Henry* (SSBN-599) as a member of the Blue Crew. While on patrol he stood watches of four hours on and eight hours off: 'Ten weeks underwater working at this pace was hard. The sonarmen developed many skills, and we were the first humans to listen to the whales. We were very active in Russian fishing fleet areas, with lots of sonar activity to monitor. But active sonar was never used, as this would have compromised our position.' Passive listening sonar was deployed, and this had to be interpreted by ear and brain without computer assistance. Giambri remembered this process: 'I loved listening and identifying ships, boats, sea creatures, all by ear. I was pretty accurate at identifying different types of civilian and military ships by the sounds they made.' [191]

Both the NATO and the Warsaw Pact submarines concentrated on remaining hidden. Detection was difficult and both sides devoted large resources to this activity. As submarines could be spotted at depths of 150 feet, they needed to operate beneath this level.

When submarine masts were up, the boats travelled at less than 4 knots to avoid spray giveaway. Their periscopes also had to drain water from the top window for photographs to be taken. This activity kept the boats at periscope depth to accomplish their task, giving opportunities for the Russian Anti-Submarine Warfare (ASW) force.

But there was another activity which added danger – snorkelling. This action was needed when the submarine was running its standby diesel engines. Fresh air was needed for this activity; however, this exposed the snorkel pipe and could also allow water to enter the submarine. This would have damaged the electrical circuits.[192]

The SSBN had masts that housed many instruments – the snort (snorkel) system, the attack periscope, the search periscope, the HF (high frequency) communications mast, the intelligence-gathering mast and the radar mast. The periscopes could also provide the range and bearing of a surface target.[193]

The Holy Loch submarines had to be particularly vigilant before they reached the open seas, as in the confined waters in and around the Firth of Clyde there was a constant danger of collisions with other vessels. Captain Don J. Ulmer commented: 'Once in open waters, we would dive, but we always had a Soviet spy trawler on our trail. They would be measuring everything associated with the SSBN, including transmissions and sounds. Sonar equipment was carried aboard these vessels, and was used to record the sound signature of each SSBN.' This caused SSBNs to avoid any shipping detected within 50 miles when they were at sea. They always operated in a stealthy fashion.[194]

There were also many fishing trawlers whose nets could easily become entangled, and Mike Giambattista remembered an incident with an Irish trawler. The boat had been dragged backwards and had cut its nets to escape from the submarine: 'Once I confirmed that this was the case, arrangements were made via the US Embassy in London to compensate the trawler's owner.'

A trawler is no match for a big SSBN submarine, and there were several occasions when an SSBN unknowingly dragged a trawler backwards for several miles. The SSBNs would be undamaged, and in fact they seldom noticed the collision. In 1987 the Irish fishing boat *Summer Morn* snagged its nets and was dragged back for 10 miles. The crew frantically tried to disengage, and when they were eventually able to break their nets free they found that a section of equipment from the submarine had become entangled with the cables which had been reeled back onto the boat. The section was stamped with the words:

> NAVAL ELECTRONIC SYSTEMS COMMAND.
>
> Mfd by Spears Associates Inc., Norwood, Mass

It was a BR-8 communications buoy, but the U.S. Navy initially denied that any of their submarines were operating in the area. The trawler skipper, Eric Culley, recalled the ordeal: 'It caught in the nets and towed us for miles. We could not cut free and were all scared of being dragged under. Thank goodness we broke free in the end.'

Although the incident was now a fact, the U.S. Navy would not confirm it. The Holy Loch spokesperson would only comment in an oblique fashion: 'All that we are allowed to say is that we don't discuss our submarine operations.' Following more negative publicity, the US Embassy in London had to admit American involvement in the incident: 'The indications are that it was one of ours …'

It was.[195]

The *Dolly* and the Victor bump[23]

The sea lanes leading from the Clyde to the open seas were always dangerous for SubRon-14 SSBN transit. Sometimes frighteningly so. On 3 November 1974 the USS *James Madison* (SSBN-627) left Holy Loch on patrol. Two hours later, Henry Kissinger, Secretary of State, received a short but worrying message from General Brent Scowcroft, the national security adviser:

I HAVE JUST HEARD FROM THE PENTAGON THAT ONE OF OUR SUBMARINES HAD COLLIDED WITH A SOVIET SUBMARINE. THE SSBN JAMES MADISON WAS LEAVING HOLY LOCH WHEN IT COLLIDED WITH A SOVIET SUBMARINE WAITING TO TAKE UP TRAIL. BOTH SUBMARINES SURFACED AND THE SOVIET SUBMERGED AGAIN. THERE IS NO REPORT YET OF DAMAGE OR OTHER DETAILS. WILL KEEP YOU POSTED. WARM REGARDS.[196]

This was a near-disaster, only 10 miles from the west coast of Scotland. The two vessels, having sideswiped one another, both came within inches of sinking. The *Madison* carried 16 Poseidon (C3) ballistic missiles with 160 nuclear warheads. The Soviet Victor-class submarine was probably carrying nuclear missiles and torpedoes.[197]

James Jinks, who wrote a history of Britain's post-war submarine service, said the message was further confirmation of a 'highly secret underwater game of cat and mouse'. He noted that the Soviet submarines were routinely sent to Scottish waters, and operated to detect, track and trail Royal Navy and U.S. Navy ballistic missile-carrying submarines as they deployed from Faslane and Holy Loch.

The incident was kept quiet for more than 40 years. It had occurred inside British territorial waters, a severe embarrassment to the UK Government. A nuclear weapons expert historian, Hans Kristensen, noted: 'It shows how easily they penetrated our defence system and threatened the biggest toy in our arsenal. The nuclear submarines could disappear in the deep Atlantic, but they had a problem when coming out of the narrow confines of the Holy Loch and travelling through the channel between Northern Ireland and the Kintyre peninsula. The big shock with this Victor-class submarine was that it was off Arran.'

---

23 Dolly Madison was the wife of President Madison, hence the nickname 'Dolly' for the SSBN.

After the collision, both boats surfaced and checked for damage, and the Soviet submarine headed back home to Murmansk. The *Madison* had a 9-foot scrape along its hull. A stronger impact would have ripped open both submarines. Repairs were carried out to the *Madison* at the dry dock, and another SSBN was extended on patrol to cover the gap in America's defences.

In the confusion of the collision, a war could have been sparked, as Kristensen noted: 'The *James Madison* was a ballistic missile submarine armed with 16 Poseidon missiles with 160 nuclear warheads. In the worst-case scenario, the collision could have triggered explosions that ignited the ballistic missile fuel and ejected or destroyed the warheads. There was also a clear possibility for a war if the crew on one of the submarines had misinterpreted the collision as an attack and decided to defend itself and sink the other submarine.'

Some crew members were close to the point of collision and have vivid recollections. Jimmy Johnson was a Blue Crew MM1 (machinist's mate 1st class): 'Remember it? Hell, I was there. Spent the entire patrol cycle aboard the *Dolly* in the loch.'

For Stephen J. Munkwitz it was an anti-climax. It was his final deterrent patrol: 'Yeah, that was fun. I was quartermaster on watch when it happened. We had just come out of dry dock from an overhaul. My last and shortest patrol.' [198]

For others it was frightening. James D. Walton, MM3/SS, was on watch and feared for the worst: 'I was in Machinery-1 on watch when it happened. I was on my last patrol and thought for a second that I wasn't going to get back to the States. It sounded like we hit a mountain.'

Donald McKesson was on watch in the MCC (mission control center) when the collision occurred: 'It rolled us to port considerably. No one knew for a few minutes what had happened. We were on pre-patrol sea trials, involved with being the target for British anti-submarine exercises. The Victor was being the typical interfering Soviet submarine and ran over us when we dived. Fortunately, he hit us at an angle rather than T-boning us, which would for sure have sunk us.'

The *Madison* made its way back to Holy Loch for repairs. McKesson said: 'We went into dry dock for several days while the hull was inspected. The collision had left a 9-foot-long dent in the pressure hull at the MCC, which was repaired by removing the cork insulation and wire-brushing the hull clean to enable it to be magnafluxed. Talk about a mess – even with two Handy Billy vacuum blowers sucking air out of the compartment to topside.'

'The skipper visited the MCC during the process and just about had a heart attack at the dust accumulation even with the equipment wrapped in plastic. We were a few days delayed going on patrol, and had reports that the Victor went home on the surface at 3 knots. Thank Heaven for HY-80! [24] I figured I had been closer to a Russian sub than any other American sailor, even if I couldn't see it.' [199]

The cause is still unknown, but Fayette L. Thornal Jr had his own explanation. He knew that a spy trawler was trailing the SSBN. He recalled that it seemed to be marking the *Madison*'s position as the Victor hit it: 'I had just hit the rack after securing the manoeuvring watch when it started. First we heard that sound like a deck hatch slamming shut – then the hit.' [200]

---

24 HY-80 is a high-tensile, high yield strength, low alloy steel. It was developed for use in naval applications, specifically the development of pressure hulls for the US nuclear submarine programme.

Such incidents occurred on a regular basis; the estimated figures for collisions involving nuclear submarines show there have been almost 40 such episodes. None have become a nuclear catastrophe and all have had cover-up stories. No cause has ever been revealed for this incident, but scholars have suggested that the Victor may have been carrying out a reconnaissance mission similar to that done by the USS *Tusk*. The vast majority of similar collisions were located close to submarine bases and tight local waterways. An agreement was drawn up between the United States and the Soviet Union in 1972, but this was regularly ignored, as seen in the 1984 collision between the aircraft carrier USS *Kittyhawk* and a Soviet submarine.

Fishing trawlers were the main problems, not the Russian spy trawlers as these kept behind the SSBNs. The trawlers were always unaware of submarines beneath them as they concentrated on their own fishing activity. So collisions were inevitable, and during the Cold War there were ten such incidents recorded in the waters north-west of Scotland. One happened on 9 April, 1968. The USS *Robert E. Lee* (SSBN-601) was submerged in the Irish Sea en route to Holy Loch and the French trawler *Lorraine-Bretagne* was fishing in the area with nets that were 200 yards long. The inevitable occurred – the SSBN snagged the nets – but the trawler responded swiftly and the nets were jettisoned. The submarine was undamaged.[201]

Another of these incidents was recorded on 7 March 1979, when USS *Alexander Hamilton* (SSBN-617) became tangled in the nets of a Scottish trawler in the Sound of Jura. The SSBN towed the trawler backward for about 45 minutes until the nets were cut. No injuries or serious damage were reported by either party.[202]

Life under the sea – the watches

Life aboard a submarine operated around a daily system of six-hour watches, during which all stations on the boat were manned. This left a six-hour period for other tasks and a six-hour period for rest. Fatigue was inevitable, as an eighteen-hour cycle is a problem for an individual's body clock. Watch-standing was not an easy task, as Bud Lewis noted: 'If you are a qualified watch-stander, you have to stand six on and six off until the new man qualifies for your watch station. That may take some time and it puts a strain on everybody.' The watch system meant that submariners had to function on an 18-hour day instead of a 24-hour day.

When at sea, the watch team controlled the SSBN. Watch teams were commanded by the dive officer. He was supported by the chief of the watch and the quartermaster, another chief. The specialist submariners on duty were supervised by the two chiefs. In emergencies the captain would return to the bridge.

The watch team members were well trained. The watch officer was responsible for the SSBN's integrity; he carried out the mission orders, plus additional orders from the captain, and oversaw all activity. The quartermaster was the keeper of the navigational chart, and constantly calculated and verified the boat's position.[203]

The chief of the watch received commands and instructions from the watch officer, and passed them to the necessary departments and personnel for implementation. He managed the activities of the enlisted personnel in the control room. The SSBN was steered by two planesmen, who manned the bow planes and the fairwater planes to maintain the course and depth ordered by the watch officer or chief of the watch.

The SSBN was a huge electrical complex which was managed by the IC (in charge) electrician. He received orders from officer and/or chief of the watch and transmitted them by the sound-powered phone system or the general announce system. He was also responsible for activating the ship's alarms when ordered. The navigation equipment was overseen by the navigation electronics tech and/or nav officer.

A fire control tech was on duty to maintain the integrity of the control room missile control panel. He also dealt with commands for changes in water and air tank balances by venting or flooding tanks.

There were two enlisted sonar watches, who, as mentioned earlier, did passive listening only. They identified, tracked and reported all non-biological contacts to the control room, and responded to orders regarding contacts. They also recorded any unusual biological or non-biological sounds encountered that might prove valuable for analysis, training or mission assistance. The sonar watches alternated in half-hour shifts to avoid boredom, strain and/or loss of sensitivity to sounds. When tracking a specific contact, the operator on the headphones remained with the contact as long as necessary. Important information was recorded, and once the boat was back at Holy Loch the tapes were sent to the Navy scientists at the APL for analysis. This examination could uncover a new Soviet submarine signature sound.[204]

Thomas Weeks was a member of the USS *Robert E. Lee* (SSBN 601) Blue Crew, STSSS 3, sonar technician. He made seven patrols; for two of these he was in the deck gang and for the other five he was in the sonar gang. The deck gang took care of topside while in port, and when at sea they were mess cooks and laundrymen, and they cleaned the heads. In sonar they listened and tracked all ships and submarines and maintained the equipment. Thomas developed his sonar skills: 'It took me a couple of years to get good at knowing what I was listening to and determining details about the ships around us – their speed, course, whether submarine or surface ship etc. With courses and hands-on training, I gradually learned to fix and maintain most of our equipment.' [205]

The work of a sonarman was not overly physical, but the need to concentrate for long periods was tiring. The sonar room was very small, and listening was both tedious and mentally taxing.

These hardships had all been foreseen and the U.S. Navy had prepared its sailors. This process began at boot camp. Recruits were physically challenged, mentally strengthened and carefully managed to serve on board a ship, submarine or shore station, or to do any other Navy job.

Mike Masishin praised the long-lasting benefits of naval training: 'In the beginning of the process, your civilian life becomes a memory really quickly. You're forced to learn discipline in a way that is rarely seen in the civilian world. You learn to perform as a team. There is individual and team learning, and there are individual and team consequences. All of this is designed to save your life and the lives of the people who work with you.'

The space forward of the engine room was known as the Cone. It was inhabited by the coners. These included the radioman who dealt with all message traffic and were security cleared to a high level. The missile technicians were also in this area. They had the sensitive task of checking the temperature and pressure of the missiles. There were other crew members such as the auxilia-rymen who scrubbed the boat's atmosphere clean, managed the waste tanks and maintained the diesel engines.

The torpedomen were the weapons masters. They maintained the ship's torpedoes and personal weapons. Jim Craig was an archetypal American patriot. Of Scots-Irish descent, his father had educated him on the threat posed by Communism. Jim detested Communism and wanted to see it fail. He got his chance to assist in this matter when he became a member of an SSBN crew. He was a torpedoman's mate 1st class, and the USS *George C. Marshall* was his first boat. His classification required him to supervise the tactical weapons and launching systems, as well as the pyrotechnics and small arms on the ship.[206]

Most SSBNs carried 12 torpedoes. But as Jim Craig recalled: 'They were technologically advanced weapons, but their handling came from the Stone Age. There was a pulley system on board the submarine. Operating this system was physically demanding. Torpedoes had to be moved from their storage bays to the torpedo tubes. The storage area was also our bunk area. We slept alongside two torpedoes – one on either side.'

Constant drills were carried out when at sea, as Craig remembered: 'Life on patrol appeared to be a series of war scenario incidents. The crew was called to battle stations, and various defensive and torpedo-related scenarios were played out. There were scenarios when launching the strategic missiles was simulated for readiness tests. Overall, drills occupied a large part of the time at sea.' Like his crewmates, Craig had been screened and cleared for the pressures associated with the mission. He was only too aware of the consequences of failure: 'It was a quite heavy burden, but we knew what the outcome would be if we lost the Cold War.'

Then there were the cooks, who were the most popular members of the crew. They produced meals every six hours throughout the voyage. Administrative matters were run by the yeomen, and health was monitored by 'Doc', the medical corpsman. All wore Dolphins.[207]

Although vast amounts of money were spent on the construction and maintenance of SSBNs, little money was used for on-board medical facilities. Initially, each boat had an assigned doctor. It was not a hard duty, recalled Mike Giambattista: 'There were 140 fit young men aboard the submarine. To fill their time, many submarine doctors became qualified as diving officer of the watch. They were on the ship's watch bill. Then the situation changed. The Vietnam War arrived. Its impact was immediate. Drafted doctors were needed in Southeast Asia. SSBN medical tasks were passed to senior medical corpsmen.'

Submariners faced constant work-related hazards. Weather and water were ever present. Snow, whether falling in the Holy Loch or at sea, posed problems for the SSBN crew. It would accumulate on deck and it caused treacherous conditions. There were accidents, and sailors fell overboard after slipping on ice. Most times a life ring was thrown to them and they were hauled aboard. 'When the boat surfaced at sea, movement on the top deck was restricted. We had the bridge manned on the sail and hardly ever sent people out on the deck. It's dangerous in open seas for people to be topside, so it was kept to a minimum,' recalled Craig.[208]

Another constant problem for crew members was the adverse effects caused when the SSBN had to use its snorkel. As mentioned earlier, SSBNs also had a diesel engine for emergency power. When it was used it had a dramatic effect, but additional air had to be provided for the engine, and this could only come from outside the boat. It came in through the snorkel mast and this was known as operating on the pipe.[25]

Snorkel air did not come in a constant stream. Inside the ship the air pressure changed significantly every minute. It produced discomfort, and was repeated endlessly for several hours. Damaged eardrums were inevitable. A new officer asked Mike Giambattista about this problem. Without saying a word, Giambattista showed him the bloody handkerchief from his pocket. His eardrums would leak after a day or two on the pipe.

Workplace accidents aboard submarines were common, but boat failures were different. Submarine accidents are the most lethal of naval accidents. Between 1945 and 1989 more than 50 such accidents were recorded by the U.S. Navy. New technology had not reduced the rate of mishaps. In addition, there have been many hundreds of lesser submarine-related incidents recorded. Only 20 per cent of these episodes have occurred in shipyards, the remainder were located around ports.[209]

Although the statistics from the Soviet Navy are not available, it is assumed that they are much higher. The U.S. Navy claimed that the Soviets have suffered 'numerous serious submarine casualties – sinkings, propulsion failures, fires and navigational accidents… In the last ten years, they [the Soviets] have had over 200 submarine accidents, some of which have been very serious.'

The squadron and its mission

By 1975 the Soviets had more than 300 submarines. But they were primitive, noisy and easily detected. Jokes were made that their crew glowed in the dark because of low standards of engineering technology. They were manned by unmotivated, low-paid conscripts with equally low standards.[210]

The Russian submarine fleet was riddled with a 'shocking level of negligence on all levels; stunning breaches of discipline; and shoddy, obsolete and poorly maintained equipment.' There were 'shortcomings of training and discipline … low morale and low professionalism.'

A Russian admiral highlighted their flaws as 'Weak combat and occupational training of the crew, specifically their unfamiliarity with ship systems, emergency procedures, and life-saving equipment.' [211]

Although their submarines could spend 70 days at sea, they were slow and noisy. In addition, the Soviet nuclear-powered submarines regularly suffered observed nuclear reactor failures. The CIA logged various instances of Russian boats being towed slowly back to the USSR. They also noted radiation sickness among the crews in these instances. One of these involved a Cruise missile submarine which was spotted dead in the water near Rockall Bank in 1978 before being towed slowly to the Murmansk region.[212]

---

25 The original snorkel concept was created by James Richardson, an engineer at Scott Shipbuilding in Greenock in 1916. He patented it, but the Admiralty ignored it. The system was eventually fully developed by a Dutchman, Jan Jacob Wichers, in 1938. It was then exploited by the Germans. (J.F. Robb, *Scotts of Greenock: Shipbuilders and Engineers, 1820–1920: A Family Enterprise.* Glasgow University, 1993 unpublished PhD thesis, p. 424.)

In stark contrast, the United States and Great Britain maintained a qualitative advantage over the Russians. They both had experienced, all-volunteer submarine crews and an excellent training regime.

Lieutenant Mike Giambattista was assigned to SubRon-14 at Holy Loch in 1961. His father had attended the US Naval Academy as a classmate of Admiral Rickover in 1927 and had ended his career as a rear admiral.

During Giambattista's Holy Loch tour, the squadron built up to its full strength of ten SSBNs. His role was communications officer. All the incoming and outgoing radio traffic was first routed to him. He had to encrypt outgoing messages and decrypt incomers. The tender's radio centres processed more than 70,000 messages per year. He maintained the secure communication links to the Royal Navy.

Before their SSBN departed Holy Loch, Giambattista recalled that the commanding officers would be notified about the ever-present Russian spy trawlers. Captain Ron Gumbert remembered this factor: 'The submarines would dive as soon as they had cleared the Mull of Kintyre to avoid the line of spy trawlers positioned off the coast of Northern Ireland. Spy trawlers were always on station off the west coast of Scotland. It was all part of the Soviet intelligence-gathering program. The spy trawler would spot the SSBN and follow behind for several miles.'

Giambattista would brief the SSBN's captain and navigator on the status of Soviet trawler activities on their track in the Minches and any adjacent waters: 'Once submerged, the 'boomers' would proceed to their assigned station by a prescribed time. Subsequent target coverage areas or changes were transmitted via encrypted messages copied to the ship via its floating wire antenna.'

On 20 March 1968, while returning to Holy Loch from patrol, USS *Theodore Roosevelt* ran aground off the west coast of Scotland. It had been taking evasive action to avoid being picked up by a loitering Russian spy trawler. In this situation precise navigation was essential, but there was an unforeseen problem. Captain Arthur Clark Bivens recalled the dramatic event: 'There was an uncharted pinnacle or wreck. The ship rammed it and nearly sank. She was saved because the torpedo room was pressurised. The *Roosevelt* switched to high alert status. There was superficial damage with no radiation leaks.' It was repaired at Holy Loch.[213]

The Clyde area was a prime target for Soviet intelligence-gathering after 1969, when Scotland became home to the UK's nuclear missile submarine fleet at Faslane on the Gare Loch, only 10 miles from Holy Loch.

The U.S. Navy had adopted a policy of 'wiping off' against these Soviet submarines. This required the American boats to confront the Soviet boats. It became a game of underwater chicken until one of the boats would back off. It also led to several collisions.[214]

The submarine squadron commander oversaw the entire U.S. Navy operation at Holy Loch. He was the commodore, and occupied the admiral's quarters aboard the tender. The squadron staff had offices on several levels of the vessel. Mike Giambattista's office had a secure entry into the briefing room, where the daily intelligence report and other sensitive issues were discussed.

Giambattista coordinated day-to-day movements of U.S. Navy vessels. He liaised with RAF Leuchars which had ASW aircraft ready to intercept any Soviet flights along SSBN routes. He also had to manage the arrival and departure of Navy cargo ships on a monthly basis. On occasion, there were emergency visits by non-SSBN submarines due to engineering problems or casualties. These submarines would have been involved in intelligence trips or SSBN protection roles.

Most of his time was taken up by the daily intelligence briefings to the commodore, the captains of the tender and the SSBNs alongside, and the senior staff officers. Information came from a variety of sources, including the Pentagon, US Naval Forces Europe (London) and the Royal Navy; it covered a range of topics, each important within the overall operating scenario. The SSBN strategic target coverage was assigned for each patrol by the joint strategic target planning staff located at Offutt Air Force Base in Omaha, Nebraska. The patrol stations were assigned via encrypted messages prior to departure from Holy Loch.[215]

Giambattista worked with a staff of 30 sailors, most of whom were radiomen. At times he had to collect sensitive documents from the US Embassy in London or visit Northern Ireland to liaise with the Naval Communications Station at Londonderry. This activity was essential to SubRon-14 activities, as Londonderry was the communications base for SSBNs.

As mentioned earlier, submariners had been well trained for their role. Their expertise was immense, but it was job-related. They had practical skills which were constantly utilised at their workplace. They followed orders and protected their country. The potential use of nuclear weapons did not cause any concerns with the SSBN crew. That was their role. The attitude of Bud Lewis was typical: 'I did four Gold Crew patrols somewhere in the North Atlantic covering a period from 1965 to 1968. Our main purpose was to remain undetected and be ready to launch missiles when ordered to do so.'

Business as usual

World events did not disrupt Holy Loch's schedule. When President Kennedy was assassinated, there was no change to the routine; mission focus was maintained. On 22 November 1963, Mike Giambattista was driving home listening to the radio, to hear: 'We interrupt this broadcast to let you know that the US President, John Kennedy, has been shot and taken to hospital in Dallas, Texas.'

When his landlady answered his knock on the door she advised him that President Kennedy had died. Giambattista phoned the squadron duty officer immediately. The petty officer answering the phone was unaware of the tragic event. But this dreadful news did not affect the operation of the squadron: 'The only visible symbol of JFK's passing was that the flags were flown at half-staff for 30 days. The fact that the vice president immediately was sworn as president, ergo commander in chief, made for business as usual in the Holy Loch. The mission was never compromised.'

4 'Industrial Las Vegas'

Blue-collar skills and trades

Site One was the location of the U.S. Navy's hard-working, no-nonsense world of
blue-collar skills and trades. A miniature shipyard alongside beautiful scenery.

This was how *All Hands*, the U.S. Navy magazine, described the Holy Loch naval dockyard in 1985. Refit Site One, one of the U.S. Navy's overseas repair facilities, was a big site, similar in size to other dockyards along the River Clyde. The complex was more than 500 yards long, with five massive cranes, two barges and the floating dry dock. It was the workplace of more than 1,500 men and women, naval and civilian, and was illuminated by floodlight every night.

Described as an 'Industrial Las Vegas,' Site One was available to its customers 24 hours a day, 365 days a year. It operated at an unyielding tempo, carrying out 23 submarine refits annually, and it enabled the U.S. Navy to operate a forward support facility closer to its targets in Russia.

There were three separate commands at Holy Loch: Submarine Squadron 14 (ComSubRon 14), the submarine tender and the floating dry dock, USS *Los Alamos*. The commander of the submarine squadron was the senior U.S. Navy officer in charge of the Holy Loch and the Fleet Ballistic Missile Submarine Force in Scotland. The dry dock, the submarine tender and the ten SSBNs reported to him. But, significantly, the submarines themselves did so only when they were in port. When at sea they reported directly to the Pentagon. The Naval Support Activity, responsible for all the leased facilities and coordination of all the support for the US military families on the Cowal peninsula, adjacent to the Firth of Clyde, also reported to him.[216]

The tenders were needed at Holy Loch to enable submarines to refit at a forward deployed site. This meant they did not have to return to home port to conduct maintenance and repairs. The SSBNs underwent refits there, which increased their availability to be at sea and within missile range, performing their strategic deterrent mission. The SSBNs needed to periodically offload missiles for maintenance, and onload new missiles that had been updated/refurbished. This was all part of a pre-planned maintenance cycle.

The first tender was USS *Proteus*. As initially it was not long enough to store nuclear missiles, a 40-foot section had been inserted amidships. It was more than 500 feet long. Its successor, USS *Hunley* (AS-31), had integrated facilities for servicing the Polaris weapons systems. It could carry out difficult tasks that had been awkward for *Proteus*, such as welding on SSBN pressure hulls and also the welding of reactor plant fluid systems. Other than a major shipyard overhaul, *Hunley* could handle any submarine repairs.

Before the U.S. Navy had entered Holy Loch, some upgrading work was done to Greenock's dock buildings and cranes. Clyde tugmasters were re-qualified to operate further upriver, and a supply of fresh water to the submarine tender was agreed. Disposal of garbage and effluent was organised, and local health staff ashore were trained in atomic medicine. A safety monitoring team was set up to measure the atomic pollution of the water.[217]

Holy Loch had been heavily used by the Royal Navy during both world wars. Pollution of the waters and surrounding seabed was inevitable. Hefty fines had been imposed along the Clyde since the 1920s.[26] The creation of Site One extended this polluting activity for another 30 years.

When Site One began operating in 1961, attempts were made to reduce noise pollution and disposal of rubbish from the onboard workshops. Strict controls were imposed to avoid nuclear contamination of the loch. These failed. Complainers were regarded as subversives, and were investigated by the CIA and UK Special Branch officers. These were the days before Greenpeace and environmental campaigners.[218]

The submarine USS *Patrick Henry* (SSBN-599) entered Holy Loch to become the first refit task for Site One. This was the start of more than 2,500 refit tasks carried out there. The tender and the dry dock were constantly in use to maintain the United States' main strategic operation. Over the next 31 years Site One was serviced by the tenders USS *Proteus* (1961–1963), USS *Hunley* (1963–66 and 1982–87), USS *Simon Lake* (1966–70 and 1987–92), USS *Canopus* (1970–75) and USS *Holland* (1975–82).

By the end of 1963, the submarine squadron had ten SSBNs. The local economy received a boost from the number of people required to support the activities of the base. Prior to this, most employment had been in farming, fishing, forestry and holiday accommodation.

The operational routine was constant and placed great pressure on the squadron's administration and logistics units. Every ten days one submarine departed on patrol and another came alongside for refit. Logistics and material problems needed to be briskly resolved. The dockyard work continued at its non-stop pace, and by the end of 1965 one hundred refits had been completed at Holy Loch.

The dock

Site One's floating dry dock, USS *Los Alamos* (AFDB-7), had crossed the Atlantic to Holy Loch in four separate sections and arrived on 1 June 1961. The construction of USS *Los Alamos* was undertaken by Seabees of the Mobile Construction Battalion 4, Detachment Kilo.[219]

The mission of the Seabee detachment at Site One was crystal clear: 'To erect a floating dry dock in Holy Loch, capable of docking Polaris submarines.' [220] For the next five months more than 500 men from Mobile Construction Battalion 4 (MCB4) assembled the vessel. The project was completed on schedule. Their attitude and training helped them to overcome the many

---

26 My father was fined 10 shillings (£450 in 2023 values) in 1931 for washing a ship's tarpaulin in the river; he was found guilty of 'polluting the waters of the River Clyde'.

problems. The expertise and ingenuity of Detachment Kilo at Holy Loch was recognised by Captain J.C. Tate, the European Commander of the Seabees. He described the Holy Loch task as: 'Definitely one of the most interesting jobs of any of the Seabee battalions.'

USS *Los Alamos* was the largest lift floating dry dock in the U.S. Navy, and it remained at Holy Loch for the next 30 years. It could handle five submarines; four of these would be moored alongside, while one was raised within the dock itself. The dry dock's name was deliberately chosen for the location in New Mexico where the first nuclear weapons had been assembled. It was manned by a crew of 4 officers and 150 men.

The dry dock consisted of a flat bottom and wingwalls in the form of pontoons. The vessel for maintenance or repair sat on the flat bottom, supported by keel blocks. The wingwalls housed the support equipment; engines, boilers, air compressors, pumps, crew berthing, galleys etc. This was a practical design, as explained by Captain Ron Gumbert: 'If all this equipment were to have been put below the dry dock floor, the space needed for it would have increased the dry dock's draft by 30 feet or more, so when the dock was flooded down, in order to dock or undock a submarine, the very bottom of the dock would be some 75 feet below the water's surface. But by keeping the support equipment in the wingwalls, the floor of the dry dock is only about 35 feet below the water's surface during the docking/undocking activity.'

The dry dock was 470 feet long and 256 feet wide. It could handle vessels of 32,000 tons, as well as providing all hotel services and electrical power. Annually it dry-docked up to 17 ballistic missile submarines.

Once completed, in November 1961, the dry dock was transferred to the commodore, Captain Schlech, and a 60-man Seabee rear echelon remained.

James Hamilton arrived in Holy Loch to join Detachment Kilo on the construction of the dry dock. He started work in charge of an LCM-6[27] boat: 'These small boats operated as tugs and were used to lay the anchors of incoming vessels. They were landing craft, 56 feet long, flat-bottomed and powered by twin diesel engines. These workboats were designed to carry 78 fully loaded marines and land them ashore in combat.' [221]

Hamilton also worked with other small boats before moving on to becoming a crane supervisor: 'Kingpost cranes were positioned on the top of the dry-dock walls. The walls were 60 feet above the water and 100 feet above the dry-dock floor. It was a long way up and a long way down. Attention to safety was needed.'

The dry dock, known as AFDB-7 (amphibious floating dry dock, battleship) had been in storage since the Second World War. Detachment Kilo had been formed in the spring of 1960 to assist in its reactivation. Construction was a difficult task. The main problem was the unrelenting weather; it is impossible to weld correctly when the entire workplace is moving in high winds. Faulty welds had to be cut out and re-welded. This took time, and shelters were built around the weld areas as work continued 24 hours per day.

Underwater surveying needed to be done for all dock works, including floating dry docks. Divers in traditional heavy diving suits with surface-supplied air examined the bottom of the loch to check for the safety of moorings and to ensure there was clearance of any obstructions

---

27 Landing craft mechanized

on the seabed. Frogmen could not have done this as the time underwater would have been too long for them.

Civil engineers recognised these problems. Ewan MacPherson had built highways, harbours and other structures, many in Scotland. Much of his military work was in wild, windy places. 'In Scotland the winter weather is terrible for this type of work. Particularly on the West Coast at Holy Loch. Work would have stopped early on many occasions because of a combination of driving sleet and minimal daylight. As the engineer I had it easy compared with the working teams. Mud, rain, sleet and snow – and always wind, lots of it! Superheroes, those guys. Similar techniques are used today for installing and decommissioning oil platforms offshore.'

MacPherson sympathised with the plight of the Seabees and the dockyard workers: 'There were unavoidable problems faced by the Seabees. Wind would have been the main factor, on the high sides of the dock when fully floating, which they were most of the time. Working in the dock, they are by nature in very exposed places off the shoreline, so catch all the weather around.'

Detachment Kilo's main task required steelworkers. Many of this group had graduated from the Davisville, RI, welding school, and they had been well trained in all types of welding. This knowledge was put to the test at Holy Loch.

The construction demands were onerous. It took almost 16 hours to raise the walls for each of the four sections. Cranes were pulled across with blocks and tackles; the main generator engine broke down and a longer working week was implemented to meet the operational date; the work schedule was pushed to six days a week and 12 hours a day; eventually it was increased to seven days a week, 12 or more hours a day.

The dock was held firm by 22 anchors, each of these weighing 30,000 lbs (~13,500 kg) and attached to 3 miles of chain. Because of the dock's strategic value, the mooring situation was constantly monitored.[222]

During their time at Holy Loch, the Seabees lived aboard the *Apple*, APL-42 (auxiliary personnel lighter), a floating barracks ship. They overcame all the problems – the weather had been atrocious, and many stores items had been unavailable – and delivered the project on time, an excellent result. The U.S. Navy commander in Europe, Admiral H.P. Smith, commended the Seabees: 'Yours is a significant contribution to fleet readiness of which you can be justly proud … Well done.'

The dockyard operations

Site One became a major U.S. Navy engineering facility. The SSBN refits were primarily conducted by the submarine tender, and the *Los Alamos* dry dock was only used for periodic maintenance, when the submarine had to be lifted out of the water with its hull exposed. During these out-of-water actions, the submarine hull was cleaned of fouling and painted, the seawater hull valves were checked, and the main ballast tanks (which are not accessible when the submarine is in the water) were examined. Also, any hull damage was repaired.

An *All Hands* writer was impressed by the industrial efficiency of the dockyard operation: 'At Site One they give whatever it takes. The job gets done every ten days – like clockwork.'[223]

New arrivals to Site One were told to be prepared for hard work. It was a fully operating naval dockyard and had all the normal departments for this task. Three or four submarines, undergoing a 28-day refit, were alongside at all times. The materiel office handled the major repair tasks and problem areas.

There was a long logistic support chain for the U.S. Navy's most important overseas facility. The workload was large, and needed excellent coordination. There were four main groups involved; the tender, the dockyard, the submarine crews and the civilian technicians, who came from American shipyards and defence contractors. The system worked well, and the squadron commander seldom needed to intervene.

The repair department had more than 450 craftsmen in ten specialised divisions. The tender workers would tackle every task, and nothing was referred back as being too difficult. In *All Hands* this attitude was emphasised: 'I didn't realise how hard they work. They end up making and fabricating things you would task a shipyard with.'

In the engine rooms, the engineers worked 365 days a year to provide the site with power, light, heat and air-conditioning. Replacement parts could not be obtained speedily – if a metal part had been ordered from a supply depot based in the USA, this would have taken three weeks – so they were manufactured aboard the tender. By using more heat than is required to power a submarine, the engineers generated the 1,275°F (690°C) needed to melt brass. This was then poured into a mould for a submarine part.

Huge amounts of reading material were produced. Technical manuals were required, as naval craftsmen had to follow the latest instructions for repair jobs. There was a press shop which worked non-stop. More than 250 print jobs were needed for each individual submarine refit. This total often rose to 450 print jobs. Damage control manuals, forms, ship's logs, photo-engraved tags were created.

There was also a library containing hundreds of blueprints and technical reference items. Every part aboard a submarine was listed, and the corresponding literature was required to provide the step-by-step procedures required for each repair task.

The welders had a specialised role, and their work was dangerous. Strict safety rules were needed as there was little space aboard submarines. Machinists' mates and machinery repairmen used precision-measuring devices to obtain accuracy within thousandths of an inch. In the optical shop the periscopes would be laid out for repairs, and six or more technicians would work on their specific components.[224]

After attending sonar school at Key West, Dave Pratt spent three years at Holy Loch, and left as an ST2, sonar tech 2nd class. He worked in the sound and vibration lab, where his job was to help to reduce noise on the submarines. His next task was in the sonar shop, which maintained hydrophones and transducers.

Submarine sound levels were recorded before work occurred. They were recorded again after the work had been completed. From this it could be determined if increases in sound levels were occurring, enabling the specific machinery to be identified and fixed. Dave Pratt recalled his escapades: 'I also crawled around the subs' superstructure with a rubber mallet, banging on things to see if they were loose and needed tack welding. Tapping superstructure supports would reveal broken welds. These would cause loose metal to bang and make noise when under way. Sound lab personnel would do this inspection, and the tender welders would do the repairs. This process required strong nerves, as the sailor had to crawl into a torpedo tube to get to an access plate to the sonar dome to reach the hydrophones and transducers. It was a stinky, muddy and worrying activity. An underlying fear was getting trapped in there when the boat got under way. Never happened, but the thought was there.'

Some essential tasks on a submarine could only be done when the submarine was out of the water. These were performed in the dry dock. The vessel would need to be placed on keel blocks for all-round access. The keel blocks were crucial components. If they were not correctly laid out, a boat could get damaged. The dry-dock crew became expert at this activity.

The dry-dock operation was spectacular. First, the dock flooded its tanks and sank to a depth permitting the incoming vessel to enter. This vessel would position itself over the keel blocks, which supported it once the dry dock's tanks were pumped out. The docked ship's entire hull was then available for inspection and maintenance.

In dry dock several specific tasks were performed: broken equipment was fixed, preventive maintenance was carried out, and ship's systems were upgraded. The dry docking enabled external hull and seawater system maintenance, hull cleaning and painting, as well as any shaft or propeller maintenance.

Once the repairs were complete, the boat would return to the water. Captain Ron Gumbert explained the process: 'When the dry-dock maintenance was completed, the dry dock sank into the water (controlled sinking), which refloated the submarine off the keel blocks, and the submarine was gently guided out of the dry dock and moved back alongside the tender to finish the refit.'

The *Los Alamos* expanded its capability and was then able to work on two separate classes of submarines. This was a major improvement, and enhanced the value of Scotland's geographical usefulness. More work could be undertaken at Holy Loch instead of sending a submarine back to the USA for maintenance. Thus the ability of the *Los Alamos* to accommodate either class of SSBN on short notice was an advantage.

Many of the dockyard refit tasks were awkward, and Seabee Joseph McDonnell remembered the long hours taken up by some jobs, such as cleaning the hull of a vessel: 'Lost a lot of liberty over that damn thing. It was so covered with barnacles it was unbelievable. Took days to get them off.'

Some dry-dock operations could be tricky, as ships had different problems. In 1968 the USS *Betelgeuse* (AK260) was dry-docked, the largest ship ever to enter *Los Alamos*. James Brandon described the operation: 'She was problematic and there were concerns about getting the basin above freeboard, but *Los Alamos* never broke a sweat coming up out of the depths of the loch with *Betelgeuse* inside.' [225]

Working on the dry dock could be hazardous.

A very anxious submariner, Alfred H. Singleman Jr, crew member of USS *Francis Scott Key*, described it vividly: 'If you have never worked in a floating dry dock, it can be a nerve-racking experience. We had to carry 21 new Polaris missile guidance packages aboard the *Key*. These were each in a large round canister that weighed about 40 lbs and were very awkward to carry … we began to carry the canisters up the stairs … after a struggle, we made it to the top of the dry dock, then started out onto the windswept, slippery catwalk. You had to use both hands to hold onto the guidance packages, so you had no hands to hold onto the railings to stabilise yourself. You could easily see through the skimpy railing to the hard deck six storeys below. The point where the two halves of the catwalk meet was held together by a simple chain. In the gusty wind, the two halves were swaying in such a way that that you had to wait for the right moment when the halves lined up to be able to cross.' [226]

The missile guidance packages were safely delivered. The perilous activity had ended. But for some bubbleheads, such as Mike Robertson, the mention of 'dry dock' still leaves him trembling, 40 years later: 'The dry dock is a huge set of pontoons that gets flooded to allow the sub to pull in. The water is then pumped out to raise the sub out of the water. The open ends of the dry dock have a metal catwalk that is then closed to enable dockworkers to pass from one side to the other.' [227]

'Once a submarine was in dry dock, it was hosed down with a high-pressure nozzle. This created a danger zone for the workers, and was called the suicide nozzle by the dry-dockers; if it slipped it would whip around and cause injuries to anyone within range.'

'Scaffolding was then erected around the sub. Pallets of sand would be placed fore and aft and blasting would begin. As the sandblasters made progress, the treated area would be painted. After the hull was blasted and the first coat applied, three more coats followed. Dry-dockers did a lot of the painting, and often worked through the night and into the next day on this gruelling, unhealthy task.'

When Martin Hastings arrived from Queens, New York, he was assigned to deck division, serving aboard *Los Alamos* from September 1966 until March 1968. He worked on the cranes and boats, sandblasting and painting submarines. Hastings believed that this work had a physical effect on the 'deck apes', as the seamen in deck division were called: 'Got there three months out of boot camp, at 17 years old. The paint was oil-based and contained anti-fouling chemicals. The fumes had an effect. This was evidenced by guys singing Christmas carols in July! They drank lots of alcohol. Lots of drinking. And fighting. Hard work. Hazardous chemicals. Harsh weather. The crew were called the Lost Animals, and were definitely a wild bunch. We called the *Los Alamos* the Animal Farm Dunoon Branch – the ship letter designator being AFDB 7.' [228]

There were many tasks to be carried out in a hurry. The Cold War was an unrelenting, high-pressure activity which placed great demands on the squadron's administration and logistics units. As soon as one SSBN departed on patrol, another would come alongside for refit. Logistical and material problems had to be speedily resolved.

The first two tenders, *Proteus* and *Hunley*, had limitations, as missiles could only be loaded or unloaded from an SSBN berthed immediately alongside; when three SSBNs were in refit, the third ship would be moored outboard of another SSBN, and the crane could not reach out to that ship, making missile loading impossible. But moving an SSBN during refit was complicated, as its nuclear plant was closed down and restarting the plant took two days, affecting work in progress.

This produced a problem for the Operations Center, evidenced by a steady stream of frustrated and angry department officers. Conflicting priorities and capacity limitations often caused a 'musical boats' situation. This meant moving SSBNs for missile loading or dry-docking.

In addition, the programme had to cope with the monthly arrival of the resupply cargo ships. Time was precious, as any refit delays spilled over on to the strategic plan. Something had to change.

Mike Giambattista tackled the problem. He produced a day-by-day, 60-day detailed plot that eradicated unnecessary activities. This schedule, speedily implemented, resulted in estimated annual savings of hundreds of millions of dollars. More importantly, it ensured that there were no gaps in the strategic requirement.

The USS *Proteus* had a crew of almost 1,500. It handled all service and maintenance tasks and had many specialists aboard. Tenders were crammed with a vast range of equipment: huge lathes and tools for working with microscopic instrument parts, electronics labs for the repair of complex missile guidance systems and submarine detection devices. There was a wide array of specialised shops – optical, drafting, printing, woodworking and plastics. The supply department stocked three times as many items as were carried by an aircraft carrier, and it sustained the needs of the ship and her subs for long periods without replenishment.

Organising this was a mammoth task. The supply department stored more than 50,000 items to be issued. Over 1,000 people had to be fed every day, and individual departments had huge workloads, such as the medical department, which carried out more than 5,000 X-rays annually.

Dr Laurel Clark was head of the medical department. As a diving medicine specialist she worked with the U.S. Navy Divers at Site One and the U.S. Navy SEALs at Machrihanish. Clark was very proud of her Scottish heritage, and a piper played at her wedding to a fellow naval officer she had met at Holy Loch. She also dived with Navy SEALs from Machrihanish and performed medical evacuations from submarines.

A few years later she was one of the astronauts killed in the Space Shuttle Columbia disaster. On the morning before the tragic accident, NASA Mission Control had played 'Scotland the Brave' as the wake-up call for Columbia's team in honour of Clark. The well-known pipe tune was also played at her funeral at Arlington National Cemetery. Minutes before the fatal explosion she had played the Scottish band Runrig's 'Running to the Light' on Columbia's internal audio system. This CD was later retrieved from a Texas field amid debris, and was brought to Scotland and presented to the band by her husband and son. One of her former Holy Loch colleagues, Commander John Szakas, remembered her: 'She was like everybody else that was there – worked hard, long days and did her job.' [229]

The powerhouse of Site One was the tender. It issued almost 4 million gallons of diesel fuel per year to the submarines and provided lubrication oil, chilled water, drinking water, steam, electrical power, telephone services, sewage services and gas services. There was a weapons repair department that handled technical services for nuclear missiles and also serviced torpedoes and smaller armaments.

The post office worked full-time handling official and personal mail, and there was also a legal service. All departments were accessed via narrow steel corridors, lit by neon lights. Working conditions were cramped, there were few portholes and most compartments had no external light.

Some sailors served aboard different tenders. Gary Flynn was a warrant officer, and was aboard the USS *Holland* as a division officer in the weapons department's electronics division:

'I oversaw the ship's armory and later the quality assurance division. I later served aboard USS *Hunley* and USS *Simon Lake* during my service as an electronics technician.'

The tender engineers were resourceful. Some would cook their own food on the exhaust manifolds of the ship's engines. This would normally be soup or cans of beanie weenies, but these treats had to be handled correctly, as Greg Kent, an EN2 supervisor on USS *Holland*, recalled: 'If you didn't open the can a little, it would blow up and be a huge mess!'

As Site One was an overseas naval base, it had to be resupplied from continental USA. Cargo was brought across the Atlantic to Holy Loch aboard US Naval auxiliary ships. These cargo (TAK) ships were vital for the Holy Loch operation, and Captain Ron Gumbert emphasised their importance: 'The TAKs brought maintenance materials for tender and submarine refits, including bulk goods such as oil, rags, toilet paper and especially frozen food to the SSBN, and replacement SSBN missiles that were undergoing a standard maintenance cycle.' The TAK would stay alongside the tender for about three days and then depart. A TAK could be alongside the tender at the same time as SSBNs were undergoing refits.

USS *Betelgeuse* was a regular visitor. It had been modified specifically for Holy Loch duty, could carry a total of 23 Polaris missiles and was dedicated to the Polaris fleet. This modification changed its mission from a fleet resupply ship to a most vital link in the Polaris programme, enabling a more efficient stowage and transfer of Polaris missiles and their components. The ship made resupply runs to Holy Loch and Rota, in Spain. Polaris missiles were its principal cargo, and it would return with missiles from the SSBNs to the USA, where they would be fully serviced.

Bill Bradford was a snipe, an E-4 machinist mate 3rd class – also known as an engine jockey – aboard *Betelgeuse* on trips to Holy Loch in the mid-1960s. He carried out maintenance on the main engines of the steam-driven ship and stood watch to keep tabs on the engines' performance. His daily routine was dirty and dangerous. He would perform repairs to steam valves and pumps. When in dock he would drain the oil from the reduction gears then crawl inside and wipe up the excess oil: 'Like taking an oil bath. The sump was about 2 feet in depth. Didn't care much for wire-brushing deck plating to clean any rust off, then applying a thin film of oil and cleaning the bilges.' He also worked on the water supply system; as fresh water is bulky and can spoil in storage, *Betelgeuse* used an evaporator that distilled sea water.

One of his shipmates was Edward Delsanto, who worked in the engine room. He also worked as a mess cook and, like most sailors, had a variety of other jobs. He was at the bottom of the work scale. He mostly cleaned bilges. They were smelly, oily and confining. And he could not escape the effects of the North Atlantic weather, especially during the winter crossings: 'High seas – and there were many in my ten crossings – posed many problems. The cargo was well secured, but the crew had to put up with the rockin' and rollin'. In high seas even basic tasks, like eating chow, were daunting. Sleeping was another experience. But at times the sea was like a millpond … one thing I remember was lying on a hatch cover and watching the stars!'

Eventually Edward Delsanto transferred to submarines, 'for adventure'. He saw how the sub sailors lived, with their camaraderie, and volunteered after talking to the executive officer, who was a former sub sailor.

Working on the tender as a female sailor

Felice Bluhm (Clauder) was a street-smart New York City girl, used to taking the subway and bus to school each day. She had lived a fast-paced life in a tough neighbourhood, somewhat oblivious to the noise, litter, crowds, smells and disassociated air from those around her who she met regularly on the transit, and never said 'hello'. She described her Holy Loch service as simply 'my experience in Scotland was a 180-degree difference to anything I ever encountered.'

She arrived in Holy Loch in 1985 and by the time she left in 1987 as HT2 Bluhm (hull technician 2nd class, a petty officer), her life had changed radically. Felice was one of the first group of female sailors aboard the *Hunley*. She came aboard from basic training with no specialism, and as she had not yet achieved a rating such as hull maintenance technician or electrician, she was classified as a striker. A striker had to search for a rate by exploring various types of jobs and by visiting shops throughout the ship. But some of the rates were not open to women.

Sleeping aboard USS *Hunley* and focused on her job, she tried not to think about the nuclear arsenal stored below: 'I was young and somewhat naïve about politics and the potential disasters which could occur. Yes, it was scary, but I was there to perform my job.'

Felice was interested in qualifying as a machinist's mate, but was not allowed to pursue this path. This protectionism changed in later years, and women are now in all rates and in traditional military male roles. But this was not the case for Felice. It was not easy for her, and she followed a slow pathway. She was a Jack of all trades and a master of none, and was initially sent to the deck division: 'During my first week aboard USS *Hunley*, I was performing odd jobs along with another female sailor, Smiddy. These included grinding the deck to remove the old paint before repainting, a task always given to lower-ranking sailors. It was noisy, dirty and boring.'

Felice and Smiddy then got the chance to assist bringing a submarine alongside the *Hunley*. To accomplish this task, the sub would throw a line to a sailor who was hanging over the side on a boatswain's chair. The sailor had to catch the line, which had a knot on the end. It was then connected to a heavy hawser on the submarine. The hawser would be pulled aboard the tender and looped round a bollard. Felice laughed as she recalled this episode: 'To prove ourselves capable sailors, we volunteered to go overboard and assist with mooring the sub. The XO was on deck watching the evolution. He was totally against sending a female sailor over the side. Despite the XO's concerns, we volunteered to be lowered down to capture the rope.'

Going over the side of a large ship in the rain, and hanging by a rope over freezing water is something Felice normally would never have done, as she hated heights. However, she and Smiddy both felt this was an opportunity to prove themselves as representatives of female sailors. They were both lowered into the heavy rain.

Slowly the sub came in, through fog. A sailor on the sub's bow had a device that shot the mooring line. He had to shoot it a several times before Felice caught it. Each time she missed, the rope would drop into the loch, so not only were they sprayed with rain but were also soaked with water from the Holy Loch: 'Eventually I caught the line, and my job was to pull up this humongous, weighty hawser, which had been dragged through the water, to be looped over the bollard. The task was exhausting. At one point, I considered giving up. However, the sailors above were cheering for us, so I tenaciously, and with great determination, completed the task.

Afterwards, the guys clapped, and gave us a 'that-a-boy' when we arrived on deck topside. The executive officer was surprised, and praised us. I think this may have been the first time the XO was exposed to females performing a strenuous, traditionally male, task.'

Most of Felice's crewmates were helpful: 'They were not anti-women. They were just cautious and keen to ensure they did not offend or harm the female sailors. Most of the men were positive and supportive when it came to the females aboard. Of course, there were those who were sexist and intolerable. However, that is true whether you are a man or a woman, and it occurs in most workspaces.'

As a striker, Felice had to go in front of a board of chiefs to gain promotion. She passed the board and was moved from deck division to the hull maintenance shop. Welding was now to be her specialism. Then male prejudice reared its head.

Felice had put in a request to have a few days of leave, as her sister had come to visit her from New York. The chief approved it. At the time, a 1st class petty officer was in charge of the shop. He told her that before she could depart on leave she had to stay past the end of the working day and weld a perfectly square box of angle iron. Felice had not gone to welding school and only knew the basics.

She stayed up all night trying to accomplish the task: 'By the following morning, I was angry and frustrated. I had been unable to complete the assigned task successfully, and my sister had arrived. At the time, I believed the 1st class petty officer was a jerk. I hated him and stayed as far away from him as possible. But that was not the end of the story. There was a twist to it.'

About nine years later, they met again when he was a naval reservist: 'At the time, I was a senior chief petty officer (E-8), whereas he had never been promoted past his rank. I taught shipboard firefighting and he was a student in my class. He pulled me aside and apologised for his behavior on the *Hunley*. Throughout the years, I had met several others who had crossed my path previously. These guys were under my supervision, as I had become the senior enlisted. They always asked for forgiveness. I did forgive them, but it gave me some satisfaction, and it was a great lesson to those who had given me hell.'

As time progressed women were accepted into different types of jobs throughout the tender. But it was not a smooth journey. Felice believed that as women proved they were able to perform a task, they were more likely to be given more responsibility and more jobs: 'But I believe women were more closely scrutinised, for if a man made a mistake it was generally overlooked. However, if a woman made a mistake it became her albatross.'

Having female crew members was a unique problem as it was a major change to naval tradition. The social conventions were not clear, and Site One had a strict no-fraternising policy. For the junior enlisted this meant that the ship was off-limits for any sort of affectionate activities. Off the ship, relationships were allowed, as long as they were deemed appropriate and discreet.

Felice recalled the effects of this policy: 'It was an awkward situation. The male sailors aboard the *Hunley* were expressly told they were strictly forbidden to fraternise with the female sailors. It was a sensitive situation for all concerned. The problem with the word "fraternise" was that it was a vague term that could be defined in an extreme manner. It took the female sailors a while to fit in, and I believe that the first women had to work extra hard to prove their worth before they were accepted.'

Tradesmen and technicians

There were hundreds of highly skilled naval tradesmen aboard the tender. It was no place for faint hearts.

When he reported to Holy Loch in 1971, Ray Conner was 17 years old. He served aboard the tender USS *Canopus*, initially in the main engine room. On his next tour to Holy Loch, in 1977, he served aboard the dry dock USS *Los Alamos* and achieved the rank of MM-2 (machinist mate 2nd class): 'My main duties included search and rescue tasks, as well as work on all propulsion systems. Damage control and firefighting are vital tasks aboard all vessels. The teams needed to wear OBA [oxygen breathing apparatus]. Different methods were applied to each emergency, such as electrical, chemical and fuel oil firefighting.' [230]

Conner wore a radiation suit for protection. All training was conducted in 'no light' scenarios, as in real emergencies lighting was usually absent. The teams had to deal with search and rescue situations on board the ship, as well as searching for anyone lost at sea, boating accidents and the like: 'Our most hazardous work concerned radiation control, when we wore radiation suits and searched for radiation leaks or hidden radioactive isotopes. I had other less hazardous duties, including checking fresh water supplies, loading, monitoring and cleaning fuel, and monitoring ballast tanks. To round off my busy life, I also worked on all propulsion systems and the fresh water pumps and turbines. On the rare occasions when I had nothing to do, I was duty crane operator. I now had lots of work and plenty of responsibility.' [231]

Dockyards are easily identified by their cranes, and Site One was no different. The cranes worked constantly, loading and unloading every large item of stores and equipment, whether it was missiles or vegetables. Martin Hastings was a crane man: 'Running the cranes was part of my job training. To get into the crane you climbed a ladder in the base then another through the cabin. The wind greatly affected the boom and the load. The cabin also had to be rotated so the hatch was accessible for the crane man. We became skilled at our job, although competence led to overconfidence. Some of us got too good. Making three moves at once was common. Running along the tracks. Raising or lowering the hook, and rotating the boom was common. With some stretching the boom could be lowered at the same time. But that was frowned upon. Keep in mind that in deck division an old guy was 19 or 20!' [232]

On one occasion a crane operator had just returned from liberty and had to drive the crane so that sailors could put a solid final coat of paint on the submarine hull to improve the speed of the boat. Martin Hastings chuckled as he described events: 'The sub sailors were on a gangway hoisted by the crane. About eight of them. They were going pretty slow, and the operator wanted to get it done. They scoffed at his goading. He threatened to dump them into the Holy Loch. They scoffed. He rotated the gangway outboard and lowered them into the drink. He then went down to the quarterdeck and stole an LCM [landing craft], which he took to the pier and left there. I think he then proceeded to Edinburgh.'

Seamen strikers filled a variety of jobs, including shore patrol, and Adam Scott spent one year doing this job. He was then assigned to the R-4 division aboard USS *Holland*, received technical training and became an electronic technician. [233]

The R-4 was the antenna repair shop, and Scott worked on the BRA-8 buoy, which was part of the radio system of a submarine. It looked like an old Second World War bomb, and was stored under the skin of the boat, behind folding doors; when the submarine deployed the BRA-8 these would open, and the buoy would be let out, attached to a cable until it was almost at the surface. But problems were ever present, as Scott recalled: 'We spent many long days and nights getting these buoys fixed and qualified for deployment aboard subs. The subs would lose them quite often. When the subs dived the cable would be cut by the propeller, so lots of work needed to be done. We had to fix any damage caused and retest them. This meant flying a buoy next to the ship from a crane, with a weight attached, so we could simulate it going up and down.'

Most of Charlie Witherow's high school classmates joined the military in 1966 – they were drafted. Only a small number were exempt from military service, and Charlie was one of these: 'At the age of 18, I decided to join the U.S. Navy and moved from my small home town in a coal-mining area of north Pennsylvania, intending to follow the route of my brother, who had enlisted for naval service three years earlier. My brother had suggested that I should pursue a career as an opticalman.' [234]

Witherow completed his basic training and then attended the opticalman A school in Great Lakes, Illinois. Opticalmen were vital members of a ship's crew, and their training was thorough: 'I learned theory, maintenance and repair of navigational equipment such as binoculars, sextants, alidades, gun sights, rangefinders. All of these were crucial to a ship's navigation. I completed more specialist training before being assigned to Submarine Repair Site One at Holy Loch – and I never left Dunoon after that. I was the chief petty officer in charge of the periscope shop as well as being the Site One indoctrination officer. To soak up more of my time, I was also the assistant quality assurance officer.'

His work was important and interesting: 'Our ship was moored out in the Holy Loch, and with the severe weather conditions, including very high winds, removing and replacing the periscopes from the submarines was often quite challenging.'

Site One, like all military organisations, needed stores. Without this crucial lifeline, the front-line activities would have been impossible. It is a fact often forgotten by those who operated on the front line.[235]

Frank Murray had already served with a submarine squadron, in Naples in 1984: 'I was ordering supplies for six submarines and was assigned to USS *Hunley*, 1984–86. I also served aboard USS *Simon Lake*, 1989–92. My final rank was E-6/SK1 [1st class petty officer and storekeeper 1st class. I was a supervisor at the Sandbank naval warehouse.' Murray was qualified to manage hazardous cargo, and did all the shipping out of hazardous materials. He also handled weapons orders and electronic items. Work at Sandbank was continuous: 'We processed military clothing, machine shop items, welding tools etc. Pallets were loaded with other materials, such as oil drums. The warehouse took delivery of ship-ordered items and was a busy place. Some of the stores were controlled items such as gyros, electronic components and other important pieces of equipment. There was tight security on the site, and access was restricted to security-cleared persons.' [236]

He made the regular boat journey from Sandbank to Gourock: 'One evening I was among a group of frightened passengers aboard a Mike boat [an LCM] in a Force 8 gale between Holy

Loch and Gourock. The boat rolled around in the 20-foot waves, and the young officer who captained the boat calmly handed out lifejackets. We all got ashore safely. The Firth of Clyde waters could be rough.'

Another storeman was Nat O'Dell. He was two years out of high school when he arrived at Holy Loch: 'I was one of many storekeepers working in the supply department of the USS *Simon Lake*. This department contained other specialists, such as ship's servicemen – laundry workers, barbers and stewards. I was immediately embraced by the professionalism of the U.S. Navy. There were high levels of training and professionalism involved in operating the base. This was a responsibility that all of us who served took very seriously.' [237]

His boot camp instructor had told O'Dell that he had served at Holy Loch and that O'Dell would 'love the duty'. He was right. O'Dell also loved a Scots lass, married her and settled in Dunoon when he left the Navy. Before marrying her, he had also headed to Vietnam with his mobile construction battalion. Because of his 'youth and naïvety' he did not give much thought to the significance of having a nuclear submarine base in close proximity to the 2 million people who lived in the Greater Glasgow area: 'I did understand that our military mission was one of being a deterrent force. I believed in the value of that mission and was proud of being part of that mission. Based on the same knowledge and support of the idea of having a deterrent force, I believe that I would have felt fine with having a nuclear submarine base in close vicinity to where I lived.'

On arrival at Holy Loch O'Dell learned an immediate lesson, along with five other men fresh from storekeeper school; this was their first sea duty aboard a naval vessel. They had been assigned bunks and were in the process of unpacking their sea bags when an announcement boomed out: '*Simon Lake* departing!'

O'Dell and his group were bewildered: 'Where the hell are we going? We just got here! I thought the ship was staying put!'

Reassurance was provided by the seasoned sailors: 'Relax fellas. It's just the captain going ashore!'

The new boys had all forgotten a simple fact from basic training – the commanding officer and the ship are referred to as the same thing. Whenever the commanding officer arrives or departs the ship, an announcement accordingly goes out over the public address system. So O'Dell's ship was not going anywhere.

He reached the rank of E-5 (SK2 petty officer storekeeper 2nd class) and over time his job became more complicated. When he had first arrived aboard, he had been assigned to the break-out crew: 'This group gathered all the supplies which had been requested by the other ships and brought them to a collection point. I was then transferred to the stock control division, and worked processing requisitions and keeping track of the supply inventory. My last job assignment before departing the ship was procuring supplies from sources outside the Navy supply chain when those items weren't readily available. I dealt with local merchants and processed invoices so that payment was promptly made.'

Movement around this large floating complex was done by small boats, but these could not handle the bad weather. Lt Giambattista was called upon to solve the matter, and sourced the Box-L craft: 'This was a specialised Army mine-laying vessel, 64 feet in length, with a pilot house containing radar and radio equipment. The two Box-Ls were much larger and far sturdier than the current craft.'

Site One used many small boats to transport personnel and supplies from the shore to the ship. Among these small boats were 50-foot utility boats. There was an LCM Mk-8 for cargo transport, and a 32-foot officers' motorboat – the captain's gig. The ship's divers had their own dive boat, an LCM Mk-6 that was designed for carrying vehicles but had been modified to serve as a dive boat. Martin Hastings was a small boat coxswain and has fond memories of one adventure: 'I was on a run for sand loaded by crane by civilians. On the way back we lost an engine. Pretty dicey. Heavy list to starboard, as the port engine, which had quit, powered the bilge pump. This meant that we could not pump out the bilge water. We got back safely but it was a struggle.'

The LCM had a three-man crew and carried out many tasks daily. The coxswain was in charge and ran the boat. LCMs were 56 feet long. They also ran to Greenock and Gourock a couple of times a day, and sailors on liberty had to be very careful about their time. If they missed the last boat back to Holy Loch they would have to sleep in the shore patrol shack on Cardwell Bay pier.

The boatmen at Site One were a hardy breed. They were tough and competent, and dealt with every odd job, often in an unconventional manner. Greggery Kunkle, a boatman, came from Chambersburg, Pennsylvania. His father had just finished a few years in the Navy Reserve, so Greggery joined the Navy and arrived in Holy Loch in 1986. As a seaman striker he was in Boat Operations (Boat Ops).

The breakout department was the warehouse part of a ship's mess department. All the food was stored there until needed. As a new sailor, Kunkle had to work on the mess decks: 'Breakout would receive an order from a ship. The items were identified and stacked on pallets, then sent up an elevator to the ship's galley or to the main deck. When the stores ran low, the monthly TAK [cargo] ships from the United States would arrive. The tender would take on so much resupply that the crates were stored in the aisles. The crew would have to walk on these pallets until they were sent out.'

He moved on to the busy world of boatman tasks. Plenty of variety here: 'No task was too trivial – or too awkward – for Boat Ops. We moved around the water between Holy Loch and Gourock all day long. I was never idle. I carried out various duties – roving patrol, bow hook, engineman, and coxswain duty for the liberty shuttles with the Mike 8s [LCMs] and the officer motor boats. I served as crew for the work boats for a wide variety of jobs around the site. I refuelled the boats and was part of the refuelling evolution when the YFNB-31 barge would take on fuel from the tender.'

Kunkle loved working with the boats and became coxswain-qualified: 'In fact, I was the only coxswain-qualified engineman. But a large amount of my time was spent in the engine rooms of the various boats, just staring at the gauges. That was extremely boring for me, as I very much preferred to be driving the boats. Eventually, I was assigned my own LCM8 boat. I loved operating boats and I became very good at it. The mechanical love of my life is, was, and always will be LCM8 #1 at Holy Loch. I wouldn't have traded her for anything.'

When the Site One tugboats were not available and a submarine needed to be moved, the Mike boats did it. There was always an officer or chief in charge of this operation, and the coxswain and other crew of the Mike boat facilitated the task. Kunkle never forgot this procedure: 'When one of these moves was scheduled, the Mike boat and crew would arrive early in the morning, tie off to the sub and then wait. The boatmen were always invited to go aboard the submarine for breakfast. This was a welcome treat, as we knew from our time mess cranking that the submarines got the very best food. So breakfast on a submarine was always a delicious treat. Being just out of high school and standing in a nuclear ballistic missile submarine thousands of miles from home, doing something as normal as having breakfast was almost surreal for me.'

Another boat operations task was regarded as routine at the time, but for Kunkle in later years it was thought-provoking: 'When a missile transfer between a sub and the tender was taking place, boat operations supplied a Mike boat and crew for the Marines to use as a security craft. Having marines armed with deadly weapons and every intention of using lethal force instantly to protect nuclear weapons never really affected me until after I had left Holy Loch. It never really sank in that I was mere feet from the most destructive weapons made by mankind. Not until later did I realise what I had been in such close proximity to. For me, it was just another workday at the loch.'

On occasions, problems arose that required a unique solution, often at the limits of safety. One day all four Mike boats had to be moved to another mooring. But there were not enough boat crews at the time to get the job done. A plan was devised to move all of them in one shot, but although it would have solved the problem quickly it was contrary to normal procedures. Undaunted, Kunkle and his colleague tied all the boats together side by side surreptitiously. Then they moved all of them together: 'There was a lot of radio chatter demanding we cease what we were doing and return the boats to the dock. Once the move had been successfully completed, I was ordered to report to the operations office. I stood outside the office while the BM2 discussed what had happened with the chiefs and warrant officer. From the angry voices on the radio, I was sure we were in deep trouble. When our BM2 finally came out, he took one look at my worried face and laughed. They were so impressed that we'd pulled it off, no one was in trouble. Of course, if things hadn't gone well …'

As oil was regularly spilled into the water it needed to be removed and this was done by a protective floating oil boom. One night a piece of the boom broke loose and drifted to shore. The roving patrol woke Kunkle and explained that he and his boat crew had to retrieve the wayward boom. His crew were in their bunks sleeping: 'I tried twice to wake up my crew, but they slumbered on. Frustrated, I went to one of the work boats and fired up the engines. I cast off the mooring myself and headed for the shore. I located the oil boom, but found a problem as it was on the shore, right at the water's edge. There was no crew aboard to assist me, and I would have to complete the tricky task on my own. I put the boat as close to the shore as I dared without grounding and tried to use the boat hook to get the oil boom. This failed and I needed to be closer. Also, the wind kept pushing the boat away from the oil boom. But the boat was a modified landing-craft and I decided to beach it. But then I found the beach was full of rocks, not sand.'

He moved ahead at low speed and lightly beached the Mike boat, worrying in case he knocked a hole in it. His gamble paid off. There was only the sound of minor scraping as the bow of the boat went ashore. Kunkle was then able to easily snag the oil boom and tie it off to the boat for removal: 'Mission accomplished; I took the boat back to its mooring. It was now time to face the music. I returned to the barge and was called forward by my boss. He told me to never do that again and to never tell anyone what I had just done. Matter closed. I don't think he realised I had beached the boat because he never said anything about that – and I never volunteered that information.'

A regular task for Boat Ops was to repair the Site One oil boom when it when it broke apart. The retrieval of the wayward parts of the boom was often an awkward task. The oil kings (boiler technicians) had to carry out these retrievals, but at times a stray piece could drift alongside vessels, complicating the removal. The recovery boat could rarely get close enough to complete the task. But Kunkle would always push harder to succeed.

Stray booms would often wedge between the tender and a submarine, making it very difficult for the retrieval boat: 'On one occasion, I worked my boat into this narrow space without hitting a single thing. It was very delicate and dicey work. But I still needed to be closer, so moved forward and secured my bow hook under the oil boom. The boat was now stuck under the stern of the *Simon Lake* and blocked by the mooring lines of the submarine and barge. My only option was to go back out the way I had come in and strip the lights off the back side of the barge's mast.'

He did so. The oil boom was secured in its proper place and the electricians were informed of their extra work.

As with all military procedures, Boat Ops had strict rules. One of these was that on any trip there had to be a qualified petty officer as coxswain, and two crew aboard. Only a petty officer was allowed to take a boat across the river. Kunkle was a coxswain but was not a petty officer, so he was not allowed to do this task. But one day this changed: 'I was assigned as the bow hook for the noon T-boat run. The boat was ready for a petty officer to take charge. The passengers had already boarded. One was an officer, who was starting to get annoyed that the boat had not departed. Boat Dispatch had called across the barge for the T-boat coxswain, but no coxswain had arrived. Tempers were rising. The officer was getting angry, as he and others had trains to catch, and the trains would not wait for a late T-boat. I made my mind up. I told the engineman to untie the boat, and I took the T-boat across the Clyde.'

The boat arrived safely in Gourock in time for the train, but as it approached the Gourock pier the shore patrol was waiting. Kunkle knew he was in trouble. The patrolman told him that the duty officer wanted him to call Boat Operations. He called and reassured the duty officer that there had been no problems and was ordered to report to the office on return. Back in Holy Loch he explained why he had taken command of the boat: 'The reason no petty officer arrived was that both of the petty officers with T-boat duty that day thought it was the other's turn to take the trip, and so neither one went to the boat. Each thought the other was handling it … it was not like I was going to take a sightseeing tour or go fishing with the Navy's T-boat.'

The explanation was accepted and operating procedures were amended. Thorough training ensured that such an event would not arise in future.

Marine traffic around the Holy Loch was constant, placing a huge demand on the local tugboats. These were expensive to use and were not always available. Once more, Lt Giambattista was told to find a solution. He applied to U.S. Navy headquarters for a large harbour tug, and within a month USS *Natick* (YTB-760) crossed the Atlantic and arrived in Holy Loch. The commodore was delighted: 'He designated me as the officer in charge of *Natick* – she had been my first command!'

Other tugs followed and became the workhorses of Site One. They were 100 feet long and versatile, towing ships, barges, submarines and other craft in, out and around the site. They also helped put out fires and broke up oil slicks.

Paul Davis was a tugboat man, who spent his first six weeks at Holy Loch in the mess and galley of the tender: 'This was a rite of passage, as a new sailor could view his crewmates and they could view him.' Tugboat men and all personnel in Boat Operations were assigned to the submarine squadron as support personnel. Boat Operations was based in a 600-foot barge, which, sitting between the tender and the dry dock, was a self-contained division: 'It had its own deck department and boatswains' mates, engineman department, oil king department, hull repair technician department and electrician department. The barge accommodated all these miscellaneous personnel.'

Paul Davis had enlisted in the U.S. Navy when he was 17 years old:

> 'I had joined the Navy to see the world and serve my country, and I was eager to go to Vietnam. I wanted to serve on a PBR [river patrol boat] or a coastal swift boat in Vietnam, but I was assigned to an aircraft carrier, where the Navy most needed young men. When I later re-joined the Navy, I asked for a carrier, as I wanted to see the Mediterranean. So naturally the Navy bureaucrats ignored my request; instead, I was assigned to a yard tugboat. I came aboard USS *Saugus*, YTB 780, assigned to the ComSubRon 14 [Commander Submarine Squadron 14] at the U.S. Navy's nuclear submarine base at Holy Loch, Scotland. I went from the biggest ship to the smallest.' [238]

Davis entered the world of non-stop activity. 'Working on the tugboat was hard, physical and dangerous, but we were proud of our service.' These squat, powerful vessels were deployed on a wide range of tasks. They worked long hours, and often went to sea to rendezvous with submarines for medevacs, classified missions and transfers of personnel. They also took part in exercises as targets, and they retrieved the torpedoes that had been used: 'Tugboat seamen performed deck duties, and stood helm watches at sea and security watches in port. There was a crew of 12: the chief, a cook and two groups – the boatswain mates/seamen and the enginemen/firemen.'

Most sea rescues involved military and civilian craft that had lost engine power at sea and needed a tow in bad weather or had a medical emergency. Rescuing sailing boats in summer was a regular occurrence, as many of these had run aground on sandbanks. The tugboat crew handled heavy waterlogged lines as thick as a man's arm; once a submarine had cast off its lines, the tugboatmen had to quickly reel them in, hand over hand, to prevent the lines being caught up in the tug's huge screw. A chief petty officer was the tug boss, and the crews, known as 'skimmers', were independent-minded and rugged, thinking of themselves as 'McHale's Navy', after the 1960s comedy TV series.

Going to sea during a Scottish winter aboard a 100-foot boat was a bracing activity; it would ride 50-foot waves and withstand gale-force winds. The skipper had to put the bow of the tug into the huge waves and ride them up and down. This was not pleasant, as Paul Davis recalled: 'Few of us were amused. If a huge wave had hit us on the side, we would have capsized and gone under quite fast. It was at times quite scary. Had we gone down we knew there was no rescue for us, as we would have died from hypothermia before we drowned.'

The boats in Boat Ops were refuelled on a daily basis from the barge. Fuelling was hazardous, and when the barge itself needed fuel this would come from the submarine tender. The tender, in turn, took on fuel from the ATK cargo ships. It made sense from a security viewpoint. The fuel and the other supplies would come from a secure military supply point in the United States. This reduced the chance of it being sabotaged. Greggery Kunkle highlighted the safety regulations involved: 'No smoking was permitted while this took place, on the tender or the barge. The oil kings secured the barge side of the hose and would be in constant communications with the oil kings on the tender while the refuelling was in process. If there was a leak or problem, steps were taken instantly to stop the flow of fuel.'

Oil pollution was easy to spot, as pools formed at the water's edge and the seaweed turned black and slimy. Site One had lots of oil, and some of it floated on the water. Oil 'donuts' were used to soak this up, but oil still polluted the loch every day. The oil donuts were checked daily and would be emptied by the oil kings. When a submarine, or any other vessel, arrived and needed to offload waste oil, Boat Ops would tow a donut alongside. They would then run hoses to it and offload the waste oil. Once they were done, Boat Ops towed the donut back out to the moorings at the head of the loch. Kunkle operated these tasks: 'The donuts would frequently sink or break free, and oil would pour into the water. This oil had to be pumped out into a reservoir, but there would still be lots of oil remaining on the water. I put an oil boom completely around the oil donut to keep the oil contained once they pulled the donut out of the water. The mess left behind was one of the dirtiest and most time-consuming jobs I've ever done. It took a long time to clean it up.'

Lots of work at Site One was carried out under water. Submarines were checked by Navy divers after returning from sea, and on most days while moored alongside the tender. The divers entered the loch to check for anything suspicious under the vessels.

Navy divers lived a lonely, dark existence. Their work was remembered by Boatswain's Mate First Class John W. Nance. He recalled his years as a Navy diver as a thrilling experience but added a touch of reality: 'This is not an easy job. Diving is both demanding and challenging. It is hard work at all times. Diving is a serious business, involving more than the pleasure of seeing the treasures of Davy Jones's locker. Diving isn't as glamorous as most people envision. There are many hazards to cope with. It's hard, demanding work and you have to be able to take care of yourself and your diving partner. Above all, you have to know your equipment.'

Divers in Holy Loch never deployed to sea with the subs, as they were members of the tender's company. They would also have other technical specialties, such as machinist mate, boatswain's mate, medical orderly.

Don McNulty was a Holy Loch diver: 'If an SSBN skipper felt a subsurface issue was a concern and insisted on an inspection of the hull, typically a shallow water diver would do this task. Major issues might require dry docking. Typical problem areas included the ship's propeller, as cavitation was always a concern. Debris between the pressure hull and the superstructure were often problematic, as were hull inlet openings for sea water etc. When other seabed matters were identified we would be lifted over the scene and jump into the water from the helicopter.'

Anne Donnelly was married to a navy diver who served on the USS *Holland*: 'I was concerned at times, as they spent very long hours on different jobs. They checked the floor of the loch and all vessels belonging to the submarine squadron and its support ships. They checked for cracks in ship's hulls and also for the possibility of Soviet Special Forces frogmen attaching mines or listening devices. I was especially worried about the night-time dives in the cold waters of Holy Loch.' [239]

From her front window Anne could see the dive lights on the tender's mast: 'When they came on late in the afternoon, I knew there would be a long night's work ahead for the divers. Once the dive lights were switched off, I would make my way to the pier to meet my husband and his fellow divers coming ashore. I would bring some hot dogs and baked beans for them. Boy, the divers were happy when I appeared with the food!' Her thoughtfulness was recognised by the executive officer of the USS *Holland*, who presented her with a written commendation.

The high standard of training maintained by the U.S. Navy was also evident in the welders at Holy Loch. They were a central component of the dockyard workforce; welding was always needed and it was a highly specialised task. Bernie Gantt remembered the expectations: 'You were supposed to be able to weld anything except the crack of dawn and a broken heart.'

At the age of 18 he had no job and had lost his driving licence, so he joined the U.S. Navy in order to learn a trade and see the world. By the time, 18 months later, he was ordered to USS *Canopus* at Holy Loch, he was a certified nuclear components welder – a big change in his life and responsibilities: 'My trade training had been long, and there were no shortcuts. Following boot camp, I was assigned to damage control school and then moved on to shopfitter school in San Diego. I was offered the opportunity for more training and took it, as Vietnam was in full swing and my alternative path would have been to go to a ship in the gun line.'

He moved on to welding school. The course started with 35 sailors and only 5 of them advanced to the nuclear-welding phase. But those who finished the long and tough course were the Navy's most valuable welders. Gantt was one of them. When he received his orders for the USS *Canopus*, he was a priceless commodity. However, at Site One, as all tradesmen had to prove their worth as shipmates, he started at the bottom.

He got all the grunt work, despite being the most highly qualified welder. But he loved it, as he was fixing submarines and knew he was the only one there that could do the job. At weekends he undertook extra training and became qualified on specialist welding tasks. But his watch-standing duties were awkward, as they were always at night. He would work until 11.15 p.m., go back to his bunk, get cleaned, change his uniform and stand watch for four hours. When the watch ended, he would change again and go back to work: 'I found myself as the only guy qualified to do these welds. I worked many crazy hours with no set liberty days. Crazy part about it was that I had to stop working on critical jobs to go clean up and stand a four-hour watch on my duty days.'

He qualified as a radiation worker and regularly had to do reactor repair work on board submarines. As a nuclear component welder, he held the highest Navy employment classification, and was required to maintain and refresh his qualifications every three months.

Nuclear welding was a specialised activity. Before workers could enter the RC (reactor compartment), the reactor had to be shut down and cooled down below 200°F (93°C). At times the welders had to work on it when the temperature was high. On such occasions, the stay time was about 10–15 minutes. In these situations their advanced skills were put to the test.

Radiation workers received doses of harmful ionising radiation and special training was required in order to limit individual exposure. When they worked on valves and piping, some worked inside glove bags. Quarterly medical checks were required, as Gantt pointed out: 'Exposure levels were closely watched, and if you absolutely had to exceed the local limits, authorisation had to be approved by the fleet commander or Admiral Rickover. This was extremely rare, and no skipper ever wanted to request this.'

On qualifying, a navy welder was certified to weld submarine pressure hulls, but not all this work was inside the vessel. They did a lot of work topside, and when a boat went into dry dock the workload tripled.

The weld shop aboard *Canopus* had almost 20 welders, and their work was non-stop, as Gantt noted: 'Most of it was expensive, and pressure was constant as every task was inspected. The senior petty officers got involved with the tough stuff. As time went on, I had qualified on every possible type of weld we had available. Some of the practice mock-ups cost $2,000–$3,000 each. If it failed inspection, it was scrap metal.'

The dry dock needed constant maintenance, as John Smith Jr recounted: 'I remember when the weather got colder the welds would crack. So they would preheat the steel before welding it. Also, they hired civilian welders to help get the job done.' [240]

During his trips to Gourock, Gantt dated a local Scots lass, and they decided to get married. As the wedding date approached, he had booked to take two weeks' leave and go to Edinburgh for the honeymoon.

A week before the wedding, a submarine was re-routed to Holy Loch for a specialist welding repair. Gantt was the only person qualified to perform this specific type of weld. He was briefed that he was still to go on leave but had to be contactable by phone at all times and be no more than two hours' travel time from the ship. He gathered the four best welders and trained them to do the weld.

For their honeymoon Gantt and his wife stayed in Largs, 20 miles from Gourock. On the second night he heard a knock on the door – it was the shore patrol. They had come to take him to the ship. As it was almost midnight, Gantt presumed he could travel in the morning, but it was a move-now order: 'I was told that the boat was waiting for us and I was going now! I went to the ship and did the weld. Of course, none of the guys had qualified, and as soon as I arrived to do the job, the chief cancelled their 24/7 qualification assignment. No one ever qualified to do that weld other than me.'

A few years later, Gantt returned to Holy Loch as probably the most qualified welder in the Atlantic Fleet. The repair officer assigned him to the QA (Quality Assurance) division aboard USS *Holland*. This was a good move, as it taught him a lot: 'I was promoted to HT1 and was no longer the junior man in a shop with two chiefs, two first classes and myself. One of the chiefs was in charge of all controlled materials on board the tender, and the other chief taught QA to the shop personnel. I was now the QA supervisor for refits, as all repair department work carried out on the submarine had to be QA-monitored. This was the application of high standards as monitoring was done by the shop QA inspectors for their respective repair shops – and my team monitored their monitoring.'

A QA supervisor was assigned to every refit; sometimes refits overlapped and then there would be two to supervise. It would be a busy period, Gantt recalled: 'Work was intense, as both captains would demand the best for their boat. This ensured that the QA supervisor was in perpetual motion, coping with the workload. The subs would be alongside for about 25 days, then out for a 2–3-day trial period. Then back in for their supply load and any final touches, before going back on patrol for 60 days. I had to sign off all welding repairs during this period. There were many, and inspections could take hours at a time.'

While on patrol, a submarine crew would produce work orders for matters that needed repair during the upcoming refit. On its return voyage the sub, once surfaced, would radio the work orders to the squadron headquarters for review and approval. Before the sub arrived alongside the tender, a team of repair experts would come aboard from a tugboat. This transfer of passengers could be exciting, as the weather was always windy and the tug had to come alongside regardless of the conditions: 'My team would get soaked by the waves. Once aboard, we would inspect the proposed work and start planning for it.'

If special materials or parts were needed, this information was radioed to the tender in advance: 'The process was started before the sub came alongside. Much of the repair work required special controlled-work packages. Documents with step-by-step instructions and signature completion steps had to be created. These were put together in preparation for starting the work. Full U.S. Navy standards were applied to every action. Top-class work was required.'

As soon as the sub tied up the refit started, and repair teams swarmed aboard with the crew showing them exactly what was needed.

Gantt worked hard to maintain QA standards, but he also branched out in his naval expertise by qualifying as OOD (officer on duty) for in-port watches. Normally this was a qualification reserved for CPOs (chief petty officers) and junior officers, but: 'I had other responsibilities. I was the at-sea flying squad leader, the guy in charge of fighting any emergency that happens – fire, explosion, collision etc.'

'This was unusual. I hardly ever got under way with the tender when she left Holy Loch on one of her rare trips into the North Atlantic or to a liberty port. They had me as leader so that we could pass our readiness inspections, which were conducted by visiting naval headquarters staff. These inspections were always done while we were moored, and this meant that I could be there. Another chief I trained took over for me when the ship was under way.[28]

But his most memorable qualification was his submariner's Dolphins: 'After working closely with the submarine crews, I got to know many of the chiefs and officers. This close liaison

---

28 The junior officer of the deck (JOOD) met every person coming aboard. The OOD (officer of the deck) was responsible for everything that happened on board, for instance the OOD monitored: how the subs were moored; how the small boats ran; what flags were flown from the mast; all announcements over the ship's tannoy; and many other matters.

enabled me to assist one sub with serious issues about its safety certification. While speaking to the captain one day, he said that I knew more about his boat than his own sailors did, and suggested that I should sit a qualification board to see if I could qualify to wear Dolphins.'

The challenge was accepted, and the commodore authorised Gantt's application. He did not have much knowledge about such matters as the steering, diving, sonar and communications systems, so he requested authorisation to go on patrol. This was refused, but he was allowed to go out on sea trials in order to do crash courses on these systems: 'At the next refit, I sat a qualification board. I'm very proud that I passed the board, since I wasn't actually a crewmember on any specific sub, and I've never gone on patrol – but I have more underway time on subs than most bubbleheads. I was presented with my Dolphins by the commodore!'

It was rare for someone not assigned to a submarine to be awarded the submarine Dolphins. Gantt gained his ESWS (Enlisted Surface Warfare Specialist) pin[29] shortly afterwards. This brought him another job; he became a member of the ESWS qualification board for the *Hunley*.

His area of questioning was the ship's damage control and fire-fighting/emergency actions. This included fire, collision, explosion, weapons drop/explosion, and radiological accident/ incident. This area was considered to be the hardest to qualify on, and Gantt had a reputation for being tough!

Because of his knowledge, Gantt was co-opted to the qualification board for in-port OOD testing. After this he moved on from standing OOD watches to become the ship's fire marshal. This meant that he was not required to stand watches on the quarterdeck. As fire marshal he had to constantly rove the ship for a 24-hour period: 'Biggest concern was making sure all trash had been dumped, and no unauthorised welding was happening after hours.'

This was strictly forbidden, as all welding had to be done to strict safety standards: 'Welding torches produced sparks, and these could start fires. Welding had to be pre-planned and authorised, and approval was given by the CDO [command duty officer)] or ship's fire marshal. This activity could involve welding on a bulkhead with an unchecked tank on the other side. Or flammable materials on the other side of a bulkhead, or around the welding area. This could cause a serious incident.'

But additional qualifications also meant additional duties for Gantt: 'I attended a special school to qualify as a "gas free engineer". This meant I had to inspect all tanks and voids to ensure they were safe for welding and other tasks. My classmates quickly realised the extra work qualification would bring and intentionally failed the exams. This left me as the only qualified gas free engineer at Holy Loch. This resulted in much additional time spent on board when others were off on liberty.'

Working in the repair department was tiring, but there was no letting up of pressure: 'Most of its personnel were working 100–120-hour weeks, and many times 30-hour stretches with one or two hours of sleep, before starting it again.' [241]

Unexpected incidents would occur during a refit. The submarine could not be delayed, so solutions would be rapidly applied. Gantt remembered one common problem activity: 'One of these situations involved a battery changeout or a 300kW generator changeout. These were

---

29 The ESWS (Enlisted Surface Warfare Specialist) pin was introduced as a way for sailors to be recognised as having proficient knowledge of their ship.

always stressful tasks that required tight coordination to get them completed on time. Sometimes a steam generator inspection was required. This was a task that was scheduled several months in advance; special teams were formed and special equipment acquired. The refit would be extended to ensure this task could be completed.'

At times, hull cuts were made in SSBNs to replace large equipment. This was a challenge that Gantt still remembers: 'The repair team had to climb more than 70 steps up the ladder from the dry dock basin to the top of the wingwall to get onboard the sub. From there you could get onboard the sub to do the work. No elevators. There were no shortcuts, although sometimes a crane lifted the equipment, but no personnel ever rode the crane.'

Working days in the dockyard were long. John Smith Jr was a 3rd-class steelworker erector who remembered the routine: 'Reveille was at 4.30 a.m.; ya ate breakfast at 5 a.m. or 5:15, then noon chow was at 12 noon. It was a long time between breakfast and lunch, so you made an extra sandwich or two and took it with you, wrapped in a napkin along with a couple oranges or apples.' [242]

But the dry dock also needed regular maintenance, and this was not an easy task. John Smith Jr recalled this: 'I was assigned to the painting crew. The entire dry dock was covered with a thin coat of asphalt that had to be chipped off with jitterbugs and air brushes. No ear protection was provided. The dry dock was then painted with a coat of red lead paint, then a coat of navy grey.' [243]

It was easy to spot the welders at work: their torch flames were visible, as were their little safety work boxes – their habitats. But there were other sailors whom nobody ever saw. They worked in the engine rooms of the tender and the dry dock. Tommy Gilbert was a Boiler Technician who served at Holy Loch from 1966 to 1970 aboard USS Simon Lake: 'I was a snipe. This was a hard job, but almost nobody knew what snipes did. We provided steam for every activity.'

Self-inflicted damage

The Cold War in Scotland was fought in a dangerous, hostile environment. Constant enemies were the wind, the rain and hazardous equipment. Lives were not lost in action but by accident, which made the loss harder to accept.

The *Los Alamos* dry dock had high sides, with a 100-foot drop to the metal floor below or into the water. There were flimsy walkways and no safety harnesses, and slips and stumbles were commonplace. Bill Edwards, engineer 1st class, recalled the death of a young crew member in 1964: 'He was known as Lightbulb on account of his smile. He fell from a height. Sad thing is that I can always recall his smile, but I can't remember his name.'

John Smith Jr recalled another dockyard accident: 'Young kid, who could climb that steel like a professional, was climbing up the steel rung ladder on the wing wall and slipped. He fell about 30 feet and broke both legs.'

Falling into the water was a constant hazard, and SF1 (shipfitter 1st class) Jim Locklear had a narrow escape. He slipped and fell overboard wearing his full welding equipment. A rope was thrown and he was pulled to safety.

Chief warrant officer Bob MacPherson was in charge of the investigation after another accident: 'A sailor, EMFN [electrician's mate fireman] Robert Dowe Hobbs from Belen, New

Mexico, was blown off the top of the dry dock. He was killed, and I accompanied his body back to the States. The Holy Loch winds were very strong at times.'

Tugs were often involved in seagoing incidents. As wind, tides and obstacles needed to be encountered safely, particularly when entering harbours, the tugs and their towed vessels needed to be perfectly co-ordinated – but sometimes they were not. Holy Loch was the scene of one such accident.

On 16 June 1964, USS *Betelgeuse* was arriving at Holy Loch from the USA with fresh supplies for Site One. Admiralty tug RFA *Empire Rosa* was on station. The ships collided. A towing wire fouled the tug's propeller, and water rushed into the tug. Rapid repairs were made. The tug was towed to a buoy by another tug, and a U.S. Navy diver cleared the wire around its propeller.

No casualties this time – a lucky break.

Accidents also happened when a ship was berthed. Bill Brown was standing boiler watch on USS *Los Alamos* in 1964 when he witnessed a metal stress fracture: 'Part of my duty was to carry out safety checks on the fuel supply. The fuel tank was a large container, roughly the same size as a small bus, and suddenly fuel spurted out of a hole. I hammered home a plug into the hole, stopping the leak, but the danger had not gone away. Fitters came down and disconnected the fuel piping. Divers went down and discovered a 3-foot crack in the hull – and all this happened with a sub in dock.'

There was a lucky escape for one sailor aboard the dry dock. A crane hook broke free and crashed through the deck into his bunkroom. Fred Saylor was a crew member who was at the scene and immediately spotted that the operator had made a mistake – it could have been fatal: 'I think the crane operator ran the boom down without letting out the No 2 big hook. So the boom actually tore off the big block and sent it to the deck. Just missed Steve Nelson, who had just got out of his rack.'

Sometimes accidents happened to unlucky sailors who were in the wrong place at the wrong time. One was hurt when a steel plate rack collapsed on him. His crewmates rushed to assist but could not lift all of the heavy steel plating. Eventually a crane removed it. He was badly hurt, and after medical treatment he was returned to the USA.[244]

The greatest danger aboard a ship is fire. Shipboard fires are often deadly and uncontrollable – and difficult to escape. Site One suffered its share of fires.

The hull techs (welders) were the primary firefighters. Every sailor is firefighting-qualified, but the HTs led the fight against fire, as Greggery Kunkle recalled: 'We were just bodies they could use to put on the hoses. Or in aiding in fighting flooding, in case that happened.' [245]

Fires were always bad news. Greg Kent was an engineman 2nd class aboard USS *Holland*. He tended the electric motor that turned the propeller shaft, and the six main diesel engines, and was also responsible for a generator. He recalled his first night aboard ship in Holy Loch when there was a fire in the forward engine room. He responded swiftly and helped fight the fire. When it was all over, his fellow firefighters welcomed him, the newcomer, to their fold: 'The fire had been caused by a cracked fuel line which was running close to full load. It sprayed high-pressure diesel fuel down the side of the engine. We had multiple fires during my tour and all were put out within a few minutes. Almost all were due to mechanical failure. Some were due to stupidity of the watch, leaving rags in the wrong place etc.' This was the cause of a fire aboard USS *Proteus* when on a training cruise in the Irish Sea in March 1962. Slight damage occurred.[246]

The engine room was always very hot, and fires started easily. Most were swiftly extinguished, as the engine room personnel, always on hand and alert, would fight these fires. They were experienced in dealing with them, although the damage control team would also send down someone to see if they needed help.

Aboard the tender USS *Holland*, there was a problem in communicating the fire alarm signal from the engine room. Greg Kent was trying to sound the alarm: 'It was a small fire on one of the main engines. I was trying to notify damage control central, but could not get through on the sound-powered phone. I finally told them to shut up as we had a Class B fire on Number 2 main engine. The fire was extinguished. The chief engineer waited for the incident to calm down and apologised when he heard the whole story. He then had a new alarm box installed in each engine room for fire, medical or flooding. These were used in the future and there were never any more problems reaching someone during an emergency.' Another example of high standards being reinforced.[247]

The *Canopus* Fire

But one fire at Holy Loch was serious.

It was November 1970, Thanksgiving evening, and the waters of Holy Loch were calm. The air temperature was below zero. The lights twinkled and all was quiet. The Blue Crew of USS *Francis Scott Key* was aboard *Canopus* ready for changeover the following day. The Gold Crew still had the ship.[248]

Suddenly smoke started billowing from the *Canopus*. Thick and acrid-smelling, it hung over the ship. The quayside was quickly wreathed in smoke, and flames started to appear. Sailors began running along the deck of *Canopus* and cries were raised. *Canopus* was on fire!

The Blue Crew had just arrived from Prestwick. The *Canopus* had a skeleton crew of mostly junior personnel on board, and the Gold Crew still had the boat. Russ Christie was on his second patrol: 'Our group was aboard *Canopus*, waiting to board the submarine. We smelled smoke and then the fire alarm sounded. The fire was some distance from our group and we stayed in our berthing. As the fire took hold, smoke was thick around the ship, and we mustered on the top deck of the tender. The *Canopus* crew called for help. They only wanted personnel who knew their way around the ship. Then all the lights went out and it became very dark. Cars began lining up on the shore with their headlights pointing towards us, and that was the only light. The decision came down to cast off one of the submarines that was tied up next to the tender – the USS *Francis Scott Key*.'

The Blue Crew commanding officer forbade anyone to get involved with the firefighting, as he was aware of the panic and confusion on board the tender. John Linville was a Blue Crew man who recalled the details: 'We piled OBA masks by the bottom of *Canopus*' bow for the tender crew to get if they needed them. I remember the confusion on the tender; there was smoke on the weather deck and lots of guys running around. We had a big welding machine aft on deck. We kept calling for someone on the tender to open the breaker on it. Finally, the chief said, "Just get rid of it!" so we pushed it overboard. I have never seen a sight like that – a fully energised 480-volt welder into salt water. Killed all those scupper fish suckers for 100 feet around the impact area.'

The crew of the *Canopus* battled with the fire, but the damage teams encountered their own difficulties. Some of the senior ratings had not used their OBA equipment for a long time, so they were out of practice and could not fit their masks. Replacement firefighters needed to be found. This took time.

The Gold Crew captain swiftly assessed the situation. He needed to remove his boat from the danger area, as the fire could spread from *Canopus*. But all of the tender crew were engaged in fighting the fire, so there was no one to deal with this urgent matter. Linville remembered the drama: 'We couldn't get anyone to cast off the lines from the tender. So we cut the lines ourselves with, I believe, fire axes. If I remember right, we cut the mooring lines down on the boat, and went upriver to tie off on the floating dry dock. I think the captain wanted as much distance between us and the tender as he could get, as the boat was in overhaul and not ready for sea.'

But casting off from the tender did not remove the submarine from danger. No tugs were yet on hand, and the next minutes were critical. Linville recalled: 'The lines from the *Key* were tossed into the bay and the power cable was cut. There were no tugs near, so the *Key* began to drift away from the tender. It drifted towards shore and looked as though it was going to run aground when a tug finally arrived, snared the *Key* and took it over to the floating dry dock, and tied it there.' A severe incident had been averted by well-practised procedures.

But when the submarine was moved, more drama occurred. While moving *Key* over to the dry dock and mooring, one of the crew members fell into the loch. He was pulled out by Gold Crew member Bob Lewis, MT2 SS: 'We reached the dry dock, and about that time the officer in charge was coming down toward me, so I told him to stay back. Instead, the officer continued forward and as we were trying to double up the line he fell overboard. I don't remember seeing him fall, but I heard the splash and since he fell aft, I made a quick decision to go into the water, and by keeping one arm around the rescue line was able to get him over to the side of the boat, where he was hoisted aboard by the rest of my line handlers. I was also pulled back aboard the boat.'

The fire on *Canopus* was now out of control, and it was burning towards the missile storage area. If that happened the missile compartment would have to be flooded, which would cause the ship to break in half. Russ Christie clearly remembered the situation: 'We now began to think of how to escape if that happened. None of us wanted to go into the freezing water, as we knew we would not make it to shore. So, we began looking for liferafts, lifejackets etc – then the word came that the fire was now under control.'

After four hours the fire abated. There was no nuclear accident. However, three sailors died; two of them had been prisoners and the other was the guard who had freed them from their cells. All had been overcome by heat and smoke before they could reach safety. Their bodies were recovered by the corpsman and fellow shipmates. The remaining sailors were upset over the fatalities, but relieved to be alive.[249]

The fire had started in the baggage storage area. No one got much sleep that night. The Blue Crew were delighted to assume command of the USS *Francis Scott Key* and leave the tender. There was extensive damage to one section of the ship, but SubRon-14 's mission was unaffected. The necessary repairs were completed and the U.S. Navy stated: '*Canopus* was never "off the line".'

This was a major incident. Fears of a nuclear accident spread through the local community. The U.S. Navy dismissed concerns that a nuclear explosion could have occurred aboard the *Canopus*, or even that a remote danger from missiles or other materials existed: 'We have drills and precautions which rule out any danger whatsoever. There are precautions against every eventuality in Holy Loch.' The records show that 'damage was extensive in the small area in which the fire was contained'.

The sailors who were there on the night had overcome their fears and fought the fire. It was a frightening event, and John Linville described it with typical vigour: 'We were told the fire got within two bulkheads of the torpedo warhead storage locker. Had it gotten there, the loch would be a *lot* deeper today. I wonder if the Brits, at any level of government, ever got the true story? – *No danger to persons or property outside the ship*, my butt!'

The Big Storm

The weather at Holy Loch was a constant problem, especially the strong winds which blew up the Firth of Clyde. High wind is always a problem for seafarers, even when they are ashore. At Site One, the Big Storm of 15 January 1968 was unforgettable. The region's worst natural disaster since records began created havoc, and the hurricane devastated the west of Scotland. Wind speeds measuring more than 110 mph killed 20 people and left more than 2,000 people homeless.

In Glasgow over 70,000 homes were damaged. Hundreds of people raced, panic-stricken, from Europe's tallest flats as they began swaying. In the River Clyde at least seven ships sank or went adrift. Thousands of trees were downed, as well as power lines, leaving the city's population of 1.7 million people in darkness.[250]

The weather in Greenock was vicious, too. A dredger capsized and sank in the river across from Holy Loch, with the loss of three crew members. The storm ripped up the Firth of Clyde, and acres of woodland were reduced to matchwood. Destroyed yachts were scattered on the roads.

Site One did not escape damage, and the tender USS *Simon Lake* was severely buffeted. Ashore, electrical lines swung wildly and most were torn from their fittings. Many crackled angrily along the ground, sending sparks into the night air. Cars were overturned, and roofs from many small buildings were torn away. Shopfronts were blown in, and telephone boxes were blown over. People rushed home for shelter – but the U.S. Navy stayed at its post.[251]

John Smith Jr was a dry-dock Seabee: 'Four Mike boats got loose. A group of us jumped into another Mike boat and went to rescue them. We tied up to it, but the cleat broke off on our boat and we had to cut it loose. The wind blew us to Gourock. The wind died down and we turned around and made it back to AFDB-7. The medical corpsman was there when we got back, and gave all of us each a small bottle of brandy. It sure tasted good.'[252]

Rick Winkler was aboard *Los Alamos*. At times it swayed dangerously as large waves crashed against it, and the walkways swung crazily. It was impossible to move around, and crew members hung onto supports. Most of them stayed below, but some had to work: 'I was in the crew's lounge when I got a call to man the port crane. When I got topside the crane's boom was swinging in the wind like a weathervane. We lowered the boom to the deck and dogged down the crane's cabin to keep it from rotating.'

Large lengths of timber were torn from the outrigger, and adjacent buildings and trees were blown over. Ardnadam Pier suffered minor damage, but overall Site One escaped major disruption and damage was limited. The sheltered nature of the Holy Loch had proved successful when tested.

The hurricane passed through quickly, and by early morning all was calm. Time to survey the damage. Officers and petty officers wearing hard hats swarmed over the site. Timber was floating alongside, and some small boats had been driven high onto the shore. These were quickly refloated, and Jack McNeelly, a Seabee, was at the centre of the clear-up: 'Our skills and equipment meant that we could help sort out the mess. Our officer had a hard time trying to prioritise the work. Every man and his dog wanted our help. It was a long couple of days before the excitement had calmed down and the mess was removed.' [253]

The missile incident

While an SSBN was in port its nuclear missiles were stored aboard the tender for maintenance and inspection. This activity was handled mostly by tender personnel. Dry-dock cranes shifted the missiles between the submarines and the tender – but this was a worrying task, recalled Ray Conner: 'They were large! Moving them slowly was paramount. All actions were scripted and performed sequentially.' Extra supervision and deep concentration were needed on this task, but accidents happened …

An alert message pierced the air: 'EMERGENCY ALPHA! – EMERGENCY ALPHA!'

Everyone paid attention. This was the highest level of warning – there had been a weapons drop! For Greg Kent, the date 2 November 1981 is etched in his memory: 'We had an incident with a missile. Now during that week we had numerous Emergency Alpha incidents with something floating alongside or some other nuclear drill. Of course, this pissed all of us off in Engineering, as we always had to stop what we were doing and come up to the mess decks.' [254]

That morning, everyone aboard knew that weapons would be moved. The weather was miserable. Lunch had just started when the USS *Holland* crew heard a large booming thud resonate through the ship. Crew members all looked at each other, puzzled, but continued what they were doing. The normal laughing and joking stopped when all of a sudden a chief came screaming into the mess decks and slammed the watertight hatch – 'They dropped a missile! They dropped a missile!'

Everyone spat out food and drink. It was at that moment that they felt the impact of what they did in the Navy. This was serious. They switched to the actions they had been trained to do in this type of emergency. Petty officers quietly took charge and all waited for information to be passed over the tannoy.

All High Alert situations had codewords. The crew knew what to do when these were declared. CONDITION ZEBRA was the highest level of watertight security: all doors/hatches in ship were secured. CIRCLE WILLIAM required all ventilation to be secured. These actions were carried out without any direction from officers or senior ratings, as this was survival activity. The crew assembled on the mess deck … and waited many hours for answers. When it was all over they were told the crane brakes had given way and the missile had dropped into the ship.

Access to the nuclear weapons division was via the Radcon (radiation control) door, where an armed marine guard checked IDs against an authorisation list. This was normally a highly controlled matter. Greg Kent vividly recalled that day: 'The marine guard never checked any IDs of sailors going into the Radcon door, as he was so scared. Apparently, there was a small fire there, and two guys who went into that area handled the situation correctly but did get radiation exposure. I do know the two left, never to come back. Everything was then hushed up for security.'

The missile had dropped 15 feet to the deck of the *Canopus*. Fortunately a safety device on the sling had prevented it from tipping over and crashing onto its side. Because the Poseidon warhead used an unstable explosive, a conventional explosion could then have taken place, dispersing radioactive material from the warhead.

The incident was not immediately reported to the local emergency services. The Navy claimed: 'There was no damage done, no injuries occurred; there was no danger to personnel.' They also refused to confirm or deny whether there were nuclear weapons on the missile. This attitude left a profoundly negative impression locally.[255]

This was a moment of significant potential danger. To this day, some crew members refuse to discuss this serious incident, as the fear has never left them.

Unwelcome legacy

Despite the best efforts of the oil kings and others, Holy Loch was contaminated. This was confirmed by official scientific surveys. A report stated:

> Following the closure of the United States Navy Submarine Base in 1992, video surveys revealed that a considerable amount of debris, largely scrap metal, was present on the bed of the Holy Loch … that a number of contaminants were present at high concentrations … Contamination of Holy Loch sediments by PCBs [polychlorinated biphenyls] and by trace metals, especially copper and zinc, was confirmed as severe but localized.[256]

There were also serious allegations regarding nuclear contamination. In one of these, the *Glasgow Herald* reported that the U.S. Navy had admitted that the paint on the USS *Sam Rayburn* (SSBN-635) was mildly radioactive when it returned from patrol in February 1984.

The Navy denied this story, claiming that the doses were within the permitted levels. This statement only added to the controversy.[257]

A former SSBN commander, Captain James Bush of the USS *Robert E. Lee* (SSBN-601), stated that radioactive primary coolant was regularly being dumped in the loch. This news sparked a political row in 1989,[258] but the U.S. Navy insisted that all of the discharges referred to were well within environmental guidelines. They stated that monitoring carried out in the Holy Loch and the surrounding area by British scientists had shown radioactivity to be at normal background levels. At the time of writing the disagreement continues.

More academic research carried out in 2004 showed that Holy Loch had significantly higher levels of contamination than other local sites in the Firth of Clyde: [259]

- 'The highest mean total CB concentration in all samples collected between 1999 and 2002 was found at Holy Loch.'

- 'Engineering firms and naval facilities around this site all involved the use and discharge of contaminants.'

- 'Highest concentrations were found at Holy Loch … only Holy Loch … would be classed as having high levels of contamination.'

After the departure of the U.S. Navy the Holy Loch waters were very dirty. Further research reported that toxic waste had been thrown overboard by the U.S. Navy and had transformed Holy Loch into one of the dirtiest stretches of coastal water in the world: 'concentrations of heavy metals, PCBs and other toxic chemicals in the loch are far higher than in other estuaries in Britain. These breached safety limits.' The American naval presence in Holy Loch had caused significant pollution and ecological damage.[260]

5 Kirknewton

– a conundrum behind the castle

Introduction

The American military lived in fear of repeating the catastrophic mistake of Pearl Harbor. Knowledge was vigorously sought about the Soviet Union. The gathering of intelligence was regarded as of 'immeasurable importance' by the chiefs of staff. After the Second World War, intelligence agencies began to proliferate, with the formation of the CIA, the NSA and new army, navy and air force intelligence organisations. Information-gathering activities increased, and the secret UKUSA Agreement of 1948 assumed great importance.[261]

UKUSA was a multilateral agreement for SIGINT cooperation between the US, the UK, Australia, Canada and New Zealand. It is also referred to as the Five Eyes. The accord formalised the 'Special Relationship' between the USA and the UK. Its importance was emphasised by General Marshall a few days after the Japanese surrender in 1945; he stated that 'the intelligence agreements and commitments with the British … will require re-examination and readjustment in the light of the post-hostilities situation.'[262]

Its existence was kept so secret that it was not even disclosed to the US president until six years later, in 1954. The prime minister of Australia was only informed in 1973, and it was only revealed to the public in 2005. Third-party nations, including Germany, Israel, the Nordic countries and the Philippines, are associate members, but are not part of the formal intelligence-sharing protocols of the Five Eyes.[263]

In 1949 Washington had been caught unawares by the Soviet atomic bomb, and nearly a decade later, in 1957, was similarly adrift with Sputnik. Greater intelligence coverage was deemed necessary. Part of this requirement took place in Scotland.

From 1950 the United States became a significant player in the field of intelligence-gathering. The detonation of Russia's bomb in 1949 had been a major shock – none of the American intelligence agencies had forecast this event. Information about Soviet activities was essential. As part of this development, the United States established three major radio spy stations in Scotland – at Kirknewton, Edzell and Thurso – as well as a high-tech strategic communications network.

Washington needed information on a global basis. Intelligence-gathering by cooperation between the UK and the US became a prominent feature, and this activity was arguably of greater importance than their nuclear relationship.[264]

SIGINT was the best method of gathering military intelligence. During the Second World War it had proved its worth, and during the Cold War its value increased. The CIA estimated that SIGINT was the source of 95 per cent of all finished intelligence data during this period. In addition, the NSA consistently devoted approximately 50 per cent of its resources to the Soviet target.[265]

Allen Dulles, former director of the CIA, had been a wartime spymaster in Switzerland.[266] He was a strong supporter of SIGINT, claiming that it was 'the best and hottest intelligence that one government can gather about another'.

In 1966 this was formally acknowledged in the United States Senate by Senator Milton Young: 'As far as foreign policy is concerned, I think the National Security Agency and the intelligence it develops has far more to do with foreign policy than does the intelligence developed by the CIA.' This statement emphasised the importance of America's intelligence-collecting sites in Scotland. In 1945 SIGINT action and its data had been protected by a presidential decree; now this information could only be released 'with the special approval of the President'.[267]

The geographical location of each SIGINT site was chosen for its convenience in eavesdropping on a target's radio traffic. The UK had extensive wartime SIGINT expertise, and agreed to sharing its sites. However, the UK could not match America's financial resources. So, because of the better US equipment, it was the NSA that carried out most of the intercepts and by the late 1980s GCHQ had almost become a sub-unit of NSA, which dictated the targets.[268]

All three of America's Scottish SIGINT sites were run by GCHQ on behalf of the NSA. The NSA paid for most of GCHQ's equipment under the terms of the UKUSA agreement and the NSA also controlled the missions.

SIGINT activity has always received the highest level of security. It was only in 1983 that the UK Government admitted its SIGINT activities and the existence of GCHQ. The UK and US governments still insist that most SIGINT records remain secret.[269]

Its value was such that President Lyndon B. Johnson insisted that the NSA should transmit SIGINT directly to the White House Situation Room. Johnson was a constant consumer of SIGINT material, using it to support the decisions he made during the Vietnam War. However, its value was sometimes downgraded. Henry Kissinger did not know enough about it, and Richard Nixon was not interested in reading intelligence material. As a result, the clarity of the SIGINT source material was overlooked.[270]

The senior KGB defector, Oleg Gordievsky, spoke about the value of SIGINT for the Russians. He stated that it was the source of the Kremlin's best intelligence data, particularly during the Cuban Missile Crisis, when its value was praised by Khrushchev.[271]

SIGINT provided important intelligence information for the United States prior to and during the 1967 Six-Day War. It also showed that in 1968 growing numbers of Soviet and Warsaw

Pact troops were being deployed along the borders of Czechoslovakia. This acted as a strategic warning for the White House, so the Russian move did not take it by surprise.[272] The Russian invasion of Afghanistan in 1980 was similarly observed during its build-up phase.

SIGINT was Kirknewton's mission. In the 1950s the main reason for an American radio spy station being based in Scotland was signals intelligence; Kirknewton had more than 500 personnel, and monitored the hotline. It was staffed by the US Air Force Security Service (USAFSS), as the USAF fully supported the establishment of ground stations to intercept Soviet radio traffic.[273]

This was a unique command. Most other Air Force units were in constant training status, preparing for a war-fighting contingency. But the USAFFS had a live, ongoing COMINT, (communications intelligence) mission, which was deemed necessary for America's security.[274]

Scottish activity

In 1949 the USAFSS began SIGINT operations and set up a worldwide network of radio masts to listen to Soviet signals. A deserted airfield in Scotland was an ideal location for this, and RAF Kirknewton, close to Edinburgh, became one of America's most important European intelligence-collecting sites.

From 1952 to 1966, American radio operators at Kirknewton listened to Soviet ships and aircraft, and tracked their positions.[275] More than 500 personnel worked on the base to intercept Russian voice and Morse signals. NSA operatives were on site from its early days, as SIGINT was its specialism. Although NSA involvement at Kirknewton was an open secret, from the outset official sources always skirted around this matter.

In August 1951 the 37th radio squadron mobile (RSM) was formed at Brooks AFB, Texas.[30] Six months later it left for Bremerhaven, in West Germany, but its mission was to occupy Kirknewton. Once background checks had been completed, it moved to Scotland in May 1952, with an initial strength of 6 officers and 39 airmen.[276]

Their early days at Kirknewton were primitive. It was a run-down former POW camp for Italian prisoners, consisting of basic concrete block buildings and a hangar. The site had no water or sewage facilities. Lt-Col Russell French, the first commanding officer, was not impressed when he made a reconnaissance visit in 1952; RAF Kirknewton was a dreary picture. But following this site survey, he confirmed that it was geographically suitable. In fact, it was an ideal location for the proposed radio intercept work. The advantages of Scotland's geographic position outweighed any concerns about facilities – the amenities of the site could be improved. Work started soon afterwards.[277]

The squadron swiftly settled into their spartan surroundings. The reality of outdoor living in Scotland during the winter soon became obvious. The winter of 1952–53 was the most severe in more than 100 years, and winterised tents were erected. Old diesel camp stoves were used for heating. The tents were used for all requirements – operations, accommodation, stores, latrines, cookhouse etc. It was a tough first year in freezing conditions, but in the second year proper

---

30 Re-designated the 6952nd RSM in May 1955, and became the 6952nd Radio Group in July 1963. Under this title it was stood down in 1966.

construction got under way; airmen moved into prefab H-frame buildings heated with small oil burners.[278]

Within months, as Staff Sgt Frederick S. Crawford recalled, there were 17 officers and 155 airmen at Kirknewton. The base eventually grew into a major listening post employing hundreds of highly trained airmen, and was a pioneer in the use of antenna configurations. Its task was to intercept Soviet radio and radar signals, and it tried out various antennae array configurations before settling on its final array of eleven rhombic antennae.

The high masts were built, and Nicol McBain, an early operator, described the layout: 'Each antenna was a single, narrow structure about 100 feet in height … the antennas were referred to as 'rhombics' – that must have been a reference to the shape of a collective array of perhaps five antennas grouped together as a unit.' [279]

McBain recalled the technical advantages of the mast layout: 'Each monitoring position had access to all antennas at all times. They were all cut for high frequency reception. The rhombic antenna system produced good results, and was quite adequate for our assigned mission tasking.'

The first USAFSS site had been at Stracathro, near RAF Edzell, in 1951. It had been staffed by operators from Chicksands, recalled George Montague, one of the early airmen. He served at three UK locations: Chicksands, Kirknewton and Stracathro. 'We were a 13 enlisted men detachment of the 10th RSM USAF … formed for service at Edzell … to operate an HF radio direction-finding station. All I knew about Scotland was that England tended to ignore the Scots.' [280]

George Montague was an intercept operator on the original Stracathro site in 1951. He copied Morse transmissions. When he worked in direction-finding, he took bearings on where the Russian transmission came from: 'When several DF [direction-finding] sites have a bearing on the same transmission, the place where they all meet is the location of the transmitter. That was our mission: to locate the position of Soviet transmitters.' [281]

The mission at Stracathro was then relocated to RAF Kirknewton, and the DF equipment was moved there.[282]

Radio messages had to be copied swiftly, so in June 1954 two stenographers – the first female personnel – arrived. They needed separate billets, and these were easily provided, as the building project had been completed. The base had now grown from the original small number to almost 400 personnel.[283]

By 1961, Kirknewton had a rhombic HF antenna farm with lots of masts, ranging from 75 to 100 feet tall. The operations building was located at its edge. It was single-storey and prefabricated, and was enlarged as the operation grew. McBain recalled the site: 'The road up from the ops building to the base was called Hurricane Road - it was wide open, being bordered by fields, and in the beautiful Scottish winter was a delight to traverse.' [284]

The base itself covered almost 50 acres. All the necessary support functions were provided. The camp was self-sufficient. It had a clinic and a doctor, but for any serious medical emergency the patient would be moved to the hospital in Edinburgh for treatment. There were early admin problems regarding pay and mail, but these were quickly resolved. Morale improved, and the positive effect was noted by Lt-Col French: 'There was an immediate drop in delinquent reporting.'

Support services such as base security and police duties were provided by the 7535th Air Base Squadron. They were a welcome addition, giving airmen more free time, and for the overworked radio operators there were no longer any extra duties such as cookhouse, fatigues and guard.[285]

However, not all of the base personnel were from the USAFSS. Kirknewton has always been linked to the ultra-top secret NSA,[286] and it was NSA officers who directed all the communications interception bases. Officially, the NSA did not actually exist until 1982, despite having been created 30 years earlier.[31] It was America's SIGINT collecting spy agency, and its charter was clear: 'The National Security Agency is responsible for providing foreign SIGINT [Signals Intelligence] to our nation's policymakers and military forces.'[287]

Both NSA and GCHQ – which, as mentioned earlier, operated as NSA's local agent – were involved at the site, but their presence was hidden. Some USAFSS personnel were aware of the liaison between the British and American agencies, but most never knew any of the details. One of them remarked: 'Upper-level officers worked closely with GCHQ in how the information was used by our two countries. This, by the way, was far above my pay grade at the time.' [288]

The NSA did not advertise its presence on radio spy sites. But some Kirknewton personnel, such as Nicol McBain, were fully aware of the NSA link. He recognised that there was a regular stream of civilian visitors. Many of these came from the Air Force, the US Embassy or civilian contractors. But he realised that some of them would have been NSA officers in disguise as he was aware that USAFSS was operationally subordinate to NSA.[289] USAFSS provided the trained personnel, and NSA provided the tasking: 'Any info about tasking, targets, sources, methods and equipment systems or processing systems was always classified.'

Kirknewton tracking data had to satisfy the NSA-specified criteria. The operations personnel performed all collection, analysis and reporting tasks, and any information deemed necessary for further analysis was retained for a discretionary period. If an incident happened again, the material was retained. If not, the security team destroyed the record. The NSA provided the criteria for events that it wanted to be reported.

Kirknewton's role remains shrouded in mystery. As far as its operators were aware, the mission of 6952nd Security Squadron was described by a bland statement: 'To provide radio relay communications, both data and voice, from US Military Organizations in the United States to US Military Units in Europe.'

As usual, regarding American intelligence collection activities, this reveals nothing. Kirknewton was a radio spy station A leading intelligence scholar has identified Kirknewton as a SIGINT centre with a target area of the Kola Peninsula. This has been officially denied, but no convincing rebuttal has been presented – in fact, the available evidence tends to support it. Kirknewton's location meant that such work could indeed be done there.[290]

The ops personnel knew that it was an intelligence-collection site. They did not directly track aircraft, although they did collect information from other sources. If an air activity met the NSA-dictated tracking specification, the operators would write and transmit a time-sensitive narrative report to DC, describing the activity.[291]

Kirknewton carried out both direction-finding and intercept tasks, as carried out at Chicksands. The principal reason for Kirknewton's existence was to track communications from

---

31 Until its existence was officially admitted in 1982, the NSA was referred to as 'No Such Agency.'

Soviet aircraft and sea vessels, and operators copied Russian and Warsaw Pact military radio traffic. The operators produced a high-quality output. Their work was successful, and George Montague described it with pride: 'What we did back then is all out in the open now. The only part that is still classified is how well we did it.' [292]

The Soviets routinely flew in the Arctic/Polar region, and Kirknewton was interested in this type of activity. When it occurred they would issue an initial report, then send follow-up reports to DC as the activity proceeded. Although some operators, such as McBain, did not recall any Soviet combat aircraft flying in the UK ADIZ (Air Defense Identification Zone) during their time at the unit, they admitted that this could have happened in the earlier days. [293]

The operations room at Kirknewton was crammed with radio machinery. Entry was restricted to the personnel who operated the equipment. Some were voice intercept ops, while others were manual morse intercept ops. Technicians were also granted supervised access, as broken equipment needed speedy repair. Lee Hendley spent a lot of his time there, for a simple reason: 'If they broke something, or their equipment failed, I was sent to fix the problem.' [294]

Lee Hendley was an air force staff sergeant (E-5) electronics repair technician. His crew were responsible for the maintenance and repair of all of the electronic equipment in the mission area of the site. He served at Kirknewton from 1963 until the base closed in 1966. His work included the classified equipment, which even now, at the time of writing, is still classified: 'As far as how my group assisted the mission, suffice it to say that if the equipment didn't work there couldn't be a mission.' [295]

Sigint could only work if it was done by well-trained, highly skilled operators. Kirknewton had these people. Their work required a great deal of dedication, expertise, flexibility and individual initiative. As such, these operators were not amenable to control by the standard rules and regulations or military-type discipline in general. Al Lorentzen, however, explained that although he and his colleagues might have been non-military in behaviour and attitude, they fully focused on the value of their mission; their 'loosey-goosey' behaviour never affected their excellent work outcomes. [296]

They had a mixture of talent, energy and high intelligence. A rigorous testing process was adopted for recruits, and as a result USAFSS was staffed by the top 10 per cent of USAF enlistees. McBain had a 20-year career in USAFSS, and was impressed by the calibre of his comrades: 'In all my years in USAFSS, I could not recall anyone stressing out. All the troops were well-trained, well-adjusted, very smart young men.'

Important questions have been raised about Kirknewton's targets. Claims have focused on the sensitive issue of its commercial communication interceptions; this radio traffic carried information which was valuable to the business interests of the United States. Investigative journalist Duncan Campbell believed that Kirknewton monitored these links, but the US Government always flatly denied this at the time.

A former operator, Jim Haynes, supported Campbell's allegation. Haynes said that he had to keep a special watch for commercial traffic, stating that his scans were targeted on key words which contained dozens of names of big companies. Haynes observed, too, that all intercept material was sent back to Fort Meade. [297]

Campbell claimed that the intercept operators at Kirknewton were monitoring commercial radio links between major European cities in 1965. These networks carried detailed economic and mercantile information exchanged by private companies, as well as encrypted diplomatic messages. Campbell produced evidence that in the operations centre the recording machines produced reams of 8-ply paper records for later analysis.

Lee Hendley recalled non-military targets being covered: 'In truth, the mission of the intercepts was not commercial transmissions, although it was done on occasion.'

In August 1975 the NSA director, General Lew Allen, gave evidence to the Pike Committee of the US House of Representatives. He freely admitted that the NSA was involved in eavesdropping on commercial radio links as well as on military radio links.[298]

The hotline

It appears that Kirknewton had an intriguing secret which placed it at the centre of Cold War communications. Duncan Campbell believed that it was part of the Washington–Moscow direct radio link: the hotline. This has never been officially confirmed – but the claim has never been disproved, either.[299]

The White House–Kremlin hotline had been set up to help prevent the outbreak of the Third World War. A direct link between the US President and his Soviet counterpart, it was the last-gasp safety device which enabled top-level talks between the two, to prevent any rash military actions by either side. Despite being depicted by film makers as a telephone line with a red telephone, the hotline was in fact a double teleprinter link. This was intended to guarantee that there would be no misunderstandings at either end.[300]

The link was set up after the Cuban Missile Crisis. During the standoff, American translators had taken almost 12 hours to decode a 3,000-word message from Moscow. And then, before the US answer had been prepared and delivered, they received another – more menacing – threat. So it was clear that the need for a direct link was urgent, and on 30 August 1963 it was set up. Known as the Molink (Moscow Link), it was tested hourly from both ends. The Americans transmitted Shakespeare and Mark Twain passages, and the Russians replied with Chekhov. The Washington terminal was operated by USAFSS personnel.[301]

Former Kirknewton staff members have stated that the hotline cable route ran close to the base. As Kirknewton was an American military telecommunications site, it could monitor the hotline's technical performance. Few, if any, other locations had the necessary security clearance for involvement in hotline activities.[302]

Lee Hendley stated that some of his colleagues carried out maintenance and repair work on the equipment. Although this separate group of technicians had been vetted for involvement with this task, he was not; its exact location was highly classified, and was only known to the personnel who worked in that section. Hendley had no detailed knowledge: 'I just know the hotline was there, but did not have anything to do with it … above my security clearance.'

As a SIGINT site, Kirknewton had top-level security and operated on a need-to-know basis. McBain believed that the communications centre, which had restricted access, would have been the ideal place for the hotline. Access to the system would be handled there by security-cleared personnel, and the officer on duty would be available to react. When I interviewed McBain he was equally vague about the details – understandable, after more than 50 years: 'The existence of the hotline was kept to a very limited number of people.' [303]

Kirknewton was an integral part of America's radio spy network, as well as a key nodule in Cold War communications.[304] It was an ideal location for the hotline technical monitoring point, as it was located on the main UK telephone network route. Both underwater cables – from the United States and from Russia – came ashore in Scotland, and Kirknewton sat at their junction.[32]

However, mystery and controversy remain …

Kirknewton's operations

On arrival at RAF Kirknewton, personnel were told that it was focused on the interception of Soviet Morse code messages and Russian-language radio transmissions. Its operators intercepted signals which were then decrypted, with copies made for various intelligence agencies back in Washington.[305]

Thirty USAFSS cryptologic radio operators were stationed in the main area of the communications compound with earphones and typewriters. Kirknewton tracked the interaction along the northern coast of the Soviet Union – both Soviet navy and Soviet merchant, military and commercial. As most of it was in Cyrillic Morse, there were Russian linguists on watch as well, listening in on the radio transmissions between submarines and their control centres. From those, analysts could determine the objectives of training missions, experiments, and could track naval movements.[306]

When John J. Moore arrived on his first tour in 1957, he was an experienced airman and a master sergeant radioman, and had served at other SIGINT stations. His work was interesting, and he emphasised they were tracking Soviet targets: 'We would pick up Russian TU-16 and TU-95 aircraft flying near to the north of Scotland. When they passed too close to our air space zone, we would inform the RAF. They would send up their standby planes to intercept the Russians and escort them out of UK air space.' [307]

George Montague operated DF and intercept activities. Both were carried out from the same operator position, and the only difference was the antenna: 'We used different antennas for each task, but the same radios. For DF we used an Adcock antenna, and for intercept used several others, but the best was a rhombic antenna.'

Kirknewton was known as one of the most technically exciting assignments for USAFSS personnel. Al Lorentzen, based there from 1959 to 1962, rated Kirknewton as the most interesting posting of his career. He enjoyed working 'eves' the most, as it was generally busy, and radio signal strength was better than during a day shift: 'I would pick up an aircraft reporting its position back to a northern Russian staging base. Down the line another operator would pick

---

32 The hotline crossed the Atlantic via an undersea cable known as TAT-1; the cable came ashore at Gallanach Bay, near Oban.

up another aircraft, and soon all operator positions would be working on this aircraft's radio traffic.'[308]

Life at Kirknewton was hectic for DF operators like Josh McInally, who worked in the operations building. He and his colleagues would receive requests for bearings on a particular target frequency. The signal would be located, a bearing obtained, and the information passed to the Morse section. The team worked a punishing schedule of hard, tiring shifts – and, worse, as he was working mixed shifts it was difficult for him to completely rest when he was off duty: 'This meant that I could not get my body into a routine as the shift start and finish times were different on many days.' [309]

Many of the operators were fluent not only in Russian but also in German, Czech and whatever other languages were needed; the intercepts covered most of Western Europe.

The intelligence analysts, working in the operations area, would read the intercept information gathered by the radiomen. Lee Hendley remembered that they would go up and down the line of Morse operators, ripping five-ply tear-sheets from typewriters, breaking the radar plots of intercepted traffic. They would then, using the big map in the operations centre, start tracking these Soviet long-range air army aircraft as they headed up towards the North Pole. At times some of the aircraft would venture into far north airspace, and Kirknewton would alert the Strategic Air Command and Air Defense Command, as America was being threatened – but the Russians always turned back.

Work at Kirknewton was done to an exacting standard. There were high-quality, well-trained personnel involved. Operators such as John J. Moore were fully aware of the high calibre of the Kirknewton workforce: 'Radioman billets needed well-educated personnel. It was a demanding job.'

Although there was lots of pressure, this was a unit with excellent morale, which led to plenty of teasing between the various flights. As McBain noted: ' "Day Ladies" was a term of endearment that Ops flight personnel used for Ops dayworkers. The sharpest people worked on days and were involved in management and evaluation of flight ops – so there was good-natured banter back and forth. But we were all part of the team, and everyone had signed on to that. It must be said that Security Service people were the smartest and sharpest people in the entire USAF – without a doubt.'

This self-confidence was a notable point about the Kirknewton personnel. Their level of expertise was often in demand elsewhere, so they were regularly detached to other locations.

James S. Richards, an intercept radio operator, was part of a detachment sent from Kirknewton to Libya in 1954. His mission was the same as at Kirknewton – to copy transmissions from his assigned targets: 'I listened in, and when an assigned target became active I copied the message. This was then passed to an analyst for action. At that time, I was too new to know where the assignments had come from. Each person knew his job and did it. We did not have to know anything else. And yes, I knew the importance of my duties, even though I was a 19-year-old kid.' [310]

But it was not all hard military work. Sometimes there were leisure activities with the British army units in the same business as Kirknewton's staff. The British operated radio stations on the sites used by earlier USAFSS teams, and visits between the two stations provided much-needed relaxation.

McBain remembered the British site at Hawklaw in Fife. This had more than 100 personnel and, as part of the US Sigint ground network in the UK, was operated by GCHQ to intercept Eastern Bloc communications until it was closed in 1988. He recalled visiting the non-commissioned officers' mess at a Royal Signals site at Hawklaw. The British NCOs from Hawklaw had been to the Kirknewton NCO mess earlier and invited the Americans to their station: 'We spent our time there toasting the Queen, the squadron and others.' [311]

At the centre of the Kirknewton site was the communications compound. Security was rigorous; only a few individuals were cleared for admission. It was protected by armed guards – an exceptional activity in Scotland. The walls of the cryptologic operations room were thick and soundproof, built to withstand attempts at forced entry long enough for the technicians inside to destroy any classified material. Within the compound, the operators were armed with submachine guns.[312]

John J. Moore, George Montague, Nicol McBain and their colleagues worked the normal gruelling shift system on watch. There were 25 of them on duty at any time. There were four teams, and they rotated through the various routines.

The United States sought information about any Soviet technological advances, and as Russia conducted trials on new equipment Kirknewton eavesdropped. The Soviet radar systems were prime targets, and the Soviet planes were tracked as they communicated with their base. Kirknewton had the capability of intercepting these transmissions, capturing fax-transmitted photographs and other information. These intercepts provided valuable information on the state of Russian technology.

Most of the transmissions were mundane. But one was significant: this message referred to submarine experimental propulsion trials as the Soviet navy tried to make their subs run much more quietly. This was a chain of events eerily prophetic of the strained standoffs that would later develop between the submarine forces of the Soviet Union and the United States.[313]

Philip C. Shackleford had been given the security task of weeding through the papers of the base commander. This involved assessing the relevance of the material and destroying certain documentation. Some of it was low-level, but some of it, top secret, would be sent to NSA for handling. One document stood out from the rest; it covered the interception of a new signal, which at the time of its reception had been deemed especially important. Three extra radio operators had been sent in from the headquarters at Chicksands to concentrate exclusively on the new signal. The times were tense. At the time of writing this signal has not been declassified.

Messages could interest various military customers. A former senior CIA officer, Douglas H. Wise,[33] explained: 'Let us take an adversary submarine. There are the people who are interested in the doctrine of undersea warfare adopted by the adversary, their tactics. Then there are the guys who care about the weapons systems on board the submarine; they don't care about the doctrine, only the weapons system: How long does it take to make it? How is it made? What is it made of? Where was it made? There are yet others, who only care about the propulsion drive: What fuel does it use? Is it traditional or non-traditional fuel? Where do they get this fuel? So there are not just one or two persons interested in the submarine; it is the intelligence community itself.'

---

33 Douglas H. Wise served as deputy director of the Defense Intelligence Agency.

Day-to-day DF and intercept material was critical to the United States' strategic posture. The strict on-site security measures in place were emphasised to all personnel on arrival and departure. McBain, in his role of security specialist at Kirknewton, responsible for the training and activity of his team, devised a wide-ranging briefing for new personnel that was so effective that he repeated it at all his subsequent bases.

Operations personnel had top secret-level clearance, and a few select technicians were cleared above this level for their involvement with the hotline. Incoming personnel, whether military or civilian, were given a rigorous briefing.[314]

But tight security was not enjoyable; it produced stress, and most personnel lied to their families about their job. A key member of the operations team recalled that when their shift was over, no matter how tense or exciting the events had been, nobody talked about it when they had left that secured area. McBain recalled this situation: 'When people in Edinburgh, or even our wives, asked us what we did for a living, we'd say we were clerk typists or some such thing. It wasn't easy to keep quiet about your business if you were married, but I think most of us did.'

Some aspects of the security culture have eroded over time. Much of Kirknewton's activities have been declassified, and memoirs have been released by senior intelligence officials. But the old guard from Kirknewton will still not talk about their work; when they became civilians they signed an agreement not to discuss these matters for 80 years. McBain was one of these. About 25 years later, he picked up a magazine which contained stories about NSA and what he and his colleagues did while working for USAFSS: 'Shocked to see it in print. Apparently, by this time, all this stuff was antiquated and declassified. Showed my wife that first article and after all these years, she found out what I did for a living when I was a young lad … I'd really never uttered a peep till then!'

SIGINT had been the only way to tackle the Russian Puzzle, and security was draped around all American SIGINT operations. This secrecy was demonstrated to McBain: 'When I left NSA/ government service and was debriefed, I was stunned when it took all day to debrief on the 36 special access programs that I had worked on during my career. Until then I had not known that I had been involved in so many secret projects.'

The lights go out

By 1966 the pioneering base on the old airfield had served its purpose and its operations were transferred to Menwith Hill in Yorkshire, which was described as the largest electronic monitoring station in the world.[315]

USAFSS Kirknewton then faded away, and as the buildings deteriorated the weeds took over. Some military training took place, but the air of mystery and excitement had gone. A poignant postscript was provided in 1991 by a retired chief who stopped by while visiting Edinburgh. Kirknewton had been basically abandoned for several years and was under caretaker status with a cadre of about a dozen RAF personnel keeping visitors away. He was allowed to tour the base, to find that all of the buildings were deteriorating rapidly. Although some of the towers on the antenna farm were still standing, the base was deserted.[316]

Unsurprisingly, Kirknewton made little impact on the locals. The importance of the base was completely unknown to them. Security controls had stopped any leaks. Its 14 years' existence was covered in a single paragraph by local historians Kenneth Roy and T.L. Hardie:[317]

> In the late fifties and early sixties, the U.S. Air Force had its Scottish base here. About 50 houses were built to accommodate the service families, but it seems the villagers reacted to the miniature invasion with equanimity. Little but the most cursory contact was established between the visitors and the resident population and, except for the occasional 'Open Day' at the camp, the Americans kept themselves very much to themselves. They did, however, put up a water-tower, which has become the unhappiest legacy of Kirknewton's brief reign as Little America.

Kirknewton was a successful pioneer radio spy station. It had been established to support an urgent strategic requirement for US military operations during the early Cold War period. It provided a listening post covering the region off the north of Scotland, an area of vital importance to the USA in its confrontation with the USSR. The United States needed early warning of Soviet military activity in the zone, and Kirknewton was an ideal location to provide this. Its strategic worth only declined when technology improved enough to make it obsolete.

Echoes of Dallas

Twelve years after its closure, Kirknewton's activities came under close scrutiny by the US Congress.

A sensational allegation had been made by a former operator, Sgt David F. Christensen: 'About a month or six weeks before I left Scotland, I picked up a link mentioning the assassination of President Kennedy.'

He claimed that his supervisor at the time had refused to forward this information to Washington DC. 'How hard I tried to get it sent out … they wouldn't send it to NSA. How I got my ass chewed for not dropping this link. Literally broke me up after 22 November 1963. Especially when I had it all beforehand.'

He said that the phone call linked the assassination plot to a member of organised crime: 'Since then have I learned that the man's name most mentioned was number four in a certain branch of organised crime at the time.'[318]

The identity of the conspirator was not revealed, but Christensen's statement suggested, once again, that USAFSS Kirknewton was listening to commercial telephone messages. The claim was investigated by the House Assassination Committee in 1978. The former supervisor was questioned, and told the investigators that the so-called phone link could have been intercepted, but 'had not been an assigned target'.

Christensen's incredible claims needed to be examined, as conspiracy stories about Kennedy's death were common. The NSA, as the custodian of SIGINT material, was tasked to check their records regarding this claim. This was swiftly completed and they reported to the House Committee, stating that they had made a thorough search of all records that might contain such information, but no communications or information relating to this event had been located. It was a short declaration. NSA had no information on this matter. No further action was taken.[319]

But questions remain. The NSA had used its own personnel to investigate its own records. No other agency took part in the investigation. Nobody was permitted to re-check the NSA's search process and results.

Many people are not convinced.[320] However, others supported the accuracy of the investigation. Nicol McBain was a day ops analyst on the Friday that JFK was killed. He cannot remember any message, and is adamant on this point: 'It was about 7 p.m. when we got the word about Kennedy's death, and we all reported to work. This allegation was made by a former operator from Bravo flight. I knew the personnel who worked on that flight. I don't recall anything about the message. Had there been a message anywhere about JFK, I would have heard about it.'

6. Edzell

– the Elephant Cage, huffduffers and wizards

American strategy

Towards the end of the 1950s the Soviets realised that their submarine Morse transmissions were being easily intercepted. They changed their system, compressed the Morse and introduced burst transmissions. In 1960 the American intercept sites did not have equipment to provide a bearing on a burst transmission, so the Russian submarines had vanished from their view and the Soviets had gained an advantage.

In response, Project Boresight was initiated, and found a solution: giant Wullenweber masts were erected on American HFDF sites. HFDF sites. Boresight became the number two U.S. military priority, the number one being the development of Polaris.[321]

Fourteen HFDF systems were installed worldwide, with the primary mission of tracking the Soviet navy during the Cold War. This became known as the Classic Bullseye, responsible for strategic intelligence collection and identifying the emitter locations. These stations had a huge layout of a circularly disposed antenna array (CDAA), popularly known as Elephant Cages.[322]

The growth of Edzell

The creation of NSGA Edzell was dramatic. There had been no master plan. An opportunity had arisen, and it was taken. On 9 February 1960 Lt A.J. Pelletier arrived at the U.S. Navy Headquarters in London to work in the communications security (Comsec) division. When he reported for duty, he was flagged down by the executive officer, Cdr Karl Koller, who told him that the captain wanted to see him soonest on an important matter.[323]

Pelletier made his way through the building, puzzled as to why the captain wanted to see him on his first day. He soon found out. Captain Lehman told him that he had heard from the

Admiralty that the Royal Air Force base at Edzell, Scotland, was being sold off, and bids would be accepted from interested organisations. Lehman had been told that if the U.S. Navy were interested they had better make up their mind immediately; otherwise, it would go to auction. Lehman told Pelletier to proceed immediately to Edzell and accept ownership of the base on behalf of the U.S. Navy.

The order was clear. Pelletier saluted and marched out, his mind buzzing. He collected his travel documents, ready to head north to complete the mission.

On 10 February 1960 he caught the train for Edzell, and next day he met with Squadron Leader P.I. Redford, who represented the commander of RAF Leuchars. Pelletier signed for the base and then, in near-blizzard conditions, the RAF ensign was lowered, then raised simultaneously with the Stars and Stripes. The base had joined the U.S. Navy.

Pelletier caught the morning train back to London. Twenty-four hours later he gave the signed papers to Captain Lehman who looked at them, and a broad smile broke out on his face as he sat down and drafted a message to his boss in the Pentagon. He showed it to Pelletier:

> ONE OF MY OFFICERS THIS DAY ACCEPTED TITLE TO RAF BASE
> EDZELL, SCOTLAND. PLEASE CONFIRM THIS ACTION SOONEST.

Pelletier was astonished. He had signed an ownership agreement for Edzell without prior approval from the Pentagon. Lehman told him not to worry, as there was a calculated reason behind his order. The bureaucrats at the Pentagon could not make their mind up about the base. The intelligence community knew they needed to have a Scottish location, as it would provide unrivalled coverage of the northern waters and Soviet naval activity. Lehman had recommended the base many months ago, but the paper-pushers had dragged their feet.[324] He had made the decision at his level. Edzell would be an excellent site. He had now forced their hand.

The powers that be came through with the authorisation. In 1960 Captain John S. Lehman became the first commanding officer of the Naval Security Group Activity (NSGA) Edzell. From its outset, the activities and purpose of NSGA Edzell have contained many ambiguities. The tone was set by the original U.S. Navy press release, which claimed that there 'would be no missiles, planes or radars' there. Although technically accurate, it misled the public as to the activities planned for the base.[325]

This, then, was how the radio spy site at Edzell behaved throughout its years of operation. There was a constant stream of denials and misleading statements. It was a site working on sensitive matters. During the Cold War NSGA Edzell, the main United States intelligence-gathering base in Scotland, was staffed by various units, including personnel from the US Naval Security Group, USMC (US Marine Corps), NSA, the Royal Navy, the RAF and GCHQ.

The USAFSS had run a similar base at Strathacro near Edzell in the early 1950s. The base at Stracathro operated the United States direction-finding activities aimed at the Russian and Warsaw Pact radio stations. The detachment personnel had moved to Edzell, lived in RAF billeting there and commuted to the DF site at Stracathro by jeep.[326]

The US Naval Security Group required plenty of room at Edzell for both intercept and direction-finding antenna fields. They also needed a large building for receiving and recording the intercepted signals, with space for a full air-conditioning system for the vacuum tube equipment, which generated considerable heat. Ancillary units and power plants were also installed on the site.

Edzell lived with endless security and cover stories. Its primary role was to detect, monitor and track Soviet submarines and radio signals in the North Atlantic zone and the Barents Sea. With a working range of almost 4,000 miles, Edzell's equipment could even reach the Caribbean, and was specifically designed to detect transmissions from submarines.[327]

The US Government expended huge sums on Edzell's operations. Its importance was recognised in 1973 when the Senate described NSGA Edzell as carrying out 'an anti-submarine warfare support mission vital to the security of the nation as part of the high-frequency direction-finder network ... this station provides communications essential to the defense of the United States'.[328]

By 1974 Edzell's mission statement showed that it was an integral part of a worldwide network developed by the United States, known as the Classic Wizard. Its remit was the collection and processing method for the Classic Bullseye system, and its task was 'to serve as part of a program to provide communications for the defense of the United States and the free world' as well as 'additional functions include monitoring transmissions procedures and research into electronic phenomena'.[329]

Edzell continued to perform its role in the strategic defence of the United States, and increased in size after 1968. An early warning complex was constructed at Inverbervie in 1978 and was staffed by Edzell personnel.[330]

The significance of Edzell's output was indicated in 1979, when its operational control was transferred to the director of the NSA (DIRNSA). Edzell's mission was to 'provide cryptologic support to commanders and units of NAVEUR, with an obligation to provide SIGINT, interpretation, advice and assistance'. There was no doubt about Edzell's strategic role.[331]

By 1985 the mission had been upgraded, and to ensure the passage of funding legislation in the US Congress a cover story had been necessary: Edzell was claimed to have been involved in supporting US Fleet units operating in the area, to have provided navigational service relating to air-sea rescue, and to have conducted technical research in support of Navy electronic projects. This, of course, was misleading. More detail would have drawn unwelcome attention to Edzell's unrivalled value as a strategic asset for the United States.[332]

But official denials could not hide the true purpose of Edzell's activities. The radio equipment was fully visible. There was a huge array of tall masts of the type normally used in direction-finding activities. The site's radomes and parabolic antennae housed interception equipment.[333]

The masts were a Wullenweber array, similar to those at all U.S. Navy HFDF Classic Wizard sites. The masts were nicknamed 'the Elephant Cage'. The inner circle was made of wooden poles similar to telephone poles, but about 90 feet high. The poles in the outer circle were made of aluminium and stood about 25 feet high.[334]

The Elephant Cage dominated the site and covered 40 acres. It took two years to construct. There was a 23-man maintenance team, split into antenna, radio and test equipment technicians.

They climbed the towers to deal with corrosion, rust, timber preservation, painting and the electrical system checks. Each antenna was a complex technical entity, with almost 1,800 separate pieces and more than 100 different connections. More than 500,000 feet of cable was in use, and the system was regularly checked by a specially designed computer.[335]

Tall masts have problems in high winds, and at Edzell this was found to be true in 1968. Many masts were blown down in the Big Storm of that year. Eric Mercato was a technician and witnessed the damage on that wild night. The roof of his billet was damaged, trees were uprooted and the area was littered with broken branches. But the main damage was at the Elephant Cage: about a quarter of the array was blown down, and this hampered the collection operation. It took several weeks to re-erect the fallen masts. But operations were not drastically affected.[336]

Any degradation of NSGA Edzell's capabilities would have been serious, as it operated at the centre of the American intelligence community. Joe Mazzafro was a U.S. Navy intelligence officer in London, who brokered intelligence exchanges between various UK and US agencies. He described Edzell's intelligence role: 'Edzell and the other US SIGINT sites in the UK exchanged information through NSA and GCHQ protocols, which were based on 'need to know'. The same protocols were followed in transactions between CIA and MI6.'[337]

He explained that the SIGINT activities were split between NSA, GCHQ and their subordinate organisations. In addition, 'robust agreements' governed the sharing of Edzell's intelligence between the U.S. Navy and the Royal Navy; both services staffed the site.

Some of the intercepted messages were dramatic. Edzell operators listened to the Israeli attack on the USS *Liberty* during the 1967 Six-Day War, when 34 Americans had been killed and almost 200 wounded. This was followed a year later by the capture of the USS *Pueblo* by North Korea. These incidents were a severe shock to the U.S. Navy cryptologist community. Richard Crispl was on watch when both the *Liberty* and the *Pueblo* were attacked: 'The Edzell operators listened to these live incidents. It was an unpleasant experience, as many of them had served previously with these men or had been trained alongside them. Emotions ran high.'[338]

The base, under the nominal control of the U.S. Navy, was home to the Oceanographic Monitoring Station, which tracked Russian naval activity in the North Sea and surrounding areas.[339]

Base security involved multiple law enforcement agencies: the MOD police, RAF police and U.S. Navy police were part of a joint effort. Confusion reigned, however, as the Americans believed they were immune to UK legal action. There was a problem with the Americans accepting the role of the RAF police – it was even challenged by senior personnel, who should have known better. MOD Constable Malcolm Campbell was regularly involved in these squabbles: 'As far as they were concerned, this was an American base with American military police and the Brits had no authority over them. But we had. They learned.'[340]

NSGA Edzell was an American operation, and it had an American commanding officer.[34] Yet as it was an RAF base with an RAF commanding officer, it contained American and British

---

34 The Status of Forces Agreement established the legal jurisdiction over military personnel and related civilians; defined the exemptions of such personnel from passport and visa regulations and customs and excise duties; set out the legal right for military personnel to patrol bases, transit the host state, wear uniform and bear arms in the host nation; and set out the cost arrangements for establishing and maintaining military facilities. It was set out in the Status of Forces Agreement 1951 and the Visiting Forces Act 1952.

military personnel, plus American dependents. So police work was convoluted at times. The MOD police duties at Edzell were a policing and security role.[341] They had full constabulary powers and would deal with complaints where military and civilians were involved. Campbell recalled the situation: 'For minor offences, the offender would be reported to the U.S. Navy Command, to be dealt with under UCMJ [the American Uniform Code of Military Justice]. However, in cases of more serious offences a report would be forwarded to the local procurator fiscal, who would either accept the report or resubmit it to the U.S. Navy for action.' [35]

Anyone travelling the road passing RAF Edzell could not miss its huge circular array of wooden and gleaming metal poles. Incoming U.S. Navy personnel such as Tom Shirley were amazed to see this for the first time. He and his colleagues were completely puzzled by the sight of the Elephant Cage.[342]

There were two main sites, the radomes and the Elephant Cage. The radomes (aka Golf Balls) were in fact weather protection for the satellite-receiving antennae inside them. They were part of the high-tech, well-funded Classic Wizard activity. At the time, most other intelligence-gathering sites worked with DOS computer systems but Classic Wizard had an Apple system; it was a prestigious activity, able to locate ground as well as sea targets.[343]

Inside the Elephant Cage was Building 300, the operations centre which handled SIGINT collection and analysis. Some of this work was also done by the Royal Navy contingent. Building 300 had two levels below ground. Entry to this area was restricted, and most personnel did not have the required security clearance.[344]

The lower deck of Building 300 housed an important facility – the calibration laboratory (cal lab). All technical equipment needed to comply with the current U.S. Navy standards. The technical maintenance personnel calibrated the electronic instruments and test equipment here. This was a crucial task, and the required standards were rigorously enforced. This meant that a meter used to measure electrical activity in the operations area was tested by an instrument in the cal lab.

Dan Flanagan was a petty officer 2nd class (E-5) radio operator at Edzell in the early 1970s. He explained the importance of this process: 'The laboratory instrument was in turn tested by another accredited laboratory instrument that was more accurate. This formed a link in a chain that goes all the way back to the appropriate level, e.g., a national laboratory. All the electronic instruments which were used in critical applications required accuracy that was traceable back to national and international laboratory standards.' [345]

Building 300 housed other top secret departments: the maintenance department and the antenna shop. There was an armoury that held all the USMC security team weapons. It also had an interesting collection of contents, as many of the Edzell sailors were hunters and had brought their own guns to Scotland. Access to it was controlled at all times, and gun owners had to book a time to collect their weapon.

Building 300's lower deck contained mysteries such as the goniometer. This was an essential tool for HFDF activity. There were 160 masts in the Elephant Cage and the signals from the masts were fed into Building 300. These were transmitted to the gonio deck. The goniometer

35 The procurator fiscal is the prosecuting authority in Scotland. The US equivalent is district attorney.

equipment was used to rapidly scan through all the antennas around the circle. This allowed fast and accurate direction finding; speedy scans were needed, because the Soviet submarines used wide-band, four-second burst transmissions to avoid detection.[346]

It was the noisiest room in the complex. As well as the goniometers, there was a huge array of fans to control the temperature. Personnel had to shout to be understood, and ringing telephones could not be heard. A simple solution was found and telephones were fitted with submarine klaxon ring tones. But people outside could also hear it. When a telephone klaxon sounded, there would be a cry of 'Dive! Dive!' from most personnel.

Local rumours grew because of these antics, as Richard Crispl discovered. He was sitting in a local pub one day, when a gentleman pulled up a bar stool next to him. The stranger got to the point immediately and told him he knew why the Americans were at Edzell. Crispl maintained his standard non-committal look and asked him to elaborate on his statement. The local lowered his voice and replied that it was well known that the Americans kept their missile submarines under the base, with access from a tunnel to the North Sea, some 10 miles away. Crispl kept a straight face as he quietly choked on his beer.

Security and secrecy were paramount. Most Edzell staff knew nothing about the gonio room. Others were aware that it had an important operational role.

Jim Luis Parham was the base supply officer. He had started his U.S. Navy career intending to become a naval aviator or a SEAL, but neither happened, so after service in Vietnam, he transferred to the Navy Supply Corps. When he came to Edzell as the supply officer, part of his role was to maintain the supply of technical spare parts to the gonio deck, which had high security status. He had to check these on a regular basis, and remembered the behaviour he encountered: 'Fascinating! Every time I walked into THE BUILDING to inventory parts … everybody hollered, "Sanitise the area!" ' [347]

Non-security-cleared personnel needed access to the lower floor for mundane, but essential tasks, namely to cash their pay cheques. The security process worked well.

Regardless of their contents, the underground levels were not pleasant workplaces. They were narrow with neon lighting and featureless concrete walls. Noisy air-conditioning ran constantly, and Willie Hogg detested them: 'It sucked, as it was in a building with no windows, but I felt like a mole too. At the end of my watch, I was delighted to step above ground and breathe fresh air.'

The watch system was the backbone of all naval activity, whether at sea or ashore. At Edzell the watch system was remorseless. It ensured that the station was always fully staffed to track the Russian ships and aircraft in its region of operations. Sailors were familiar with the rhythm of the watches. Work continued throughout in the DF shack, as recalled by Jimmy Grier: 'There was a constant chatter of Morse Code and the rhythmic clacking of teleprinters. It was in near-darkness, to better read the DF scopes, and the soft orange glow of the scopes enhanced its shadowy air of secrecy.'

Operators liked the fact that they were awake and working while the rest of the world slept. They knew they were doing very important work, tracking vessels of the Soviet Navy and merchant fleets. Tom Shirley enjoyed the routine, and learned a lot in this environment as his watch supervisor was a real taskmaster who insisted on continuous attention to duty. The instructor and his assistant had devised an intensive on-the-job training programme. This was invaluable after the pre-set school training already undertaken, as the Edzell veterans brought new operators up to field speed, ready to immediately step into their task. Another example of the never-ending attention to high standards which characterised America's Cold War activities in Scotland.

Keith Collie was an HFDF operator – a 'huffduffer' – at Edzell, and the shifts he worked were unrelenting: 'The rest period was essential. However, even that was not all rest. The real naval world always intruded with additional tasks.' [348]

The typical DF watch section was composed of four men and a petty officer section leader, recalled Mac McInness. DF work was not physically tiring, but two or three times during a shift there would be a lot of activity. For the rest of the time, the operators would scan through the frequencies looking for transmissions and call signs of interest.[36]

Personal administration had to be done, and this absorbed an operator's free time. Sleep deficit arose, as McInness remembered: 'The short turnaround between most watches was a busy period. By the time an operator had returned to the barracks (or home), showered, changed clothes and got something to eat they did not have eight hours off to rest before going back to start all over again. After a series of watches had concluded it took some time to catch up on sleep.' [349]

This was the routine at Edzell, and its CTs (cryptologic technicians) lived in this fragmented fashion. They tolerated the stress and, like McInness, got on with the job. His personal routine was buttressed by his patriotism: 'With other operators monitoring the radios, we were able to get up from our position, walk around, get coffee or just stretch. I never felt I lost efficiency during my shifts, as the job we did was both exciting and rewarding. I only felt the need for rest without the sounds of Morse code in my ears and eyes on a scope when I was off duty, headed to the barracks or home. It's like working a stressful job in civilian life five days a week. You look forward to weekends off to rest and relax. I would say one reason I never felt tired or exhausted on duty was the fact I was doing something positive to defend my country.'

The watch routine was a rigorous existence, with even more disruption for the USMC operators, as they also had to do Marine Corps training in their rest periods. There was also another factor which could not be overcome, as Dale Reemett recalled: 'The day/night cycle that far north meant that you could literally go days, or even weeks, without seeing daylight.' [350]

At this time the USMC were keen to widen the job spectrum to women. Louise Glen arrived at Edzell in 1977 as a 19-year-old corpsman taking part in a new project.[351] She had been posted there to see if a female corpsman could work in what had previously been a men-only environment. Yes, it was possible for females to work at Edzell. The female facilities were initially basic, but they improved quickly. The experiment was a success, and other female marines joined her.

Although the Company B marines were cryptologists, they maintained marine battle training standards, as recalled by Reemett: 'As marines, we would often go on runs down the long strath, through the Blue Door, and into the river for a … soprano-making river run in boots and utilities … next day we would be cold warriors, doing Cold War stuff – prepping for a run through the gas chamber … and the following day we would spend a morning of rappelling from beneath a train bridge.'

---

36 In radio communications, a call sign is a unique designation for a transmitter station, i.e. a ship, aircraft, ground station or vehicle.

The Edzell equipment was high technology: the workplace was not. Keith Collie recalled that it was certainly a *Cold* War environment: 'It was freezing in those spaces, due to the large mainframe tube-based computers. We usually wore our work jackets on watch.' [352]

Operators on watch would go hungry for eight hours. Unbroken concentration was important, as Dale Reemett remembered: 'There was plenty of coffee for eight hours. But no food. Most of the time you ate before and after the watch, and not much during your shift.' The work was hard and relaxation was valuable. During their rest period, operators needed some free time to sleep without interruptions: 'At the end of a midwatch we'd take the bus back along the old runway, have breakfast at the galley, then walk over to our Quonset hut and sleep the day away. Even with their severe lack of amenities, those Quonset huts now stand out fondly in my memory.'

Tired operators needed undisturbed sleep, but single men slept in barracks with individual beds in one large room. There was no privacy. Mac McInness reflected on this system: 'Accommodation was not allocated by watch sections. It was haphazard. There always seemed to be someone sleeping in the room. It was unusual for such an important matter to be treated in an off-hand manner.'

Like all military installations, whether basic sites or high-tech facilities, Edzell's lifeblood was supplied by the stores department. With more than 3,000 military personnel and dependants, plus vast amounts of equipment and a large base area to be maintained, there was a huge demand for stores at Edzell.

CDR Parham's team consisted of two junior officers and about 50 UK MOD civil servants. His department was responsible for all personal property, shipment of household goods, logistics and stock control, finance, disbursing pay and stocking the galleys; such matters accompany all military units. The majority of his time was concerned with logistics and finance. He chased after high priority spare parts and dealt with the prioritisation for funding. There were many conflicting calls on his budget.

Parham was aware of the base mission. His job was to ensure that the electronics, such as magnetrons, circuits etc., were ordered, delivered and replenished. Many were very high priority. He explained the role of NSGA Edzell: 'The mission of Naval Security Group Activity Edzell was often described as a big ear listening to the Soviets. Almost all the base personnel, CTs, were cleared for SI [Special Intelligence], one of the highest security clearances.'

It was always busy. Christine Pine has vivid memories of the supply department, and recalled that 'just about every person smoked in the office. It was like living in a fog.' She was a storekeeper, and her duties involved stock control, receiving and delivering materials and procuring contracts. She handled medical and office supplies, communications equipment (lots of which was classified), repair parts and materials for all departments. She was involved in contracts activity, which consisted of liaising for local services, local equipment and public works.[353]

Although storekeepers handled all the technical resupply matters, only the supply officer knew these details. Pine was not one of those who needed to know, but she fully realised the importance of such secrecy. Her knowledge of the unit's programmes was so little that she just went along with the flow. It was her job and she got on with it. She did not understand one iota of what was going on, and did not comprehend the big picture either: 'Those of us who were not CTs, SISS Zulu, Classic Wizard or SPECCOMMS [Specialist Communications, Edzell's specific missions at the time] just did our support part. I was a storekeeper in the supply department.'

Leisure time was treasured. Pine remembered sitting in the lobby of the barracks, watching The Muppets on TV: 'How funny to see all these adult American Cold War warriors crammed into that little area and having a good time!' [354]

Edzell operations

The Naval Security Group developed the Wullenweber array system to detect, monitor and plot the location of Soviet submarines and other radio emitters in the Atlantic and Pacific oceans. SPECCOMMS was a classified programme that intercepted submarine communications and located them.[355]

In the 1960s a group of ELINT (electronic intelligence) satellites was launched by the United States. Edzell was one of the monitoring stations for these satellites. This work was done by the SISS Zulu section within the Classic Wizard department. It was yet another highly classified activity.

Edzell was part of the Naval Ocean Surveillance System (NOSS). The data being collected had to be immediately relayed to operators elsewhere, as the ships that had been detected would be constantly changing position. Chief Arne Simonsen was the NOSS operations chief at Edzell: 'We provided real-time special intelligence to national intelligence agencies, aligned allied intelligence agencies and deployed Naval vessels and aircraft.' [356]

NSGA Edzell was described as the European base the Americans would least like to lose. Its mission was to monitor the Northern Seas and the European continent. A former operator recalled that they listened to Soviet land-based radio stations, the Soviet navy and Soviet merchant ships.

Although its operational control lay with the NSA,[357] few Edzell personnel were aware of the NSA linkage. But Dale Reemett, an operations supervisor, knew about it: 'The naval security group activity, Edzell, was considered an out-site of the NSA. We were tasked by the NSA.'

Eric Mercato was able to shine a light on the shadowy involvement of the NSA at Edzell and other sites: 'The NSA were the customers; NSGA Edzell were the producers. The NSA set the SIGINT task, and Edzell set about accomplishing it. It was a relationship similar to a client and project management.' The NSA technical teams would arrive at Edzell to monitor and maintain some of the newest equipment associated with the task: 'They would turn up in groups of ten or so, and remain here for four or five weeks. They came here to assist delivery of the mission. Then they would return to Fort Meade [in Maryland].'

CTs only had a need to know about the various sensitive matters limited to their own area of work. It was common knowledge among Bill Carpenter's group that secret material was being transferred to NSA headquarters in Washington DC. The reason for this was obvious: 'Everybody and their little brother wanted to know where the bad guys were.'

The movement of the classified recording material was organised by the security specialists. Eric Mercato was involved in tasking the couriers, and most days would despatch to Fort Meade packages of sensitive material which had been collected from the operations centre. The U.S. Navy couriers would take them to the courier section at Prestwick Airport for onward secure despatch. This was a well-practised process. A couple of large mailbags were sent each time.[358]

The courier section at Prestwick was a sub-unit of NSGA Edzell. Prestwick was a two-hour drive from Edzell, and there were always two couriers on the NSA run. At Prestwick the classified bags were collected by an authorised NSA courier with high-level security clearance; he would sign the paperwork, and the Edzell personnel would hand over the sacks. There was a daily transatlantic flight to Washington DC from Prestwick, and Edzell material was carried on these flights. Some incoming classified material was unloaded at Prestwick.

Although he was security-cleared, Eric Mercato had little knowledge of the other operations. He was privy to their collected information, but this was for security purposes: 'People did not talk about their jobs. It was possible to be aware of the activities they were carrying out. However, nobody talked about the details. There was no small talk on these matters.'

Yet despite the strict security regime, the KGB had good knowledge about Edzell's activities and this was highlighted in 1993 when a Russian military magazine published full details of the Classic Wizard programme. Although this information would probably have come from a different source, Edzell's cloak of secrecy had been pierced.[359]

Dale Reemett was a member of a USMC unit at Edzell. He was a member of Company B, USMC: 'My unit supported intelligence-gathering. We were trained as radio operators for intelligence-gathering. We were nicknamed 'ditty chasers', and staffed the Collins R390 receivers and copied Morse code traffic on typewriters. There were other marines in the operations room, alongside U.S. Navy personnel who worked at the HFDF console.'[360]

These Edzell marines sat quietly at their workstations for long hours. Concentration was required. Reemett recalled that his unit observed military customs and courtesies such as saluting officers, and stood monthly personnel inspections, barracks inspections and the like. Otherwise, they were very much a group of technicians who happened to wear uniforms to work. They were casual and informal, and they addressed one other by first names, often by nicknames. There was no cheering or whooping either.

The chance taken by Captain Lehman had paid off. Edzell attracted other units, and in 1970 Detachment 370 USAF arrived. They were part of Project Clear Sky, the anti-nuclear weapons treaty monitoring process. As usual, their arrival was described in a bland fashion, as part of a weather research and radio propagation project.[361]

They monitored atmospheric nuclear tests carried out by the Soviet Union, and their activities were top secret. Malcolm Campbell often saw members of Detachment 370 at work and at leisure, but despite close involvement in providing protection for the American groups, the security culture was so strong that he never found out any details about the various missions. 'I never knew for sure what the various departments' missions were and never asked, as the Americans were very sensitive about these things. We would chat about the weather, sport, local events and other matters, but they never let slip any information about their task.'[362]

Secrecy led to the growth of rumours about Edzell's activities; one topic which received regular attention was the Black Projects. These were highly classified projects, unacknowledged by the US Government. Some of them, such as early reconnaissance satellites and high-altitude spy aircraft, were linked to intelligence-gathering.

Marion Summers had been a junior USAF officer working with a small group from the U.S. Air Force signals intelligence group. She said: 'Although NSGA Edzell was primarily a Navy assignment, USAF people were sort of lost/screened behind the larger projects. All of it was classified and compartmentalised. It was special information, concerning the Black Projects.' [363]

The training regime

Excellent equipment and well-trained operators were fundamental to the success of NSGA Edzell. The U.S. Navy and the other contributing units ensured that their personnel had been properly trained before reaching the base. Eric Mercato summed this up: 'You don't *join* any of the intel services, at least not in the Navy and the Marine Corps ... you're hand-picked by your instructors at early stages of your training.' During his basic marine training, Mercato had shown advanced language and problem-solving skills. Further technical specialist training followed.[364]

The service men and women at Edzell were among the cream of the crop. They had scored very high on their entrance exams and had been selected to serve at important intelligence-gathering sites. These valuable people were offered large re-enlistment bonuses to stay on, and as further encouragement to them to do so, the Navy relaxed the normal rules of military discipline for them.[365]

The Edzell radiomen and technicians had undergone a long training process, which produced first-class field operators. High standards were essential to operate the site effectively and maximise its geographic advantages. Its personnel had started out by attending a boot camp where they had been given aptitude and intelligence tests. Those who achieved the highest ranking in these tests were vetted for security clearance. Successful candidates were invited to attend further training.[366]

At that time, Morse code was the basis of cryptography. It was the fundamental requirement of a Navy CT, and all CTs had to master it. The full mastery of Morse code was a relentless activity: every day new letters had to be learned, and every week copying had to become faster until it was an automatic response. High speeds had to be achieved. All code was copied on a typewriter, as it became too fast for longhand.[37]

Bill Carpenter remembered his training. Students would sit in one large room learning the 26 letters and 10 digits that made up one version of international Morse code. 'I became competent – regularly competent – and kept pace as the speeds increased. Five words a minute. Then eight. Then ten, twelve and so on. Graduating speed was twenty-two words per minute, and by then I had met and exceeded the threshold comfortably, and actually enjoyed what I was doing. I became that code-copying fool.' [367]

A different route was followed by A.Q. Morton, who had completed his degree at Pennsylvania State University in June 1968. He then, having received his dreaded draft notice, chose to

---

37 I achieved a copying speed of 16 wpm (words per minute). The Edzell personnel and others achieved 30 wpm and above.

enlist in the U.S. Navy rather than be drafted into the Army and sent to war in Vietnam. After completing basic training, he was sent to the US Naval Communications School in Pensacola, Florida. Having been an amateur radio operator (ham) for six years – so he was proficient in high-speed Morse code – and freshly out of college, he graduated at the top of his class. The top graduate had a choice of being posted to any U.S. Navy Security Group Activity in the world. He chose Hawaii. However, after learning that a close friend had received orders to Scotland, Morton changed his selection to the US Naval Security Group at Edzell.[368]

Dan Flanagan also attended Morse school in Florida to learn his job skills: 'For the first 10 weeks or so we were taught the Morse code. I already knew it, as I was an amateur radio operator. At the time I could copy about 30 words per minute with a pencil. My instructor didn't believe me, so I had to demonstrate it to him. I then learned to type out the code on a mill [typewriter] during that time, and helped the instructor to grade tests.'[369]

As the Russians used the Cyrillic alphabet the American operators needed to learn this too. One day Flanagan's instructor moved the class to another room with rows of mills, and when they pulled the dust covers off their mills, they found the keys had the Cyrillic alphabet on them. They spent the second half of the training copying Cyrillic Morse on their mills. They were also taught the importance of maintaining security and not divulging classified information. This was a constant theme of the CT service.

When Dan Flanagan completed his training he was posted to NSGA Edzell. He returned to Pensacola to be trained for six weeks on HFDF and become a huffduffer.

Arne Simonsen had always been interested in the world of radios, and was aware that there were many radio-linked jobs in the Navy. As a youth, he had been an amateur radio operator, so he joined the Naval Reserve while still in high school. The Navy determined that he had the skills to become a CTR (collection) striker. This meant that he was required to have a top secret special intelligence clearance. He was sent to CTR A school, and upon graduation was transferred to NSGA Edzell.[370]

HFDF activity

DF work was procedural. The operators identified the target, took a bearing and pushed a button, sending the bearing back to the USA, where it would be cross-fixed with other bearings on the same target sent from other CT sites. Operators such as Mac McInness would watch the screen and scan the frequency ranges until a target was discovered: 'The watch routine consisted of sitting with headphones on, paper and pencil ready, a cup of coffee to hand and a cigarette.'[371]

The operators scanned the target frequencies provided by the NSA. Target call signs came via a 60 wpm teletype machine, and the target results went back via teletype. The busy times happened two or three times per watch, when ships called into their base to give their DPR (daily position report). This activity kept the operators extremely busy. The target base lined them up one by one, and after they were logged in each ship was then called to give its DPR. McInness remembered the result: 'When this happened, it produced mass confusion, lots of activity and great excitement.'

Collection and analysis were done on the same floor in Building 300. The collection team occupied one end and the analysis team the remainder. There were no windows, no doors, no offices; the staff needed to be able to move freely across the floor to listen to other transmissions.[372]

The Edzell operators followed specific Soviet units. They searched the frequencies the Russians would use, and identified specific Soviet operators. The analysts' task was to look for the interesting bits of these transmissions, so, as they sat at their individual collection stations they printed out the transcripts to study them.

The intercept operators had come through highly structured training, and their attention to detail produced high standards. Surprisingly, however, the analysis team had an unstructured training syllabus. They wrote technical reports and intelligence reports, but there was no rigidly formulated training programme which handled an operator's transition from collection duties to analyst. The training was on the job, intuitive, as the Soviets did not have strict radio discipline. They were, however, creatures of habit, so the Edzell crew could identify individual Russian operators. Reemett was trained in this manner: 'Our training consisted of reading old intelligence reports and becoming familiar with the patterns which were established. We realised that the more experienced analysts were good at this aspect of the job, and we learned from them.'

Newcomers were mentored by senior radiomen, who passed on the frequencies to be monitored. 'Operators became more proficient the longer they worked on their task,' noted Jimmy Grier, 'and then they passed on this high level of expertise.' [373]

During periods when nothing of interest was occurring, operators such as Keith Collie would scan through the frequencies known to be used by targets. As soon as one was found to be talking to its control centre, its call sign and frequency were passed to Control. If Control was interested in the target, they would send the details out to the net via the teletype. The bearing would also be submitted. External stations would multiply the effort to gain success.

By 1965 the original direction-finding equipment at Edzell had been upgraded. This new equipment was far more accurate. McInness remembered the changeover: 'We were switched to the new operations site with its large circular ring of antennas.[38] The equipment was new and operated the same as the old, but the O-scope was more defined and accurate. The target area coverage produced better results, especially for the ASW system. The identified Russian submarines would then be tracked until intercepted by ASW assets.' [374]

In the ops room there were three duty stations for HFDF operators. The first of these required the operator to change the 'tyres' – large Ampex reel-to-reel 1-inch tapes. The target radio frequencies were recorded on four separate recorders, each of which was backed up by a library of 96 large tape spools – digital storage was many years in the future.

This was the start point for CT operators when they arrived at Edzell. On each system there was a two-minute lag between the record heads and the playback heads. That meant that if a transmission of interest was detected, it could be played back in near-real time within that two-minute window. The machine heads had to be maintained, as recalled by Morton: 'In between each change, you used large Q-tips to clean and lubricate the record/playback heads. This was

---

38 The antenna array at Edzell was listed as an AN/FRD10 (FRD = fixed ground radio direction finding).

the most monotonous, boring duty. Technology had its limits, and staying awake on a mid-watch was challenging.' [375]

Keith Collie outlined more details of the ops room process: 'We kept a watchful ear on Russian ship and plane movements in support of early warning. One group captured strings of encrypted Morse code messages to be deciphered by, I think, the T-branchers. And there were also the 'matmen,' the CTMs[39] who fixed the equipment they claimed we abused ... ha!'

Another operator task involved taking bearings on intercepted signals. Edzell's mission was to locate and fix targets, and tasking was triggered by incoming tips from another HFDF site in the European zone that had intercepted the target transmission. The incoming tip automatically set a receiver to the Morse signal. For Collie, this was an interesting moment; he would then listen for that target to repeat its call sign. When this occurred, he would record its bearing by manipulating a cursor on the O-scope. The target would normally be repeatedly calling a Russian control station, and, as he described it, 'We would be waiting patiently to hear 'DE', dah di dit-dit [the international phrase for 'this is']. The payoff would be hearing what came after that, which would be the four-letter call sign of the sender.'

During this transmission, the CT operator would try to get the best possible bearing. Collie explained: 'When you had confirmed the sender's identity and obtained a bearing, you pushed a button to send that bearing back to Norfolk to be cross-fixed with a report from another HFDF site.' [376]

He moved on from this task to another stage in the process: tip-off operator. His Cyrillic alphabet skills now came in useful, as these frequencies transmitted Russian Morse messages, and the tip-off operator could identify the target transmissions by its use of Russian and the Cyrillic alphabet: 'Before arriving at Edzell, I had learned how to read the Cyrillic alphabet and copy it. Whenever, I found such stations, I passed the call sign and frequency to the DF console operator. A bearing was then taken on it.' [377]

Finally, Collie moved to the DF console task. When he had received call signs and frequencies from the receiving operators he plotted the bearings. Once the frequency was tuned in, the operator identified it on the O-scope by placing a cursor over the signal blip, then the computer program made an accurate measurement of each bearing. It took about a minute for the different bearing measurements to converge, and this action would provide a location for the signal.

Although these actions were computerised, precise input was required from the operators. The bearing was passed to the main DF console, where the control supervisor had an important role, as Dan Flanagan remembered: 'I collected bearings from the DF console operator and sent the call signs and frequencies of stations of interest over the RTTY [radio teletype] machine. This was connected to all the other DF comms stations on the network around the world.' [378]

Edzell listened in to northern and central Russia, and also covered the waters off the east coast of America. The operators would be listening to the communications from Russian ships and planes, and the Cuban 'fishing boats' operating off the US east coast. These were identified as Russian spy vessels and, as Morton explained: 'We monitored the Russian navy, the Russian

---

39 Cryptology technician maintenance.

merchant navy and the Warsaw Pact shore stations. We also intercepted coded traffic and took DF bearings.' [379]

An important element of NSGA Edzell activities was the top secret specialist programme known as SpecComms. This group was responsible for locating Soviet submarines operating at periscope depth in order to use their HF communications. 'This made them vulnerable to American detection,' said Willie Hogg. 'We intercepted these transmissions, but no signals were sent by Edzell during this activity. It was strictly a receive-only operation.' [380]

Hogg had been an ET who spent four years at Edzell in the 1980s. He had worked in SpecComms, and he confirmed that his team relayed this information to an outside location. Secrecy prevented him from revealing the name of this location; all he could say was that they covered the HF band on a multitude of frequencies: 'We covered one specific area of the world for our mission, and we only listened to transmissions. Then we would then relay this info elsewhere.'

But Hogg did not know how Edzell gathered its intelligence material: 'Our coverage was mainly aimed at the North Sea, the Barents Sea and northern Russia. Being an HF system, this coverage extended at least 1,000 miles due to its high-gain antennae.' Hogg confirmed one element of Edzell's activities: 'SpecComms needed direction information from the submarines, so we had equipment in our spaces that would provide this information.' [381]

Edzell was not a stand-alone organisation. It was linked to other elements of the Classic Wizard system, and McInness recollected that there was a phone link to a British site somewhere in England. Periodically the Edzell team would be asked to provide a bearing for a signal that GCHQ were tracking. When the target was found, Edzell would give the bearing information to the person on the phone. No questions were asked.[382]

The huffduffers' job was to catch the Soviet vessels' call signs. Each Soviet ship would send to its headquarters a DPR including a weather report, location, course and speed. The Edzell team compared this information to the details they had gathered on the targets. The operators had learned tracking while at DF school; it was an essential skill. To keep track of the Soviet vessels, the team members wrote the call signs on paper tags and stuck these to a tracking chart in the operations room. This was constantly updated as Mac McInness recalled: 'Our division officer would come in each morning and stop for a long, thoughtful gaze at the Soviet vessels I'd stuck on the tracking chart.' [383]

Flanagan also worked in the area where digital communications were monitored. These were highly classified at the time, as their use was limited to special forces and strategic communications. Russian digital communications were of particular interest, as it was believed that critical information was being transmitted in this high-tech mode. Occasionally he listened for Soviet satellites, and his search zone covered a wide geographical area: 'Russian shore stations I remember were in Moscow, Vladivostok, Murmansk. I'm sure there were others – maybe Arkhangelsk, Saint Petersburg – but the prominent ones I recall were Moscow and Vladivostok.'

When activity was slow, Flanagan and other operators would scan the HF spectrum for signals of interest and pass them on to the DF console in the other room: 'These signals would be put out on the network. With experience, one learned to identify signals of interest. These could be recognised by call sign, by use of the Cyrillic alphabet, by use of coded letter groups – usually five-letter groups, but not always. Or they could be identified by the bearing and a combination of all of the latter.' [384]

A standard group of frequencies was monitored, and the Edzell operators learned a lot about the constant weakness of Soviet radio discipline. An experienced operator could identify the Soviet operator on the other end. Their sending was usually fast: 25–35 words per minute. Different operators had different 'fists' – that is, differences in their Morse sending characteristics such as speed and swing (i.e. Morse character timing). Slower Morse was sent with a manual key, and faster speeds were obtained by using semi-automatic ones.

The Edzell equipment had become faster and more accurate. It became easier to use. The new system was known as Classic Owl, and operators needed to return to the United States to be trained. The training was held at NSGA Winter Harbor, Maine. It was a long course, 182 days, and special security screening was required.[385]

Dale Reemett worked in Sigint analysis and … Royal Navy intelligence staff also worked in Building 300. Reemett was the supervisor of the collection room in this building. He handled Morse, machine Morse and voice communications as well as the radio frequency ranges ELF, HF, VHF and UHF. The Soviet information was transmitted in encrypted Morse.

Reemett had access to many intelligence reports, and one of them told a shocking story that demonstrated the brutal reality of the Cold War. This document narrated the loss of the Soviet submarine *Komsomolets* on its first operational patrol in 1989. She has been off the coast of Norway in April 1989. This area was constantly covered by the Edzell operators, and the radio traffic was intercepted.

Komsomolets had 69 crew on board. Fire broke out and most of the crew abandoned ship; 42 were lost. Soviet rescue aircraft and a Russian fish factory ship attended the scene. The U.S. Navy offered to assist, but this offer was declined.

During this incident, the Soviet response had been callous. The Russians would not take American offers of help. All external assistance and humanitarian aid offers were rejected. The boat and crew were sacrificed, and ideology triumphed.

It had a profound effect on Reemett: 'This intel report was instrumental in helping me understand their ruthless mindset toward us, toward their own service members, and toward their mission.' [386]

It was a harsh lesson for Reemett and his colleagues, but it helped them to realise the power of propaganda within the Soviet armed forces. Unsurprisingly, it entrenched their own hostility to Communism.[387]

Arne Simonsen worked in the processing and reporting division, alongside the Russian linguists who translated the intercepts before they were passed to the analysts. He was assigned to a three-man office whose task was breaking codes and ciphers. But his team had just one U.S. Navy Russian linguist, and patience was not one of Simonson's strong points: 'I quickly got tired of having to run over to an officer who was a Russian linguist, so I re-enlisted for basic Russian language training.' [388]

Most intercepted messages were routine and helped to build an overall bigger picture. None of them were noteworthy, though, until one night in 1990, when Reemett was sharp enough to note some significant details. His team realised that what they were copying and writing was not a routine message. Something big was happening; there was far more activity than normal. It was strange and unusual. Reemett wrote a significant report. It was one of the first indications of the beginning of the collapse of the Soviet Union.

He co-authored this report with a U.S. Navy E-5 Russian linguist. They laboured all night, writing furiously as events unfolded. At one point they realised they would not have the time or the wherewithal to properly format the report. However, the details were so important that they ignored this. When it was finished, they checked it over one last time, and forwarded it to the watch officer. 'I'll never forget his response: he looked over his monitor at me, over his glasses, and said, "Sergeant Reemett, is this *your* shit?" '

Reemett nodded. The report was forwarded as required. The next day, word was received from higher command that Reemett and the linguist were to be officially reprimanded: 'The day after that, the same command, now seeing much more from other sources, reversed course, telling him to belay the reprimand and instead present both of us with commendations – Bravo Zulus.[40] We had been right with our intel analysis and subsequent report.'

The activity on watch was systematic and well planned: some departments monitored local frequencies in the North Sea, and others monitored further afield. Most of the Soviet radio traffic was not encoded, and manual Morse code copiers listened to it. The frequency ranges being scanned were from 2 to 32 MHz. There were bands of frequencies where different services were licensed to operate. Reemett remembered that commercial shipping was assigned a separate range of operating frequencies, different countries were assigned call signs: 'For example, Canadian call signs started with C, US started with N ... there are exceptions for the military.'

Some Edzell departments monitored the North Sea sector frequencies. The classified departments, such as Classic Wizard, monitored further afield. Manual Morse code copiers listened directly to unencrypted Russian unsecured traffic. There were also other high-tech collectors who listened to other Russian communications. Outside agencies sent information to Edzell, and Eric Mercato recalled how this was handled. It could be done by getting reports from an AWACS (airborne warning and control system) aircraft on a ferret flight. It could be provided by a submarine collecting data, or even by American satellites. All of this was of use, and the analysts would sift through the material and make comparisons. This information monitored everything, from 'what Soviet weapons were turned on in Siberia to whether or not there were 10,000 people smoking outside in Petropavlovsk at any given time. The absence of such a regular activity would have been noted by the intelligence analysts.' [389]

Mercato had arrived at NSGA Edzell as a USMC cryptologist knowing very little about Scotland. He had been told it had a nationalist movement. It was during the era of the IRA terrorism, so personal security was at risk, and individuals needed to be wary and prepared. For Americans this meant one thing – carry a gun. Eric qualified as a sidearms expert, and laughed as he recalled the outcome: 'Scotland did not become another Northern Ireland ... but I did get a shiny new pistol expert shooting badge to wear on my dress uniform.'

---

40 US Navalspeak for 'Well done!'

Maintenance of equipment

One of the bastions of Edzell's operational success was its equipment. As this was always fully maintained it produced excellent results, regardless of its age. Most of it was maintained by civilian contractors, many of whom had worked with this equipment as members of the United States Navy. Continuity of expertise was a principal factor, so this process was of fundamental importance and it was rigorously applied. The equipment consistently worked to its fullest capability because of the amount of maintenance it received. Mac McInness recalled: 'the electronics we used at that time were so antiquated, and it's amazing how well they worked and how accurate they were.'

At Edzell there was no off-time for the equipment – it was used 24/7 – and Mercato's task was to keep the communications circuits up and running between Edzell and its distant ends. He inserted codes into the system to ensure that the data being transmitted off the base was encrypted properly. He maintained the multiplexers that jumbled the communication channels from place to place. He also sorted messages and carried out the maintenance on all the technical hardware that sent and received classified messages to and from the base.

Henry George worked with the Classic Wizard programme.[390] He was a civilian software engineer who had come to Edzell in 1983 for the deployment of Increment 3. He had previously installed this software at other U.S. Navy Classic Wizard stations, and explained his role: 'My deployment at Edzell included software installation, and the training and operational support of Navy personnel. Although I had full security clearance at Edzell, my access was strictly limited to the Classic Wizard site. I trained the sailors on the new capabilities that had been installed. The operational support consisted of answering questions while the system ran with the new software. I also tried to document and/or fix issues when new features did not work as planned.'

Nevertheless, the need-to-know rule applied to George, despite his high-level security clearance: 'All of the secret operations on the base were a mystery to me. I knew nothing about them. I was clueless as to operations. I was a technician with a 'scope and a soldering iron. And a tube checker.'

This restriction applied to other technicians. Jimmy Grier, for instance, knew little about sending secret codes and other data back and forth to the NSA. Although he had been taught about the top secret cryptographic level systems that were directed at spying on Russian submarines and fishing trawlers, his detailed knowledge was directed to the maintenance of this equipment. He had little knowledge of the secret work carried out by other shipmates: 'Funny to think that some dude standing at the urinal beside me was carrying top secret cryptographic material. But then I was 19 or 20, and a noobie.' [391]

In the military world, operational methods are constantly revised and improved. While Grier was at Edzell there were continual changes to the collection process. The Russians kept changing their methods to communicate with their nuclear fleet. Edzell monitored and broke the Russian code and methods, but the Russians changed it again. In response the Americans needed to improve their chances of gathering transmissions of secret code from subs and Russian fishing trawlers. Grier recalled: 'They developed receivers that captured thousands of frequencies, and recorded them to tape for further analysis. They were like a DVR [digital video recorder], which records all the shows on all the channels. These wide-band receivers were a step up from thousands of guys spinning radio dials around the world. My job was to keep those things aligned and working.'

This was another example of the ability of the United States military establishment to nullify Russian operational methods by the production of better technology.

The ongoing improvements in intelligence-gathering technology brought further changes. Earth-orbiting satellites were launched by various nations. The time had now arrived to check on such activity. In October 1993 a top secret American unit, Detachment 2, 17th Space Surveillance Squadron, arrived. This unit operated sensors for the low-altitude space surveillance system until the base closure in 1996.[392]

In the 1960s and 1970s, from its base in Thailand, the unit had tracked Soviet missile launches. During the 1980s it had provided low-altitude space surveillance before moving to Edzell.

Space surveillance was – and is – an important strategic activity. By the 1990s the United States had found it essential to conduct a rigorous space monitoring programme. This enabled them to determine the capabilities of potential adversaries such as Russia and China. The data obtained could predict the orbits of objects in space and include warnings of potential collisions or attacks on American military satellites. In addition, the data could also alert US military units that they were about to come under surveillance by Soviet or Chinese satellites.

Surveillance was conducted by a collection of radar and optical sensors, using advanced electro-optical telescopic equipment. There was a series of worldwide ground stations, all linked to the Space Defense Center at Cheyenne Mountain, Colorado. This was the nuclear-hardened command centre. All data from the Edzell unit was sent back to Cheyenne Mountain for processing and analysis.

Sensor equipment for the surveillance squadron was housed in radomes similar to those at Edzell. Each location for a surveillance squadron base was specifically chosen, as its equipment's operation was degraded by such factors as fog, atmospheric pollution and light pollution from cities. Edzell was free of these restrictions and it was therefore deemed that the base and its supporting elements were suitable for the surveillance programme.

Edzell had moved to the front edge of technological intelligence-gathering.

To protect the area occupied by this unit, armed UK personnel were deployed. This was an unusual occurrence in the United Kingdom. It was the MoD Police who were made responsible for the external security of the base and their role as armed officers was to respond and cover the site whilst the USAF staff checked out the internal situation.

This specialist unit added a new dimension to the base security plan. Campbell was a working witness to this dramatic change: 'We as a force had been trained to carry firearms, and in times of heightened security we would carry them. When the USAF Det 2 arrived, they required a two-man armed response to any alarm condition, so after that we were permanently armed.'

Edzell was a true house of secrets. There were different levels of security clearance. If an individual did not need to know about a specific programme, they knew nothing about it. Pat

Cronin recalled that Edzell security was severe: 'The U.S. Navy Security Group had the best security in the business, a fact of which I was very proud! I wasn't allowed to ask the guys I served with any questions about their activities throughout the building. It wasn't until many years later that I found out that a lot of the stuff we did was really real. I found that out by watching TV and reading books. Even the name of the relevant systems was classified top secret. At our debriefing before leaving Edzell, we had to commit to not divulging anything about it, including its name.'

Edzell worked on top secret activities and imposed a stringent security regime. Campbell recalled that nothing was ever talked about. He encountered breaches of physical security by Greenpeace activists who tried to access the base. But although there were minor security infractions or incidents linked to not following proper procedures, security was very tight inside the workspaces.

Operators never talked about their job, and family and friends had no idea about the importance of the work. An individual's background had been thoroughly checked when they were in communications school. McInness remembered the security process: 'My family was never contacted, so I was curious if anyone did a check. I found later that my friends, employers, clergy, teachers and coaches were all questioned before I was given a security clearance.'

Despite being the home of NSGA Edzell, it was still a British site. It was a joint operation, and Jack Jackson noted that British individuals worked alongside the Americans: 'It was the special arrangement that we had. Can't go into much more than that. British military worked with us very close.' At the time of writing, information is still restricted.

There were special security officers (SSOs) at Edzell to supervise its crucial activity. Jackson was one of these; he was the personnel and physical specialist for the Elephant Cage and Classic Wizard facilities. He also did work with the Marine Corps on the base. The SSOs sustained the secrecy regime; they checked activities and kept on top of all security-related matters. They spent most of their time supporting the various operations and projects to maintain the controlled status of Edzell. They ran security education programs, logistic flight coordination and the Armed Forces Courier Service. They were also responsible for specific physical processes. 'Yep, we were busy, and I remember quite a few Sunday hours spent on site to make Monday mornings tolerable. Some Mondays greeted us with 40 or 50 Action Item messages.' [393]

Jackson's duties included checking and repairing electronic locks and the destruction of classified material. He emphasised that CT work needed strict discipline. This was because achieving the CT rating and advancements was difficult and required background checks, personal integrity, a decent education and an enormous amount of reading. A CT was responsible for protecting all the classified material and information being handled. Maintaining the security of classified material was not an extra job, but was a basic part of an individual's assignment: 'Nearly every detail surrounding the CT world,' said Jackson, 'from administration to operations and repair, needed dedicated technicians with high-level clearances. It was important material, which needed to be protected constantly. Just think how little the job would mean to the Navy if the classified material was not given the security protection required. Secrecy has been the trait most prized among cryptologists'. [394]

On specific occasions higher security clearance was granted. These were mainly associated with equipment repair and maintenance, as Jimmy Grier described: 'At Edzell, they had wide-band receivers, all solid state. The most secure room had cryptologic equipment, so I was not allowed in. But when the KS7 capacitors started failing, I was given emergency clearance to replace the hundreds of capacitors on the circuit boards.'

A.Q. Morton learned strict security awareness at Edzell. When he went home on military leave in the USA he visited a friend who was also an amateur radio operator. His friend's receiver was tuned to a frequency in one of the amateur bands. While they were talking, Morton heard a signal which was transmitting Cyrillic code groups. It was faint, but definitely Russian. Immediately – but casually, so as to not draw attention to his action – he reached over and tuned the receiver away from that channel. The Russian station was transmitting an encrypted message on a non-standard frequency: 'I guess my CT training about the importance of security worried me. I didn't want my friend asking questions about it when he realised it was not an amateur radio station.' [395]

It was officially stated that NSGA Edzell was part of the American SAR (search and rescue) system. This was in fact true, and Mac McInness recalled such tasks: 'As Edzell was part of the air–sea rescue system, there were rare times when we were asked to track a MATS [military air transport service] plane on the way to, for example, the Azores that had possible mechanical problems.' [396]

Despite the draconian security regime at Edzell, anomalies occurred, and Dale Reemett chuckled when he spotted Edzell photos on various websites many years later. At the time there had been signs everywhere, stating clearly that taking photographs was strictly prohibited. Submarines, too, were highly classified then, as now: 'I'm finding it hilarious that there are *so* many pictures of subs from Holy Loch. And *so* many pictures of life at Edzell.'

The Russian threat

Edzell would have been high on the Russians' Cold War target list. As a major American intercept and DF station, it was part of the NATO High Command network. In addition, it operated a top secret submarine tracking system, and was a link for presidential wartime communications. Just as the United States targeted Soviet military communications centres, the Soviets targeted similar American facilities.

However, the Edzell personnel appeared to be unaware of this. Former staff were surprised to discover later that NSGA Edzell had been a probable Soviet target. They had known that nuclear weapons sites were prime targets but had not realised that communications centres were also on the list. Its personnel had believed that it was a relatively small base and dealt mostly with communications. There were no nuclear weapons at Edzell. Eric Mercato was the one who had been ambivalent about the threat posed to Edzell and the adjoining area: 'I understood the nature of the technology that we were using to communicate and monitor, and I understood the importance of our mission. The threat of nukes or a Russian attack was not something that I ever considered on a local level … it was a global thing.'

But Mercato and others had been aware of the threat from Russian Special Forces. Dale Reemett and other marines from Edzell were detached to Holy Loch to assist with its closedown in 1992 and he returned with an interesting souvenir: 'As reward for our work, we were each allowed to take three books from the base library. One of mine was a book about the Spetsnaz. I had sometimes thought that they could attack Edzell.'

Reemett was correct about the Spetsnaz threat, and Douglas H. Wise explained that Spetsnaz would definitely have been involved in this type of activity. They would have engaged in small acts of disruption such as ambushes, felling trees to block roads and sabotaging power supplies: 'This would have degraded Edzell's activities and terrorised the local population. It would have gained a few days for the Sov subs to cross the GIUK Gap.'

But on the outbreak of a hot war Edzell would have had to counter another, more serious, danger. General Sir Rupert Smith identified this threat: 'Soviet airborne troops could be used in a parachute assault.' This had already been recognised by the CIA in 1965.[397]

Edzell was an essential base for the strategic defence of the United States, as it tracked Soviet ships and submarines coming through the GIUK Gap, a region which would have been the centre of any early hot war activity. As the United States dominated the Gap with its radio spy stations, the Soviets would have needed to wrest control of Edzell for their own purposes. Edzell was vital military ground.

Miscellany

NSGA Edzell needed top talent. Its personnel had been specially selected and were the best from the U.S. Naval Security Group and the USMC intelligence community. Grier and others stressed the elitist standing of its personnel: 'We were evidently chosen to serve at these communications intelligence installations based on our exam scores. The Navy also dispensed with nearly all the bullshit drills and inspections. Fed us well and pampered us. Nearly all my shipmates, like me, were college educated to some extent.'

The cryptologists at Edzell were a valuable resource for the U.S. Navy. They had exceptional skills, and the Navy did not want to lose them. But the sailors wanted to be promoted. This concern was recognised in 1960 by Allen Dulles, Director of Central Intelligence, so he instructed that armed forces cryptologists should have proper career paths. In 1966, the U.S. Navy launched a petty officer academy at Edzell to help retain these highly trained personnel. Bill Carpenter, an instructor there, regarded it as one of the highlights of his tour at Edzell: 'I taught Naval Customs and Traditions in that school, as sailors were promoted from the junior (E-1–E-3) ranks to that of a petty officer. I enjoyed it hugely.'[398]

Despite the controversy attached to intelligence gathering, there were no anti-American protests at the base. Carpenter did not witness a single aggressive incident while he was there: 'There was nothing political.' This relaxed tone was observed by other Edzell veterans. McInness remembers that CND protesters would occasionally gather outside the base for a token gesture. On a few occasions across the road from the entrance to the base there would be a Ban the Bomb protest. There were normally less than 20 people, mostly young, with protest signs. It was a gentler age: 'You would wave to them and they would wave back. All was very peaceful and friendly. Nothing like what goes on today.'[399]

The radio masts at Edzell were visible for many miles, but there was little external awareness of its existence. Willie Hogg and his colleagues were surprised that few people outside the locality knew anything about the existence of the base: 'Most people I ran into didn't know the base at Edzell existed. People down south, in England and lower Scotland, hadn't even heard of it.' [400]

There have always been allegations about the base eavesdropping on non-military communications. These arose because NSGA Edzell's mission had been explained to the US Congress in 1980 as being a radio station that could 'listen for American or foreign broadcasts'.[401]

In addition to its main HFDF role, Edzell is also believed to have hosted a USAF solar observatory from 1990. Such observatories were used for noting solar events which could affect long-distance communications.[402]

NSGA Edzell was a place of mystery and rumour. Some of this was created by official statements and some by the inevitable gossip mill. The radomes were part-futuristic and part-menacing, and the site was protected with heavy loops of barbed wire. This was scary, and visitors did not have a clue about its interior, fuelling stories about spies, satellites, submarines and espionage. Edzell remained an enigma throughout its lifespan.[403]

Closedown

The Edzell operation closed down in 1997. Work continued on the mission until the final watch, and then its activities were moved to RAF Chicksands and RAF Menwith Hill, both in England. This was the U.S. Navy's last hurrah in Scotland; 37 years of duty there had ended.

The last watch section commander was Royal Navy Chief Petty Officer Edward Knox, and he reaffirmed the status of the operation: 'At Edzell I noted the variety of other intelligence agencies present. This was new to me, but it showed that it was a very important station. There were military and civilians there. Not just USN and RN, but other US military and others.' [404]

Regardless of any official evasiveness, Edzell's importance was summed up by Arne Simonsen: 'Every NSGA facility had a cover story. But it is commonly understood that we provided real-time special intelligence to national intelligence agencies, aligned allied intelligence agencies, and naval vessels and aircraft. We also deployed CTs and marine equivalents on special missions aboard US Naval vessels.' [41]

Edzell participated in the Cold War's important radio intercept activity. Even 30 years after the Cold War ended, few are willing to discuss Edzell's role, significant as it was. A former commanding officer at NSGA Edzell was tight-lipped about Edzell's intelligence role.[42] He stated: 'Information about intelligence gathering, submarines and contributions of Edzell etc. were and are for good reason still mostly classified. We cherish our fond memories of times gone by, but to the normal reader they would seem mundane.' [405]

A similar reluctance was displayed by Jim Hart, a former U.S. Navy intelligence officer. He had served two tours in the UK and had regularly been involved with Edzell. His reticence speaks volumes: 'This is a difficult subject to discuss in an unclassified environment.' [406]

---

41 CTT, CTR and CTI ratings, CT personnel, go through Special Background Investigations (SBI) every five years in order to hold a Top secret/ Sensitive compartmented information clearance (TS/SCI).

42 This officer became Commander US Naval Security Group.

Eventually the NSA revealed Edzell's Cold War activities in an official history. This left no doubt as to who had been in charge there, admitting that 'Edzell was a most important intelligence-gathering centre between 1960 and 1997'. It confirmed that NSGA Edzell had been operated by the US Naval Security Group, a branch of the NSA. Edzell had performed a variety of functions for the U.S. Navy, including the Naval Ocean Surveillance satellite system, also known as Classic Wizard or White Cloud, whose principal task had been to monitor and track Soviet submarines in the North Sea. Its importance was highlighted by the visit of the United States National Security Advisor Kenneth Graffenreid in 1984. He came to the UK to visit the US Embassy and Edzell.[407]

Edzell was deservedly known as the NSC's European showcase.[408]

7 Thurso

– the starting gun

Introduction

Thurso's mysteries were hidden on the north coast of Scotland in a remote area which was wild and empty, and stunningly beautiful.

The people of Scotland and even some of the base personnel were unaware of its pivotal and potentially chilling role during the Cold War. The grim reality was that it was the U.S. Naval Communications Station Thurso that would relay the President's command to fire the starting gun for the Third World War. The base had two key roles: it tracked Soviet submarines in the Northern Seas, and it was the US Government's principal European transmitter to its submarines.[409]

The Big Stick, a radio mast more than 600 feet tall and visible to distant ships, loomed over the local area. Its job was to broadcast messages to American submarines in the Northern Seas. Its messages were one-way only; no reply was needed, as these were the nuclear missile launch instructions. If the President decided to start the firestorm, the order would go out via the Big Stick. On receipt of the message, SSBN commanders would commence the firing sequence.

The missiles, ready in their tubes, could be launched within 15 minutes, programmed to head to Russia, with their target details locked into their guidance system. The nominated officers would, as mentioned in Chapter 3, vote to proceed with the launch – and mayhem and annihilation would follow. Millions of people would be killed, cities would be destroyed and civilisation would be laid low.

It was Thurso's personnel who made this scenario possible. The base was a vital stage in the process of creating nuclear devastation for Russian cities – and for everyone at Thurso, as well.

American strategy

During the Second World War Thurso had been a SIGINT station, and at the end of the 1950s its strategically important location was needed again; America's SSBN fleet from Holy Loch would be operating in the Northern Seas. Radio contact was essential, but there were no American-staffed bases in Norway to provide this because in peacetime no foreign troops were based on Norwegian soil. So a communications gap had to be filled, and Thurso fitted the bill. A radio station at this location could support the uncovered Northern Seas zone, boost FBM fleet communications and assist the ASW programme.[410]

In the Northern Seas ASW was important as it would keep any hot war away from the shores of the USA. ASW activities could locate, identify and destroy Soviet missile submarines on their way to attack the United States. But the Russian submarines would have to be identified before they crossed the GIUK Gap, the principal submarine battle zone. Thurso could support the GIUK Gap strategy.

The decision to establish a U.S. Navy base at Thurso had been announced using double-speak and evasion. The 1961 Pentagon press release stated that Thurso was not 'designed to serve Polaris submarines'. It was declared to be a tracking station for American ships, a US base for the north of Scotland. Thurso was to be another link in the Distant Early Warning (DEW) line and would have the responsibility of keeping track of U.S. Navy radar picket vessels (DERs). These ships would have berthing facilities at Scottish ports. During the Cuban Missile Crisis in 1962 several of them moved south to perform the same function.[411]

The U.S. Navy had learned the value of radar picket ships during the Second World War. These ships provided early warning of incoming aircraft. In the waters around Scotland their primary mission was to look out for Soviet aircraft approaching the North American continent. Their secondary mission was surveillance of ships, including submarines on the surface.[412]

This cover story obscured the fact that the base could track Russian submarines while those enemy vessels were submerged. This information was hidden deep within the main agreement which dealt with the basing of the US Polaris missile submarines in the Clyde. That was the big story, and the small print about Thurso went unnoticed. In fact, Thurso's significance was talked down by stating that the communications station was a small radar facility to fill the gap in the system.

This subterfuge was deliberate. Defense Secretary Robert McNamara had agreed that the details should not be made public – or even, indeed, notified to the United Nations, as was required by international agreement: 'The UK has proposed and we agree, that in view of military security requirements it is not intended that the agreement regarding these facilities should be registered with the UN or otherwise be made public'. The British Government merely issued a bland statement confirming that an agreement had been made.[413] The final sentence of the press release mentioned that a considerable part of the land involved would be available for grazing, giving the impression that Thurso was a low-level, unimportant backwater.

But the mention of the DEW line in the Pentagon's press release was another clue to Thurso's importance. When Soviet submarines left Murmansk or Kola, American aircraft would track them. This tracking task would then be passed to the British planes in the UK sector, and they would receive tracking information from Thurso's intercept activities. Radio intercept activity always means that intelligence-collecting is taking place. The confirmation of Thurso's intelligence-gathering role was provided when GCHQ staff moved there. As at Edzell, GCHQ worked in conjunction with, and under the direction of, the NSA.[414]

Thurso grows

By 1970, Thurso's mission was stated: 'To manage, operate and maintain those facilities, equipment and devices and systems necessary to provide requisite communications for the command, operational control and administration of the Naval establishment'. This was a clever example of the cover story about Thurso's role.[415]

In November 1971 A.Q. Morton arrived at the U.S. Navy Radio Station, Thurso. At that time it was a small base, with only 90 personnel; within a few years it would double in strength. Morton recalled: 'The base was equipped with HF transmitters to transmit to U.S. Navy surface vessels in the North Atlantic and the North Sea, and LF transmitters used for one-way transmissions to U.S. Navy submarines. The vertical antenna for the LF transmitter stood well over 500 feet high and could be seen for many miles on the flat coastal terrain. At night it became a good landmark for ships sailing the Pentland Firth. Part of the radio station was a receiving facility located in a small building at Murkle, about 7 miles east of the transmitter site.'[416]

In 1972, *All Hands* described Thurso's activities as follows: 'A small part of a massive communications complex, the Defense Communications System. The system links Navy, Air Force, and Army communications facilities together with the NATO communications system. Additionally, Thurso provides a wide range of services to U.S. ships operating in the North Atlantic and North Sea areas, as well as to British and other NATO ships'.[417]

Thurso expanded its activities in 1977, when it assumed the full range of operations of the U.S. Navy transmitter at Londonderry. This had been the main U.S. Navy communications station in Europe, and was linked to the SSBN fleet. But during the mid-1970s Londonderry was a centre of terrorist violence, and the US Government was desperate to avoid an incident at the base; its closure would have caused a serious strategic problem, as the radio link to the nuclear submarines had to be maintained. Thurso assumed this role.

Thurso already supported SSBN activities, including the LORAN-C navigation system, which was upgraded in the 1970s for use by SSBNs. Codenamed Clarinet Pilgrim, it was a vital element of America's strategic package, and the Scottish stations at Thurso and Edzell, which had both operated the previous Clarinet Betty system for LORAN-A, were participants. Thurso and Edzell also linked the Transit satellite navigation data to the SSBNs in the northern waters.[418]

Once Thurso became the main U.S. Navy transmitter for Europe, then it, combined with the hilltop relay stations in the north of the country, was able to guarantee links to the SSBNs in the Norwegian Sea patrol areas. The Tacamo aircraft, with their 10-kilometre trailing antenna, also communicated with Thurso.

The U.S. Navy communications stations at Thurso and Edzell were involved in providing ground resilience links for the Tacamo/Silk Purse wartime communication systems, providing further evidence of the geographical importance of these Scottish bases to US strategic operations.[419]

The base activities

The sites at Forss and West Murkle were crammed with equipment. Their machinery operated 24 hours a day and required regular maintenance and repair; this was the main task for Morton and his fellow technicians. The problems caused by the teletype machines were often difficult: 'There is not much to say about working on teletype machines except that they sometimes posed a complex electromechanical challenge.'

The Public Works Department, responsible for site maintenance, had a contingent of civilian joiners, electricians, masons, riggers and mechanics. The U.S. Navy used local labour for non-critical tasks, and relied on the Seabees and its American civilian contractors to carry out all sensitive work.

Steve Cady, then an E-5 Seabee, construction electrician 2nd class (CE-2), recalled the work carried out: 'There were mechanics, equipment operators, electricians, plumbers, builders, engineering aides etc. They provided front-line support for the daily operations of the base. The watch sections were tasked with inspections of the equipment throughout the base, as well as for the fire house and fire engine.'[420]

Unlike other workers within the various buildings, the Seabees did not have the necessary security clearance, so when vital equipment required attention, this was awkward. The Seabees, responsible for the electrical plant, needed regular access, as the operation of the base depended on this running properly. So Cady needed an escort for access to this equipment. The Seabees' most important duty was to race to the EP (electrical power) building when there was an unscheduled power outage. Cady recalled the complexity of this activity: 'We had to manually sync four 500kW generators to restore power to the base. We trained so often I could still do it in my sleep!'[421]

Craig Capaldi was a Thurso Seabee utilitiesman 1st class, responsible for the base plumbing, air-conditioning, boilers, commissary refrigeration and generator operation. He was also a fire truck operator, but the security culture limited his knowledge of the classified activities: 'We were escorted at all times when getting into restricted areas. I still don't know what was happening in there.'[422]

Callouts could happen at any time during the day or night, and precise resolution was essential to the continued smooth functioning of the mission. Steve Cady recalled the excitement of those incidents: 'As you can imagine, the adrenaline was peaked when you're wakened in the middle of the night from a dead sleep. Off we'd hustle to the EP building, into a giant room where all four generators are screaming in unison and sounding like a 747 jumbo jet taking off. We had eight minutes to get them all running in parallel and online! We were a crack team. At the time we held the record for the quickest operation – at just under two minutes. We averaged four to six minutes.'

A potential Cold War scenario created another task for the Seabees – and this was a matter of survival for the base. Had the base been attacked by the Russians, the water supply could have been cut off or contaminated by nuclear or chemical attack. Cady remembered the Seabees' task of building the 55,000-gallon water tank buried beside the guard room. This would provide safe water to the base.[423]

By the end of 1973 there were more than 200 sailors on the base, plus 80 civilian staff. The original agreement in 1960 had specified only 80 personnel, but the mission continued to expand. Thurso was important to the United States' strategic defence. It linked the Pentagon to the SSBNs and tracked Soviet submarines.

The riggers

Thurso's main asset was the Forss radio mast, visible from almost 40 miles away. The huge mast needed regular maintenance of its cables and electronic cabinets. It was more than 600 feet high, and the only way to the top was by climbing it – a formidable challenge, whatever the weather.

The riggers needed to have a good head for heights and a good sense of humour. This challenging task was carried out by a specialist civilian team, the antenna crew, nicknamed 'the A Team' after the popular TV series. They had their own motto: 'Through wind, snow or rain, the job will get done!'

John A. Lang was the assistant public works officer, and remembered their activities. Thurso's riggers were out in all weathers, keeping the 38 antennas in perfect operating condition. He described them as quiet and impressive: 'When they got to the base of a mast they never seemed to have any need to talk to each other. After picking up their tools they got on with the job. The chief rigger, Bill Luke, explained that his crew had worked together for so long that they no longer needed to waste time talking about what to do – they all knew. Bill Luke was the team's antenna specialist, and his reputation is known throughout U.S. Navy TELCOM. He came to Navcommsta UK in 1973, after working for the BBC as an antenna engineer. The others had similar backgrounds.'[424]

During his time at the base, Luke was a climbing icon; his name and exploits have passed into legend, as recalled by Kathleen Scollan, a civilian employee: 'Bill Luke ... could certainly scramble up these antennas. He was as fearless as Superman and as agile as a monkey.'[425]

The riggers wore climbing boots, waterproof clothing and a waist harness, recalled rigger Robert Schissler. 'But this slowed the rate of climb, meaning we would get colder, wetter and more fatigued. The climber would take a long time to reach his objective. Once the rigger got two-thirds of the way up it was really cold. But the worst part was that it took twice as long to go back down. My hands started to cramp, and fitting my feet into the small steps was much harder than when going up.'[426]

There were constant difficulties when cleaning the mast, as Schissler remembered: 'It was covered in sea salt. This lowered its performance, and it had to be removed by hand. Riggers used mops of fresh water to do this. The spray from the waves and high winds also coated the insulators. We had to carry the mop and bucket up the mast with us.'

But there were other dangers: a climber could be injured. Schissler recalled one incident: 'When the system was at full power one rigger drew 3-inch sparks to all his fingers when he touched some copper sheeting on the mast walls. It took weeks for his burns to heal. Thurso's medical facilities were minimal. There was only a Navy corpsman to treat patients, and then they were referred to the local civilian medical system.'

Mast-climbing was dangerous. The training was run by a safety supervisor who would ensure that the technician knew where the safety equipment and clothing were located and how to use them. The precautions for working on the antennas, including climbing them, was taught by experts from the United States. These specialists would certify Scottish civilians on the antenna crew as technicians and trainers.

Climbing the Big Stick was a nerve-racking experience; some could become petrified, and many reported that they remained afraid of heights. But there was a bonus, as Bob Till explained: 'I climbed the tower several times. That is one hell of a climb – but the view!' However, this was small comfort as the view was only visible on clear days, and climbs had to be made in all weather conditions.

The Big Stick had a hypnotic effect on the sailors stationed at Thurso, and some of them would attempt to scale it. They were not expert climbers, and most did not succeed. Nobody fell off, but many got tired and frightened. Some sailors would take part in a spontaneous attempt; if successful – and few were – they would take lots of photographs at the top of the mast. It was a Thurso emblem, and one marine used it for his re-enlistment ceremony: he and his witness climbed to the top of the mast, where he took his oath.[427]

The value of the rigger's role was bluntly described by John A. Allen: 'The antenna crew would be out working even in stormy weather, keeping the antennas in tip-top shape. Without them, Navcommsta UK could not have operated.'

The fire crew

Like the other sailors at Thurso, Wally Nerring had additional jobs. On his arrival to run the payroll office, he was asked a simple yes/no question: Can you drive a standard transmission automobile? Wally answered, 'Yes,' and was given a military driver's licence – and extra work: 'I drove the furniture trucks from base to the navy housing, I did drive the fire truck a couple of times, but my usual firefighting role consisted of running the charged hoses into the grass.'[428]

As the local civilian fire station was small and served a wide area, it was clear that outside help would be slow in arriving to tackle any fires. So a base fire crew had to be formed, and on-site courses were run by the civilian fire marshal and Seabee instructors. Wally Nerring was trained on one of these courses: 'I remember that this training was intense and very good. All the duty sections became fire teams, and if a fire broke out I would drive the fire truck.'

Their high standards were shown during Wally's tour at Thurso. At one point the base had prepared for an IG (inspector general) inspection.[43] All aspects of their work had to be flawless. One of the items for inspection was the firefighting drills: 'Suddenly the fire siren sounded Warn of a Fire. The fire crew sprang into action, and everyone performed flawlessly. However, this time it was not a drill – an actual fire had broken out in the galley dumpster. The team raced to the scene and extinguished the fire in minutes. The IG team checked that task off their task list, much to our relief. I don't remember the civilian safety and fire marshal's name, but he was amazing at what he taught us Yanks.'[429]

---

43 IG inspection – an external inspection carried out by higher command.

The fire crew training was indeed thorough. For four days the fire marshal and the Seabee instructors put the students through an intensive programme of classroom instruction and practical training. At the end of the week a written and oral examination was set – but the real test came on the last day, when the students faced simulated firefighting situations.[430]

The instructors would have arranged a number of surprises, including a training room on fire. This set was so hot that when the door was opened smoke and flames exploded outwards. It was quite a shock for some of the students. This realistic training was long remembered, as standing in front of a blaze with a hose-line, wearing breathing apparatus and seeing nothing through the smoke, was a frightening experience.

The course delivered this training superbly, and many Seabees declared that the SCBA (self-contained breathing apparatus) training was the best they had known.[44] Students became reliable firefighters, and a lot of their fears and concerns disappeared; they felt that should an emergency arise they would be competent enough to deal with it. The high standard of training was maintained, and firefighting ceased to be a major concern.

Seabee Toby Swain drove the fire truck at times. He found it always good fun to charge around the base with the lights on and the horn blasting. Nobody ever got in the way. He enjoyed it, apart from one occasion when a callout caused him to miss the Seabee Ball. By the time the emergency had ended and the vehicle had been cleaned and stored in the firehouse, it was after midnight. Swain was too late for the ball.

Londonderry closes

At the end of 1977 Thurso underwent a dramatic change, and moved up to major league status. The 'local disagreement' in Northern Ireland had left the U.S. Navy with no choice but to move its operations from Londonderry to Thurso.

Earlier that year, the commander of the U.S. Navy had made a decision, as the situation in Londonderry had become worrying. Bombs, bullets and beatings were common, and the unrest showed that it was unwise for the American base to remain there. So all of its activities were relocated to USN Thurso. There was no political difficulty in Scotland, and the Scottish Office welcomed the proposal, noting that they could see nothing but advantage from the proposed development.[431]

Londonderry's commanding officer, Captain Tom McKeown, was called to a meeting in the Pentagon. There were senior officials present from the State Department and the British Embassy. The message was blunt: 'We have a serious matter on our hands … we need you to carry out a critical mission … the President himself wants us to close the base as soon as possible … he is concerned there will be an attack on the base, and the nation will be pulled into conflict over there.'

The decision was speedily implemented; Londonderry was closed, and transferred its strategic operational capability to Thurso. McKeown recalled that Thurso was upgraded to provide communications support between submarines and ships in the North Atlantic, the Baltic and the Mediterranean.

---

44 SCBA – self-contained breathing apparatus, standard wear for firefighters.

In addition, Thurso transmitted intelligence and early warning data to the USA. McKeown listed other activities: 'We also operated communications relay between ships and submarines. To do this we would receive a message from a ship and transmit it to the submarine from our big mast. The ship could not communicate directly to the submarine. Thurso had this specific capability. We also provided ship-to-ship relay through our very high masts.' [432]

Two hundred personnel from Londonderry moved across with him, and Thurso's name was changed to reflect its new status; it became U.S. Navy Communications Station UK (USNavcommsta UK). This was an important naval occasion; a ceremony with pomp and circumstance was held in the base gymnasium, overseen by Captain McKeown.

One of the transferring crew was Janet Dixon, who proudly recounted that she had been one of the NCS Thurso plank owners, as she had been stationed in Thurso when it was commissioned from Naval Radio Station Thurso to Naval Communications Station United Kingdom. She remembered: 'It's a symbolic measure, really. In the wooden ship days, the decks were made of wood, specifically on the quarterdeck. In theory if you are a plank owner, you own one of the planks that make the quarterdeck. When the base closed, I tried to acquire my plank, but to no avail.' [45]

Another plank owner was technician Raymond John. His role was to troubleshoot system problems and to get the equipment operational. He recalled Thurso's mission: 'It was mainly for radio relay purposes. This involved message traffic and fleet broadcasts to US and NATO ships operating in the North Atlantic. In addition, Thurso had a low-frequency transmitter for communicating to FBM submarines.' [433]

Thurso operations

Thurso's importance after 1977 was highlighted by former SubRon-14 officer Mike Giambattista. Once an SSBN from Holy Loch had submerged on patrol, all communications to it from the Pentagon went via Thurso: 'Thurso was the primary transmitter of the launch messages. SubRon-14 was not in the loop as far as communications with SSBNs on patrol was concerned; we never initiated a message directly to an SSBN. But once it had surfaced, in transit to or from Holy Loch, we did communicate with it, sending messages via Thurso.'

In addition, American intelligence information was downloaded at Thurso from US spy submarines such as USS *Tusk*. These boats regularly entered Soviet waters on intelligence-gathering missions, probing the Russian naval bases at Kola and Murmansk. These spy missions tested the Soviet ASW measures around the naval bases. This was observed, and intelligence data was then transmitted to Thurso.[434]

Thurso's personnel – whether radiomen, technicians, Seabees, supply, administrative or medical staff – were highly skilled, and had been hand-picked for this important mission,. They had been trained and selected by the U.S. Navy in the same manner as those who served at Edzell.

---

45 Plankowners: certificates are given to all active duty personnel stationed in a ship or base when it is being commissioned.

There were two separate sites at Thurso. The personnel working at Forss had a vague idea about what was being done at West Murkle, and it was the same situation for the West Murkle personnel. From 1963, Forss and West Murkle provided secure LF command and control communications with SSBNs.[435]

The transmitter site at Forss, west of Thurso, was a large site, with the Big Stick and 16 smaller masts. It communicated with the SSBN fleet. At West Murkle was a much smaller receiver site. The sites were separated by about 7 miles of flat, windswept clifftop countryside. This created a feeling of isolation at each site, as Chief Johnny Moore recalled: 'West Murkle had a very large room that housed the equipment and several supporting offices. The people who worked at Murkle would associate with the other Thurso departments, but they were very isolated … so there were times when we didn't see the Murkle folks for long periods of time.' [436]

West Murkle carried out DF operations which identified and tracked Russian naval vessels, particularly submarines. The Russian transmissions were intercepted, and the details were recorded and passed to the other NSA-controlled sites in the North Atlantic network. This was vitally important, as the Soviet submarines had to be picked up before they could cross the GIUK Gap; any that slipped the net would be difficult to find later. Ed Martin, one of the early staff, commented: 'During the sixties we used basic equipment without the high-tech scanners and suchlike that came along later. But the Red subs were primitive, and we could always follow them. I believe they improved later, in the seventies and eighties.'[437]

The transmitting operation was at Forss. Moore recounted: 'There was a transmitter deck with the HF and LF transmitters. The tech control centre patched up the transmissions. All of the receivers were at West Murkle.'

The satellite communications division operated from West Murkle, and Janet Dixon worked there as a radioman 2nd class. Her job was to listen for radio signals emitting from American ships and submarines sailing the North Sea. When she found one she would tune in a receiver to a viable frequency, connect it to an antenna and attempt to initiate communications with the ship. Once communication was achieved, Thurso could receive message traffic from the ship: 'In the meantime, the transmitter site in the main base at Forss would tune up a transmitter to this frequency, and message traffic was sent to the ship. All of this was coordinated through the base technical control. That's kind of the gist of it.'

These operations were controlled by the communication watch officers, who had a wide remit, as Moore narrated: 'They were expected to know what every piece of radio equipment was, how it worked, how it connected to other pieces of equipment and systems (both local and worldwide), plus its limitations and what to do in case of failure of equipment. We used terrestrial and radio frequency communications. We operated mostly in the LF, HF and UHF ranges.' [438]

Watch-standing – repetitive and monotonous – was the lifestyle of the sailors at Thurso. As communication watch officer, Moore worked the normal eight-hour watch system. He would do this for three rotations and then have 80 hours off: 'Because of the low number of people stationed at NRS Thurso, when someone asked for leave it would shake up the whole working staff. Any time someone took leave, the watch had to be augmented.'

Moore was impressed with the equipment used at Forss; they had transmitters, receivers, teletypes and other peripheral equipment to perform their function. They also worked with computers. Moore recalled: 'The tall LF antenna supported the main mission, and there were also RLPAs [rotating log periodic antennae], which operated in the HF spectrum and were part of America's worldwide HF system.'

After attending radioman school in San Diego, Kevin McCoy worked in the message centre at Forss on fleet relay matters: 'Messages would be received and would be re-transmitted via radio teletype to the American and NATO ships in the area.' [439]

All the data was in the form of a constant stream of encrypted data going back and forth over the microwave link. The transmitters were continuously on the air except during scheduled maintenance or repair. But it was not all official U.S. Navy activity, as Morton recalled: 'We did have one teletype machine on the transmitter deck that continuously outputted an Associated Press newsfeed from the United States.'

The Big Stick was needed to speak to the submarines, as without it they had to come up to periscope depth to communicate. This would have made them vulnerable to Soviet detection and tracking. They had to stay in deeper water to remain undetected and receive their missile launch orders. The Big Stick technology was able to transmit to these depths.

For many sailors, their service at Thurso was an unforgettable time, and this was very true for Joe Coia. After 14 years in naval service, he was an E-6 petty officer 1st class, but in an instant his life was radically changed: 'I lost my service at Thurso, as I was hit and ruined by a Gunn coal truck. I was on the sidewalk at the end of Kennedy Street, right before the local school. Then the truck hit me.'

Coia suffered serious injuries, and this effectively ended his naval career. He had been a radioman, providing communications with naval assets in Thurso's area of responsibility. During his tour, he had rotated through various communications tasks within the departments. He had worked as the lead petty officer in the message centre, then moved over to tech control, where, in both it and the message centre, there were about 40 radiomen.[440]

NCS Thurso had various departments, and their personnel operated as a team. Moore recalled the contributions made by the other sailors: 'People in the different departments had different functions to perform. The administrative department made sure that everyone knew when they were to prepare for advancement testing or for correspondence courses. They also managed personnel records. The public works department made sure that the lights stayed on, and that the roads were passable in the winter.'

Some sailors, such as Stan Ogrodnik, were the pioneers when new concepts were introduced – in his case, satellite downloads. Ogrodnik was first posted to Thurso in 1967, and returned as the satellite controller at Forss. The training for his new role took place in the USA: 'The course was a basic classroom course: a few printed books, and lots of handouts. No equipment, only classroom theory. The curriculum was based on the old satellite systems. These satellites would pass from horizon to horizon, and the ground antenna would follow them. When the satellite would be getting out of sight, the ground terminal would swing back over to pick up another orbiting satellite.' Ogrodnik applied his new skills to help maintain Thurso's excellent reputation: 'What we learned as satellite controllers was the mathematics [trigonometry] to calculate the azimuth, elevation and power needed to get a usable signal up to those orbiting satellites.' [441]

Security

Although the two sites at Thurso were top secret, the physical security management was surprisingly relaxed, and access to the Forss base was wide open – but a high fence surrounded the operations building; entry to this was restricted to the personnel with the necessary security clearance. Similar restrictions were in force at Murkle. But neither location had a dedicated security force.

The operations buildings were staffed 24 hours per day, and watchkeeping duties included security patrols of the site. Any unauthorised intruders would be handed over to the Thurso police. Michael R. Ellis, in charge of base security during his tour, remembered some incidents: 'The antenna fields were on open grazing land. Sheep were there, and locals – and drunks – would occasionally trespass. The aim of this was to be able to claim that they had breached the base security. Others would claim that they could have been terrorists, thus able to destroy the antenna fields. This might have seemed far-fetched, but it was accurate.' [442]

But this light touch approach was misleading; there was a much stricter step-up policy for base security, as Ellis recalled: 'During security incidents there was serious back-up available. The UK Government had agreed that if the base needed protection the UK military forces would provide it. The US base was not US property – it was UK property, and had a UK military radio call sign: GXH.'

The military protection force was based in HMS *Condor* in Arbroath, home to 45 Commando Royal Marines, one of Britain's crack military units. They were tough, lightly armed and fast-moving, and although they were more than 150 miles from Thurso they would have come in fast, by helicopter. [443]

Global events had a direct effect on the security status of the base. The United States was seen by some as the world's policeman, and had many enemies. Any threats had to be taken seriously. A late-night phone call introduced Steve Cady to this scenario: 'I remember getting a call in the middle of the night, and was informed that the United States had just gone to war with Iraq: Desert Storm. I arrived on base to find concrete barriers staggered down the road leading into the base. I was then put in charge of building fighting positions with sandbags.' Cady did not go home for three days. But despite the tension, he retained his sense of humour: 'There was a shortage of sandbags for the barriers, and we eventually ran out of them. I told my supervisor we could have gotten more if we had not blown up the warehouse in Iraq!' [444]

Mark Bubs Whitten worked in Message Center Tech Control, and during the first Gulf War was on the auxiliary security force (ASF): 'The base was on lockdown, and we had not been home for three days. Our team slept in the Chief's Club, on the floor. Conditions were basic, which means miserable. It was around 3 a.m. and it was extremely cold. To the astonishment of the security force gang, the local baker, Eric Drummond, came in early and gave us all soup in a Styrofoam cup, just to warm up all our bones. Needless to recount, spirits rose immediately.' [445]

Thurso had to be permanently protected against potential acts of sabotage. Guard duty was shared by all personnel. Ben (Wylie) Northcutt from the supply department was regularly involved in this. He was never an integral part of the security and communications section, but he had a part in providing security on base. Many of the administration personnel served as officers of the day and he served as shore patrol approximately every 10–14 days: 'It was during this time that I felt a true sense of supporting the mission of our base. During shore patrol we made hourly rounds of the facility during the night hours of a 24-hour operation.' [446]

As the physical security officer at Thurso, Ellis had a busy job: he had to ensure that the base complied with all regulations issued by U.S. Navy and Thurso's commanding officer: 'This required me to check infrastructure such as fencing, alarms, locks, security cameras, security signs etc. I also monitored the security clearance procedures. All operational personnel needed to have up-to-date security status. There was lots of paperwork involved.'

The security regime produced its own problems. George McKenzie, a local electrician, recalled one incident: 'I could only supply power to the edge of the perimeter fence; internal connection and distribution tasks were done by Seabees.' But most of the Seabees did not have the security clearance needed to get close to the operations rooms, so when they took the cabling into these areas they were escorted by a radioman. They had to repair all the faults: 'There were always electrical faults, as there was so much heat generated in the building. We didn't have any difficulties – only waiting for the escort.' [447]

Seabee Craig Capaldi carried out maintenance tasks. Some areas were closed off, and he was also escorted at all times: 'I only worked inside the secure area when the air-conditioning, heating or plumbing systems had malfunctions. Then they sanitised the areas I was working in because of security clearance requirements.' [448]

Thurso's sensitive material had to be kept secure. Its classified documents were valuable and had to be handled correctly. All base personnel, whether military or civilian, had various levels of security clearance. Michael R. Ellis supervised this activity. Comsec was his constant nightmare; there was just so much material that had to be protected against loss, mishandling and unauthorised disclosure. He had a rigorous process for destroying documents; this was done by secure burning by either Ellis himself or the duty officer. There were lots of classified registers to be checked at the end of each week. Then he had to resolve any deficiencies, whether these were documents or equipment parts: 'We were given a Comsec inspection by U.S. Navy London every six months, and this always found omissions. Comsec was simply a never-ending activity.'

Jim Hart was a U.S. Navy intelligence officer: 'I was given the unenviable task of doing Comsec visits … Overnight train … Then spend the night and do the inspection … if they fail, spend the next day training, so they can pass the next day.' [449]

All of Thurso's activities had high levels of security. This was so tight that former personnel still refuse to divulge any information.

Safety training was a continuous matter; accidents and lost working days had to be avoided. This was the beginning of the health and safety era, and each department developed its own training syllabus. Ellis was involved in this: 'The training sessions had to be held at least twice a year. Each department focused on safety practices relating to locations within their own units.' As a result, accidents lessened and injuries became infrequent. So much so that in 1985 the commanding officer was able to report: 'We have not lost one working day to injury in the past year.'

Another part of Michael R. Ellis' role was to deliver training courses in firefighting, first aid, safety, intruder search and seizure, minority awareness, and equal opportunity. However, the equal opportunities training encountered resistance within the U.S. Navy.[450]

During the 1980s the U.S. Navy had begun to admit more female sailors. RMC (SW) Johnny Moore remembers the change that had taken place within the service: 'I would think that during the mid-1980s there were females in every department.'

Louise Pass, RM2, was a female sailor who worked at Murkle and then moved into tech control: 'Technicians controlled how the system worked. We analysed the overall condition of the system and corrected deteriorating elements. We also set up systems for use by radio operators to send and receive messages. Our job was to make sure the system was in good working condition, and we would carry out maintenance to make sure that weak components had been amended or replaced.'

For Sarah Murphy, Thurso was a new experience, especially its different climate. She was an electronics technician, and it was her first duty station. She was there in 1982 and 1983, and worked on communications equipment at the main site. Like most recruit sailors, Murphy, when she enlisted, did not have a specialist trade in mind: 'When you first enter the Navy, they give you a battery of tests to determine what ratings you qualify for and let you know about availability and a little about what it entails, then you choose. I chose to be an electronic technician.' [451]

Thurso personnel carried out a professional job for their country, but their reward – namely their salaries – fell short of their high standards. All pay matters were dealt with from Londonderry, but this was hardly ideal. It was only when Wally Nerring arrived in April 1977 that the new payroll office opened.

This was an important step for the sailors at Thurso. It boosted morale, as the disbursing office was now there on base. Nerring recalled the problem he faced: 'Prior to this, some of the personnel had not seen their pay records for more than a year. We were very busy the first year. Overall, our presence meant that they were able to concentrate on their job of communications.' [452]

Patrick Derham sat in the financial hot seat from 1986 to 1989, as a PN1 (E-6).[453] He took care of sailors' pay, advancement exams and travel arrangements. The personnel were still paid by cheque, and had to cash them into dollars or pounds as needed. Some deposited their cheques into American or Scottish banks or credit unions: 'All seems very mundane until someone's pay is messed up. Hard to do operational jobs with precision and accuracy when you're concerned about money and providing for your family. Especially the junior sailors.'

Royalty and kilts

Scrabster, 2 miles from Thurso, was a regular port of call for the Queen and her family aboard the Royal Yacht *Britannia*. The Queen Mother was a Scot who regularly stayed at her nearby Castle of Mey for a month or two, and many personnel were able to catch a glimpse of the royal family visiting the area each year. Jo Hunding recalled *Britannia* coming in every year, and she was able to watch it from the back of the transmitter deck even though she was on duty.[454]

Another royal watcher was Susan J. Smyth Shelvock. She had come across from Londonderry, and was a Thurso plank owner. When the royal family came ashore she was able to see them: 'I remember the Queen's yacht coming in to Scrabster in 1978. I had a good viewpoint and was able to click off some good photos. A nice memory.'[455]

But the base's association with Scotland was not always appreciated by senior command. Particularly when a Scottish-themed activity was featured in the *Daily Mirror*, one of Britain's mass-circulation newspapers. Red Mann recalled this episode with a chuckle. It was the Fourth of July 1977. The crew had wanted to celebrate Independence Day with a swagger, and as so as many of them owned kilts that they wore them to work that day. The officers formed them up and organised a parade. There would have been a short ceremony in any case, but they thought this should be part of the proceedings. There was a local press reporter and photographer. The crew marched past the commanding officer, Captain McKeown, who took the salute. The crew marched off and got back to work. Then the trouble began, as Red Mann recounted: 'The photograph was taken up by the *Daily Mirror*. They had 2 million readers. We replaced the Page 3 girl in the *Mirror* on 5 July 1977. Story was about the American cousins celebrating their independence. What a great day it was! There was a bit of a furore when CINCUSNAVEUR saw this, being that kilts are not an authorised part of the uniform.'[456] A severe sense of humour failure, no less.

Closedown

By the early 1990s technology had advanced and Thurso's days were numbered and it closed on 4th November 1992. Seabee Pat Bealin remembered the closedown: 'It was a sad time for the crew who loved the base.'

Prior to leaving Thurso the U.S. Navy had arranged for a local stonemason to build a Caithness stone cairn, near the clifftop, which contained a time capsule. The cairn's inscription stated:

> Here once stood United States Naval Communication Station,
>
> United Kingdom, 1962–1992.
>
> Supporting the fleet was our mission, world peace was our goal

U.S. Navy Radio Station Thurso and U.S. Navy Communications Station UK had served their purpose. The base had searched the Northern Seas for Russian submarines, and identified them and tracked them as they passed through the GIUK Gap. Most importantly, communications had been maintained with the SSBN fleet.

Thurso's fundamental importance was emphasised by Mike Giambattista: 'The communications staff at SubRon-14 would make regular trips to Thurso. The SSBN mission depended solely on the communications link from the President. Face-to-face chats between both ends of the structure were essential. Any problems were resolved swiftly, and confidence would be restored. When I was a staff officer at Holy Loch it was my most important task.'

Navcommsta Thurso had been a crucial link in the American high command network, and therefore a Soviet target. Communications centres, particularly vital radio bases, would have been principal objectives in Russian efforts to blind the American SSBNs.

Thurso's importance was highlighted by the perceived threat from the Russians. Official UK Government records have revealed that it had been expected that in the event of war the Soviet Union would obliterate much of Caithness. In addition, the renowned historian Peter Hennessy stated that the Russian target would have been the U.S. Navy submarine communications station at Forss.[457]

If war had indeed broken out, the UK chiefs of staff had expected the Soviet Union to launch one or two nuclear warheads at the Thurso base, each with a yield of 500 kilotons. (By way of comparison, the atomic bomb dropped on Hiroshima had an estimated yield of 12–18 kilotons.) The Russian rationale was starkly described by the UK Government as 'in a strictly military plan, our nuclear strike airfields and associated installations would have the highest priority, as they offer the greatest threat'.[458]

8 An essential military activity

– anti-submarine warfare

Introduction

During the Cold War the United States had four principal reasons for using Scottish bases: strategic retaliation by the Holy Loch SSBNs; intelligence-gathering at Edzell and Kirknewton; staging posts for the airborne reinforcement of Western Europe; and anti-submarine warfare (ASW) operations. American ASW planes flew from Scottish airfields, and their armaments, including nuclear munitions, were stored in Scotland.

Because of political limitations with Iceland and Norway, Scotland was a key component in guarding the GIUK Gap. The U.S. Navy used Scotland as an alternative location to Iceland, an indication of the importance of geography in international strategy.[459]

American strategy

Submarines had a vital role in the superpower navies. The submarines were involved in intelligence collection, confronting enemy submarines and delivering missile attacks. So ASW was a major component in US strategic policy; the United States needed to track and deter the Soviet submarines that were trying to reach firing positions around the coasts of the United States. Scotland, with its radio spy stations and airfields, provided a good platform for the American ASW activity in the North Atlantic.

In the 1960s, the Soviet Navy expanded rapidly and underwent a 'fundamental reorientation of naval strategy'. Following this the Russians could then target any supplies of fighting materiel being moved from the USA to Europe. Loss of this materiel would have caused serious disruption to NATO's northern defence. The Soviet leader Khrushchev claimed that Russia's submarines could block America's ports and fire missiles onto the American landmass. The Soviet naval mission had become 'the delivery of nuclear warheads to the continental United States'. Accordingly, the Soviet submarine fleet increased dramatically, to support this mission.[460]

By 1975 the Soviet Union had more than 200 submarines. The United States had 95 – but these were of superior quality. The Soviet Navy had 54 SSBN boats and 175 attack submarines (SSK/SSN). More than three-quarters of these new Russian boats were posted to the Northern Fleet at the Kola Peninsula. Their route to confront the United States took them through the GIUK Gap. This Soviet build-up ensured that the Scottish bases were permanently in the front line [461]

Because of this huge Russian naval construction programme, NATO focused on ASW in the Atlantic as a priority task. The U.S. Navy strategic doctrine stated: 'It will be essential to conduct forward operations with attack submarines, as well as to establish barriers at chokepoints using maritime patrol aircraft, mines, attack submarines, or sonobuoys, to prevent leakage of enemy forces to the open ocean where the Western Alliance's resupply lines could be threatened'.[462]

Up to the mid-1970s, the US and the UK held the advantage in ASW activity. Although the Russian submarine fleet had increased in numbers, its technology was basic – and noisy.

The Soviets introduced Victor III-class nuclear-powered attack submarines, which were fitted with acoustic equipment that threatened US and British undersea dominance. This improvement came from the superior manufacturing technology that the Russians had illicitly acquired from Norway and Japan. The Red Navy also adopted new tactics; near American underwater arrays the Russians would operate older, noisier submarines, masking the passage of their newer, quieter ones. The reason for these dramatic changes remained a mystery until the 1985 arrest of U.S. Navy warrant officer John Walker; it turned out that he had been passing naval intelligence to the Soviets since 1967. His betrayal had a devastating effect, and its discovery caused the United States to rethink its ASW strategy.[463]

By 1989 the Soviet submarine construction programme had accelerated, and they were building submarines at the rate of one every six weeks. Their fleet had swollen to 349 boats, so the Royal Navy worried that they would run out of torpedoes before the Soviets ran out of submarines. However, only 34 of the Soviet boats were of the latest design. The United States and Great Britain still had more top-quality submarines and crews than the Soviets, and this balance never altered.[464]

In 1986 a new NATO ASW strategy was adopted: the 'forward diversion'. The U.S. Navy decided that the best ASW policy was to attack Soviet submarines in the shallower seas north of the GIUK Gap, in order to prevent the Soviets from getting through it to intercept the American convoys. So the US and UK submarines moved north of the GIUK Gap, to exert constant pressure on the Soviet SSBNs transiting that zone. This change was possible because of the great advances of technology deployed by the American submarines.

To counter this, the Russians had to withdraw their best attack submarines from the open North Atlantic. These had been used to threaten the American and UK SSBNs transiting to their firing positions in the Northern Seas, but now the Soviets had to protect their own SSBNs in this northern zone. This change of strategy also increased the cost of ASW for the Russians, as they needed to produce more boats to protect their missile-carrying submarines, as well as those required to harass the American and British SSBNs.[465]

The U.S. Navy now guarded the GIUK Gap with the aim of containing the Soviet submarines. American carrier hunter/killer groups, long-range land-based patrol aircraft, submarines and the Sound Surveillance System (SOSUS) were used to detect Russian boats transiting the gap, and deal with them.[466]

The SOSUS consisted of large, fixed arrays of hydrophones laid across the floor of the North Atlantic, and it transmitted information on Soviet submarine movements to the nearest ASW headquarters. Mines were available to seal any gaps. The LORAN-C system also played an important role in this strategy by accurately identifying an enemy submarine's location. All of these elements had Scottish operational facilities.[467]

Additionally, the Holy Loch SSBNs also needed protection when in transit to their patrol zone in the Northern Seas, and to achieve this a fully co-ordinated ASW programme was required. The Scottish radio spy stations were integral to this ASW concept, and the airfields at Prestwick and Machrihanish played an important role as well.

An ASW master plan was implemented. Cold War sub-hunting was complex and expensive, and it required detailed coordination between all ASW platforms. There was round-the-clock tracking of submarines. These activities were controlled by the Commander ASW Force Atlantic (COMASWFORLANT), from his base in Norfolk, Virginia. Patrol aircraft were dispersed to various sites, and the radar picket ships (DER) also contributed. Information from tracking stations such as Edzell came to the headquarters, and tasks were passed to each sector of the force.[468]

This Cold War Battle of the Atlantic was summarised by Admiral James Stavridis, former NATO senior commander: 'What was the Cold War like in the Atlantic? First and foremost, it was a battle for control—really complete surveillance and the positioning of strategic and tactical assets—in the Greenland-Iceland-United Kingdom [GIUK] gap. This zone of thousands of miles of empty ocean became critical strategically. Thus, in the Cold War, there was a constant maneuver between the Soviet Union (and its Warsaw Pact allies) and the NATO forces led by the United States for the control of the gap.'[469]

These active ASW measures could locate, identify and destroy missile submarines on their way to attack the United States. Intelligence information from Thurso and Edzell would enable American SSNs to attack the anti-shipping Soviet SSK attack submarines. Both of these radio stations were major players in this activity with their direction-finding systems.

Scottish activity

In October 1962 the true level of Soviet submarine development in the Atlantic was revealed. The Soviet replenishment ships spotted in the Azores were in that region to resupply the submarines heading to Cuba. Soviet submarines were now operating in the western Atlantic, close to mainland USA. This was a wake-up call for the ASW community. During the Cuban Missile Crisis, the Scottish bases tracked Russian submarines for 23 days, and in the following years this level of involvement became normal.[470]

The Soviets needed to combat the American ASW plan, and they implemented their own ASW strategy: after 1965 a permanent AGI (spy trawler) was assigned to Holy Loch. These seaborne spy stations gathered intelligence on SSBN deployment rates, time on patrol, schedules and readiness states. This information was invaluable in tracking the American boats. The huge Eastern Bloc fishing fleet based at Ullapool in the 1970s and 1980s had many spy trawlers. These vessels relentlessly tracked Holy Loch SSBNs in the northern fishing grounds and along Scotland's west coast.

The North Atlantic was a major concern for Washington as this was the transit route for the Soviet nuclear submarine fleet. ASW aircraft regularly patrolled this zone. They flew out of bases in Newfoundland and Iceland to cover the GIUK Gap, and were specially adapted for long flights of ten hours or more. Extra fuel tanks were fitted, and radomes carried air search radar and other electronic equipment.

Prestwick and Machrihanish played a regular role in the ASW air campaign. Their geography had pushed them into the front line of Washington's defensive strategy. Kinloss and Stornoway also handled occasional ASW air sorties.

Operations

Anti-submarine warfare (ASW) procedure was straightforward. American aircraft would track Russian submarines leaving their bases at Kola and Murmansk. Thurso and Edzell would then provide communications and tracking data. Without the Scottish facilities, major ASW activity would have been hindered.[471]

One of the best ASW platforms was the P-3 Orion aircraft. Its primary mission was to pinpoint Russian submarines, principally by dropping sonobuoys in locations identified by Edzell and Thurso, and then analysing the signals received. These underwater microphones tracked every movement of the enemy vessel. Occasionally, the P-3s would drop small depth charges, forcing the subs to surface and identify themselves.[472]

The P-3 ASW squadrons were based at Keflavik for two weeks, and in bad weather would switch to Prestwick, Machrihanish or Kinloss. These squadrons were well practised in regular deployments from their home base. Don Staunton, a P-3 crew member, remembered the process: 'Today, I am still amazed by how the squadron could expeditiously pack up all its gear into collapsible metal footlockers, load aboard three Air Force C-141s, fly nine P-3Cs, and deploy far away to start immediate ASW operations. The ASW program was a coordinated Allied effort, and many countries contributed significant forces to the continuous Cold War efforts to hunt and track Soviet submarines.'[473]

He explained the mission of his unit: 'Norwegian P-3s initially tracked Russian subs as they transited around the Kola Peninsula, and turned them over to the US. Our mission was to locate and/or track the subs (missile or attack) as they proceeded south, to determine whether they were heading toward the G-I [Greenland–Iceland] gap, which meant they were headed deep into the Atlantic or via the I-UK [Iceland–United Kingdom] gap, to head down towards the eastern Atlantic, or possibly by Gibraltar into the Mediterranean. VP [fixed wing] squadrons[46] were focused on tracking Russian missile boats, which were a key strategic threat to the US.'[474]

---

46 VP squadron: seaplane patrol squadron.

Their ASW patrol flights lasted for 12 'boring, tiring, and repetitive' hours. These long flights were undertaken in order to detect Russian submarines on the edge of the Greenland ice pack. When this happened, a cumbersome process had to be initiated to launch the sonobuoys to track the boat: a hatch had to be opened on the aircraft, then a safety net had to be erected and the launcher brought forward. This was an awkward process at any time.[475]

Two types of sonobuoys were in operation: passive and active. The passive buoy provided the direction of the target, and the active buoy then detected its location. Tyler Rogoway, a U.S. Navy P-3 pilot, recounted a story about the active type: 'For decades this buoy has been called a Cadillac by aircrews, because rumor has it that when initially built the buoy cost so much it was nearly as expensive as a new Cadillac.'[476]

P-3 crews were briefed three hours ahead of take-off time, and then began the pre-flight checks for the aircraft. If any systems caused concern during this process, the 12-man crew would move to the standby aircraft. Hard work would then normally ensure that they met the assigned take-off slot – essential in order to be on station in time to relieve the active patrol aircraft. Don Staunton noted the high standard of teamwork displayed on each mission: 'I was extremely impressed by the entire squadron's determination and total focus on its mission of prosecuting Soviet submarines aggressively and maintaining passive sonobuoy contact.'[477]

It was difficult to locate the Russian submarines. The intelligence information was useful, but for success the P-3 crews had to adopt the correct tactics. Chris Bowen was a P-3 tactical navigator: 'As a tactical crew, most of the time we did not know the larger context of who was where, like the theatre ASW planners in an HQ. Most of the time we were given an area and some generic guidance on what was likely there. Sometimes we were given specific information on a specific hull number present, but most times not. In some cases a submarine was already being tracked, and we would go out and rendezvous with an aircraft already on station and take over when they were out of fuel or sonobuoys. So sometimes we were alone in a larger area and were simply searching for a possible target; other times a target had already been detected and we went out to take over from another aircraft.'

During these flights, the P-3 crew analysed the signals produced by the sonobuoys. AVCM (Ret.) Jim Cole was a combat air crew (CAC) member on such flights, and he recalled their success rate: 'I have five to ten times the computing power in my iPhone 6 than was in the man-sized CP-901, so after getting a hot contact in ASW, it was very rare for a crew of a P-2 or a P-3A or B to still have contact when going off station. The opposite was true of the P-3C – when it got a sniff, with a competent crew it hung on.'

The P-3 sensor operators analysed the signals received from the sonobuoys. They could recognise the difference between underwater noises and those given off by a submarine. Their expertise was impressive; from the different sounds produced by the submarine, they were able to identify its country of origin, class of submarine, course, speed and depth.

Don Staunton recalled the range of equipment carried on ASW sorties: 'In the late seventies and early eighties the aircraft carried 84 sonobuoys: 36 internals, and 48 externally mounted in the belly; the buoys could be set for one, three or eight hours' life. Each search coordinator had different buoy deployment tendencies. For example, when our pilot Lt Stump started to lose contact, he would let loose what he called a 'rain of steel' – many buoys – to try to regain contact.'[478]

A normal ASW mission lasted around 12 hours: the aircraft could fly more than 1,000 miles, pursue a submarine for four hours, and fly back to its home base. The ASW flights were hard work for the crew. However, the 12-hour flight needed an additional 5-hour preparation. The long hours of low-altitude anti-submarine tracking were demanding for the crew. Flight engineer ADJ1 Tom Beaman recalled that the cabin's power and air-conditioning were crucial to maintaining top performance from the complicated equipment on board: 'This required constant monitoring, as any deterioration would adversely impact the sensor information.'

The P-3 crewmen were thoroughly trained for their task and Beaman recalled that: 'flight engineers had to complete a 19-week specialised training school.'[479]

The P-3C weapons bay routinely carried a nuclear depth-weapon – the Mark 45 torpedo. Authority for nuclear release was a team effort. Tyler Rogoway remembered the procedure for launching these weapons: 'There were nuclear arming panels where both pilots would insert their firing keys and provide dual concurrence to release the nuke.'[480]

Tim Beaman noted the high standard of competence of the crews: 'The crew were required to requalify annually through a process similar to the Dolphins procedure for submariners. In-flight training was constant, and all personnel were security-cleared.'[481]

There were also two surface radar picket stations (DER/AGI) – one to the west of Iceland, and one to the east of it. The DERs maintained a cycle of about two weeks on patrol followed by two weeks in Greenock or Rosyth for upkeep, stores and fuel. Occasionally Thurso was used. As they were permanently stationed in a wild weather region, the DERs needed constant upkeep. One of these radar pickets, USS *Brumby* (DE-1044), was towed from Greenock to South Carolina after damaging its steam generators in November 1972. Significantly, it was not taken to Site One, as the Holy Loch facility was reserved for the submarine mission.[482]

Barrier patrols were tiring and difficult. Admiral Hyland said of them: 'It was those people in the seaborne part of the barrier that really had some rough weather to go through. In the middle of winter in the North Atlantic, there isn't a more difficult or unpleasant place to be.' The weather was always severe, and when USS *Roy O. Hale* (DER 336) was heavily damaged in a fierce storm in February 1962, 13 crewmen were injured. After three weeks in Greenock for repairs, *Roy O. Hale* resumed its patrol duties and operated further south a few months later as part of the ASW barrier during the Cuban crisis.[483]

The Holy Loch operation was a prime target for Soviet ASW missions. This problem increased in importance after 1971, when the UK Polaris submarines arrived at Faslane. The Russian spy trawlers would track the SSBNs as they exited from the Clyde, and Soviet reconnaissance submarines would attempt to tail them into the Northern Seas. The same procedure would occur on the return passage.

The U.S. Navy was confident that the SSBNs were able to elude pursuit once they had reached deeper waters, but protection was needed against this harassment. The development of suitable helicopter platforms improved NATO's ASW capability. From 1970 Sikorsky Sea King Mark 6 helicopters were flown from HMS *Gannet* at Prestwick; their primary role was to provide ASW defence of the Clyde area, to protect Holy Loch and Faslane.[484]

Summary

Scotland provided excellent ASW facilities for the U.S. – intelligence gathered at Scottish sites and airfields on Scottish soil contributed to the success of this crucial mission. A vital segment of the NATO ASW plan was thus ensured.

Mike Lacey
(*Mike Lacey*)

Captain Don Ulmer
(*Don Ulmer, Facebook*)

Mike Giambattista
(*Mike Giambattista*)

Mike Masishin
(*Mike Masishin*)

Captain Ron Gumbert
(*Ron Gumbert*)

Philip Giambri
(*Philip Giambri*)

[Above] Polaris Missile Launch from USS *Andrew Jackson* (SSBN-619) viewed by President Kennedy on board the USS *Observation Island* (AG-154). (*U.S. Naval History and Heritage Command Photo L55-15.02.07*)

[Left] Crewmen handle line as USS *John C Calhoun* ties up alongside her tender USS Canopus at Holy Loch, Scotland, 18 May 1972, to end The One-Thousandth Undersea Ballistic Missile Submarine Patrol (*U.S. Naval History and Heritage Command Photo 1151620*)

Bernie Gantt, centre, with his
sister and brother (*Bernie Gantt*)

Sharon Hahn
(*Sharon Hahn*)

Paul Davis
(*Paul Davis*)

Felice Bluhm
(Clauder)
(*Felice Clauder*)

Gary Flynn
(*Gary Flynn*)

Greggery Kunkle
(*Greggery Kunkle*)

Ray Conner
(*Ray Conner*)

Charlie Witherow
(*Charlie Witherow*)

Frank Murray (*Frank Murray*)

Dave Pratt (*Dave Pratt*)

Edward DelSanto
(*Edward DelSanto*)

USS *Los Alamos*
(AFDB-7) at
Holy Loch,
Scotland, with a
ballistic missile
submarine
(SSBN)
inside, circa
the 1980s. USS *Simon Lake* (AS-33) is in the left distance. (*US
Naval History and Heritage Command Photo NH 98381-KN*)

USS *Hunley* with two submarines coming alongside
(*JOC Fred J. Klinkenberger - U.S. Defenseimagery.mil*)

USS *Holland* (AS-32) moored in the Holy Loch, Scotland (*U.S. Naval History and Heritage Command Photo L45-126.08.01*)

[Left] USS *Saugus* (YTB 780) with crew on deck *(U.S. Naval History and Heritage Command Photo L45-255.02.1)*
[Right] USS *Hunley* (AS-31) tied to a mooring buoy at Holy Loch, Scotland, circa April 1966. She has two submarines, an LCM and other vessels alongside *(U.S. Naval History and Heritage Command Photo NH 96830)*

Dan Flanagan
(Dan Flanagan)

Keith Collie
(Keith Collie)

Admiral Bill Studeman *(U.S. Naval History and Heritage Command)*

Lee Hendley
(Lee Hendley)

Arne Simonsen
(Arne Simonsen)

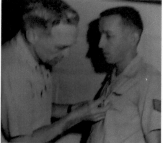

[Left] Jim Louis Parham with Edzell tug of war team. (*Jim Louis Parham*)
[Right] George Montague being awarded the Distinguished Flying Cross
by General Stapleton, Commander USAFSS, 1968 (*George Montague*)

[Above] Collins R-390 Receiver – the work
horse for Edzell CTs (*Dan Flanagan*)

[Right] DF Console O-scope (*Dan Flanagan*)

[Above] The Operations Building at Edzell, surrounded by the Elephant Cage (*Dan Flanagan*)

[Right] Magnetic tape recorders at Edzell – the tapes had to be changed every 15 minutes (*Dan Flanagan*)

[Below] The legal clerk at Edzell – an important individual (*Dan Flanagan*)

[Right] Racks of R-390 receivers at Edzell (*Dan Flanagan*)

Colin Maclean in red jumper with
UN in Israel (*Colin Maclean*)

Philip E Gillock
(*Patrick P Gillock*)

[Left] Kirknewton Ops Room (*RAFkirknewton.com*)

[Right] 37 RSM Headquarters Kirknewton, 1953 (*RAFkirknewton.com*)

[Above] NCO Academy USAFSS
Kirknewton, 1957 (*RAFkirknewton.com*)

[Left] 6952nd RSM Able Flight HQ,
1955 (*RAFkirknewton.com*)

David Gow
(*David Gow*)

Keith Bryers
(*Keith Bryers*)

Alan Kinghorn
(*Alan Kinghorn*)

[Left] Genetrix Gondola and camera equiptment (*Peebles Collection*)

[Right] Boxcar recovers a Genetrix balloon (*US Air Force Photo*)

C-119 Boxcar (*USAF Museum*)

Bill Broome
(*Bill Broome*)

Chris Carlson
(*Chris Carlson*)

Fred Ver Planck
(*Fred Ver Planck*)

Terri Sanders
(*Terri Sanders*)

Alec McMahan
(*Sandy McMahan*)

Ron Swart
(*Ron Swart*)

Gan Starling
(*Gan Starling*)

Ken Waringa
(*D.G.Mackay*)

Howard Tillison
(*Howard Tillison*)

Jim Madison
(*Jim Madison*)

Two-man Klepper Canoe (*US DoD photo*)

Sketch of the station's facilities, engraved on copper plate, and presented to Admiral Thomas B. Hayward, Christmas 1980 (*U.S. Naval History and Heritage Command Photo NH 93835*)

Mark Bubs Whitten
(*M. Whitten*)

Michael R Ellis
(*M.R.Ellis*)

Kevin McCoy re-enlists at the operations floor in Thurso (*Kevin McCoy*)

Louise Pass
(*Louise Pass*)

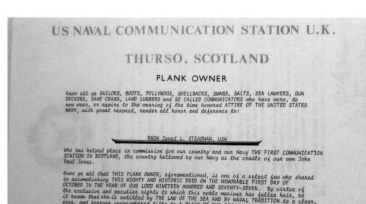

[Above] Janet Dixon
(*Janet Dixon*)

[Left] NCS Thurso plank-holder certificate
(*Janet Dixon*)

Soviet spy trawler, Scottish-registered BF 346 at Ullapool (*Mike Archbold*)

Sikorsky UH-19 from Exercise Hop-a-Long (USAF Museum)

Mike Archbold
(*Mike Archbold*)

USN personnel en route to USA through
Prestwick Airport, 1972 (*Dan Flanagan*)

Bob Broff
(*Robert S.Broff*)

[Left] USS *Patrick Henry* (SSBN-599) underway along the River Clyde *(US Navy Photo)*
[Below] Systems check of Polaris Missile Compartment, USS *John Adams (U.S. Naval History and Heritage Command Photo L55-15.02.08)*

[Above] Transfer of a Polaris Missile between USS *Patrick Henry* (SSBN-599) and USS *Proteus* (AS-31) at Holy Loch, Dunoon *(US Navy Photo NPC 1053952)*

[Left] CDR Laurel Clark *(NASA photo ID S96-16627)*

[Above] Soviet factory ships in Loch Broom.
One of these would have been a full-fitted
SIGINT station *(Bbc.co.uk, Noel Hawkins)*
[Left] Balloon shortly after take off *(US Air Force)*

Grumman HU-18B Albatross Seaplane used by 67 ARS at Prestwick
(National Museum of the United States Air Force)

Lockheed P-3B Orion *(US Naval History and Heritage Command Photo Bu-153433)*

9 Links in the chain

Introduction

Napoleon was frank about the role of communications in military matters: *The secret of war lies in the communications.*

During the Cold War, Scotland hosted a large American military communications network which dealt with presidential wartime communications, space missions, satellite links, military command, SSBN links, SAR and direction-finding. When early versions of digital technology were developed they were deployed on these sites.

Most of the communications stations were located on high ground, and were operated and maintained by American military personnel. These links were essential elements of the United States' Cold War infrastructure.

American strategy

The fundamental requirement for the United States' perimeter defence strategy was for the Pentagon to rapidly communicate with its vital components. This strategy was underpinned by its nuclear triad: SAC bombers, ground-based missiles and SSBNs. Reliable communications were of paramount importance. The first two legs of the triad were mainly based in the USA, where communications were guaranteed, while the submarine response fleet had its European bases at Holy Loch and Rota.

In addition, other networks were required to deal with the ongoing daily passage of routine administrative, logistical and operational traffic.

The communications system needed to be able to survive a nuclear exchange. The NCA control centre was located at Cheyenne Mountain, Colorado, but this was a long way from

Europe and as long-range transmissions were subject to the limitations of the available technology, intermediate rebroadcast facilities were necessary to guarantee the integrity of the strategic plan.

By 1960 both Eisenhower and the UK Government had agreed that there was a need for an American communications network to be located in Scotland. This would be able to coordinate a variety of activities. In particular, communications had to be improved for SSBN boats.

Submarine communications were an extremely difficult matter; the boat had to stay as deep as possible to avoid being detected by Soviet air observation or radio intercept. But radio waves cannot penetrate water easily. Both the United States and the Soviet Union researched this problem, and both came up with similar results. The Russian transmission site – enormous – was based well within the Russian landmass, but this solution could not be applied in the United States. It would have been astronomically expensive, as well as providing a first-strike nuclear target for the Soviet Union. An alternative solution was required. This was provided initially at Londonderry and then, after 1977, at Thurso.

The NSC (National Security Council) pointed out that the FBM fleet could be nullified in a conventional war by 'attacks on supply ships, bases, communications'. Cryptographic capability was limited, and there was little interoperability between the different communications systems in use; there had to be a network capable of fully supporting political and military needs. Day-to-day military communications had to be guaranteed.

The Pentagon specifically needed a reliable last-ditch system which would connect the President to military commanders on the ground. It had to be secure, jam-proof and survivable. Part of this required a presidential airborne command post.[485]

A specific wartime command network was created: the Silk Purse. It was designed to ensure guaranteed communications between the NCA and American military commanders in various locations.

Throughout the Cold War the United States military operated a robust airborne command and control organisation, which, known as Tacamo (Take Charge and Move Out), linked the NCA to senior military commanders. The Tacamo system was a survivable communications network for use during nuclear war, and was tested on a continuous basis to ensure its operational readiness.

A presidential command post (ABNCP) aircraft was airborne at all times, as directed by President Kennedy when the system came into service in 1961. The initial aircraft used were C-130s specially adapted for this task. By 1974 the aircraft had been updated to a Boeing E-4 which included a trailing antenna more than 5 miles long.

The aircraft carried a battle staff headed by a general or flag officer, the Airborne Emergency Action Officer (AEAO), whose team was on standby to assume interim authority if the NCA command centre was destroyed or immobilised. Because of their grim role the two planes were referred to as the Doomsday planes.[486]

Tacamo supported the Silk Purse command network and controlled the SSBN missile launch information. The concept was simple: in times of crisis, the President and his staff would move to a designated airfield, board the Tacamo aircraft (then known as Nightwatch, and later designated Air Force One) and take off.

The major United States military commanders had a similar capability. Each of their airborne command posts replicated the presidential aircraft. All were linked through a series of Tacamo airborne relay stations and were part of the Silk Purse network. Both Thurso and Edzell were ground stations for this system.[487]

The Tacamo aircraft flew constant training sorties to guarantee the operability of the system. One of the Tacamo squadrons, the 2d Airborne Command and Control Squadron, was located at RAF Mildenhall in England and flew its mission over Scotland every month. This route was essential, as Scotland was a major component of the priority network for the Allied Command Europe Highband (ACE High) system. Scotland also operated the guaranteed link to America's Europe-based SSBN submarines. The continuous operability of these vital Scottish communications links was fundamental to the defence strategy of the United States.[488]

The U.S. Navy devised a working solution for communicating with its SSBNs, and it came into operation in the mid-1970s. To provide this network, six major VLF transmitters were constructed worldwide. Thurso was the main U.S. Navy transmitter in Europe, as its geographical and geological location enabled it to communicate with submarines, specifically the FBM boats. All of these transmitters were part of the Silk Purse command network system.[489] Thurso's VLF/ELF transmitter ensured that SSBNs could be connected to the NCA as required. The Tacamo network aircraft, with their trailing wire antennae, were linked through Thurso.

When the presidential command post took to the skies, the other twelve Tacamo aircraft were already airborne. These aircraft were permanently on a 15-minute alert status, and Captain Vern Lochausen described his days as a Tacamo pilot: 'What it meant to be a Tacamo sailor in the Cold War was to be on alert, get the call and rush out the aircraft, not knowing if this was it, the real thing, the time when we would have to do what we trained to do and know that having done that the world and life as we knew it would not be the same again – and yet we did, and would go and do just that.'[490]

Chico Buffone was a Tacamo sailor: 'I served as an enlisted airborne communications system specialist on one of the mission teams. We were part of the NEACP/Nightwatch group.[47] NEACP was one component of the network which ranged from Europe to Asia. We would send or retransmit EAMs [emergency action messages] from the NCA over our airborne survivable system to all commands.'[491]

In-depth training was a feature of the Tacamo role: 'Our specialised training consisted of a formal 19-week tech school, then up to a year of on-the-job-training under an instructor-rated crew member. We did have to possess a very high security clearance.' He recalled the routine and its strains: 'Alert tours were scheduled and rotated between the crews. We had a crew of about 75 members. We would get no-warning callouts to maintain our edge. During the Cold War, you always wondered if the klaxon was training or real. An alert klaxon could be a fast taxi, then either a return to alert pad or a many-hours-long flight. We wouldn't know which until we took off.'

During peacetime, these networks carried a wide range of traffic. Most of this would still be required during wartime. There was a need to simplify the number and types of communications networks which were essential once a conflict was under way. These were

---

47 NEACP: National Emergency Airborne Command Post; Nightwatch was its codename.

identified and grouped under the Minimum Essential Emergency Communications Network (MEECN). This system was able to provide continuous communications in a nuclear situation, and guaranteed a one-way passage of messages to the nuclear commanders. The network was resistant to jamming, and could operate in a post-nuclear environment. The MEECN systems formed the technical basis of the Tacamo activities and were practised rigorously during training flights.[492]

The MEECN system operators also trained annually in Europe, and the Scottish networks were vital. During these training exercises, MEECN messages were transmitted through Thurso. EAMs from the NCA would also be broadcast to the SSBNs in the northern waters via Thurso's transmitter – a rehearsal of its primary wartime role.

The Russian military were themselves also fully aware of the prime importance of communications. This was laid out in simple terms in the *Great Soviet Encyclopaedia*, which stated:

> The main mission of military communications is to ensure that commanders and staffs at all levels are able to maintain continuous control of subordinate forces under any conditions and to communicate signals to the forces at the proper time concerning the threat of enemy attack and the implementation of combat readiness.[493]

The United States' communications networks in Scotland

To support the Pentagon's essential command and control needs, more than 30 American communications sites were erected in Scotland, including many small hilltop stations. These remote sites were links in a network that ran from Washington DC to Naples in Italy.

At that time, NATO had different military communications systems. Some were based on commercial networks, but these were vulnerable and insecure. It had been to counter this shortfall that the ACE High system was constructed. This enabled the Pentagon to speak directly to the Supreme Allied Commander Europe (SACEUR), who was always an American four-star general or admiral.

ACE High included a fixed NATO radio communication and early warning system. The system was a combined UHF troposcatter/ microwave radio system, which enabled the radio traffic to be passed across great distances. It was a huge network, which opened in 1958 and was still operating in 1988. ACE High was the biggest communications project of its kind ever undertaken, extending from Norway to eastern Turkey and linking nine of the then fifteen NATO countries. There were 49 troposcatter stations and 40 microwave stations. Five of these stations were in Scotland; at Mossy Hill, Collafirth Hill and Saxa Vord, all in Shetland, then Long Haven Hill and a major interconnect site at Mormond Hill, both in Aberdeenshire. The entire network extended across a distance of 8,300 miles. Each site had a huge dish antenna. The equipment used huge reflectors and aerials more than 50 metres (~160 feet) high.[494]

It was designed to provide 'reliable, secure and virtually instantaneous communications' for SACEUR by connecting both the military and national headquarters to ensure that command and control could be exercised effectively by the NCA.

The deployment of this NATO-wide communications network to Scotland was integrated in a hush-hush fashion. The separate computer information link required for SACEUR was also transmitted via the Scottish stations.

These Scottish sites were in the essential category for US strategic communications. Most of the sites were unstaffed, and their equipment was maintained by American personnel. Their maintenance and inspection cycle was continuous, and small teams would visit each location to complete the necessary tasks to ensure the reliability of the system.

Edzell was a key component in this communications web. A network of radio station sites ran between Mormond Hill, Edzell, Inverbervie, Kinnaber, Latheron and Thurso. Their operational integrity was safeguarded by the UK Government. The special status of these sites was notified to the relevant local authorities, who had to refer the planning applications for any proposed works, such as the erection of masts, buildings, roads, fences or houses, in their vicinity to the UK Government for final approval.[495]

Technological improvements meant that the ACE High network was upgraded to microwave use. It became part of the Digital European Backbone (DEB) network, and by 1969 the UK Wideband Microwave System (UKWMS) was completed, linking Edzell to Londonderry. Edzell's inclusion was an indication that the communications supporting its SIGINT mission had been incorporated into this protected network. The relevance and importance of Edzell in this context could not have been clearer.[496]

After 1970 there was a microwave link to Thurso from Edzell. This used several repeater stations, with the longest being 75 miles between Kinnaber and Mormond Hill.

Kinnaber, 10 miles from Edzell, was a manned site.[497] It had a maintenance team consisting of five Navy personnel and civilian contractors from the equipment manufacturer. The Navy team consisted of a chief petty officer with about five electronic technicians and one person to maintain the mechanical equipment. During normal weekday working hours, most of the assigned personnel were at the Kinnaber site or at a link site performing routine preventative maintenance.

A.Q. Morton recalled his time at Kinnaber: 'The site was a small building which looked like a converted farmhouse with a large tower supporting microwave dish antennas. Inside was a large control panel that monitored a microwave relay network. The network connected the U.S. Navy sites in Scotland (Thurso, Edzell and, I believe, the submarine base in Holy Loch) with the US Naval Communication Station at Londonderry, Northern Ireland. From there the link was connected to the United States.'

The Kinnaber control panel monitored the operating status of all the other microwave sites in Scotland. Morton recalled the procedure: 'If for example, the primary receiver at Kirk o' Shotts near Glasgow (call sign GXH15) were to fail, the secondary receiver would still be online to maintain the link. A panel light and audible device on the control panel would indicate the primary receiver was out of service at the Kirk o' Shotts site. At that time a voice control channel over the link was used to talk to Londonderry to advise them that a team was being dispatched to resolve the problem. Once at the site, they used the voice channel to communicate with Kinnaber and/or Londonderry while the failure was being resolved.'[498]

Kinnaber was also the central point for maintenance of the network. Working in shifts, the team members monitored the health of each mountaintop relay site, maintained verbal communication with Londonderry via the network, and performed periodic preventative maintenance and calibration at each site. Morton recalled that: 'If a fault was detected at any site, they immediately drove to the site to fix the problem. If a site was more than 100 miles away, they stayed overnight in a nearby hotel.'

This involved a patently unsuccessful attempt at subterfuge, as Morton remembered: 'To not draw attention to ourselves, we were directed to wear civilian clothes. I liked that, but thought it strange because we really stood out, sporting military haircuts and driving a large American pickup truck with *U.S. Navy* stencilled on the doors, not to mention our American accents.'

All the microwave links were located on high ground, often on the same site as BBC television transmitters. 'Each site consisted of a small windowless building, a microwave tower with antennae and a generator/battery building for back-up power. Inside each building was a rack of microwave equipment consisting of two complete receiver/transmitter systems. The second system served as a backup to keep the link operational at all times. If this occurred, power interruption batteries kept the system on the air until the generator came on-line.'

Morton added: 'The tower height and antenna size for each site varied according to how high the local terrain was and how far away the next microwave link was. I remember the site somewhere south of Ayr having the highest tower and the largest antenna to cover the path across the Irish Sea to Northern Ireland – 110 miles to Londonderry.'

Most on-site time was spent on scheduled routine maintenance. Generators were serviced and run, fuel levels were checked, and the microwave equipment was adjusted to nominal operational parameters. The fault warning system gave a general idea what main component (e.g., receiver, transmitter) was faulty, and a replacement component was carried by the maintenance team: 'When a main component was replaced, it required in-system testing and alignment. The test equipment required to perform those operations (i.e., frequency counter, meters, cables, tools) were also carried to the site.'

The sites were very reliable. The occasional malfunction usually involved going to the site and performing a frequency or level adjustment, as Morton recalled: 'If a component could not be adjusted back into service, a replacement component was installed and adjusted likewise. The defective component was returned to Kinnaber/Edzell, where the civilian manufacturer technicians fixed the problem. During my time at Kinnaber there were never any malfunctions due to weather or vandalism.'

Morton recalled that despite their strategic function, the sites were not completely stand-alone, as they used commercial power from the grid. But also: 'Each site contained equipment and a generator. The generator was only used if a power failure occurred. I believe that if a power outage occurred, the site automatically went to battery power. Then if it was on battery power for a set period of time, the generator automatically went online.'

Morton could not recall any instances of a site reverting to back-up power due to a commercial power failure: 'I do recall watching the mechanical service technician starting and testing the generator during routine preventative maintenance site visits.'

Lee Hendley was another technician who recalled this activity during his service in Scotland: 'During my tour at Kirknewton I did visit other sites in Scotland in my job as an electronic maintenance repairman.'

Until 1964, each of the United States military services operated their own separate communications networks. This was inefficient and, in a wartime situation, would be difficult to protect. These separate military networks were combined to form the Automatic Voice Network (AUTOVON). This was a wholly military system, with appropriate physical defence measures to resist enemy attack. It enabled high-level users, such as the President, the Secretary of Defense and the Joint Chiefs of Staff to 'provide rapid, worldwide command and control communications for the NCA and other high-priority subscribers, as well as other military and diplomatic users.' There was no doubt about its importance.[499]

AUTOVON was the most important telephone communications project undertaken by the Department of Defense. High-level users could access the worldwide network, while others, less important, were limited to their local area. The overseas section of the system, eventually completed in 1970, formed the final segment of the US strategic command, control and communications framework, C3. Although this major strategic communications network was routed through Scotland, its installation was not publicised.

Scotland had a line of unstaffed AUTOVON links. These were located at Latheron in Caithness, Inverbervie in Aberdeenshire, Kinnaber near Montrose, Craigowl Hill in Angus, East Lomond in Fife, Kirk o' Shotts in Lanarkshire, Browncarrick Hill near Ayr and Sergeant Law near Paisley. AUTOVON was upgraded in the 1970s, using the new digital system which had been introduced. This upgrade provided secure voice and data capability. The network was also linked to the DEW line at both Fylingdales and Londonderry until 1977.[500]

Because the Arctic/North Pole region was the shortest route for a Soviet air attack on the United States, the DEW line had been constructed across Alaska, Canada, Greenland, the Faroes and Iceland to defend against this threat. Its purpose was to provide early warning to enable American bombers to take off in time, and for the land-based nuclear missiles to be launched. However, the DEW line could only detect incoming bombers. It could not detect missiles. So to handle this requirement the Ballistic Missile Early Warning System (BMEWS) was developed.[501]

The original specification for the BMEWS in 1958 had proposed a site in Scotland. In 1963 Thurso, as it was geographically suitable, was considered as a possible link in this upgrade of the DEW line. A decision was taken to occupy the site, and Secretary of State Dean Rusk described the site as 'a scanning and tracking capability, a central-computer and display facility, and communications' which would boost the DEW Line. It was not confirmed, as it would only have provided a 'marginal' improvement, but the site was subsequently fully exploited to serve other needs of US strategic policy.[502]

To resolve the missile-detection problem, in 1960 the North Atlantic Radio System (NARS) was introduced as an extension to the DEW line. NARS, which could detect missiles as well as aircraft, stretched from Iceland to Fylingdales in Yorkshire (Site 45).

Its Scottish terminal was at Mormond Hill (Site 44). This was connected to RAF Buchan by a 70-mile line-of-sight (LOS) link. Mormond Hill was home to a large collection of tropospheric scatter antennas operated by small detachments of the USAF and the British Army. There was also a British Telecom mast and three buildings: a radio complex, a composite building and a power supply building. Later it was upgraded by the installation of a ground-to-air link, part of the Apollo space mission network.[503]

Summary

During the Cold War, Scotland provided an essential common platform for U.S. — military requirements. This ensured that the NCA was able to communicate in wartime vital matters as well as in peacetime day-to-day activities. Scotland's geographical benefits were once again fully exploited.

10 A Fog-Free Airfield

Introduction

During the Cold War, Scotland was a convenient base for US military units to confront the Soviet Union on a daily basis.

The SSBN fleet at Holy Loch was the centrepiece of this strategic jigsaw. Edzell and Thurso added weight, with their intercept and direction-finding capability, to the unrelenting ASW campaign that was waged around the waters close to Scotland. Other units based in Scotland added a strategic matrix of communications stations to the American war chest.

The United States also created reserve air bases at Stornoway and Machrihanish. Personnel and materiel passed across Scottish shores. Nuclear and conventional weapons were stored on the west coast, and its wild country was an ideal training area for US special forces.[504]

American strategy

The Pentagon needed more airfields in Western Europe. The US already had strike airfields in England, France and West Germany, but others were required to service strategic movement and directly support ongoing operations. Military air operations had to be kept secret. Scotland was ideal.

During the Second World War thousands of American aircraft had passed through Scottish airfields. Post-war, these airfields became valuable to the American Cold War strategic plan. They had a specific advantage, being close to the sea and well away from big cities – and Russia was within range for the spy planes which flew from these airfields.[505]

The U.S. Navy and USAF were flying ferret reconnaissance flights from the UK in 1951. These flights would fly very close to Russian territory and collect data. Many came through

157

Prestwick or Machrihanish on their return journey, as these were valuable refuelling points before the long flight back to continental USA. As both airfields were listed as emergency bases, this activity placed them on Russia's target list. Although Machrihanish was unlikely to have been part of any ferret flight plan, Prestwick was regularly involved.[506]

Aircraft from the 117th Tactical Reconnaissance Wing had passed through Prestwick on their way to their UK base at Burtonwood.[507] Its effectiveness was noted for future use.

By 1956, Khrushchev had boasted that Russia was developing nuclear missiles. However, the United States had no way of examining this claim. Throughout the 1950s, few UK/US agents had returned from the USSR, and air reconnaissance was now seen as the best solution. The United Kingdom, and Scotland in particular, was ideally placed to handle these flights.[508]

The Russians had constructed Arctic airbases, and they installed a radar chain across the zone containing their nuclear facilities. Transmissions from these long-range search radars and fighter control systems could be intercepted by American aircraft flying in the region.[509]

So, American military units moved into Prestwick and Machrihanish. These units did not overshadow the local community, and they housed activities which could be hidden from public view.

Both airfields were ferrying points, and helped with the rapid movement of American troops and aircraft into Europe. Machrihanish was also home to U.S. Navy SEALs and U.S. Navy minemen. The U.S. Navy also flew ASW missions from the base. By 1980 the UK had a highly developed ASW capability, including nuclear depth charges, which were stored at Machrihanish.[510]

Both airfields played a daily role in the crucial ASW campaign. Their geography had pushed them into the front line of Washington's defensive strategy which aimed to prevent Russian submarines from getting too close to the east coast of the United States.

Prestwick – the good weather airfield

Prestwick had a Second World War history of operating as a transatlantic destination for American aircraft. More than 20,000 planes had been delivered through the airfield during those wartime years, and Cold War reinforcement strategy made heavy use of this well-proven link.[511]

Weather conditions enabled Prestwick to operate scheduled flights to the United States, and in the early post-war years, it had been the bad-weather alternative for London Heathrow. In 1948 American aircraft involved in the Berlin Airlift passed through it as well. John Watson was a young boy at this time: 'The airfield was full of big planes going to Berlin. It was an exciting time for us local youngsters.' The US contribution to the airlift, Operation Vittles, made constant use of Prestwick and almost 500 sorties were flown from the base.[512]

Between 1950 and 1990, Prestwick was also an important USAF facility in support of NATO activity. In 1949 the runway was resurfaced and extended to 7,000 feet; by 1960 it had been lengthened to 9,800 feet.

In 1951 it was reactivated for USAF use, for air-sea rescue tasks. It also handled full-scale NATO reinforcement exercises when large numbers of aircraft flew from the United States to West Germany. These REFORGER (Reinforcement of Germany) activities needed a servicing point on their route to Western Europe. Prestwick was a perfect location for this because of its good-weather characteristics, and it was developed into a Military Air Transport Service (MATS) base as one of five support units in Europe.[513]

The airfield continued to grow in importance as an American facility, and in 1956 MATS sent 1602 Air Transport Wing to Prestwick to support all USAF elements on the base. Detachments of 18th Weather Squadron followed, to be joined by 1267 Airways and Air Communications Service (AACS). MATS also opened a separate terminal to handle the large number of American military passengers who came through the airport in transit to European duties. After the end of 1960, U.S. Navy personnel began to arrive for Holy Loch and other bases in Scotland.

The MATS presence at Prestwick lasted from 1951 until its final closure in 1992 when the Holy Loch base closed. Initially, the 1631st Air Base Group USAF had arrived, to manage the traffic between USA and Europe. New buildings were erected to accommodate them and provide for the passengers on those flights. Prestwick now provided full aircraft maintenance and accommodation for all the American aircraft and personnel. Then in 1952 the 67th Air Rescue Squadron arrived and more accommodation was added. The airfield had reverted to its wartime role – a haven for transiting American military personnel.[514]

In July 1952 Prestwick's fog-free capability enabled the completion of the first transatlantic crossing by helicopter: Project Hopalong. Two USAF Air Rescue Service helicopters had touched down five times en route between Westover AFB, Massachusetts, and Prestwick. The two Sikorsky H-19 aircraft arrived from Iceland, having flown a nonstop helicopter distance record of 947 miles on the final leg in just over ten hours. This test demonstrated the possibility of ferrying helicopters over long distances.[515]

This was a significant aviation milestone. The first transatlantic helicopter crossing was a test of the capabilities of rotorcraft to deploy rapidly over long distances. USAF ARS (Air Rescue Service) Captain Vincent McGovern had flown on 96 rescue missions in Korea. He devised a plan to ferry two H-19s non-stop across the Atlantic. He had deduced that if the Cold War turned hot, the US forces in Europe would need hundreds of helicopters. The cheapest and fastest way to get them there would be to fly them across the ocean.[516]

The helicopters were stripped and fitted with three 100-gallon fuel tanks to boost their total fuel capacity to 480 gallons. Duckbutt Alla, a converted B-17 Flying Fortress (SB-17) carried rescue equipment and provided advance weather information and navigational guidance for the helicopters over the Atlantic. This was an early example of Operation Duck Butt – an airborne navigation relay system for USAF aircraft en route to Europe and the Middle East.

There was also an SC-54 transport, carrying spare parts, mechanics and observers. Other ARS escort planes took station along the route, and the final leg was covered by a C-47 and a Grumman Albatross from 67 Squadron. The pilots were ARS personnel.

The escort aircraft also acted as navigators, providing a positional signal to the helicopter pilots every 15 minutes. After an official welcome at Prestwick, the helicopters flew on to West Germany. Apart from its historical significance, this first transatlantic flight had proved that it was possible to deliver rotor planes from America to Europe by this method.[517]

During the Cold War, Prestwick was the courier transfer station for the dispatch of Edzell's intelligence information to Washington DC. It was also used as the changeover station for crews for the Holy Loch submarines, and was used by most American military personnel travelling to Scotland.

More than 40,000 American servicemen and servicewomen passed through Prestwick. One in particular has been widely remembered – Elvis Presley, en route for military service in West Germany in 1960. Elvis was commemorated inside the terminal building with a photo montage and the Graceland Café.[518] That café is no more, but at the time of writing there's an Elvis Presley bar airside.

The American expansion at Prestwick included the construction of a large storage area for cargo, the arrival of a small USAF unit which handled passenger transport (mainly SSBN crew turnaround) and the SAR service covering the East Atlantic. By 1961 the SAR's role also included involvement in the rescue of US spacecraft and these tasks were carried out by 67 Air Rescue Squadron.[48] In 1966 the runway was, as mentioned earlier, extended again to serve the growing needs of the USAF and conform to the US military specifications of the time.[519]

Prestwick had given excellent support to the air rescue mission. But in 1967 the situation changed and 67 Squadron was reassigned to Moron AFB in Spain, to provide more immediate rescue cover for the higher number of nuclear-armed American aircraft operating over Europe.[520]

Prestwick operations

In 1951 the U.S. Navy launched Project Magnet to survey the earth's magnetic field. This was a major programme to support the United States' global magnetic modelling and charting requirements. Prestwick was a convenient refuelling and servicing point for the survey of the Northern Seas, and aircraft from this activity were commonly seen on the airfield.[521]

In 1953 aircraft from the 1370th Photo Mapping Wing of MATS were based at Prestwick. The unit had sole responsibility for the USAF's aerial mapping photography and electronic surveying. The threefold mission included worldwide precision photomapping, electronic controlled photomapping and aerial electronic geodetic surveys.[522]

Such information was of vital importance, and the Scotland–Norway Sea zone was given top priority. A ground station was set up at Saxa Vord in Shetland, another was located at Warth Hill near Thurso, a third was set up at Mormond Hill and a fourth on Fair Isle. Chuck Hart, a former 1370th airman, described the mission activities at each site: 'It was operated for a 90-day period by four USAF personnel. The station used a 50-foot mast antenna, and the surveying aircraft would fly at intervals over the station at low altitude.' RB-50 aircraft were based at Prestwick to carry out the mission. These Superfortress bombers had been converted for reconnaissance activities and carried cameras for that purpose.[523]

In addition, from the early 1960s through to the mid-1980s, Prestwick regularly hosted aircraft from Oceanographic Development Squadron Eight (VXN-8) which were involved in missions across the Arctic ice cover. These aircraft gathered information to assist U.S. Navy submarines during under-ice operations.[524]

---

48 In 1965 it was designated the 67th Air Recovery Squadron, and finally, in 1966, as the 67th Aerospace Rescue and Recovery Squadron.

Air transport

President Kennedy gave an indication of Prestwick's importance in its military air transport role in his 1961 State of the Union address: 'I have directed prompt action to increase our airlift capacity … to any problem at any spot on the globe at any moment's notice.'[525]

Most of this air transport activity involved moving new aircraft to other American bases in Europe and elsewhere, but there were also regular large army formation exercises to practise the replenishment of Western Europe. The 1963 Exercise Big Lift was one of these, and many USAF planes carrying army personnel, equipment and vehicles flew to Europe. This would result in more than 40 aircraft parking overnight at Prestwick and became a regular occurrence. This exercise was a vital Cold War diplomatic activity, helping to reassure America's NATO allies that if a conflict arose they would not be abandoned.

In 1963 Deputy Secretary of Defense Roswell Gilpatric explained its purpose:

> This Big Lift exercise will demonstrate our ability to project our military power far more quickly over far larger distances than has ever been the case in the past. By employing such a multi-base capability, the US should be able to make useful reductions in its heavy overseas military expenditures without diminishing its effective military strength or its capacity to apply that strength swiftly in support of its worldwide policy commitments.[526]

Prestwick was nicknamed 'the Window' because of its tremendous weather record. It had a reputation as the most fog-free airport in the UK, and handled many military and civilian diversions each year, sometimes with aircraft en route for Paris and other Western European military destinations. Its busiest diversion period came in 1959, when severe weather forced many aircraft to fly to Prestwick; one day, 88 aircraft used the airfield, and on other days between 16 and 59 aircraft would touch down. Many of these were USAF flights headed to other destinations. According to Peter Berry, a former Prestwick air traffic controller, the relieved air crews all had a similar thought as they landed: 'Prestwick – safe at last!'[527]

Fighter aircraft had limited fuel capacity and on flying eastwards from the US would refuel in Iceland before attempting the leg to Prestwick. Additional fuel would be loaded to cover the final leg to France and West Germany. The aircrew would stay overnight at Prestwick.

Many of these transiting aircraft would require mechanical attention, so the Northrup Aircraft Maintenance facility was established. This was also used to carry out regular servicing of American and NATO aircraft from other European bases.[528]

The USAF also used Prestwick for its weather survey operations. These were crucial for the ferrying missions of fighter aircraft bound for Europe. Boeing WB-50D aircraft were regular visitors, along with the Boeing Superfortress KB-50J tankers which carried out the essential aerial refuelling of these single-engine aircraft. Prestwick's location, close to the Great Circle, hence the shortest, air route from central Europe across Iceland to North America, meant that it became a preferred refuelling stop. Aircraft such as Lockheed EC-121H Constellations, part of the Airborne Early Warning system, were often sighted on the tarmac. Prestwick was an essential element on the transatlantic route.[529]

Prestwick also became involved in the United States DEW System. There were zones which produced gaps in coverage and in 1963, the US Naval Research Laboratory was tasked with producing a 'radar system ... for the primary purpose of surveillance and tracking of aircraft within the USSR and the secondary purpose of detection of missile ... launchings'. This was the Madre system, an OTH (over-the-horizon) solution. Two proposed sites were investigated – Prestwick, and Elâzığ in Turkey – and it was the Turkish location which was eventually selected.[530]

Prestwick's main strategic importance was as a transit point for Holy Loch personnel. Although many other American servicemen and servicewomen came through the airport, it played a key role in the turnaround of submarine squadron personnel from Holy Loch. SubRon-14 and its associated units were only two hours by road and ferry from the airport, and because of its good-weather capability it was used in preference to the nearer Glasgow Renfrew Airport.[531]

The main troop lift task at Prestwick was the movement of submarine crews to and from Scotland and the United States. By the end of the Cold War, more than 40,000 Holy Loch personnel had flown through Prestwick.

One of these was Mike Giambattista and his first duty flight in 1961 was unforgettable. He boarded a USAF C-137 Stratoliner at Quonset Point, Rhode Island for the journey. The aircraft was a basic-level military Boeing 707 with minimal interior comforts. Mike, a submariner, was familiar with the endless routine of crew tests aboard operational submarines, but it had never occurred to him that the Air Force also operated in this fashion: 'Unable to sleep, I stumbled to the cockpit. Inside, the entire crew of five wore training hoods. They were receiving commands from another officer, who did not wear a hood. This was a readiness inspection, checking out the crew's ability for "blind flying" – using only instruments when an aircraft cannot see through clouds or mists. Excitement for me, but no problem for the crew.'

The military transport flights to Prestwick were long and boring. Gary Flynn was one of the travellers on their way to Holy Loch: 'No one flew commercial at that time, February 1966. I arrived on a Navy MATS flight, along with a submarine crew. Our flight had originated at McGuire Air Force Base, New Jersey. The small Prestwick terminal was clean, warm and welcoming.'

Mike Lacey, another submariner, recalled his military journeys to Scotland: 'It was quite a trek, involving ferries and buses as well as aircraft,. I don't remember any panics at the airport, but I'm sure there were some – with 140 submariners, there are always some.'

Prestwick's accessibility was also demonstrated by its use during Operation New Tape, in response to the Congo Crisis. Between 1960 and 1964, American military flights came through regularly, carrying UN troops, food and materiel, as well as evacuating refugees.[532]

Many Scottish civilians worked for the American units at Prestwick. Neil Gow and his father both worked at the airfield for more than 40 years. Their employer was NWA (Northwest Airlines), the official US forces carrier. They had a ringside view of the American operation, and Gow recalled: 'We used to load and unload the aircraft. The passengers were mostly from the base at Dunoon. We also attended the USAF open days, as well as working at Adamton House, the U.S. Air Force headquarters.'

Special missions

Prestwick was not just a transport hub. The airfield was also important to the United States because of its ability to support special air missions. These National Reconnaissance Office (NRO) flights were undertaken in the UK by aircraft from the 1st Weather Reconnaissance Squadron (Provisional) passing through Prestwick.[533]

By 1967 the CIA were desperate to crack the mystery of the Soviet missile sites located at Tallinn in Estonia. They needed to know if these missiles could hit targets in Western Europe. Photographs were required; the U-2 spy plane had been specifically developed for this type of operation.[534] But there were unavoidable operational difficulties associated with this aircraft.

Flight distances were long, so in-flight refuelling was necessary. But there were problems: as spy flights lasted for more than ten hours their pilots would be tired, and the refuelling procedure meant that the tanker aircraft, Boeing KC-97 Stratotankers or Boeing KC-135 Stratotankers, needed to reduce speed as the spy plane, approaching from the rear, would enter the tanker's engine turbulence zone, a delicate manoeuvre, especially as the U-2's wings were frail. Two planes had already suffered from this problem; their wings had broken off and they had crashed.

Nevertheless, the U-2 continued to be refuelled inflight, as this extended its range from approximately 4,000 to 8,000 nautical miles (7,400 to 15,000 km) and extended its endurance to more than 14 hours. An additional oxygen cylinder was also carried to combat the problem of pilot fatigue. It also meant that alternate refuelling airfields were critically important.[535]

So Prestwick was designated as an emergency refuelling point. A KC-135 refuelling aircraft from 903 Air Force Refueling Squadron was pre-positioned at Prestwick. The alternate refuelling bases for U-2 flights were at Goose Bay in Labrador, and Keflavik. The refuelling would be carried out by airborne delivery from this tanker aircraft or on the ground, if necessary.

One of these missions was memorable.

On one U-2 mission to Tallinn, the return in-flight refuelling had been scheduled to take place above Prestwick, and the CIA weather experts had provided a positive weather forecast. The Prestwick cloud ceiling was good – it was expected to exceed 1,000 feet – and the visibility was at least 2½ miles. Since any storm tracks generally bypassed this area, this meant that other clouds would not normally penetrate the aerial refuelling altitudes.

In the event of aircraft malfunction, the U-2's pilot had instructions to land at Prestwick. A cover story had been devised for the flight: he was to describe himself as a Lockheed civilian test pilot on a test flight of the aircraft's inertial navigation system. The aircraft was fitted with the equipment required to support this story. A map-destruct mechanism was fitted in the aircraft, to be activated if necessary, and there were dummy maps showing a fictional transpolar flight route. The pilot had filed no flight plan and the aircraft carried no markings.

Many valuable photographs had been captured, and 'the signals emitted by the Tallinn radar' were intercepted by equipment on board the aircraft. On the return flight to Loring AFB in Maine, more fuel was needed, so the airborne refuelling took place, as planned, above Prestwick. The pre-positioned recovery team then packed its equipment and moved out.

The mission was a great success. The CIA were able to identify the purpose of the Tallinn installation: it contained defensive missiles which could shoot down American nuclear bombers from long range.

This was not the first time that Prestwick had been involved in spying missions …

On 29 September 1952, a USAF spy flight, code-named 52-8, sprung a fuel leak. This became critical and as the aircraft proceeded offshore along the west coast of Norway, the pilot contemplated setting course for Prestwick or Sola. He could not make it back to base in Germany. He could not ditch. A decision was needed to save lives and protect the mission.[536]

His radio operator obtained a forecast at Prestwick as a 2,000 feet ceiling. This was hopeful, and the aircraft peeled off towards the airfield. But as it turned out the approach to Prestwick was hazardous; persistent low cloud was a major problem, and the pilot could barely see the runway. His fuel supply had, however, dried up, so there was no time for other actions. He had to trust his skill. He succeeded and landed at Prestwick, to refuel safely.

'That Others May Live'

The Atlantic Ocean was wide, and dangerous for those who crossed it, whether in the air, on its surface or beneath the waves.

The USAF Air Rescue Service (ARS) provided a search and rescue coverage for military and civilian incidents. The ARS reorganisation in 1952 resulted in Prestwick hosting the largest squadron in the service, with a total of more than 30 aircraft and 400 personnel.[537]

This unit provided coverage halfway to Iceland in the north of its zone, and halfway to the Azores in the south, as well as across all of the European NATO countries. Search and rescue assistance was not exclusively for military purposes; it was applied equally to any entity requiring this service, and 67 Squadron worked alongside RAF Coastal Command.[49]

The squadron's mission was twofold: first, to support and rescue aircraft involved in high-altitude reconnaissance operations, and second, to support Operation Duck Butt – an airborne navigation relay system for use by American aircraft en route from mainland USA to Europe and the Middle East. Routine search and rescue services were also provided to all aircraft in its region.

Bob Broff, a former 67 Squadron radio operator, explained these roles: 'Although we were based at Prestwick, 67 Squadron could be called out to rescue tasks far away from Scotland. We were part of a worldwide rescue service for military and civilian incidents.'

He remembered the regular flights when 67 Squadron acted as navigation beacons as part of Operation Duck Butt: 'As the NATO mission updated, the older USAF fighter aircraft (F-84 and F-86) were replaced by the F-100. These single-seat aircraft were provided with navigational aids by ARS aircraft, which were staged along their chosen route. The squadron flew this mission in our zone of the Atlantic.'

At Prestwick, each SAR aircraft had six trained crews operating on a rotational 24-hour alert watch. The alert crew wore flight suits carrying express privilege badges for the dining hall, snack bar and movie theatre. Alert status was maintained on a 24/7 basis, and in the event of an operational scramble the standby crew would automatically take over as the next alert crew.[538]

---

49 RAF Coastal Command was commanded by a three-star RAF officer – that is, an air marshal.

SAR crews had to be trained in low-level extraction (LLE) techniques for its task of behind-enemy-lines recovery in the event of a crashed reconnaissance aircraft. This mission was performed by flying low enough to remain undetected by land-based radar, penetrating for up to 200 nautical miles behind enemy lines and returning safely with all members of their downed aircraft. The techniques were practised by all SA-16 Albatross seaplane crews on a monthly proficiency basis, using Northern Ireland and the Scottish Highlands.

This activity was recalled by Bob Broff: 'Part of the monthly training for the SA-16 Albatross crews was a flight to Lough Neagh in Northern Ireland. Pilots honed their skills by taking off and landing in the fresh waters of this large lake. Additional training activities such as hooking up to a buoy and picking up survivors in a dinghy were also performed. The local RAF base provided a ramp to taxi up from the lough, and hot meals provided the crews with the taste of British hospitality.'

Broff remembered the excitement of this training: 'Launched from Prestwick, crews flew up to the Highlands of Scotland – the mission planning required avoidance of populated places to avoid detection – and descended to follow the terrain. During one such flight, a farmer on an extension ladder fixing the roof of his barn looked down in amazement at a passing SA-16 Albatross. We practised this in Norway as well.'

The squadron had a wide area to cover, and training was often carried out far from Prestwick. On one occasion, an SA-16 Albatross was training near Stavanger in Norway when an emergency arose. Bob Broff recalled the affair: 'There was a fluke in a returning satellite. It had been launched from Vandenberg AFB in California, and was to return from orbit for a splashdown in the Pacific Ocean. But a malfunction in the thrusters had caused the capsule to crash land in the Norwegian-controlled island of Spitzbergen.' Recovery of the capsule was now imperative and a rescue operation was mounted.

'The mission required special diplomatic clearance, and it would require more men and equipment than the Albatross could carry. A SAM [Special Air Mission] C-130 turboprop was dispatched from Germany and joined the SAR crew awaiting at Bodø, Norway. Diplomatic approval was granted by the Norwegian Government for one aircraft to land and take off at Spitzbergen. The SAM aircraft and crew landed and launched their snowmobiles for the recovery of the capsule. But it was reported that the capsule had been seized by the crew of a Soviet spy trawler which was now at sea. The SAM recovery team returned empty-handed.'

The rescue missions for 67 Squadron were varied. In early 1959 when the klaxon sounded the alert crew were scrambled to intercept a U.S. Navy freighter, USNS *General Maurice Rose*, in the North Atlantic. A medical evacuation had been requested. The patient, an US Army enlisted man, had undergone ruptured appendix emergency surgery. Unfortunately, pneumonia had set in and the ship's surgeon wanted him to be taken ashore as soon as possible. Weather conditions were poor.

Turbulent weather was nothing new for the *Rose*. 'It was known for rough crossings of the North Atlantic,' remembered Sergeant 1st Class Cyrille G. Desrosiers, who had travelled aboard the ship as a passenger to and from military duty in Europe.[539]

The casualty had to be collected and transferred to hospital for intensive care. The collection was a tricky matter, as the ASR (air-sea rescue) aircraft would have to make an open-sea landing, then operate a ship-to-aircraft transfer – a well-practised, but difficult technique.

Bob Broff was the radio operator: 'Immediately after take-off, I made contact with Prestwick Oceanic to obtain the ship's position, heading and speed. This information was necessary for the navigator to plot an intercept point. I made several attempts to contact the *Rose* using Morse code. Once contact was established and good lines of communication obtained, information was passed between the *Rose* and our rescue aircraft.' It had taken nearly three hours' flight time before the ship was sighted.

'The North Atlantic is not the most friendly environment for an open sea landing. However, that day King Neptune smiled and was kind to all concerned. The landing was textbook, as Captain Dibert was one of the best of the best. While the flight engineer prepared the hatch, the PJ[50] launched his rubber dinghy with the lanyard attached.'

'Meanwhile, the patient was loaded onto the pilot boat of the *Rose*. When in range, I fired the Lyle gun, shooting another lanyard to the pilot boat. This allowed the pilot boat crew to pull our rubber dinghy to them and make the transfer of the patient to the PJ. The dinghy was then pulled back to the seaplane safely. This manoeuvre keeps the boat, raft and aircraft free of collision.'

The patient was brought aboard the Albatross and made safe. The engineer secured the hatches and the aircraft prepared for take-off. But … 'Now, King Neptune started to stir up his domain. Because of the waves, we were unable to attain sufficient speed for lift off.'

However, the many training sessions had covered eventualities such as this. Bob Broff carried out the first stage in this process: 'We requested the *Rose* to clear her decks [prepare for action].' The USNS *General Maurice Rose* was then pushed to maximum speed. Meanwhile on the Albatross four JATO bottles,[51] to assist take-off, were loaded onto their racks on the outside of the fuselage.

'With the seas now less threatening, flattened by the passage of the *Rose*, Captain Dibert pushed the throttles forward. When the amphibian was at near lift-off the four JATO bottles were ignited and the Albatross climbed swiftly, clearing the deck of the *Rose*.

'Prestwick Oceanic Radio requested to know if we had sufficient fuel for a landing at Dublin, Ireland, rather than Belfast. It was confirmed that we could make Dublin, and the course was set. Within a few hours we made our landing there. The patient was transferred to an awaiting ambulance and then to the hospital for Intensive Care. Mission accomplished, and praise given by the American Embassy for our expert rescue. We took off from Dublin with swollen hearts. We had lived up to our motto – "These things I do that others may live".'

At the time of this rescue, the weather had already claimed a victim, noted E-6 Ralph Baker, who had been a military passenger aboard the *Rose*: ' Four days out of Bremerhaven we hit some really icy, stormy weather. None of the troops were permitted above deck for two days. It was really rough. A Russian trawler struck an iceberg and was sinking north of us. We were about to divert to the SOS when another ship reported being closer than we were, and they had diverted to the aid of the sinking ship. I had pretty well settled down from anxiety and fear before all this happened, then for the next several hours it was stressful.'

Some ARS rescue missions involved rock climbing, and joint training was held with mountain rescue teams. Hamilton Anderson, a member of the RAF Mountain Rescue Service,

---

50 The PJ crew member was a parachute-trained, first responder medical specialist.

51 JATO – jet-assisted take-off – was a way of helping overloaded aircraft into the air by providing additional thrust in the form of small rockets.

recalled one of these trips: 'We flew to Iceland with 67 ARRS for snow and ice training. We also went to the top of the glacier and back in record time.' [540]

The Air Rescue Service was tasked with the search for and recovery of space hardware and the support of all manned space missions beginning in 1961. In view of its expanding role in space flight support, the Air Rescue Service was re-designated the Aerospace Rescue and Recovery Service (ARRS) on 8 January 1966. [541]

The ARRS was also deeply involved in the NASA space programme. SAR crew members provided capsule and crew recovery during the Mercury, Gemini and Apollo programmes, as these missions used the ocean as a landing platform. The coverage continued into the age of the Shuttle.

USAF operated a safety training programme for the air crews and the astronauts. This programme was delivered at Pensacola, Florida. Bob Broff recalled this activity: 'The air crews worked with the astronauts on this aspect of the space mission. The USAF, U.S. Navy and USCG were part of this rescue force. Para jumpers would jump into the ocean close to the downed capsule to commence the rescue process. They would place the flotation collar around the space capsule and await the arrival of the heavy-lift helicopter. When this was overhead, they would connect the capsule to the lifting hook. 67 Squadron supported all of these flights, and an alert crew was ready for this activity. The squadron was also on alert for all U-2 flights.'

But the aircraft from 67 Squadron were not themselves immune to problems. In December 1953 a serious incident occurred at Prestwick. An SAR SB-29 Superfortress was on a training flight carrying an airborne lifeboat underneath its fuselage; the aircraft suffered a runaway propeller and had to divert to the airfield – but the main landing gear could not be lowered because of the lifeboat. The pilot managed a successful emergency landing. No fatalities were incurred, but the lifeboat was squashed. [542]

One notable rescue mission in this period involved the loss of a USAF DC-3 which was flying across Spain. It crashed into the sea with the loss of all lives aboard. One of the passengers was a USAF general who had been carrying top secret documents. Russian spy trawlers operated off the coast of Spain and were heading towards the crash site. Bob Broff remembered the excitement: 'These vessels carried Russian navy divers and would have attempted to reach the wrecked aircraft on the seabed. 67 Squadron was scrambled along with other rescue elements and all headed for the scene. Para jumpers and dinghies were dropped to secure the area. U.S. Navy divers arrived and recovered the briefcase containing the vital documents.' [543]

The bodies were also brought to the surface.

Summary

Prestwick had continued its association with United States military activities during the Cold War. All of its involvement was successful, whether in routine matters or in emergencies. Its competence was always a safe bet for Pentagon planners.

11 ~~Machrihanish~~

– A very long runway, minemen and SEALs

At the western edge of the Mull of Kintyre, Machrihanish is mainland Scotland's closest point to the United States.

The airfield is remote and was originally only used by a tiny number of planes. This changed significantly during the Second World War, and the airfield expanded rapidly. Renamed HMS *Landrail*, it was one of the three busiest airfields in wartime Britain, providing air cover for the Atlantic convoys. After the war the airfield became redundant, but during the Korean War it was reactivated for pilot training.

As Cold War tensions increased during the 1950s, Machrihanish was needed again. In April 1959 it was announced that the airfield would be upgraded to support US and NATO operations in the Clyde area and the wider Atlantic. Its location was strategically important, providing aircraft immediate access to the North Atlantic to support naval operations. It was also valuable as a stopping point for transatlantic military flights.

Secrecy followed this decision and public use maps were censored to show the runway in its old form. The airfield underwent major reconstruction for NATO purposes in 1960–62. Additional land was purchased. The bulldozers moved in, and the four existing runways were converted to a single new runway to allow large aircraft to use the upgraded airfield. The runway was now 10,000 feet – the longest in Western Europe. The base was renamed RAF Machrihanish, and its main role was stated as an American reinforcement airfield for large aircraft and spy flights.[544]

Machrihanish could service large numbers of reinforcement aircraft en route to Western Europe. Its long runway was specifically constructed for this task and the first planes were spine-chilling. They were the huge Vulcan bombers of the RAF's nuclear strike force. Their job was to fly to Russia, armed with the UK's nuclear bomb, and create chaos.

Tom Hillman was an RAF NCO who held a high-level security clearance. He had a front-row seat as these menacing aircraft used the airfield: 'Aircraft like the Canberra nuclear bombers used Machrihanish for training. We always had a nagging doubt that it might not be just a training exercise.'

NATO-related development continued and Machrihanish was designated a Master Diversion Airfield. In 1968, the U.S. Navy established the Naval Aviation Weapons Facility on the site, designed and built to hold nuclear weapons. Machrihanish was not an operational station and no flying squadrons were based there. However, it came under the command of NATO's SACEUR, to be used as a forward operating base. The airfield's refuelling capability enabled American nuclear bombers to refuel there, and this made it a probable Russian target.[545]

As far as the locals were concerned, however, the construction of the longest runway in Western Europe merely signified more employment and economic benefit.[546]

Development – here come the Yanks

As the runway improvements took place, the Americans increased their presence on the base. First of all, in 1964 a NATO fuel depot was constructed at Campbeltown, four miles from the airfield. The OFD (oil and fuel depot) served a dual function: it stored diesel for the Royal Navy and NATO vessels, as well as aviation fuel; RAF Machrihanish was one of its clients.[547]

The OFD facility was regularly used by U.S. Navy ships. In 1970 Howard Tillison was a midshipman aboard USS *Marias* (AO-57), a fleet oiler, and recalled his visit: 'We went into Campbeltown, Scotland, a NATO fuel depot, several times to take on fuel oil, aviation gasoline and JP-5 [jet fuel] to transfer to the other ships in our hunter-killer ASW group.'

Machrihanish had two factors that made it an important base for the United States military. It was remote, so military activity was screened by the long distance (140 miles) to the heavily populated Glasgow region. It was also, literally, on the edge of the Atlantic, the hotspot for U.S. Navy activity. The ASW aircraft and weaponry could be located at the base.

The first U.S. Navy unit to arrive was the Mobile Mine Assembly Group 2 (MOMAG 2) from RAF Mildenhall in Suffolk, in 1967. By March 1968 another U.S. Navy unit had moved to Machrihanish. This was the Naval Aviation Warfare Facility (NAWF) Machrihanish. They were an explosives ordnance disposal (EOD) detachment, part of the Atlantic Fleet. As a Navy bomb disposal squad, their task was to render safe all types of ordnance, including improvised, chemical, biological and nuclear devices. Life was becoming interesting in Kintyre.

As usual, a cover story was released about them. Their role was described in a gentle, harmless-sounding manner: they were to receive, store, maintain, issue and tranship classified weapons in support of the U.S. Navy and NATO operations.[548] This was military doublespeak. The classified weapons were in fact nuclear torpedoes, so sleepy, remote Campbeltown was now in double jeopardy – it was a Russian target and could self-inflict an on-base accident … Ground Zero Kintyre.

In 1968 the airfield was redeveloped and the naval aviation weapons facility compound was constructed. This was more than 160 yards long and had three rows of flat-roofed concrete sheds for ammunition storage. The sheds were subdivided into compartments with airtight doors, designed for the storage of naval nuclear weapons such as depth charges and munitions for use in ASW. The compound also stored U.S. Navy sea mines. These munitions came under the control of Momag 2.

The airfield's role was now stated to be an American reinforcement airfield for large aircraft and spy flights.[549]

Finally, in 1974 a United States Marine Corps detachment came to Machrihanish, to provide nuclear weapons security. Prior to this, security had been provided by U.S. Navy personnel, but the USMC moved in, to protect what was now a doomsday arsenal. But the locals knew nothing about the nuclear weapons on their doorstep – they worked daily on the base, in blissful ignorance of its devastating capabilities.

Machrihanish activities

From 1957 the United States had implemented a policy regarding the storage of nuclear munitions in other NATO countries. The United States military were responsible for providing appropriate personnel for the technical custody and surveillance of these weapons. The host nation, in this case the UK, had to provide the physical facilities and guarantee the external security of these storage sites. In addition, the host nation was responsible for providing housing and administrative facilities. This arrangement explains the dual responsibility for nuclear munitions security at Machrihanish.[550]

Ken Black was part of the back-up team for added security, and was aware of the P-3 Orion aircraft and their armaments. He had observed the loading and unloading of the immensely destructive nuclear depth charges and recalled that the 'items' were moved around from Machrihanish for regular maintenance and inspection. He would patrol their storage area with a loaded weapon: 'I saw the Orions sometimes, and also some transport aircraft which were used to move the items elsewhere.' [551]

RAF corporal Tom Hillman was also well informed about the P-3 Orions and their ASW mission: 'I was aware of P-3s etc … I remember I had to draft air movement instructions. All aircraft movements required this paperwork – routine or special, made no difference.' Hillman noted that the majority of personnel on the base were Americans: 'There were only 140 UK service personnel on camp; the other 200 plus were Yanks.' [552]

Derek Gillies also recalled the P-3 Orions: 'I knew about ASW. We had P-3 Orions from the States, and also Dutch and German planes. Depending on what they carried we occasionally had USMC guarding them, with us providing mobile patrols around the area. The anomaly was that the Dutch had trade union reps. If it was too cold or wet, the Dutch airmen and airwomen would leave us to guard their aircraft, as their union reps wouldn't let them. So it was okay for *us* to get cold and wet through!'

He also recalled its nuclear storage facilities: 'As far as I'm aware Mach was the fallback for USN and USMC at RAF St Mawgan. We had a secure storage area that in the past had been used for nukes, and RAF Police recruits came up and spent three weeks practising nuclear security training and hill walking and teamwork exercises.'

A former RAF munitions officer, Peter Mason, had the job of checking the ammunition bunkers at RAF Machrihanish, and confirmed that there was definite evidence of the presence of nuclear munitions during this time. Investigative journalist Duncan Campbell is certain that nuclear munitions were stored there, as Machrihanish was listed in 1984 as one of five UK locations which stored American nuclear weapons. He claimed that the base was a repository for nuclear depth bombs to be used by British, Canadian, Dutch and American ASW aircraft operating in the North Sea and North Atlantic. In fact, Machrihanish stored B57 nuclear depth bombs – slim 15-inch-diameter cylinders designed to be used against submarines, and set to explode above, on or below the surface.[553]

The SEALs of Argyll

By 1981 the quiet atmosphere of the base had changed dramatically. A special breed of warrior had come to Machrihanish. American Special Forces arrived, and the base now had a front-line unit. Where SEALs went, danger followed.

The U.S. Navy SEALs had a fearsome reputation. Their selection process was extreme. Only the most determined sailors made it to the end. They were the U.S. Navy's crack special forces and they were given the toughest tasks. Their name terrified the enemy.

Direct descendants of the wartime frogmen, SEALs destroyed enemy shipping, wrecked port and harbour facilities, and blew up bridges, railway lines and communications centres. They went to war by parachute, submarine, naval ship or land vehicle, and operated close to enemy lines. They were a world-class fighting unit which trained seriously, and Kintyre was an ideal location for them. They came to Machrihanish for a specific reason. They needed to train constantly to be ready for immediate deployment. The west coast of Scotland provided an ideal training environment and there were few locals to observe their activities.

Jim Madison was part of a 16-man SEAL platoon that lifted off from Naval Air Station (NAS) Norfolk, Virginia, one night in October 1981: 'Our ultimate destination was RAF Base Machrihanish to start a six-month deployment in the European theatre. We deployed as part of NSWU-2[52] RAF Machrihanish.' This was an unaccompanied tour.[554]

Nothing was too difficult for the SEALs. They could have flown into Machrihanish. Instead, they arrived by parachute. Their first jump into Scotland was a static-line equipment jump, landing on a drop zone just north of the runway. They moved to the base to meet up with the aircraft to unload their operational and personal kit which had been stowed in storage boxes and on pallets. This was unloaded and stored in the platoon spaces located in the airops building: 'Once our op gear was secured, we moved to the HQ building, where we assembled in the Operations Department briefing room. There the commanding officer briefed us about the unit's mission and what was expected of us.'

Most of the SEAL teams started their deployment in Scotland by parachute. In later years, others would make a 'rubber duck' water descent; a large rubber dinghy (CRRC)[53] was secured

---

52 NSWU 2: Navy Special Warfare Unit 2.
53 Combat rubber raiding craft, with a capacity for ten passengers.

to a wooden platform with a cargo parachute strapped over the entire load. It was deployed off the ramp of a C-130 aircraft and followed by static-line parachute jumpers who would then climb aboard the dinghy when it hit the water.

The SEALs operated from the Gaydon hangar at the top of the airfield. This building was a fully equipped mini-base, including internal crane attachment points to lift small boats. When vehicles were unloaded from incoming transport aircraft, they went directly into a large hall alongside the building. These specialised premises were described by Jim Madison: 'Our compound included an internal 25-yard indoor firing range, parachute training equipment and drying towers for the parachutes.'[555] SEALs worked hard and played hard. Machrihanish had entered a new era.

The handover phase between SEAL teams was important. The resident SEAL team knew about the task. The incomers did not. Rapid transfer of knowledge was vital. For the next few days, the newcomers would muster for briefings, equipment exchange and other tasks. Once the resident platoon had departed, the new platoon began their intensive training.

The serious work got under way with Exercise Sgian-dubh.[54] This was the incomers' welcome to Scotland, with its rugged terrain and severe weather. Scottish mountains are tough, wet, windy and steep. As SEALs needed to hit the ground running in wartime, hard peacetime training helped to produce similar stress. After receiving the warning order, the SEALs would set out to plan for the exercise. This consisted of a maritime insertion by small surface craft, overland movement through the rugged Scottish countryside, observation, and HF radio communications from the field to NSWU-2 headquarters. Jim Madison recalled its effect: 'This initial field exercise always met its primary objective of SEAL operators becoming acclimatised to operating in Scotland.'

Special Forces treated all training as war, and they practised scenarios in a realistic manner. The only difference was that the exercise 'enemy' personnel were not killed. They were merely roughly treated, tied up and exposed to severe weather conditions.[556]

Unlike the huge training reservations in the United States, Scottish training areas were open countryside. Therefore, live firing could only be done within specially marked military firing ranges, a change of culture for the Americans.

Some elements of SEAL training were fascinating and the two-man canoe training was especially rigorous. This involved the Klepper folding kayak. It was collapsible and portable, and new to the SEALs. The learning process was robust and frightening. Campbeltown Loch is a sea loch four miles east of Machrihanish and it became memorable for the SEALs, as Jim Madison remembered: 'They taught us how to put the kayaks together on the shores of Campbeltown Loch. We then attempted to paddle out into the loch, regularly with horizontal sleet blowing in our faces. The waves were high and many of us were not successful. Thankfully, we were wearing our wetsuits during our maiden attempt. After a couple of hours, though, most of us managed to stay afloat despite the horrendous weather conditions.' The techniques for operating the Klepper canoe were new, but before the three-week block of training was over all the SEALs would master it.

Most of the Klepper training sessions consisted of overland movement with the pieces of the kayak carried in backpacks. The SEALs would move to a small loch north of Campbeltown, where

---

54 Sgian dubh: Gaelic for black knife; pronounced ski-an *doo*.

they would assemble the kayaks and paddle from one end of the loch to the other. They would then break down their kayaks, strap them to their backpacks and patrol to the next loch, as Madison recounted: 'We repeated the procedures until we had travelled overland and paddled through five separate lochs. This was a cross-country trek, with heavy backpacks, of about 10 miles.'

This was the easy phase. Machrihanish Bay sits on the Atlantic Ocean, where mighty waves roll in from 3,000 miles away. It is the finest surfing beach in Britain. Heaven for surfers, but hell for SEALs. The next phase included a canoe transit around the Mull of Kintyre. In those days, there was little health and safety cover for this 30-mile sea journey on the Atlantic Ocean. Launching at Machrihanish Beach, they would conduct a surf passage in the Kleppers.

On the beach they learned how to effectively cache and camouflage the kayaks. During the third week of the course, there was a tough 30-mile kayak transit. The entire exercise was scheduled to take between six to twelve hours, depending on the sea state. A support team travelled in the CRRC – the only safety boat. Madison retraced this route: 'We put in north of Machrihanish Beach on the west coast of the Mull of Kintyre. From Machrihanish Beach we'd continue around the south end of the mull then travel east and then north to complete the journey in Campbeltown Harbour.'

The SEALs would often hit heavy, dangerous seas around the Mull. Madison recalled this test: 'We started out in the early morning and headed south towards the Mull. The seas would begin to brew, with winds often exceeding 35 knots. Huge gusts would almost flip the safety boat over. The Kleppers would head for the beach and attempt to come ashore. It was a struggle to get everyone ashore safely as we fought to get the kayaks through the surf zone and onto the beach. Kayaks would capsize and the occupants would battle to drag their kayak through the surf. Kayaks would be wrecked, but the SEALs always came ashore in one piece.'

This local area training prepared the SEALs for the tougher conditions further north. The Highlands have 4,000-feet mountains, with steep sides and harsh terrain. A four-man reconnaissance team would be inserted into the area by helicopter for a four-day exercise. The mission was to observe the only road running through the mountains and then carry out an untried extraction technique.

A fully inflated CRRC would be placed on a wooden platform. As it was too big to fit into the extraction helicopter, it would be deflated slightly. The purpose of the exercise was to prove the concept that a CRRC could be launched from a helicopter. So, the dinghy was pushed through the helicopter doors and hit the water with an almighty splash, Jim Madison watched anxiously and wondered if its engine had been damaged. The extraction crew were two SEALs who had jumped into the water from the hovering helicopter. They surfaced 10 feet behind the boat, climbed in and checked that everything worked: 'Huge relief at our end. Whoops of delight all round. They made their way to our location and collected us. That was the first ever successful deployment of the technique now called the Soft Duck.'[557]

Training continued, and the SEALs moved in their small boats to an area of open water. They now began a bizarre, but exciting, new activity. While on station, a specially modified C-130 flew over and parachuted a package into the water near them. The SEALs recovered it and began to assemble its contents: a small inflatable boat, a balloon hooked to a tether line, and a bottle of helium gas to inflate the balloon.

The commanding officer and another SEAL, dressed in special harness suits, scrambled into the boat. They attached themselves to the line then inflated the balloon, which rose to approximately 500 feet. The line had red flags to guide the aircraft. The scene was set.

The show got under way and Madison watched anxiously: 'Everyone waited with bated breath as the C-130, equipped with what looked like a pair of scissors mounted on its nose, made its approach. The scissors released the balloon and at the same time enveloped the line, and the two men were up and away. We could see the two men as specks at the end of the line as they were being hoisted toward the tail end of the aircraft. They were eventually recovered through the open ramp of the C-130.'

This extraordinary adventure replicated an amazing stunt featured in the James Bond film *Thunderball*, when 007 was whisked from the water by a low-flying aircraft. This apparatus was called the Fulton Recovery System.[558]

But life at Machrihanish was not all excitement. There were also mundane matters, such as getting around the airfield safely. Madison found out that to get from the south side to the north side of the base, he had to cross the runway: 'This was always an anxious time. There were traffic lights at both ends of the runway. If the lights were red, it meant that an aircraft was getting ready to land or take off. But most of the time the lights remained green because there was minimal aircraft traffic.'

The SEALs were prominent because of their physical activities. Sean Boland recalled: 'Most of their morning workout had already begun a couple of hours before their weight-training workout and a full kit run on the beach. This was their daily routine; the weights were leisure!'[559]

SEAL training was spectacular – parachuting, James Bond stunts, sea canoeing and kayaking on local lochs. It was tough, it was frightening, and as lots of it was done in daylight their concealment skills were clearly splendid, as there is little local memory about these hair-raising activities. The SEAL teams remained invisible.

Minemen, bunkers and bumpy roads

The U.S. Navy deployed sea mines to form a floating obstacle to Russian ships. The deadly mines were stored at RAF Machrihanish and at the NATO Armaments Depot (NAD) in Glen Douglas.

These locations were important, as they provided secure safe storage and immediate deployment of assets to operational U.S. Navy units. Remoteness from centres of population was an additional advantage, and local knowledge about both sites remained vague.

Built between 1962 and 1966, NAD Glen Douglas was the largest weapons storage base in Western Europe. More than 40,000 tons of missiles, depth charges, conventional shells, grenades and rifle rounds were stored there. A jetty was built nearby, on the edge of Loch Long, and connected to the depot by a military road. It also had its own railway line.[560]

Construction had been halted due to a stand-off between two UK government departments over a flock of sheep owned by the Duke of Montrose. One department owned the site and the other was responsible for the sheep. Work stopped and tempers rose. The bureaucratic war over sheep was eventually resolved by a brisk message from the Admiralty: 'The Admiralty have been running a sheep flock for eighteen months… our job is to run ships, not sheep!'[561]

Before Glen Douglas was completed, U.S. Navy London had faced a serious safety matter which needed to be resolved quickly. The naval mine dump at RAF Mildenhall, in Essex, was in a dangerous condition as safety rules had been ignored, and the local population were at risk.

LTJG Toby Horn was a member of MOMAG 0321 Bravo detachment at RAF Mildenhall. He was summoned to London and ushered into a briefing room. Two senior officers were inside and technical drawings for Construction Site Arrochar Scotland were scattered on a table. The briefing was short, and Horn's task was straightforward. Study the drawings, take the night sleeper train to Glasgow and make his way to Glen Douglas. Inspect the site and make a decision – was Glen Douglas suitable as a replacement for the inadequate storage site at Mildenhall?'[562]

Toby Horn had noted this poor standard of safety at Mildenhall. It was one of the several times in his career that he had seen blatant disregard for the rules, but – as with the other times – there was no alternative. This would now change.

Horn made his way 450 miles north and arrived at Helensburgh railway station. From there, a naval staff car took him over the nearby hills to Glen Douglas. It was an interesting journey and left an indelible impression. He learned that Scottish roads were different, particularly in remote rural areas. As he left the main road, the car seemed to point its way skyward. The road seemed at times to be as steep as 45 degrees. Horn's first thought was of coming back down that drive with a truckload of explosives and no brakes. The road was just a single-track one, but when he recalled the journey he remembered that there had been occasional passing places cut out of the cliff face. His first trip was a little scary.

He carefully inspected the site. Although not completed, it was suitable, and he returned to London. Back in the briefing room it was crunch time. He gave his positive report on the Glen Douglas site. It had none of the limitations of Mildenhall. Mines could be delivered by sea to Glenmallan Pier, three miles away. The senior officers listened quietly without interruption. No technical questions were asked. The captain smiled broadly and stood up. He spoke directly to Horn: 'Thank you, Lieutenant. You have just saved the Navy's ass. You're in charge of this. Now get going.'

Glen Douglas was staffed by MOD civilian personnel. Horn spent the next few days examining the infrastructure at the base. He visited the navy dock, and the buildings and magazines in the compound. There were more than 50 magazines; they were huge, almost like aircraft hangars, and cut like caves into the hillside. Each was fed by a very narrow road which would make vehicle movement difficult.

Other mineman units then became involved in the project. Ron Swart's MOMAG detachment moved from Charleston, South Carolina, to Mildenhall in June 1967. Their task was to decommission the bomb dump and make the area safe. Swart, who was an MN3 at the time, was not surprised, as the safety measures at Mildenhall were so poor: 'The bomb dump was in the middle of a farm. It had enough explosives to rattle windows in London, about 80 miles away.' [563]

The mines move in

The mines reached Scotland by air, road and rail from Mildenhall, and by sea from the United States. Once in Scotland they had to be stored at both Machrihanish and Glen Douglas. The logistics were complicated and underfunded.[564]

When the move began in earnest, the minemen were using C-130s and local trains to move the material, along with flatbeds and other trucks borrowed from the USAF at Mildenhall. Their cooperation had been secured by drafting one of the minemen, Glenn Troutman, a star football player in high school, to play football for the Air Force on Sundays down in London.[565]

A return road trip of almost 1,000 miles was required to transport the mines from Mildenhall to Glen Douglas. Some of the mines then needed further transportation to Machrihanish. Horn remembered moving material by truck up to Machrihanish. On the first run, six minemen drove three 5-ton trucks. They had little idea of how to get to Machrihanish and slept in the trucks on the banks of Loch Lomond. The following day they reached Machrihanish around lunchtime.

When the first shipment of mines arrived by sea from the USA, the ship moored at Glenmallan Pier, which served Glen Douglas. The construction of the new magazines had been completed on time and the minemen were ready. Hold covers were taken off and pier cranes dipped down inside the ship's belly and pulled the mines out one by one. These were loaded on to the RNAD[55] lorries and trucked up the long steep road into the depot magazines. The work was done with ammunition trailers so wide that they could hardly fit onto the narrow roads. Apprehension was a major factor throughout the activity.

Mines destined for Machrihanish had to be trucked over 100 miles from Glen Douglas. There was only one road, and it was of simple construction. The problems for heavily laden military transport were obvious. The road was narrow with sharp turns, and crossed many small hump-backed bridges. Quaint, but hardly the ideal road to transport explosive-loaded mines. Not only that, but the road could be easily blocked by a fallen tree or a landslide.

The easiest way to transfer the mines from Mildenhall was by air, and eventually one C-130 aircraft was assigned for the task. Minemen loaded the aircraft and it flew to Machrihanish, taxied close to the mine store compound and unloaded the cargo with engines running. Twenty minutes later it took off, back to Mildenhall for the next load. These mines were then stored in the mine bunker. The biggest headache was the storage of the mines in the small magazines. Horn recalled that minemen had to put them in the doorway and then wedge them round the corners. They called this the 'jam stew' method, but it worked.

The rest of the move was an operation worthy of Sgt Bilko or McHale's Navy. Horn chuckled at the memory: 'There were two C-130s from Rota allocated to us for the transfer, but one was swiftly withdrawn from use, with several major flight maintenance issues. The second was kept flying by Lt Josh Cumshaw's inventive acquisition efforts, which included a "re-allocated" engine. All done by mineman ingenuity.'[566]

When the air cargo mines were unloaded at Machrihanish, they were divided into two consignments. One stayed at Machrihanish, and the other was moved to Glen Douglas along the many miles of tricky roads. George Bellairs, a regular military driver on this journey,

---

55 Royal Naval Armaments Depot

remembered one of the worst stretches: 'This was at the top of the Rest-and-be-Thankful Road, which connected Loch Fyne to Loch Long. It was always a busy road, even in those days, as it linked Glasgow to Oban. It was all along the side of a very steep mountain and was used for stock-car racing up the steep hill.' His description was hair-raising: 'The road was all twisted like a snake's body. Large vehicles had to creep along it and ignore the steep drop on one side. There were hairpin bends everywhere. They did a lot of reversing.' [567]

Lack of air transport meant that the remaining Mildenhall loads had to go by rail. Once again mineman ingenuity was applied. There were 60 more large mines of the Mk 52/55 models still to transfer, and Lt Cumshaw came to the rescue. He deployed USAF trucks to get the mines to the railhead without authorisation from USAF bureaucrats.

Once at their final storage location, the mines had to be serviced, inspected and maintained. This was the job of MOMAG 2. During maintenance, internal and external components were tested to make sure they worked. If something required painting or grease, it was painted or greased. A typical work week would entail bringing the mines that were due for maintenance to the maintenance building. They would be disassembled into their component parts, and tested, cleaned and replaced as necessary, then reassembled and returned to the bunker for storage. The total quantity of mines stocked at each facility, Machrihanish and Glen Douglas, were divided into maintenance lots.' [568]

Commander Swart's USN mining group was responsible for the Glen Douglas and Machrihanish units. He recalled the importance of maintenance: 'Just like the regular maintenance of a car, airplane, boat or house, all naval mines in storage were rotated through the mine maintenance facility on a cyclic schedule. This ensured their readiness for use at all times. It was the reason for having the minemen stationed in Scotland; their presence guaranteed that the mines were correctly assembled and ready for use if needed. The minemen would complete this maintenance using electrical and mechanical testing equipment. They would assemble the mines and make them ready to be placed in the water. The completed mines would then be delivered to minelaying aircraft, submarines or surface ships.'

There was always a quantity of mines prepared at any given time, ready for issuing in the event of hostilities. The Machrihanish mines were primarily designated for aircraft delivery, and those at Glen Douglas for submarine delivery. When mines were moved between Glen Douglas and Machrihanish, it was done by the MOD. However, no armed mines were moved from either site. They were armed only once aboard their deployment platforms – ships, submarines or aircraft.

Mine maintenance was dangerous work. One mistake could cause an explosion. Mines and their mooring cables were coated with dangerous substances and needed to be handled carefully. Work was hazardous, especially if the mineman wasn't properly covered by gloves and face protection. Many suffered from burns and then cancers later in life, due to their exposure to PCBs. Thomas W. McKenzie, a mineman, was part of the team which closed DET2 at Machrihanish in 1995: 'The 57s were coated in PCBs. We were told about it; warned of it constantly by the Quality Assessors, in fact.' [569]

Ron Swart recalled the working environment: 'Military service is often very hard and hazardous for those who serve. The combination of young sailors, heavy machinery and high explosives could be a toxic combination at any moment, and was always worrisome – and required a lot of safety training. I know of several cases of death through carelessness and shenanigans. One was a case of operating a vehicle in an unsafe manner and another death resulted from the unsafe operation of a forklift.'

Minemen suffered physical damage but continued to serve: 'There were quite a few missing fingers among the enlisted population due to detonators and mechanical equipment.'

CDR Swart highlighted the problems caused by the PCBs on the mine mooring cables: 'Potential exposure to the cable would have been during maintenance, but much greater if they were preparing an exercise/practice on moored mines that had been planted via submarine.' This type of activity was common at Glen Douglas.

MOMAG 2 handled most U.S. Navy mines, including the CAPTOR (encapsulated torpedo). This was the prime deep-water anti-submarine naval mine, and Ron Swart remembered working on these at Glen Douglas: 'We kept them configured for submarine launch. We also had all the other mines, both air- and submarine-delivered.' [570]

The CAPTOR storage facility was a tight fit, and care was needed. The building could accommodate four tractor-trailers (articulated lorries). Swart noted how this activity was carried out: 'These would drive into the magazine one at a time, complete a U-turn and back into their parking lanes. They would always be unloaded or loaded inside the magazine; weapons were never loaded onto trailers and stored in the open areas, even within the protective berms.[56] Safety was paramount. This was a different approach from the earlier days at Mildenhall.'

MOMAG required technical services, and these were provided from Site One at Holy Loch. The submarine tender provided calibration services and supplies for the unit. Twice weekly a technical team would drive from Machrihanish to Holy Loch, and a similar journey was made from Glen Douglas.

As the Cold War came to its end, a decision was taken to empty the bunkers at Glen Douglas. In 1993, USS *Nitro* deployed to the eastern Atlantic for ammunition rollbacks from Glen Douglas. Its mission was to carry ammunition and weapons such as Cruise missiles, bombs, artillery shells and small arms. The crew worked hard on these trips; for example, over 2,000 lifts of ammunition were onloaded from the bunkers in Glen Douglas in less than five days.[571]

USS *Nitro* returned to Scotland in March 1994 to finish the removal of the remaining ammunition from NAD Glen Douglas. Grant Hoefer was skipper of USS *Nitro* 1993–1995, and remembered these visits: 'I took the *Nitro* on two trips to empty the Glen Douglas bunkers. We bulk loaded two shiploads, loading outdated or ancient ammo out of Glen Douglas back to the US for disposal at an ammo depot.'

Frank Murray was transferred from USS *Simon Lake* at Holy Loch to Glen Douglas for his final posting. He was part of the team loading the weapons to be taken back to USA: 'We loaded cruise missiles, which were 25 feet in length, six per lorry. The lorry then moved to the pier at Glenmallan, as the missiles were too big to be taken through the depot railway tunnel.' [572]

This detail at Glen Douglas was hard work. Normal military requirements were in place, and all personnel, including Frank, were on duty watch every four days. This was difficult, because

---

56 Berms were mounds of earth designed to deflect explosive blasts.

there were only eight sailors on the team, the other being mostly weapons technicians: 'Every fourth day I spent all day at Glen Douglas. We packed up hazardous items for shipment back to the USA. These included hazardous liquids, nitrogen gas cylinders, oil drums and empty paint tins.'

Willie Hogg, an electronics technician from Edzell, was also deployed there. He was assigned to USS *Nitro* (AE-23) to work on the radar and VHF, HF and UHF equipment on board. He visited Glen Douglas three times on this assignment: 'There was a pier for ships in Loch Long, so we could moor at the pierside to load up. It took six months to completely empty the bunkers.' [573]

Mach memories

Gan Starling was a mineman. His first impression of Machrihanish was comical. Despite the airfield's military importance, there was a small civilian airport at the south end of the base, out of sight of the SEALs' hangar and the nuclear ammunition bunker. Landing there was adventurous: 'The base at Machrihanish had no less than a 10,000-foot runway, built as it was for Vulcan bombers. Yet the dinky Logan Air bush plane that I flew in on from London still managed to bounce its wheels once in the grass ahead of the tarmac. And I think they overloaded the plane a bit with luggage. I say that because they had to bring out a saw-horse to prop up the tail before they could turn the engine off.' [574]

Starling was the MOMAG transportation petty officer. His duties required him to travel to other locations such as Holy Loch, Glasgow, Glen Douglas, Prestwick and Edinburgh. He fondly remembers his adventures: 'I got around a lot, but that included mastering the fine art of siphoning diesel fuel. I also got to drive a tractor with ten forward speeds and three reverse.'

The station fire crew also handled the safety matters for the civilian flights to the airfield. Former RAF fireman Shaun Boland recalled this activity: 'On occasion, Beatle Paul McCartney would get a VIP private landing, as he had a farm a few miles away. Other duties involved the special aircraft that would land on occasion (although this was officially denied). These aircraft and their cargo would be looked after by the contingent of U.S. Navy that we shared the base with.' [575]

RAF control

The RAF were responsible for all flights at Machrihanish. Their personnel worked in a series of jobs including flight operations, base protection and firefighting.

Tom Hillman was an RAF NCO with a security clearance high enough to permit him to work in the communication centre. He was responsible for all aircraft take-off and landing messages, as well as other messages related to the base. He handled these using encryption and decryption methods. This paperwork would increase when military exercises were taking place: 'Much of this would involve Special Forces troops being parachuted into the sea. These were normally SEALs and UK Special Forces.[57] Other training exercises could require base blackouts and runway blackouts.'

---

57 Confirmed by my own personal experience.

Many of these blackouts were for low-flying Hercules to practise dropping troops. The aircraft also had to practise flying onto the airfield in darkness without any runway lighting. Part of this hair-raising activity also involved taking off in the dark. Machrihanish was not an out-of-sight base; it remained an important airfield for operational and training matters.

Machrihanish was a valuable Cold War site, and as it was involved in various classified activities, good physical security was necessary. Base security was a joint operation. The Americans had two types of police, recalled Derek Gillies, who served in the RAF Police at Machrihanish in the 1980s: 'The SPs [service police] were more security-oriented, protecting special sites and weapons, like their task at Greenham Common and elsewhere. The others were called LES [law enforcement sensitive] and were just that – cops who dealt with crime etc.' [576]

The level of security around the American compound was impressive. Although Gillies mixed socially with SEALs and minemen, outside of leisure contacts security was tight: 'I could go the next day to the SEAL building and my 'friend' would still ask to see my ID card before letting me in, even though we'd shared a few beers the night before.'

He described his time there as 'unpaid and unloved'. This was because of the structural reality of his job. In order for RAF Police JNCOs[58] to be able to tell the junior ranks what to do, they were all given the rank of corporal – but they were paid at their own rank, even when it was lower. Their primary roles were the maintenance of good order and discipline of all ranks. They also covered security by controlling the main gate and patrolling the airfield and buildings to check that no classified material was left unsecured. They were also armed. This was an indication of the importance of Machrihanish: 'We were armed with 9mm Browning pistols at Mach.'

The American units had their own police force to patrol their own facilities. These were constantly patrolled by armed American military personnel. This was unusual, as authority to carry loaded weapons was seldom granted in the UK. It highlighted the importance of the base.

Exciting rumours and fairy tales

Remote locations easily attract wild rumours and conspiracy theories.

The existence of the very long runway at Machrihanish spawned an equally lengthy list of fantasy claims about its activities. Bob Lester served there during the 1990s and was asked by many people about the Aurora super-secret spy plane. He remembered that most of the locals were convinced that the airfield had a secret underground bunker. His response was simple: 'All of this was … crap. There was no Aurora, no underground bunker. Hell, one of the theories at the time is that the black hanger (Gaydon) had a false floor and a super-secret C-130 gunship hidden below!'[577]

He had no time for tales of special forces guarding the base because of its top secret aircraft: 'As for security, it was RAF police; the gate guards were made up from normal station personnel, MT drivers, fitters, air traffic control, supply, fire service etc. All very boring stuff.'

Dick Yarby worked at Machrihanish and dismissed these mysterious tales about secret installations. He pointed out that there were three U.S. Navy facilities on the base in addition

---

58 JNCOs – junior non-commissioned officers, i.e. lance corporals and corporals.

to the RAF facilities. These were NSWU 2 (SEALs), MOMAG 2 and NWFD Machrihanish. He confirmed that the base was guarded by RAF Police (not USN SEALs or any other US personnel): 'I was there for a good long time. I was never abducted by aliens. I never saw any "strange aircraft", there was no super-secret underground facility – the airfield's only about 14 feet above sea level as it is!'[578]

Even the Space Shuttle has been associated with Machrihanish. Because it had a runway long enough to accommodate the Shuttle and get it airborne again, there have been claims that it was a certified emergency landing site. However, I have not found any source that can confirm this.[579]

Summary

Machrihanish gave long service to the United States Military. It provided an excellent hub for replenishment flights and for refuelling tasks. Anti-Submarine warfare missions were regular activities from the base. In addition it supported the full-time workload of special forces and naval mine logistics. The airfield's refuelling capability enabled American nuclear bumbers to refuel there. NATO ships were also able to take fuel at Campbeltown, helping to make it a probable Russian target according to the UK chiefs of staff.[580]

12 The spying game

Introduction

For 45 years the Soviet Union was America's most important intelligence target. The US military presence in Scotland, with nuclear-armed submarines, top-level communications links and radio spy stations posed a direct threat to Russia. The Soviets needed to find out more about these activities.

Intelligence-gathering from both sides was at its height as each feared the other's nuclear strength. While the United States used huge radio spy stations, the Soviets used KGB agents and spy trawlers. Russia operated the largest fishing fleet in the world, with more than 4,000 oceangoing ships which provided support to Soviet naval units, including intelligence reports on Western naval activities.[581]

East and West deployed thousands of personnel in the war of information, costing hundreds of millions of dollars.

American strategy

The United States Government assessed the Soviet threat in stark terms: the USSR was considered to be 'the center of opposition to American policy, and the one power menace to American security. Thus, the need for knowledge of the USSR transcend[ed] all other intelligence requirements'.[582]

The feeling was mutual. From 1947 onwards, Soviet political and intelligence leaders regarded the USA as their main adversary. The KGB had almost 750,000 personnel, and its most important section was the First Chief Directorate, which pursued foreign intelligence. In Scotland its targets were obvious – the nuclear submarine base at Holy Loch, and the radio spy stations.[583]

The American and British governments were well aware of the threat posed by Soviet spy trawlers. Whitehall implemented steps to deal with it in 1964 by noting:

> since 1958 more than 30 trawler-type vessels, laden with electronic equipment, catching no fish and unashamedly designed to pick up communications and electronic intelligence, have been identified. Some of the vessels may be capable of underwater intelligence gathering. Their activities ... have caused us growing concerns ... inside the sea areas around the UK ... there is a strong presumption that Soviet vessels, especially COMINT/ELINT trawlers, are spying.[584]

Activity in Scotland

When the United States moved military installations into Scotland, these bases became targets, and Soviet intelligence gathering took place around them. Russian special forces also had a new theatre of interest. and their actions in Scotland persisted throughout the Cold War.

Soviet fishing fleet officers held reserve navy commissions, and its vessels assisted Russian naval spying operations. Soviet trawlers poked their noses into US naval operations and British military activity around the British Isles, and from the 1960s they paid particular attention to Holy Loch. This was highlighted by the CIA in 1965 when they reported that the Soviets had maintained surveillance of Holy Loch with intelligence trawlers and submarines.[585]

CDR John Murphy was a U.S. Navy intelligence officer. He observed that in technical terms any Cold War Eastern Bloc navy vessel could be a potential spy ship: 'The decrepit-looking fishing trawlers were the biggest problem, as they obstructed US naval activity on a worldwide basis'.[586]

Murphy noted that although these vessels looked like 'godforsaken pieces of junk,' they were operated by talented and capable crews containing scientists and SIGINT operators who were fluent in English. The skipper would be a Soviet navy commander or captain who would previously have been aboard, for example, a destroyer in the Soviet Mediterranean Squadron. All of the crew would have been fully screened by the KGB.

The spy trawlers lived in the open, and no attempt was made to hide them. From 1977 their Scottish base was at Ullapool, a small fishing port in north-west Scotland, with, at the time, a population of less than 600. The Cold War arrived when three Bulgarian trawlers berthed in the port, followed by several Russian trawlers a year later. All carried radio antennae on their rigging and superstructure. East German trawlers quickly followed, and by the mid-1980s, more than 90 Eastern Bloc vessels were anchored locally. Ullapool's population had now more than doubled. Some estimates placed it close to 7,000 during the klondyker years.[59] [587]

Not all of the trawlers were involved in spying, but all carried a KGB officer aboard, and any useful information was passed back to Moscow. The spy trawlers were known as *tralschiki* to the Russians and *tattletales* to the Americans. They carried an extensive array of sensors and related equipment. Some of the factory ships were fully fitted out as SIGINT stations.[588]

---

59 The klondykers was the local name for the influx of Scandinavian and other factory-fishing boats which frequented Ullapool.

The Soviet concept of specialised trawlers was affordable and easily deployed. The boats had excellent seakeeping capabilities, and competent crews were assigned to them. Nearly all Russian ships also carried a political officer – *Zampolit* – aboard, who would be in daily contact with Moscow.[589]

Some of these Soviet vessels carried Scottish fishing boat registration codes. This happened because any codes that were not allocated to existing boats were available for purchase, so the Russians could buy the codes and display them on their boats. In one instance a Scottish registration was even borne by a spy trawler festooned with SIGINT antennae; the original bearer of the code had been broken up in 1953.[590]

The Soviet arrival in Ullapool had the same side-effect as the American arrival elsewhere – a huge boost to the local economy. John MacKaig was a shopkeeper in the town: 'This was the start of an economic bonanza for Ullapool, and all local businesses expanded their trade significantly. There was never any trouble whatsoever. However, they [the Russians] were obviously wary about being in a capitalist country. We were wary of them also.'[591]

The huge Soviet presence was a good opportunity for the UK and US intelligence agencies to recruit defectors. The KGB took preventative action, as MacKaig recalled: 'I observed that when one of them [seamen] went to the toilet in a public place, e.g., hotel, public bar, shop, they were always accompanied by a specific person who waited outside the cubicle. We later learned that these individuals were the commissars. Their task was to ensure that the seamen did not defect.'

This KGB control was also observed in action by Mike Archbold, whose family lived in Ullapool. He recalled the foreign fishing fleet arriving during October and leaving by February: 'There would be in excess of 40 vessels at any one time anchored north of Annat Bay. At night it looked like a city. The CalMac Ullapool/Stornoway ferry would have to thread its way through the Eastern Bloc vessels. Many of those vessels went home for Christmas, but there would still be a dozen or so at anchor over the holiday period.'[592]

He remembered: 'Every day you could see the little red lifeboats pottering past Rhue on their way to Ullapool to collect stores from the local shops.' This was a boom time for these shops, recalled MacKaig: 'Although some local shopkeepers were invited aboard on occasion, contact between the fleet and locals was controlled and somewhat limited. Local doctors would sometimes go out to the ships if there was illness or a casualty. But even so, access was always controlled.'

A dramatic incident involving the Russians was recounted by Mike Archbold: 'One evening a Soviet boat ran aground close to the lighthouse. Quite why it was so close is unknown, as they usually anchored well away from there. An emergency call was made, and the local police, an ambulance and the volunteer coastguard team were scrambled to the scene. They set up their breeches buoy, but their offers of assistance were declined by the Russian vessel. The emergency team continued to stand by until another Russian ship towed it off.'

No explanation was given to the locals. Douglas H. Wise believed that it was a classic case of a sensitive vessel being kept away from probing British eyes: 'It could well have been a fully fitted spy trawler. These look pretty normal from a distance, but closer inspection would have revealed its SIGINT equipment, mainly radio antennae.'

It was another reminder to the locals that Ullapool was now a spy zone, similar to Berlin and Belfast at the time. There were plenty of intelligence operatives in those locations, and Ullapool had joined the list.[593]

Defection was a problem, particularly for the East German authorities. The Russian, Bulgarian and Rumanian trawlers would return to their home ports, but the East German ships would remain in Ullapool. The crews would have to change over via Glasgow airport, and some of them seized this opportunity to defect. A former UK intelligence officer analysed this behaviour: 'There were often East German defections in port. But this did not mean that these sailors became British agents.' [594]

The KGB were ruthlessly effective against defection, as John MacKaig remembered: 'The Russian authorities did not suffer from this behaviour. All their seamen had to be aboard ship before darkness. They did not attend local ceilidhs, although we attended discos and meals on their ships. Every ship had a commissar who ranked beside the captain.' John was also aware of the clearly identifiable KGB presence aboard the Russian fishing fleet: 'We had a good relationship with the Russian seamen. Their officers were polite, well-educated and friendly. Many were Westernised. Many spoke up to five languages.' This description fits the recognised profile for Soviet intelligence officers.

The task of monitoring the Russian espionage activities was handled by the British intelligence agencies, as explained by intelligence insider Alan Judd.[60] He pointed out that the presence of the Soviet ships was well known to MI5 and GCHQ: 'It wasn't just the subs they were spying on – they were monitoring our military radio traffic when we were in Northern Ireland.'

Judd described the counter-espionage steps taken by the UK. The task of monitoring the KGB identities, movements and activities would have fallen to the local Special Branch (SB). They would have reported up the chain to MI5, probably via MI5's liaison office in Edinburgh. SB would have been operating out of Glasgow or Inverness. They would have recruited local sources – traders, people working in the port – to report on the Russians. The SB officer would most likely have gone up there once a month to debrief them. There would also have been an SB officer based with the Ullapool police.[595]

The presence of American military bases in Scotland, especially the submarines at Holy Loch, led to this intelligence agency proliferation. Prior to this time, Ullapool had only attracted geologists. It was now bristling with British and Russian spies.

Spetsnaz

The American bases in Scotland were all prime targets for sabotage forces. The Soviet Spetsnaz units operated in similar fashion to U.S. Navy SEALs, the SAS and the SBS. They were ruthless and highly effective. The Spetsnaz mystique was embroidered by claims by a Soviet defector, Viktor Suvorov. A former GRU agent,[61] he claimed that Spetsnaz used condemned criminals from the Gulag system for real-life combat training to the death. This inflated their reputation.[596]

---

60 Alan Judd, authorised biographer of Mansfield Cumming, the founder of MI6.
61 GRU: Soviet military intelligence.

The threat from Spetsnaz was considerable. Douglas H. Wise outlined the possibilities of their use in Scotland. He pointed out that the unconventional warfare role and capabilities of the Spetsnaz could have been used in several ways. Firstly, in advance of hostilities or during times of increased tension, they could have been given a strategic reconnaissance role to observe and assess the state of readiness or preparation for action at critical NATO facilities in Scotland. Based on their assessments, Spetsnaz could have been given a mission to mine the approaches and departures from Scottish bases.

In the most extreme cases, Wise believed that this could include interdicting the roads leading to and from Scottish facilities by the use of small bombs. He noted an important point: 'Clearly this would be very provocative and come with great risk, but the Soviets have a different risk tolerance than we have here in the West. Spetsnaz would conduct direct action and execute commando raids and attacks on Scottish facilities.'

They would also have conducted ambushes and targeted assassinations of local leaders and local citizens who worked at the bases. Wise emphasised the effect this would cause: 'There would have been destruction on the bases, and locals would have been reluctant to travel to do the repairs. This activity would have disrupted the deployment of ships and aircraft or the conduct of SIGINT collection from Scottish locations. It would have degraded NATO's ability to posture and prepare for war, frightened the local support population, and freed up Soviet forces for other, harder targets and large-scale combat.'

Spetsnaz and sleeper agents were a real, live threat. The UK and US intelligence community knew that a network of Soviet agents in deep cover lived normal lives in local neighbourhoods near American bases.[597] Their weapons and explosives would probably have been in place, smuggled in by trawlers. The Ullapool spy fleet could bring in weapons hidden in boxes which then could have been distributed around Scotland by Soviet Bloc long-distance lorry drivers.[598]

These activities formed part of a long-term Soviet infiltration strategy. Intelligence sources outlined the preparations being taken by the Russians: 'For some years, the Soviets had been burying secret caches in Western countries. They could be used to conceal anything from small nuclear devices to arms and explosives for use by agents prior to any hostilities occurring.' These agents had been in Scotland, and elsewhere in Britain, since the 1970s. The KGB had been directed to recruit local people to assist their agents already in the UK. Their task was to identify vital installations to be attacked by Spetsnaz units.[599]

A former senior British Army officer in Scotland, Brigadier Rory Walker, highlighted the vulnerability of the important Scottish bases. He pointed out that Spetsnaz operatives would have carried out detailed reconnaissance of their targets in the guise of long-distance drivers. France, Greece, and Italy all had large and active communist parties at the time. The truckers' unions were heavily infiltrated, and it was easy enough to substitute Spetsnaz agents for regular drivers on container runs across Europe. This would have given them the opportunity to make overnight stops close to Faslane, Holy Loch and several other sites and communications centres. All would have been key targets for pre-emptive strikes.[600]

The main effort in the hours preceding the outbreak of hostilities would have been mounted by teams of Soviet Spetsnaz commandos, the Kremlin's equivalent of the SAS. The Soviet high command had more than 30,000 of these highly trained soldiers available; assaults on well-defended locations such as Holy Loch and other defended bases were judged too important to be left to a handful of local agents. In addition, as noted by Alan Judd: 'There would probably also have been a coordinated anti-nuclear (anti-Western) campaign in the run-up, protest marches, attempts to blockade etc. Like Greenham Common.'

By the mid-1980s the KGB had established a foothold for this activity, as revealed by a high-level KGB defector, Oleg Gordievsky. The KGB had been using Ireland as a training ground. This enabled their sleeper agents to familiarise themselves with British life before they moved across the Irish Sea to bigger targets.[601]

In the 1970s. the Northern Seas had become a top intelligence target. The Soviet Northern Fleet operated in this area, and the Russians feared that Western oil platforms would monitor Soviet submarines and surface vessels. Intelligence matters in this area came under the direct control of the KGB chief, Yuri Andropov, who became Soviet leader in 1982. The Scottish bases were directly involved in this war game.[602]

At the same time, British spy trawlers, too, were operating in the region. The UK had been using these boats in the Northern Seas throughout the 1960s and 1970s. At times they would be used as cover for a spy submarine, disguising its sound signature from the listening Soviet ASW vessels. One of these trawlers was the MFV *Gaul*, which sank without explanation in 1974. The truth emerged many years later in *The Guardian* newspaper – the *Gaul* had been a spy trawler. Its crew of 36 had been lost. The article revealed that it was MI6 that had been supervising this operation to spy on Russian ships and submarines during the 1960s and early 1970s; MI6 had finally admitted that spy trawlers had been operating close to Russian waters, and always carried one of their officers.[603]

Radio spy stations in Scotland were an obvious Russian espionage target. America also had radar-detection ships using Rosyth, Thurso and Greenock. A lot of British/American intelligence community resource was deployed in the Scottish locations. Many agencies were involved – CIA, NSA, DIA, USAFSS and NSGA by the Americans. The UK used the assets of GCHQ, MI5, the Royal Navy and the RAF in support of these missions.[604]

All these agencies were involved because of the complex nature of intelligence-gathering. Wise gave an overview of the intelligence-collection process: 'Targeting is a collective enterprise; it is very much a team sport. A target involves not just the resources of one agency but the resources across 18 agencies of the American intelligence community, plus the various UK assets.'

The Scottish bases had a distinctive role in monitoring their maritime zone. The intelligence material they collected was important for the United States. Wise pointed out: 'Intelligence was gathered from many sources, embracing high frequency direction-finding, satellites, human intelligence, operational intelligence, electronic intelligence and other sources. This data was collected by whatever the mission was, and whatever DOD[62] or government entity was the final customer. The intelligence collectors worked hand in hand with the analysts to create the data for the final customer.'

Wise commented directly on the close liaison between the NSA and GCHQ: 'If you are talking about the early days of Sigint in the UK it is difficult to separate GCHQ and NSA, who

---

62 DOD: Department of Defense.

were commingled; a SIGINT site, which I will call Site Alpha, might have half of its staff from GCHQ and the other half from NSA. The targeting is done between those two organisations; the tasking of themselves is done internally.'

Although these American SIGINT sites were located in Scotland, it was the United States that directed their operations. By the late 1980s, GCHQ had in reality become a sub-unit of the NSA, who controlled the target list. But the UK also needed a share of the data collected. Intelligence co-operation was a delicate subject and Wise was able to shine a light on this matter and the question of its ownership: 'The desire, in my experience, is to share more often than not. We, the US, take a look at the information and see what is needed for our partners to have access to this information, what is their ability to protect our information.' [605]

He highlighted the fundamental understanding involved; if the United States had given the UK all the information they had on the target, they expected the UK to share with them all the information they had collected on it. It was an essential requirement: 'I have to work this with my British counterpart. I cannot afford a violation of the sharing policy.'

The Walker spy ring and its effect on Scotland

America's Cold War activities in Scotland were dealt a devastating blow by one of the most notorious spy rings in history. Vital work at Holy Loch, Edzell and Thurso was sabotaged when a US communications specialist sold the U.S. Navy's innermost secrets to Moscow. The KGB head in Washington DC, Boris Solomatin, described John Walker as 'the kind of spy who turns up once in a lifetime'.[606]

Walker's betrayal of his country was staggering. It was the greatest-ever breach of security in the history of the U.S. Navy. His espionage went undetected for almost 20 years, and enabled the Soviets to decipher an untold number of U.S. Navy encoded messages.

As a senior radioman, Walker had served aboard the SSBNs *Andrew Jackson* and *Simon Bolivar* at Holy Loch during the 1960s. He had operated equipment that was also in use at Thurso and Edzell, and his betrayal greatly impacted the work being done at these Scottish bases.

Walker's stolen secrets enabled the Russians to make advances in technology, and gave them insights into submarine operations, signal codes and surveillance techniques. As a result, the Russian submarines' sound signatures became quieter, and this made them more difficult to detect. Mike Giambattista later explained that in addition to revealing the location of American SSBNs, the Walker gang passed on technical information which allowed Russian submarines to improve their performance.

Walker's spy ring stole copies of U.S. Navy operational plans and many more top secret documents. This meant that the Soviets knew the details of every SSBN patrol that left Holy Loch. There was always a spy trawler lying in wait, and a Russian submarine ready to take up their trail. A major spy war was being played out in Scottish waters.

Senior KGB defector Oleg Kalugin credited Walker with a massive contribution to Soviet knowledge. He pointed out that Walker had provided them with a huge intelligence bonus by showing them how to monitor American fleet movements. In Kalugin's opinion, Walker was 'by far the most spectacular spy case I handled in the United States'.[607]

The stolen information impacted on the entire Scottish spy station operation. Coding-key information sold by Walker compromised the Classic Wizard operation at Edzell and Thurso. Messages from the Big Stick radio mast were also breached. Submarine-tracking information was decoded by the Russians, and the Soviet subs were able to slip away unobserved.

The radio stations intercept adopted meticulous processes to maintain the integrity of their operation. Eric Mercato was one of the Edzell technicians who did this work: 'I keyed cryptographic keys into the equipment to ensure that the data that was being transmitted off the base was encrypted properly.' But unknown to the U.S. Navy the Walker gang had already sabotaged the system.

Following Walker's arrest, the HFDF equipment at Edzell and Thurso was upgraded and codenamed Classic Owl. All operators had to be retrained. Radical changes were introduced to COMSEC, explained former Navy intelligence officer Joe Mazzafro: 'My personal recollection of the biggest (and most effective) change was the Navy going service-wide to two-man control all the time for any crypto materials.'

It was because of Walker's information that Russian submarines had changed their radio procedure. But at the time Jimmy Grier and his colleagues had assumed this to be improved Russian radio security: 'The Russians kept changing their methods to communicate with their nuclear fleet. We monitored and broke their code and methods, but then they changed them again.'

Admiral Bill Studeman, Director of the NSA when Walker's activities were being revealed, gave an estimate of the damage that had been caused: 'It had a major effect ultimately on the systems and crypto-control and handling across the whole of government, and dramatically accelerated the remote keying programs to get the humans out of the loop, and to modernise US crypto systems. Frankly speaking, the Walker espionage case was one of the most significant and consequential compromises ever experienced by the US Government, so its impact went way beyond Edzell.' [608]

The Russians needed to test Walker's information. This was done when North Korea seized the USS *Pueblo* in 1968. The incident was pre-planned, to capture the *Pueblo*'s coding machines. Walker's information was proved to be correct, and Russia could now read U.S. Navy codes. He had handed over encryption techniques, manuals and key cards used to transmit secret messages on cryptographic equipment.[609]

Even the routine, unclassified, SSBN radio messages were priceless to the Soviets, as there were no other reliable sources of information about the American SSBNs. This information revealed the general pattern and area of SSBN operations. The breach had uncovered details of SSBN techniques, sound signatures, radio frequencies and call signs. The compromised radio traffic was listed by Mike Giambattista. It covered the routine details of SSBN operations: 'The unclassified transmissions related to inbound transit ETA, notice on any critical repairs/spare parts needed, request for berthing assignment etc. Outbound transit transmissions were rare. Perhaps the only useful intel for the Russians was noting arrival/departure dates and times.'

Any vital information broadcast from Thurso and Edzell would have been encrypted. However, although the weapons readiness tests were randomly timed, the fact that messages had been sent out would have alerted the Russians, telling them that the SSBNs were maintaining their intense programme of testing and training.

The wide-ranging effect of the Walker spy ring was summarised by Wise, who rated the Walker espionage case as a critical blow to the United States. 'Walker and family, because of their USN service, compromised processes and procedures for the submarine and surface navy part of the US nuclear deterrence as well as a portion of the land- and air-based part of the deterrence triad.'

Wise detailed the impact of this betrayal: 'As a result of the Walker treachery, the USN had to rebuild much of the command-and-control architecture to include encryption systems ... Edzell, Thurso and Holy Loch were a significant part of the US and NATO deterrence ... the operations in and out of those facilities were significantly affected.'

This opinion was supported by Professor Richard Aldrich, a leading intelligence scholar: 'Walker ... inflicted horrific damage upon Western SIGINT and COMSEC operations.' [610]

Holy Loch in the frame

Not all Soviet undercover activities were as dramatic as the Walker case.

After 1961, although Holy Loch and its activities became a target for Soviet espionage, the overt counter-espionage effort was unusually small. In fact, it appeared to be a one-man operation, as Mike Giambattista recalled. One day he was approached by Naval Investigator Jimmy J. Jones of the Naval Support Detachment, who was looking for help. Given the frequent questioning of the sailors in certain locations in the area, Jones wanted equipment to monitor these activities. He suspected they were sponsored by the Russians.

Jones ordered a variety of surveillance equipment – listening bugs, recording devices and special cameras. Surprisingly, he did not have a budget for these items, but his order was fast-tracked and arrived within two weeks.

Naval intelligence investigators were attached to all Navy and Marine Corps facilities. In the main they would be involved in background investigations for security clearances. At Holy Loch, Jones' chief concern was to monitor the behaviour of U.S. Naval personnel.

In view of the prime importance of the Holy Loch activities, there would have been a strong, but covert, counter-espionage effort mounted by the British and American intelligence agencies. Wise recounted how this operation would have been implemented: 'The Naval Criminal Investigative Service would likely have the lead for the CIA, since these were naval facilities and the individual concerned would be a military member or a civilian. MI5 would be the lead agency for the UK.'

An early test for Site One's counter-espionage procedures occurred in 1963. The annual Scottish Trades Union Congress was held in Dunoon, and among the international guests was a large delegation from the Soviet Union. KGB agents were present in all its political, cultural and economic delegations which visited other countries.[611]

Many Scottish trade union officials were members of the Communist Party of Great Britain (CPGB), and their sympathies lay with the Soviet Union and its foreign policy objectives. One of these Communist officials, Mick McGahey, leader of the National Union of Mineworkers in Scotland, delivered a notable speech opposing Polaris.

The Soviet delegation was housed in the Queen's Hotel. As a result, SubRon-14's commodore, Captain Syverson, placed this building out of bounds.[612]

The KGB hotel

During John Walker's time at Holy Loch, another real-life spying drama emerged. East German Peter Dorschel, a former merchant seaman and ship's cook, had regularly visited the UK and had married a British woman. When he was at home on leave in East Germany, KGB agents had approached him with a proposition.[613] They wanted Dorschel 'to obtain information from local US service personnel regarding fleet movements and facilities at their Polaris nuclear submarine base at Holy Loch.'

The KGB would provide funds for him to buy a small hotel in the Holy Loch area. Deploying him there would be risky, however, as he had not been trained in espionage tradecraft, and if captured he would be jailed. Despite these initial fears, he accepted the offer.

Dorschel bought a hotel close to Hunter's Quay, near Holy Loch. He befriended various local people, including bookmaker William McAffer and American sailor Garry Lee Ledbetter, and recruited them. The trio's spying careers were, however, short-lived; all were arrested.

At his trial in 1967, Dorschel was accused of inciting McAffer 'to obtain documents which might be or were intended to be directly or indirectly useful to an enemy, for a purpose prejudicial to the safety or interests of the State.' The evidence was overwhelming. There was no defence. His lawyer, playing the sympathy card, described Dorschel as 'a little fish … if this is how foreign espionage in matters as important as nuclear submarines is conducted, we have little to fear from it'.

The jury convicted Dorschel and he was sentenced to seven years' imprisonment. Ledbetter was court-martialled and jailed for two years. No charges were brought against McAffer. He claimed that he was working with MI6. The authorities ignored this claim, but he walked free.[614]

The Dorschel affair had been stupid. Its proponents had taken a huge risk for a small gain and their agent was now behind bars. Site One sailors thought it was absurd, and one of them, Martin Hastings serving aboard *Los Alamos,* commented: 'Along about that time, 1967, they grabbed some guy selling plumbing plans to Russian spies.'[615]

However, this was in fact a classic espionage move, as plumbing plans were valuable information. The KGB had taken a chance that did not pay off. Douglas H. Wise analysed the case: 'It displayed a lack of agent cover in the locality. The KGB took an unusual risk, and were exposed. The Dorschel case is a perfect example of casting the net wide. The collection undertaken by the KGB, as I said, would include direct surveillance, indirect collection, the use of trained/recruited agents and the use of untrained sources (such as Peter Dorschel).

'While the risks of an amateur getting caught are higher than those of a trained agent, the KGB probably had no choice, and they would have calculated that if he were to be compromised (as he was) the blowback on the Soviets would be small. Using such an agent shows how important to the KGB the wide-net collection effort was, and it also indicates that they did not have a good source near Holy Loch. They approached him back home, incentivised him and tasked him. He was encouraged to develop his own network of sub-sources, which of course was his undoing.'

Alan Judd agreed with this assessment of the Dorschel case: 'The official statement reads plausibly. Interesting that the KGB was prepared to spend significantly [buying a hotel] on such a flimsy case. Suggests they might not have had many other assets in the area. It would be interesting to know how it was discovered – my guess is that the bookmaker informed Special Branch who got MI5 (not MI6) involved. SB would have made the arrest.'

Judd also pointed out that the KGB later planned to cause major disruption in Holy Loch: 'I recall another incident regarding the Holy Loch submarine base. The KGB considered activating a plot to cause local damage. It had been put to them around 1970 by one of their London officers, Oleg Lyalin, who subsequently defected to us. Luckily they didn't use it.'

'Luckily' because Lyalin's plan would have caused major problems; he had been described by the senior KGB defector Oleg Kalugin as a person who planned spectacular incidents 'as bizarre as any of those devised by the CIA to kill Castro … when he [Lyalin] defected, the UK expelled 105 Russian agents … this was a severe shock to the KGB and the senior Soviet leadership'.

While the KGB had few local agents, there would have been a strong counter-espionage effort mounted by the British and American intelligence agencies. It would not have been an American-only operation; to the Americans Scotland was foreign territory so they would have used the good links between their own and the British security agencies.

Douglas H. Wise explained the CIA's involvement: 'If a US person had been recruited by the Sovs, CIA officers would be acting with MI5 on the case. But it would have been an MI5 case.'

The *Waverley* and the taxi driver

In 1975 the Russians carried out a ridiculous overt espionage attempt at Holy Loch. Jim Findlay and his friends had just finished high school and were aboard the paddle steamer MV *Waverley*: 'There was a discount offer for school parties on the *Waverley* and four of us created the Hillhead High School party. We were aboard the paddle steamer for a leisurely voyage down the Clyde to Holy Loch. There were plenty of people aboard, probably about 100 or so.' [616]

The *Waverley* cruised down the Clyde from Glasgow: 'When she arrived at Holy Loch, two or three guys dressed in archetypical long black coats appeared on the foredeck with 35-mm cameras, long lenses and tripods, and pushed other passengers aside to get to the rail. They appeared to be speaking Russian.'

Jim and his friends watched in astonishment: 'As *Waverley* sailed round the US floating dock, these guys continued to take photographs, unhindered and unchallenged by anyone. The *Waverley* left Holy Loch and these guys disappeared below. We tried to have a look at them during the rest of the trip, but they sat in a tight group ignoring us. They disembarked at Broomielaw with the rest of the passengers. We still talk about them – the day we met the KGB aboard the *Waverley*!'

Neil Gordon was one of the school group, and many years later still remembered his excitement: 'I think it was the way they were dressed that attracted our attention in the first place. Wish I'd taken photos of them at the time!'

This was a bold step by the Russians, as their agents were restricted to travel within the London area. Alan Judd commented: 'They could travel beyond the 30-mile limit provided they gave notice and gained permission. A trade (fishing?) delegation to Edinburgh might be more likely, but they'd have either used hidden cameras or pretended to be photographing nearby fishing boats.'

The U.S. Navy was aware of the potential espionage risks, and provided counter-espionage briefings in case sailors encountered Russian sympathisers. Greggery Kunkle had a memorable taxi ride in 1987 after collecting his pay cheque at the Holy Loch base. He climbed into a cab at the end of the pier and told the driver to take him to Innellan. The driver started chatting to him. He asked a lot of questions about what was going on at the site. At first, they seemed like harmless questions and, not thinking, Kunkle answered a few of them: 'I was an E-2 or E-3 at the time in boat ops and knew very little info of any value to a spy. I had other things on my mind and I wasn't really thinking about the conversation with the driver.' But the questions got more and more specific, and warning bells started going off in his head. He tried to offer false information to his probing questions, but then remembered that his training told not to do so.

Kunkle was now suspicious and alert: 'His questions were far more specific about things at the site than any other cab driver had ever asked me before or since. I could tell he was fishing for information about the base. I quickly decided to shut up and just play dumb. I responded with 'I don't know' to his last few questions, and he finally gave up asking me any more once he realised I wouldn't answer them.'

Kunkle had felt worried: 'Was this really a spy? Or an American who was testing other Americans? I'll never know the truth. All I know is I was very nervous for the rest of that cab ride. I went out of my way to walk around Innellan for some time before going home. I was young and inexperienced, so perhaps I was being overly paranoid. I can look back now and laugh at myself over this.'

But the reality of the Cold War had come home to him: 'This was the first time that the full weight of what the United States was doing in Scotland hit me – how serious this little adventure of mine actually was. This wasn't some story I was reading in a book or seeing in a movie. I was *living* it. I was in a foreign land, a tiny part of a gigantic machine facing another enormous machine, with decades of nuclear tensions between them. Being a minuscule part of such a colossal thing had been extremely exciting. This little experience with a possible spy was a cold reminder to me that it could also be equally terrifying.'

Confronting the Victor

Soviet submarines prowled close to the Holy Loch on spying missions. On 27 January 1973 the Soviets came inside the Inner Clyde area. A Victor-class submarine had been detected near the Isle of Colonsay, 50 miles from the Scottish shore. The Royal Navy was called in.

FROM FIRST SEA LORD: A SOVIET NUCLEAR POWERED SUBMARINE HAS BEEN DETECTED IN THE NORTHWEST APPROACHES. YOU ARE TO SAIL FORTHWITH AND SWEEP THE RUSSIAN FROM OUR WATERS.[617]

The nuclear-powered fleet submarine HMS *Conqueror* was assigned to confront and remove the Soviet intruder. The Soviet purpose was obvious – the Victor was there to act as bait for the countermeasures. The Inner Clyde zone was the Royal Navy's backyard – but they and the U.S. Navy operated in the Barents Sea, the Soviet's backyard. '*Conqueror* spent four days luring the Victor away from the Clyde approaches. This was done by a combination of active sonar and making the vessel noisy like an SSBN,' recalled LT Roger Lane-Nott, the navigator.[63]

This was a dangerous activity, as it would reveal *Conqueror*'s exact position to the Victor. *Conqueror*'s skipper, CDR Chris Ward, noted: 'We were all quite nervous about that. What I wanted to do was to try and make it like we were really going out on patrol. We closed to within 500 yards. I felt that if we got about a half-day's steaming away with him stuck behind me, then that would be absolutely fine. That would leave enough clear water for our submarines without any interference from him.' Ward's plan worked, although both submarines passed close to one another: 'Eventually we got this incredible noise of the submarine going over the top of us.' He passed responsibility to the airborne ASW aircraft and signalled the Admiralty:

> MISSION ACCOMPLISHED. SOVIET SUBMARINE HAS BEEN LURED INTO THE ATLANTIC AND DISENGAGED. OUR WATERS ARE SANITIZED. AM PROCEEDING IN ACCORDANCE WITH PREVIOUS ORDERS.

Nevertheless, the Soviets had gathered a lot of information about the defence systems protecting Holy Loch.

But the most memorable and daring Russian spy mission to Holy Loch could have started the Third World War.

And it was the information leaked by the traitor John Walker that had led to the 1974 collision between the SSBN USS *James Madison* and the Soviet Victor-class submarine in the Clyde. As mentioned earlier, the *Madison* incident had occurred inside British territorial waters, a severe embarrassment to the UK Government, as the Russians had clearly penetrated the Holy Loch defence system and threatened its prime asset, the SSBN fleet.[618] But although his handiwork was all over this incident, it took years before the true reason was uncovered.

Scotland was involved in the Cold War espionage campaign because of the presence of the Holy Loch submarines and the radio interception sites. Most people were, however, unaware of the Great Game being played around them at the time.

---

63 As Rear Admiral Lane-Nott, he later served as Commander Operations and Flag Officer Submarines. During the Falklands War in 1982 *HMS Conqueror* sank the Argentinian battleship *Admiral Belgrano*.

13 The test

– mission accomplished

The world on edge

The Cuban Missile Crisis in 1962 was the most terrifying time of the Cold War. The Soviets had moved nuclear missiles into Cuba, and President Kennedy had ordered that they be removed. For the next ten days the world watched and waited, wondering if the Soviets would comply, or if the United States would invade Cuba – or if nuclear weapons would be unleashed.

Both superpowers increased their state of military readiness. Navy, army and air force units moved to immediate standby condition. The Third World War appeared imminent. Part of America's most important actions during the crisis were the strategic retaliation preparations and intelligence-gathering activities in Scotland.

Those Americans who were aware of Scotland's part in this drama were based at Holy Loch, Kirknewton, Edzell and Thurso. Others at Machrihanish and Prestwick were operating their contingency plans. Scotland was firmly in the front line.

The crisis had begun when Raul Castro, brother of the Cuban leader Fidel, had visited Moscow at the start of July 1962 to discuss an arms build-up in Cuba. Knowledge of this meeting was captured by the NSA, and alarm bells rang in the White House.

Castro's visit was a vital piece of strategic information. Following it the Soviets had agreed to ship 60 nuclear missiles to Cuba and once there this cargo was unloaded under cover of darkness. Additional intelligence revealed that the Russians had developed a new radar system and had installed this equipment in Cuba. This radar could pick up the high-altitude U-2 spy plane. Therefore, future US flights across Cuba were now endangered. This raised questions as to why the radar equipment had been positioned in Cuba, and what the Cubans were trying to hide.

Information about Cuba became the highest priority. In July, Secretary of Defense McNamara ordered the radio spy stations to concentrate on the Cuba problem.

This order meant that the Scottish stations at Kirknewton, Edzell and Thurso were now fully involved. They had to search for Russian vessels making their way south through the GIUK Gap and the North Sea. The Russians needed a fleet of more than 70 ships to transport their 44,000 troops to Cuba for Operation Anadyr, and these were now being tracked by the Scottish spy stations. This increase in sea traffic resulted in twice as many Soviet ships being monitored during the July to September period. At the Scottish bases all leave and all courses were cancelled.[619]

The United States intelligence community began an intense scrutiny of Cuba and the flow of ships from Soviet ports. Spy planes tracked these vessels and spy stations intercepted their radio traffic. U.S. Navy air patrol squadrons kept a close watch – as did their counterparts in Scotland, Iceland, Nova Scotia, the Azores and Bermuda.[620]

At the start of October Kirknewton and Edzell were tasked with Cuban targets by the director of the NSA.[621]

History has recorded the Cuban Missile Crisis as having occurred for a total of 13 days, from 16 October to 28 October 1962, the 16th being the day after photographic intelligence had confirmed the existence of Soviet medium-range ballistic missiles in Cuba, and the 28th the day Khrushchev directed the dismantling, and the return, of the offensive weapons in Cuba.

But the story began long before that.

Two years earlier, in September 1960, communications intelligence, collected by the NSA along with its three military cryptologic agencies, had provided the first indications that Soviet arms were being transported to Cuba aboard cargo ships. Similar reports later revealed high-level visits from a Soviet arms export chief to Havana as well as the purchase of Soviet helicopters by Cuba.

By July 1962, Raul Castro's Moscow trip had been identified and tracked. The associated signal traffic had been intercepted and this SIGINT information helped to prove that the USSR was shipping missile parts to Cuba. The source of this information was probably Edzell, noted the NSA: 'It is likely that the information on Raul's trip was the product of an NSA listening post in ... Scotland.'[622]

Early in August, Kennedy had separately received personal intelligence data about the true nature of the cargoes from a very senior source. This information, highly classified, was made known only to Kennedy.[623]

By the middle of August, Scottish bases had tracked many Soviet vessels heading towards Cuba. U.S. Navy reconnaissance flights photographed these vessels, showing that they were carrying weapons on their decks. Many of the vessels steaming towards Cuba were high out of the water, so intelligence analysts were initially convinced that they were empty. But then a U.S. Navy analysis of this evidence concluded that they could be carrying cargo which was bulky but lightweight – such as missiles. These Navy analysists, familiar with cargo profiles, had identified the probable contents. But precious days had been lost.[624]

The crisis gathered momentum. On 4 September 1962, JFK made a statement regarding the Soviet supply of military equipment to Cuba. He was now aware of the plans to airlift large numbers of SCUD-B and FROG missiles to the island: 'The United States Government has information ... from a variety of sources ... the Soviets have provided the Cuban Government with ... a number of ... missiles ... they have also been providing extensive radar and other electronic equipment.'[625]

The Soviets continued their build-up in Cuba, and on 11 September the NSA reported to the President that 'Soviet leaders have put their strategic forces on their highest readiness stage since the beginning of the Cold War.'[626]

The Russian forces included nuclear-armed units. The situation was reaching boiling point, so General Curtis LeMay, head of the SAC, wasted no time. He was in command of more than 2,000 bombers, each armed with doomsday weapons, and he directed his staff to produce an operations plan. The U.S. Navy did likewise. The Pentagon reported to Kennedy that the U.S. Navy and USAF 'both have made detailed target studies.'[627]

The USA had huge numbers of nuclear-armed aircraft, but these planes, scattered at bases overseas, would have taken many hours to reach their targets. They would also need to refuel at some point. Many of them would have staged via Scottish refuelling air bases.

As previously stated, Scottish airfields featured as part of the Pentagon's strategic response to the Cuban crisis. The original long-term strategic plan had required secondary runways to be added to the airfields at Prestwick, Machrihanish, Kinloss, Leuchars and Lossiemouth. Wick was also needed as a B-52 refuelling base for SAC bombers en route to Moscow, so in 1955 its runway had been extended to handle the USAF B-52 Stratofortress fleet, and additional storage and control facilities had been added.[628] Needless to say, by 1962 USAF planners recorded that Wick was now certain to be a target for the Soviets.

American aircraft would have been within range of the Soviet air defence system for a lengthy period. Nuclear bombers, hundreds of them, were ready to visit Scotland en route to Russia, with many of them never to return.

By mid-October, NSA reports showed how the Russians were reacting to the situation. This was bleak news: 'On October 15th, the Soviets initiated a precautionary, preliminary alert, perhaps because Soviet Premier Nikita Khrushchev feared that U.S. intelligence had discovered the missiles.'[629]

All U.S. Navy HFDF sites had been involved from the early stages. From long before the time when Kennedy made his famous speech, on 22 October, they had been fully operational as America's 'Big Ear': all Soviet sea activity was monitored; ships were identified and their positions plotted. The USA had had an advantage from the start. This was crucial.

Mac McInness recalled this time vividly: 'I don't remember the exact month, but all vacations and travel were cancelled, and we were put on a three-section watch. Don't know exactly where that came from, but for many weeks you worked an eight-hour shift, had eight hours off and then back to work for another eight-hour watch.'

Rest time had been curtailed. But there was no other information. The Cuban problem was being kept under wraps. Operators were puzzled. McInness recalled: 'When it was later revealed, all the activity and urgency was explained. Everything during your watch seemed more urgent and seemed busier, a lot more activity from control than what you were used to. Don't get me wrong, you were always busy either looking for targets or following targets directed from the control centre. I don't remember any increase in tensions, probably because we weren't completely aware of all the things going on at sea. You knew what your part of the mission was and concentrated on that without thinking about what was outside your immediate world.'

The target spectrum had been narrowed. The NSA needed to advise the President on the flow of Soviet shipping to Cuba. It also needed to identify the ports of departure. This information would enable CIA local agents to focus on these locations and uncover more relevant material. American planners would then add these ports to the target list. The daily intelligence material sent to the NSA from Edzell and Kirknewton increased.[630]

The Scottish spy stations were part of the direction-finding network which tracked Soviet merchant ships and submarines sailing across the North Atlantic towards Cuba. Throughout the crisis, radio interception was crucial, helping to support the information produced by the U-2 flights over Cuba.

Submarines armed with nuclear missiles would be the key to the outcome. Both sides had this capability. Khrushchev had thought his submarines were his winning cards, but Kennedy revealed their exact locations to the Russian leader and informed him that they were all targeted for nuclear destruction. The American ASW forces had been directed to the precise locations of various Soviet submarines because the commanders of those boats had made the mistake of raising their antennae to transmit their position reports by burst transmission, and the Boresight stations, including Edzell, had intercepted those signals and begun tracking the boats.[631]

Several of the Scottish-based Atlantic Fleet radar picket ships were diverted from their routine early warning and submarine detection role to Cuban targets. On 22 October they made a major breakthrough. A U.S. Navy ASW aircraft observed a Russian replenishment ship, *Terek*, refuelling a submarine in the zone north of the Azores. This was the first time such activity had been spotted south of the Northern Seas.

The radar picket ship USS *Mills* (DER 383) had been en route from the USA to Greenock, to take up its regular GIUK Barrier patrol duties. It was immediately diverted to follow the *Terek*, which then headed away from Cuba towards the Northern Seas. Further pursuit was supplied by USS *Roy O. Hale*, which was returning to patrol from Greenock. These Scottish-based ships ensured that *Terek* was constantly harassed and unable to resupply any other Soviet submarines during the crisis.[632]

The emergency had a direct effect at the Kirknewton and Edzell spy stations. The routines at these locations were changed. Tension mounted. From early October, base security was stepped up. At first there was no explanation, and rumours ran wild. Some personnel believed there was a threat from Soviet Spetsnaz units. Others thought that Edzell was too small and insignificant to be attacked.

Once Kennedy had made his speech all was revealed. All military police on the bases – including the RAF Police, US Marine Corps Police and U.S. Navy Police – were now armed. Additional firing range practice was introduced; every armed security policeman fired at least 100 rounds of live ammunition. Arthur Grant, an RAF corporal at Edzell, remembered: 'We were issued with submachine guns. It was a bit like a war film. These guns were similar to Tommy guns. Their accuracy was just as poor. But the worst part of the weapons firing was the effect on our ears. There was no ear protection equipment in those days. Nowadays live firing is done wearing huge earmuffs for protection. Not for us then. All we had was cotton wool. It kept out some of the noise, but we were still rather deaf for a few days afterwards.' [633]

It was the Holy Loch SSBNs that were the crucial factor in this crisis; the Soviets could neither see them nor intercept their missiles. This capability was the game changer for Kennedy. His hand was much stronger than Khrushchev's, and the Soviets knew it. Scotland was now at the centre of the crisis.

The SubRon -14 commander, Captain W.F. Schlech, and his staff were fully involved in the build-up of the Cuban Missile Crisis. The procedures at Holy Loch were replaced by preparatory measures, as Mike Giambattista explained: 'We had been receiving detailed intelligence on the transit of ships suspected to be carrying missiles to Cuba … I can't recall precisely when, but by mid-September our daily intel began tracking the transport of Soviet missiles to Cuba.'

His daily Intel briefings had contained information showing the rapidly escalating emergency. The crisis had meant that all submarine activity moved at a faster pace. Peacetime regulations had been curtailed. Engineering tasks had been accelerated: 'As the crisis grew, the typical 28-day refits were cut short for the two SSBNs alongside, with only repairs to inoperative equipment; routine maintenance repairs were rescheduled for the next refit. Nuclear submarines always conducted 'fast cruises' of two to three days, which were conducted alongside the depot ship, to start and test the reactor plant prior to departure. These were reduced to one to two days, and the three-to-five-day sea trials were conducted en route to the patrol areas. One inbound SSBN had its patrol extended and did not return to Holy Loch until the termination of the crisis in late October.'

At this time there were six Holy Loch submarines at sea. They were all in their designated launching positions, but the U.S. Navy's commander, Admiral George Anderson, had to provide more firepower, because in order to put pressure on Khrushchev, Kennedy required a full hand. He needed all the submarines from Holy Loch to be out and active. So Admiral Anderson ordered two incoming Holy Loch SSBNs to return almost immediately to their assigned patrol areas in the Norwegian and North Seas. [634]

The increased refit pace was a surprise to the returning SSBNs, as they did not know about the crisis; during their patrol they had maintained radio silence. They returned to be confronted, when they berthed, with Defcon 3 military readiness level, indicating an increase in force preparedness well above normal readiness.

The captain of the *Abraham Lincoln*, entering the Firth of Clyde, responded swiftly when Mike Giambattista came aboard from a Mike boat with the news, Mike remembered: 'I told the commanding officer that his refit period had been amended. Instead of having 12 days to refit, he now only had 12 hours. He grimaced, chuckled and nodded in agreement. He quickly briefed his executive officer, and they set about re-planning the refit.'

Captain Mortimer, the XO, recalled the dramatic change of plan:

'We were supposed to go on patrol in twelve days. The Squadron 14 officer came aboard and said that we had twelve hours before departure. All the stores we needed were to be loaded immediately. He said that we should not expect to get back in two months. We are going to send you out there and when it is over you will do your regular sixty days. We ended up doing 76 days. Fortunately, we learned after a week or so that there was not going to be any shooting war. Did we realise how serious the situation was? We sure did. At least once a week we would get an artificial attack simulation.' [635]

The pressure continued for weeks aboard USS *Abraham Lincoln*. Mortimer noted:

'We would receive information from our communications channels. Everything would be real, except that the keys would not be inserted. When we had our first Weapons Readiness Test on this emergency deployment, the skipper said don't worry about anything, this is just a normal drill. After a couple of weeks, we realised that these were just drills every time. But running through our minds was the thought that if there was a real launch scenario, there would not be a lot to come home to at the end of the patrol. We were feeling a little bit strange about the situation.'

It was the high-water mark of Mortimer's career:

'This was the only time during my ballistic missile service that I had the feeling that this could be real. All the other times I believed that there was enough deterrent on both sides to keep the peace.'

Abraham Lincoln returned to sea within 15 hours of berthing. The fast pace of the new refit programme produced the required results, as Mike Giambattista remembered: 'This condensed activity enabled SubRon-14 to have seven SSBNs and 112 missiles in total, on station by 22 October. Another one was added a few days later – the USS *Thomas A. Edison*.' [636]

The amended turnaround schedule at Site One was carefully managed. It gave the dockyard full focus on one SSBN at a time. Work continued 24/7. Mike Giambattista recalled the emergency scheduling: 'SSBNs made inbound and outbound transits for the Cuba campaign, singly. We never had SSBNs arriving or departing within three to five days of each other at any time.' This change to the scheduled refit activity would have been noticed by the KGB agents in the local area, and they would have reported the changed situation. Moscow would have realised that Kennedy was serious.

Holy Loch was a strategically vital site and the Russians needed to know what was happening there. They would therefore have run a large espionage effort, noted Douglas H. Wise: 'During any major crisis with the West the KGB would have mounted a worldwide collection effort. This would have been to determine our plans and intentions. By casting the net wide, the KGB would have increased the amount of information flowing in and made their analysis and assessments better as to what we intend to do at each stage of the crisis and how we would do it. They would have had agents reporting on observed behaviors (or lack of behaviors), as well as attempting to overhear indiscreet discussions. The KGB would also have activated their agent networks to report back.'

By 22 October the US had the maximum number of strategic submarines at sea. The critical message was passed to Kennedy from the Chairman of the Joint Chiefs of Staff, informing him that the Holy Loch submarines were now in their allotted positions.[637]

Both the United States and the Soviet Union had raised the stakes. Military preparations were at a very high level. Intentions were clear from this increased activity. The tension grew steadily every day, and the Dunoon residents were very frightened. They were not the only ones, of course, but they knew they were sitting ducks, squarely in the Soviet sights.

The Man from DC

At the start of October, the Chief of Naval Operations had placed a transatlantic call to the commodore of the submarine squadron. The conversation was brief. The commodore informed Giambattista that the President was sending his senior adviser to Holy Loch. In fact, he would arrive the following day. Matters were now serious …

The transatlantic flight from New York landed at Prestwick and the passengers dispersed. One individual, a tall, slender American with short black hair, paced the arrivals hall, clutching his briefcase as he waited to be collected.

His name was Ken O'Donnell. A White House adviser had described him as: 'perhaps the most trusted and influential of that tightly-knit band around the President. O'Donnell had a hand in virtually every crisis in the Kennedy White House, from the Bay of Pigs to the Cuban missile confrontation.' He was the President's chief of staff.[638]

The collection of O'Donnell from the airport was low-key. Giambattista and the driver used a standard Navy automobile. There was no staff car, no flags on the vehicle and no U.S. Navy police escort. The meeting at Prestwick involved a handshake. There were no salutes, no fuss and no commotion. Nothing was done to attract attention. At Gourock the captain's gig collected them. This relaxed approach continued at the base. Giambattista recalled the situation: 'O'Donnell's arrival and departure were low key and unobtrusive (he was alone), and his visit lasted a couple of days.'

During that time, Giambattista was instructed to conduct the 'standard' briefing. This was based on the most recent intelligence material: 'The Operations Center, located on an upper deck in *Proteus*, had a single entrance. This room contained a working area with two desks and had whiteboards on one bulkhead. The entrance to the briefing room was via a door on the after bulkhead of the Operations Center. The briefing room was about 15ft × 15ft, and had an overhead projector and screen.' The commodore, the *Proteus*' captain, and the operations, weapons and engineering officers were present. All were curious to hear from the mystery guest.

The briefing room normally held eight or nine officers for routine meetings. Now they were about to participate in a momentous session. Up to that point the crisis had meant a lot of work and little sleep. And Defcon 3 had been set. This was an indication of possible future warlike action. All doubt was removed by O'Donnell's presence at the briefing. The President intended to use SUBRON-14 for real.

Once inside the briefing room, O'Donnell explained why he had come to Holy Loch. Giambattista recalled his mission statement: 'He wanted to see up close and personal the readiness and capability of the SSBNs, their command structure and launch procedures as well as the flow of intelligence to Holy Loch. His mission was to see first-hand the readiness and procedures to deploy the SSBNs.'

The Man from DC had their full attention. The gravity of the situation was now apparent.

Giambattista remembered the scrutiny O'Donnell gave to each item of the briefing. 'He was a quiet man who seemed to speak out of the corner of his mouth. He did not take many notes.' The submarine squadron was fully in the picture regarding the intensifying crisis and its own role in that crisis. O'Donnell and the commodore held further talks. He left the following day to return to Washington DC. Mission accomplished. The President was reassured that SubRon-14 would be up to the task if called upon.

One of the ironies of O'Donnell's visit involved Prestwick's status as a refuelling and servicing point for international air travel, in that Russian flights were regular visitors there. Even as O'Donnell was passing through Prestwick, he was sharing its facilities with Soviet military personnel on their way to reinforce the Cuban garrison. An increased number of Soviet IL-18 flights had passed through Prestwick to Havana. Pressure was put on the British authorities to cut off this access route for Soviet personnel, but the flights continued.[639]

By mid-October the Holy Loch submarines were under the direct command of the White House, as Mike Giambattista explained: 'Once the SSBNs had been deployed … we had little or no further communication with the various chains of command. It was a case of watch and wait. Not pleasant.'

Strategic Air Command had moved its warplanes to Defcon 2 status for the first time in its history. This decision put hundreds of nuclear-armed bombers, as well as American-based ICBM sites, at immediate readiness to attack Soviet targets. The Russians would have done likewise. It was a critical time for humanity.[640]

It was now clear that Kennedy held the dominant position over Khrushchev. The Holy Loch submarines were the United States' sole SSBN force. They were ready for purpose.

On the evening of 22 October President Kennedy gave his famous televised address to the American people, explaining the situation. Mike Giambattista recalled the tense build-up to this stage: 'In mid-October, after the last SSBN had deployed, *Proteus* was directed to prepare to depart Holy Loch on short notice. This came on 22 October.'[641]

This speech had a marked effect on the Russians' military posture. They immediately went on an 'extraordinary high state of alert'. Their emphasis was now on air defence – but their offensive forces did not step up to this level. This was significant. Khrushchev was showing Kennedy that the Russians would not strike first.[642]

The *Proteus* crew had rushed to prepare the ship for departure from the Holy Loch, and Gerry Pursley, an engineman, remembered the events: 'There was no travel allowed to Greenock. Then, all of a sudden, the decision was made and we were gone. We didn't even have enough time to make the ship secure for sea.'[643]

Proteus slipped her moorings in darkness during Kennedy's speech. When the Dunoon residents awoke the next morning they were alarmed to note that it was gone. Fear was high and there were cries of anger and disbelief. Brian Wilson recalled his thoughts at the time: 'There was always an awareness of what Holy Loch represented, even if it wasn't dwelt upon. The most vivid example was at the time of the Cuban Missile Crisis, when the depot ship *Proteus* left the Holy Loch under cover of darkness and went out into the Atlantic somewhere. Even though she was gone, there was a particular feeling of being in the front line that day, and I can certainly remember exactly where I was at the moment the ultimatum had been due to expire.'

Young sailor James Rapata was taken aback. He had missed the ship. He had stayed overnight in Dunoon, and when he returned the next morning the ship was gone. Tom Law, a Strone native, also had a vivid memory. His father, who lived on the banks of Holy Loch, called him at work in Glasgow to tell him that the entire Holy Loch 'kit and caboodle' had gone overnight, and he was wondering what had happened. Linda Wheeler was a local resident whose father served on the *Proteus*. She remembered watching it slip down the Firth of Clyde and wondering if it was ever going to come back.[644]

Proteus carried the staff of SubRon-14. Their work was now done and communications to the individual submarine commanders would now come via the Tacamo aircraft and the trailing-wire antenna system. Edzell, Kirknewton and Thurso remained fully staffed and deeply involved in the crisis. And the people of Dunoon could only wait – and worry.

The *Proteus* was en route for a safe berth in the Western Isles. This was a Zulu berth, a pre-arranged anchorage for the dispersal of ships during a crisis. But as its seagoing preparations were still incomplete, the consequences were soon obvious to those on board. In addition, it had had two submarines alongside at the time, with work parties on deck, rapidly loading stores before they headed to the Northern Seas. Axes were used to chop away their mooring lines, telephone cables, and water and sewage pipes. Short notice had arrived. *Proteus* set out for an epic eight-day voyage into terrible weather.[645]

The sudden departure of the tender surprised James E. Hodges: 'I'll never forget getting under way during the Cuban crisis. We must have gotten about 20 minutes' notice, and I had to tie down the missile crane hook as we steamed out of the loch.' [646]

Life aboard *Proteus* changed dramatically. The tender contained built-in danger areas which were harmless when the ship had been at anchor in Holy Loch. But when it took to sea those areas were exposed. Joseph Schmidt recalled his adventures at that time: 'There were waves of 50 feet over the top of the ship and it was pretty scary. We had to secure one of the machine shops as one of the machines broke loose. The machines weighed a ton or more, and they were sliding all over the deck. It was dangerous work.' [647]

Because of the rapid deployment, the gantry cranes had not been lowered and stowed on board, so they threatened to destabilise the ship. Gerry Pursley remembered the voyage: 'The seas were pounding us non-stop, and the ship almost rolled over several times. The decks were constantly awash, and it was a survival exercise for the crew. All the stock in the metal shop broke loose and rolled around. Our biggest fear was that the ship would break in half, as it had been modified with an extra section inserted to contain the Polaris missiles. This was the weak part of the ship's structure. Eventually the skipper told us that he was attempting to turn the ship into the waves to prevent this from occurring.'

These problems persisted throughout the voyage, noted Pursley: 'Equipment fell on top of the engines and we could not remove it to safety, so we had to lash it down to prevent further damage. The weather was terrible, and we could not see the sky as waves broke over the ship. This was a big ship, 500 feet long, but the propellors were out of the water lots of the time. This caused the engines to overheat and cut out. We had to restart the engines, and only three of the four were now working.'

As the conditions deteriorated, the skipper, Captain Ray DuBois, decided to moor in Tobermory, on the Isle of Mull. However, the ship was twice the length of the local ferry boats which normally berthed there. Mike Giambattista described the event: '*Proteus* never moored. She did try to anchor in Tobermory Bay, but the skipper decided that the harbor was a wee bit small, so he exited and we remained under way until we returned to Holy Loch.'

As the tender made its way northwards through the Minches it had been shadowed by Russian ELINT (electronic signals intelligence) trawlers. These vessels had good seakeeping capabilities. This characteristic was significant, and they were able to track the tender to the Isle of Mull.[648]

The rapid departure of *Proteus* caused great anxiety among the crew because as far as they were aware they were going to war. One of them was George Klein, a new crew member. Until that time, he had worked aboard the ship moored in Holy Loch. Then the Cuban crisis exploded. His life changed overnight, and he encountered tough sea conditions, great international tension and political agitation: 'In October 1962, we received orders to get under way. The North Irish Sea isn't fun that time of the year. Needless to say, this was one nervous, scared puppy.'[649]

During the absence of the *Proteus*, the local population believed nuclear annihilation was nigh. This was a common feeling throughout the central belt of Scotland and was true even for people who lived 40 miles away. Lizzie Lamb was a young girl who expressed this terror: 'I remembered feeling very frightened as a child, in the midst of the Cuban Missile Crisis, at the thought of being vapourised [sic] by a Russian missile because we lived within spitting distance of Holy Loch (Motherwell).'[650]

When the subs returned, the people of Dunoon were reassured. But fanciful conclusions were drawn from these events. Locals believed that Dunoon was no longer a target for Soviet missiles, as the submarines and tender had departed during the crisis – an understandable, but incorrect, conclusion. Holy Loch was always a target for the Soviets; the SSBNs were the United States' most important weapons system. They could not be ignored.[651]

Perhaps the best summing up of the *Proteus*' voyage through the storm came from Gerry Pursley, who proclaimed: 'When we returned to Holy Loch and tied up, I did not want to go to sea again.'

The crisis unwinds

Kennedy's threat worked. The crisis was resolved and no military force was used. The strategic value of Scotland's geographical position had been well demonstrated. Holy Loch's SSBN squadron carried the ultimate threat, and the radio intercept stations had kept the Pentagon fully informed.

Although the SubRon-14 boats and USS *Proteus* returned to Holy Loch, SubRon-14 still had a role to play in the resolution of the crisis. The USSR had to remove its missiles from Cuba and the USA had to remove 15 Jupiter missiles from Turkey, creating a gap in the American defences. SubRon-14 provided the solution, and Mike Giambattista remembered his involvement in this event: 'I was assigned to brief Captain James B. Calvert, the State Department's naval liaison officer, on what steps would be necessary to deploy SSBNs to the Mediterranean. The removal of these missiles had created a gap in Washington's strategic plan. As a result, USS *Ethan Allen* commenced patrols in the Mediterranean in December. The gap was plugged from Holy Loch.'

This solution led to claims being made that one of the Holy Loch FBMs had been on patrol off the coast of Turkey during the campaign. Mike Giambattista does not think this was the case: 'It is possible that unbeknownst to us in CSS14 that an SSBN could have been diverted to the Med without our knowledge. However, based on my briefings with Captain Calvert after the crisis, SSBN deployments to the Med were only then going to be implemented. I did read each patrol report of every SSBN, and I saw no evidence of an SSBN being diverted to the Med.'

At the end of the crisis the support provided by the Scottish spy stations was officially noted. The U.S. Navy Commander-in-Chief Atlantic, Admiral Dennison, highlighted the importance of the SIGINT contribution to the overall success of the mission: 'I should like to take this opportunity to mention the very significant contribution which SIGINT in general – and the National Security Agency in particular – have made toward support of Atlantic Command.'

He left no doubt as to its vital importance to the senior command: 'In the present situation SIGINT has been one of the most important single factors in supporting our operations and improving our readiness. Your fine support is much appreciated.'

The Director of the NSA emphasised this point: 'While you mentioned NSA in particular ... the Naval Security Group ... deserve[s] a lion's share of the credit.' [652]

The Navy Unit Commendation was subsequently awarded to *Proteus* for its performance in completing all the necessary tasks to enable all SSBNs to be on station by mid-October. But the squadron headquarters staff, who had organised all of these activities, had been excluded. Mike Giambattista had stepped up to solve the problem: 'I spoke with our administrative officer, LCDR William O. Thomson. He had served under Fleet Admiral Chester Nimitz at the end of the Second World War and knew the ropes. We prepared the documentation and submitted it.'

Giambattista possessed useful background information about Thomson; his middle name was Orkney, which revealed his Scottish connection; he was just one generation removed from Scotland. Thomson was most sympathetic to the efforts made by those based in Scotland, and approved the application.

The Russians had placed nuclear missiles in Cuba. They were to have been launched by the local Russian commander if he had deemed it necessary. But the truth was that the Russian missiles were stone age compared with the Polaris weapons. The Russian missiles would have reached mainland USA if their low-tech guidance systems had worked properly, and they would probably have detonated on impact. But they could not be targeted accurately, as they did not have a reliable guidance system, and most would have failed in some way. But just one could have brought nuclear devastation to some spot in the southern states. It never happened.[653]

In 1962 the United States had possessed a three-pronged nuclear deterrent; it could be delivered by air from the bombers of the Strategic Air Command, by land from silos sited in continental United States, and by the submarines from Holy Loch. The Cuban Missile Crisis provided SubRon-14 , the Scottish spy stations and radar picket ships with their real-life trade test. All passed with distinction. Scotland had justified its selection as a strategic location.

14   The final curtain

Until 1952 the United States had used Scotland as a logistical safe haven. Thousands of American warplanes had crossed the Atlantic to Scottish airfields, and the U.S. Navy had used anchorages on the west coast of the country. But none of this had been linked to front-line operations. This changed in 1952 when the Russian threat compelled the US to use Scotland for its important ongoing front-line strategic military activities. This continued until 1997, when the US Government closed its last base in Scotland. Those 45 years of military activity highlighted Scotland's strategic value to Washington.

The Kirknewton radio interception station had been established to cover a vital strategic area. The information it collected was flown back to Washington DC. The UK had allied itself firmly with the USA, mainly for continued access to the nuclear power secrets the UK had helped to develop during the Second World War, but also because the UK had advantages to offer which were vital for America's strategic defence. It could provide anchorage for the U.S. Navy's first Polaris submarine base and listening stations to cover the vital GIUK Gap; it could service U.S. Navy early warning ships and anti-submarine warfare aircraft; and it could provide a logistics link to the US military forces in Western Europe.

The Scottish bases fitted into the US strategic defence posture. Holy Loch SSBNs at sea, on receipt of Presidential orders from the transmitter at Thurso, could launch missiles to attack strategic Russian targets. The radio intercept site at Edzell was a key component in guarding the GIUK Gap and tracking Soviet vessels. Part of this role had previously been carried out by Kirknewton.

There were sound practical reasons for basing American SSBNs in Scotland. The boats based there could spend another 14 days on patrol instead of transiting to and from the east coast of the United States. Refit Site One, through its ability to service the speedy and efficient turnaround of their crews, also removed the need for the construction of additional SSBNs to ensure full coverage of strategic targets in the Soviet Union. This factor was of immense value to the Pentagon's budget; savings in this area could be utilised elsewhere.

During the Cold War, Holy Loch submarines provided more strategic deterrent patrols than those from any other location. This was highlighted in April 1987, when USS *Mariano G. Vallejo* (SSBN 658) carried out the SubRon-14's 2,500th deterrent patrol.[64]

The Scottish bases also, as mentioned earlier, achieved the political purpose of providing reassurance to America's European allies that they would be supported in the face of Russian aggression. The dark-hulled nuclear-missile submarine squadron at Holy Loch was the most prominent symbol of the American military presence.

The United States operated a professional, well-trained military machine at its Scottish bases. Its relationship with the local communities was excellent, and all the sites were regular recipients of community service awards.

Apart from the early days of the SSBN squadron at Holy Loch, there was no large-scale opposition, nor were there any protests, at any of the bases. Submarine Squadron 14 and its permanently assigned units were awarded the Meritorious Unit Commendation by the U.S. Navy for exceptional performance of assigned missions in 1975, 1983 and 1987.

The US military forces in Scotland initially included draftees, but in later years it became a full-time professional military force. Their high standards of competence never varied. This was their greatest strength. There were no poorly trained elements. All units produced top quality results. This was underpinned by a training culture which produced high-quality personnel for all tasks, who had been fully trained on long, US-based courses to achieve the desired results. The U.S. Navy operated to a training mindset which had stemmed from its superlative performance in the Second World War. By 1945 it had become the largest naval force in history, commanding 3 million well-disciplined sailors – yet three years earlier 90 per cent of those sailors had been civilians.[654] This high standard had been achieved by relentless training.

The American targets were clearly defined, and the SSBNs had to patrol a designated area of the Northern Seas in order to permanently threaten Russia. The intercept stations had to monitor Soviet air and naval activity in the area.

Intelligence information was gathered from Edzell, Thurso and Kirknewton. They covered a specific zone in the Northern Seas, and their targets were Soviet surface, subsurface and air movements. Edzell and Kirknewton also intercepted private, commercial and diplomatic messages.

An enormous amount of information was collected and sent back to the USA for analysis. But how much of it was useful? This is virtually impossible for me to answer, as the use of intelligence information was, and still is, hidden by layers of secrecy. Plenty of raw data was gathered from the three sites in Scotland and sent back to the USA for analysis. Nothing has been revealed about its usefulness. However, in the one instance where this intelligence material was known to be used – the 1962 Cuban crisis – the Scottish bases played an important role and were highly commended by senior military staff.

---

64 Holy Loch operated from 1961 to 1992. Rota operated 1964 to 1976, Guam operated 1963–1981 and undertook 398 patrols; Kings Bay, Georgia, began operations in 1979, continued throughout the Cold War, and at the time of writing is still operational.

A fundamental question was raised by the presence of these American bases: did they bring an additional military threat to Scotland? The bases at Holy Loch, Edzell, Thurso and Machrihanish did so. The UK military locations in Scotland were already on the Soviet target list, and the additional American sites would have joined them on it.

As the Soviets, like everyone else, were principally concerned with self-protection, they would undoubtedly have liked to eliminate the significant American threat points in Scotland. But there appears to have been a corporate ambivalence to this matter from both Scottish and American sources. The locals on Cowal, when questioned for a 1974 poll, showed little fear of a nuclear strike from Russia: only 20 per cent expressed concern.[655] This demonstrated the continuing power of the cover stories regarding the bases. However, reality belied this cosy picture. It was the Soviet communications centres that were targeted on first strike by the American Strategic Integrated Operating Plan (SIOP). This priority was a standard military concept, and the Soviets would have prioritised likewise.

Willie Hogg had worked on classified equipment at Edzell, Holy Loch and Thurso. Hogg and his fellow Americans believed that keeping America out of harm's way by installing an obvious target for Soviet aggression in a foreign country was an acceptable idea. He was surprised to discover that Edzell would have been a Soviet target; he had not realised that communications centres, as well as nuclear weapons sites, were definitely targets: 'What makes you think that Edzell was a prime Soviet target during the Cold War? It was a relatively small base, and was mostly just communication … there were no nuclear weapons at Edzell.'

Holy Loch and Edzell were obvious Soviet targets. Thurso, too, had been critically important to the Soviets, as it would have transmitted the nuclear release orders. The Soviet Union had seven airborne divisions which were particularly suited to the rapid seizure of such lightly defended enemy targets.[656]

General Sir Rupert Smith pointed out this reality: 'If Norway's coastline, in particular Bergen and Stavanger, was in Soviet hands and nuclear release looked likely, they might very well want to seize a foothold in the British Isles as well as disrupt nuclear communications. In which case I would seize Kirkwall airfield by airborne assault, with another group landing in Thurso to destroy the communications.'

This assault would have had the benefit of surprise and would have been launched far from Scotland's shores: 'Mounting would have taken place in Russia, possibly Murmansk, and the approach would have crossed Tromsø, the Lofoten Isles, Bergen, Stavanger, Kirkwall, Thurso. The flight would be low-level, using the coastline to shield the aircraft from radar. The assault would have close air support and the targets might have been bombed in advance of the drop.'

The U.S. Navy was well aware of the threat of a Soviet missile strike against its SSBNs at Holy Loch. As mentioned earlier, during the Cuban crisis in 1962, the *Proteus* was removed from the danger zone while President Kennedy was giving his public address. Mike Giambattista was not surprised by its departure: 'This was already written into our SOP [standard operating procedures]. It was our pre-planned response to such a situation.'

Machrihanish, Prestwick and Shetland airfields could have been follow-up targets for Soviet missiles, denying them to the America-based SAC flights and UK Vulcan bombers. Although this would have been an inconvenience to the Pentagon, it would have been catastrophic for the local communities.

The additional danger to the civilians around those bases was well illustrated by the 1974 collision between the USS *James Madison* and the Soviet Victor-class submarine, and in 1981 by the *Canopus* missile drop incident.

The strategic advantages of the Scottish bases continued until 1997, when the U.S. Navy closed its final Scottish base at Edzell. These closures were the result of advances in technology. Better equipment, such as satellites and more advanced SSBNs with longer-range missiles, had reduced the benefits of Scotland's geographical location. The end of the Cold War in 1989 hastened a Fortress America mentality along with a desire to reduce overseas military costs. The Scottish bases became victims of this policy.

These changes meant that by the 1990s Scotland had ceased to retain its original value as an American strategic asset. The United States could now base its SSBNs in home waters, and could reach targets in Russia from mid-Atlantic. Its intelligence gathering could be delivered by satellites.

Holy Loch, Kirknewton, Edzell and Thurso had been important American strategic defence bases simply because politics and geography had meant that their tasks could not be accomplished elsewhere. However, technology had advanced with the introduction of the Trident SLBM, as well as improved satellite reconnaissance.

The Trident missile was a major factor in this change process. As it now had a range of 6,500 nautical miles, the SSBNs could launch their missiles from locations much closer to continental USA. Transit times were significantly reduced, and these boats could now be home-ported in mainland American bases. The Holy Loch FBM squadron was deactivated and its SSBNs redeployed to Kings Bay, Georgia.

Captain Ron Gumbert gave a further reason for the closure of Holy Loch: 'I would say that Scotland's US SSBN support mission was no longer required because of the advances in ballistic missile technology – but also that the elimination of the US presence in the Holy Loch was more political and cost-driven than the change in its strategic value. Scotland ceased to retain its *perceived* value as an American strategic asset.'

The original SSBN fleet, the '41 for Freedom',[65] was due to reach its end-of-life stage in the late 1980s. A new fleet was designed and constructed, with longer-range Trident missiles. Captain Gumbert explained the benefits of the new boats: 'The first of these new SLBM submarines (designated the Ohio / Trident class) commenced its first patrol in October 1982. As more Ohio class submarines were commissioned and could commence patrols, older classes of submarines were removed from service and the demand for forward refit sites was reduced and eventually eliminated.

'Therefore it was clear, as early as 1981, that the days of Fleet Ballistic Submarine Refit Site One/Commander Submarine Squadron 14 in Holy Loch were numbered. By 1988, targets previously assigned to the Holy Loch SSBNs began to be reassigned to the newly constructed SSBN squadron at Kings Bay, Georgia. The Holy Loch boats were now at their end of life.'

The political climate had also changed, as Captain Gumbert noted: 'In 1989 the Berlin Wall came down, and there was an eagerness on the part of Americans to reap the "peace dividend".

---

65 41 for Freedom – nickname for the U.S. Navy's first FBM fleet of 41 nuclear missile submarines.

What followed in the United States were several BRAC [base realignment and closure] commissions. The closures program had a large political component, and with bases being closed across the US there was considerable scrutiny placed on overseas facilities.'

In 1990 Submarine Refit Site One at Holy Loch was slated to be shut down before June 1992. This was not, however, a sudden decision, as Captain Gumbert explained: 'The elimination of the SSBN mission from Holy Loch had been a long-term strategic goal. Forward-basing fleet ballistic missile submarines is expensive and creates local security challenges for the nuclear weapons they carry. From a technology viewpoint, basing SSBNs in the continental United States is a prudent measure. In addition, many in the United States opined that with the elimination of the Soviet Union as a threat there was no need for a submarine refit facility on the other side of the Pond.'

In the late 1980s the U.S. Navy decided to reduce the number of submarine tenders (specifically, by not building new ones): 'So the question was "Where do we need to put the two tenders we intend to keep?" Holy Loch was not one of the locations.'

Thurso's role as the main European transmitter was absorbed by new sites elsewhere. The U.S. Navy constructed two ELF (extremely low frequency) radio transmission facilities to communicate with its deep-diving submarines. These facilities, which were at Clam Lake, Wisconsin, and Republic, Michigan, were operated by the Naval Computer and Telecommunications Area Master Station Atlantic.[657] Thurso was no longer needed.

Intelligence coverage of the GIUK Gap remained essential, but this task could now be carried out via satellites. Their information needed to be downloaded by ground stations, and the largest radio intercept station in Europe was built at Menwith Hill in Yorkshire. The Edzell and Thurso missions moved there. The hotline switched to a secure radio mode and was no longer routed through Scotland. America's Scottish-based spy fraternity moved out, as did GCHQ and the other associated UK units.

Intelligence-gathering was dramatically affected by the swift advance of technology. Douglas H. Wise explained its impact: 'By the mid-nineties, the United States had launched many earth-orbiting satellites. Some were for scientific purposes, but many of these had military and intelligence applications, for either navigation or reconnaissance. These satellites were developed, launched and operated by the NRO, whose existence at the time was highly classified. Many of these satellites provided valuable SIGINT collection for NSA. Much of the intercept, and the entire HFDF role at Edzell and Thurso, could now be done from space. The collection from these satellites was excellent – far superior to those from the Scottish bases. Consequently, the United States began the closure of its intercept networks, including the Atlantic system. Its remaining station, at Rota, was closed in 2005.'

Support for this view was provided by Alan Judd: 'Changes in monitoring sites are usually driven either by technological change (collection methods etc) or by long-term changes in requirements and targets. In this case it looks like technology was the driving factor, as the United States still retained the same targets.'

The closures created serious economic setbacks for the local communities which had hosted the American personnel for more than 30 years. Brian Wilson described the effects of the Holy Loch closure: 'It left a huge gap in the economy when they left, and Dunoon has never really recovered from that.'

For almost half a century America's Scottish bases were in the front line, ever vigilant and fully involved in daily operational tasks of strategic importance. The cutting edge of the Cold War had been based in Scotland. Nuclear Armageddon could have been initiated by the United States military forces based there.

Dangerous times centred on their activities, especially the Cuban Missile Crisis. The world faced great danger, and the Scottish units performed their tasks to the highest standard. Scots and Americans lived together and worked together. They would have died together.

And the memories linger on …

'Ae fond kiss' [66]

The American personnel in Scotland were a long way from home. They were in a foreign country, and their presence had totally changed some sleepy Scottish towns. Local life had been disturbed and this could have caused resentment and annoyance. But it did not. The locals took the Americans to their hearts.

Russ Christie, MT1 Blue Crew, went into town one day.[658] His experience summed up the locals' attitude to their American guests: 'I had a rare day off in Holy Loch, so I put on my dress blues and headed to Dunoon for some shopping. To get there you took the launch from the tender to the beach, then down to the pier to catch a ferry to take you over to Dunoon. I got on the ferry. Suddenly I felt a quick tap-tap on my back. I turned around and all I saw was a middle-aged woman walking away from me.'

'A few minutes later, tap-tap on my back. Again, I turned around and another woman was walking past me. She did not say a word, just kept walking. Now I'm from a big city and I know when I'm being screwed with. Not long thereafter came another tap-tap, so this time I spun around quickly and asked the woman going by, "What *do* you think you're doing?" – in a rather sarcastic tone, I might add.'

'She stopped, turned towards me. She smiled at me and said, "During the war, we'd tap each of the stars on the sailor's back. It was our way of saying *Thanks, Yank, and good luck*." It left me speechless. All I could say was "Thanks". I was stunned by this random act of kindness. It left a very lasting impression. If I could relive any single event in my eight-year navy career, it would be that one.'

---

66 'Ae Fond Kiss' – poem by Robert Burns.

Epilogue

'At the tail end of the Cold War, not everything was by the book.'

The Cold War was a serious business. But the military mind can find humour in any situation. At Edzell, Greg Wright and his colleagues had concocted an elaborate ruse to play on a newly arrived marine. New personnel were vulnerable to these pranks, as they were eager to impress, and usually had little rank to push back with. This marine was an ideal subject. They set it up over weeks – leaving cryptic messages lying near his position on the ops floor, as well as whispered conversations just within earshot.

When the marine had been properly prepared, they enacted the prank. He was told to go to the roof of Building 300 to await a canister of 'classified intel' dropped from a satellite – the trick being that this was the only way to retrieve real, actionable intelligence without it being mucked about by external personalities, agencies etc. That night, Wright took him up to the roof. All was working fine, when the victim asked: 'Sergeant Wright, what if it lands on my head?'

This was in the dark, on a midwatch, on the roof, at the moment when the other joker was busy heating a spare gearwheel with his lighter. Wright had to think on his feet, and later reported: 'I managed to stay afloat, barely, by telling him that each pole of the Elephant Cage had a transponder on top, which allowed the canister to target the exact centre of the circle. Which we weren't at. So unless it was off target, there was no risk of him being hit on the head.'

The hot gearwheel was then tossed up onto the roof. The young marine found it, and sprinted it down to the ops floor, literally dumping it onto the watch officer's desk, snapping to attention and announcing his achievement. This was in front of every person on watch that night, who all began a slow handclap …

But the story did not end there. In later years it took an amazing turn. The young marine would often tell the story at Christmas dinners, at Easter Sunday gatherings and at bars with friends and family. His brother (also a marine) had married a film maker. After she'd heard the story a few times, she remarked: 'Wouldn't it be great if this were made into a short film?'

They contacted Wright, and together they put together a pretty accurate script. This was then made into a short film and premiered in 2018 at the San Diego G.I. Film Festival. With both the victim and Wright in attendance.

So the Naval Security Group Activity at Edzell, Scotland has been immortalised on the big screen. Wright chuckled at this outcome: 'The film adaptation of this glorious prank is ... fantastic. Poignant, believable, funny as hell, and faithful to the spirit of marines giving one of their own an initiation unlike any other. If you'd told me then – there – that three decades later we were all going to relive this in a movie, I'd have referred you to the base Substance Abuse Counseling Officer.' [67]

---

67 *Satellite Drop* – an official selection for the 2017 Copa Shorts Film Festival, the 2018 GI Film Festival San Diego, and the 2018 American Warrior Music and Film Festival, amazon.com/Satellite-Drop, 10 May 2019.

List of abbreviations, acronyms, initialisms

AACS	Airways and air communications service
ABNCP	Airborne national *command post*
ACE High	Allied Command Europe Highband
ADIZ	Air defense identification zone
AE	Ammunition ship
AEAO	Airborne emergency action officer
AFB	Air Force base
AFDB	Auxiliary floating dry dock
AGI	Analytical Graphics Inc
APL	Auxiliary personnel lighter
ARRS	Aerospace rescue and recovery service
ARS	Air rescue service
ASF	Auxiliary security force
ASG	Air support group
ASR	Air-sea rescue
ASW	Anti-submarine warfare
AUTEC	Atlantic Undersea Test and Evaluation Center
Autovon	Automatic voice network
AWACS	Airborne warning and control system
BM	Boatswain's mate
BMEWS	Ballistic missile early warning system
BRAC	Base realignment and closure commissions
CAC	Combat air crew
CDAA	Circularly disposed antenna array (Elephant Cage)
CG	(U.S.) Coast Guard
CGHQ	(U.S.) Coast Guard Headquarters
CIA	Central Intelligence Agency
Cinclant	Commander in Chief, Atlantic
Cincusnaveur	Commander-in-Chief, U.S. Navy, Europe
CND	Campaign for Nuclear Disarmament
CO	Commanding officer
Comaswforlant	Commander ASW Force Atlantic
Comint	Communications intelligence
Comsec	Communications security
CPGB	Communist Party of Great Britain
CPO	Chief petty officer
CRRC	Combat rubber raiding craft
CT	Cryptologic technician
CTI	Cryptologic technician interpretive
CTM	Cryptology technician maintenance
CTR	Cryptologic technician collection
DASO	Demonstration and Shakedown Operation
DEB	Digital European backbone
DEFCON	Defence condition
DER	Radar picket escort ship
DET	Detachment
DEW	Distant early warning
DF	Direction-finding
DIA	Defense Intelligence Agency

DPR	Daily position report		communications network
DVR	Digital video recorder	MFV	Motor fishing vessel
EAMs	Emergency action messages	MM	Machinist's mate
ELF	Extremely low frequency	MN3	Mineman 3rd class
ELINT	Electronic intelligence	MOD	Ministry of Defence
EMFN	Electrician's mate fireman	Momag	Mobile mine assembly group
EN2	Engineman petty officer 2nd class	MT	Motorised transport
EOD	Explosives ordnance disposal	NAD	NATO armaments depot
EP	Electrical power	NARS	North Atlantic radio system
ESWS	Enlisted surface warfare specialist	NAS	Naval air station
ET	Electronics technician	NATO	North Atlantic Treaty Organization
ET1 SS	Electronics technician 1st class, ship submersible	NATS	National Air Traffic Services
		Navcommsta	Naval communications station
ESWS	Enlisted Surface Warfare Specialist	NAWF	Naval aviation warfare facility
FBM	Fleet ballistic missiles	NCA	National Command Authority
GCHQ	Government Communications Headquarters	NCIS	Naval Criminal Investigative Service
		NEACP	National emergency airborne command post
GIUK Gap	Greenland–Iceland–UK Gap		
GRU	Glavnoye Razvedyvatelnoye Upravlenie (Chief Intelligence Office)	NOSS	Naval Ocean Surveillance System
		NRO	National Reconnaissance Office
HF	High frequency	NRS	Naval Radio Station
HFDF	High frequency direction-finding	NSC	National Security Council
HMG	Her (*during the period covered by this book*) Majesty's Government	NSGA	Naval Security Group Activity
		NSWU	Naval special warfare unit
HT	Hull technician	NWA	Northwest Airlines
IA-PVO	Istrebitel'naya Aviatsiya-Protivovozdushnoi Oborony (Air Defence– Fighter Aviation)	OBA	Oxygen breathing apparatus
		OFD	Oil and fuel depot
IC	In charge	ONI	Office of Naval Intelligence
ICBM	Intercontinental ballistic missile	OOD	Officer of the deck
IG	Inspector general	ORSE	Operational reactor safeguards examination
Intel reps	Intelligence reports	OTH	Over the horizon
JOOD	Junior officer of the deck	PCBs	Polychlorinated biphenyls
KGB	Komitet Gosudarstvennoy Bezopasnosti (Committee for State Security)	PJ	Pararescueman
		PN	Personnelman
Lcdr	Lieutenant commander	PVO	Protivovozdushnoi Oborony (Air Defence)
LCM	Landing craft mechanized	PX	Private telephone exchange
LES	Law enforcement sensitive	QM	Quartermaster
LF	Low frequency	RAF	Royal Air Force
LLE	low-level extraction	Radcon	Radiation control
LMS	Loran monitoring station	RC	Reactor compartment
Loran	Long-range navigation	REFORGER	Reinforcement of Germany
Lormonsta	Loran monitoring station	RMC	Regional maintenance centre
LOS	Line of sight	RPA	Rotating log periodic antennae
Ltjg	Lieutenant junior grade	RN	Royal Navy
MATS	Military Air Transport Service	RNAS	Royal Naval Air Station
MCC	Mission control center		
MEEMS	Minimum essential emergency		

RSM	Radio squadron mobile	SSBN	Ship submersible ballistic nuclear
RTTY	Radio teletype	SSN	Ship submersible nuclear-powered
SAC	Strategic Air Command	SSO	Special security officer
SACEUR	Supreme Allied Commander Europe	ST2	Sonar tech 2nd class
SAM	Special Air Mission OR System Area Monitor	SubRon	Submarine squadron
SAR	Search and rescue	TAK	T, transport; A, auxiliary; K, cargo
SB	Special Branch	TM	Torpedoman
SBI	Special background investigations	TOTO	Tongue of the Ocean
SCBA	Self-contained breathing apparatus	TS/SCI	Top secret/sensitive compartmented information
SF	Shipfitter	UCMJ	Uniform Code of Military Justice
SI	Special Intelligence	UHF	Ultra high frequency
SIOP	Strategic Integrated Operating Plan	UKWMS	UK wideband microwave system v
Sigint	Signals intelligence	USAF	US Air Force
SISS	Station Information and Security System	USAFSS	US Air Force Security Service
SK	Storekeeper	USCG	US Coast Guard
SLBM	Submarine-launched ballistic missile	USMC	US Marine Corps
SOP	Standard operating procedures	USN	United States Navy
SOSUS	SOund SUrveillance System	VP	Fixed-wing patrol (*as against* VF = fixed-wing fighter)
SpecComms	Specialist Communications		
SP	Special projects	XO	Executive officer
SP	Service police	YFNB	Large covered lighter, non-self-propelled
SPs	Service police officers		

ENDNOTES

1 Simon Duke, *United States Military Forces and Installations in Europe* (Oxford: Oxford University Press, 1989), 190, 343 & 347–8.

2 Gustav Schmidt, *A History of NATO: The First Fifty Years* (3 volumes) (New York: Palgrave, 2001); Email NATO Archives to author 2 Aug 2016; Baylis John, Anglo-American Defence Relations 1939–1984: *The Special Relationship*, Second Edition (London: Macmillan, 1984), pp. 40–1 & 78. Baylis, John, *Anglo-American Relations since 1939: The Enduring Alliance* (Manchester: Manchester University Press, 1997): Miller, David, *The Cold War: Military History* (London: John Murray, 1998). Also, Chris Chant, *Submarine Warfare Today* (Wigston: Silvermark Books, 2005), 8, 9 & 13.

3 Gunnar Gunnarsson, 'The Impact of Naval Developments in Iceland', in *Soviet Sea Power in Northern Waters*, eds. John Skogan and Arne Brundtland (London: Pinter Publishing, 1990), 92.

4 Charles Stephenson, *US Airforce Reconnaissance Flights over the Soviet Union 10 January–6 February 1956: The Genetrix Balloons* (Osprey Publishing, 1 May 2001), http://www.ospreypublishing.com.

5 'GRANDSON / GRAYBACK / GENETRIX / ASH CAN / MELTING POT', A History of Balloons & Ballooning, accessed 6 November 2019, www.airvectors.net/avbloon_3.html.

6 FRUS, 1950–1955, The Intelligence Community, 1950–1955, Document 229.

7 'Eden to Eisenhower, 20 August 1955', PDF Read Book Page, accessed 10 June 2019, Eden to Eisenhower, 20 August 1955, 1955_08_19.pdf

8 FRUS, 1950–1955, The Intelligence Community, 1950–1955, Document 249 December 27, 1955; National Archives, RG 59, Central Files 1955–60, 711.5261/12–1555. Top Secret. INR Files: Lot 61 D 67, Genetrix.

9 US Intelligence on Europe 1945–1995, Commander 3rd Air Force, to USAF Chief of Staff, 15 October 1954, Brill, National Library of Scotland.

10 U.S. Air Force Cable, COMDR 3 AF to COFS USAF, 29 October 1954, Top Secret, NARA; Brill, National Library of Scotland, accessed 15 January 2020; also, 1st Air Division (Meteorological Survey) Strategic Air Command. Final Report Project 119L, Top Secret. CIA-RDP89B00708R000500040001-0: 11.

11 U.S. Air Force Cable, COMDR 3 AF to COFS USAF, 29 October 1954, Top Secret, NARA; Brill, National Library of Scotland.

12 1st Air Division (Meteorological Survey) Strategic Air Command. Final Report Project 119L, 9.

13 US Intelligence on Europe 1945–1995, Commander 3rd Air Force, to USAF Chief of Staff, 15 October 1954. Brill, National Library of Scotland, accessed 15 January 2020.

14 Gregory W. Pedlow, and Donald E. Welzenbach. *The Central Intelligence Agency and Overhead Reconnaissance: The U-2 and OXCART Programs, 1954–1974* (Washington DC: History Staff, Central Intelligence Agency, 1992), 84–88; Donald E. Welzenbach. 'Observation Balloons and Reconnaissance Satellites'. *Studies in Intelligence* 30, no. 1 (Spring 1986): 24.

15 'GRANDSON / GRAYBACK / GENETRIX / ASH CAN / MELTING POT'. B.D. Gildenberg, 'The Cold War's Classified Skyhook Program: A Participant's Revelations', *Skeptical Inquirer*, Vol. 28-3 (May/June 2004): 38–42.

16 Pedlow and Welzenbach. *The Central Intelligence Agency and Overhead Reconnaissance*, 7.

17 'GRANDSON / GRAYBACK / GENETRIX / ASH CAN / MELTING POT'.

18 'GRANDSON / GRAYBACK / GENETRIX / ASH CAN / MELTING POT'. also, Gildenberg, 'The Cold War's Classified Skyhook Program: A Participant's Revelations', 38–42; also, 1st Air Division (Meteorological Survey) Strategic Air Command. Final Report Project 119L, 19.

19 [3.0] Cold War Balloon Flights 1945:1965, Airvectors.com, accessed 6 November 2019, airvectors.net/avbloon_3. html; also, 1st Air Division (Meteorological Survey) Strategic Air Command. Final Report Project 119L, 19.

20 1st Air Division (Meteorological Survey) Strategic Air Command. Final Report Project 119L, 113; Welzenbach, 'Observation Balloons and Reconnaissance Satellites', 21.

21 Welzenbach, 'Observation Balloons and Reconnaissance Satellites', 21–28; 1st Air Division (Meteorological Survey) Strategic Air Command. Final Report Project 119L, Top Secret. CIA-RDP89B00708R000500040001-0: 39.

22 1st Air Division (Meteorological Survey) Strategic Air Command. Final Report Project 119L, Top Secret. CIA-RDP89B00708R000500040001-0: 12.

23 Roy K. Jonkers, 'Cold War Balloon Intelligence', AFIO Weekly Intelligence Notes 40-98 (20 Oct. 1998), accessed 3 January 2021, http://www.his.com/~afio/.

24 'Cold War Balloon Flights 1945:1965'.

25 'Cold War Balloon Flights 1945:1965'.

26 Cold War Balloon Flights 1945:1965; Gildenberg, 'The Cold War's Classified Skyhook Program: A Participant's Revelations', 38–42.

27 FRUS, 1950–1955, The Intelligence Community, 1950–1955, Document 249 December 27, 1955.

28 'Eden to Eisenhower, 20 August 1955', PDF Read Book Page, accessed 10 June 2019, Eden to Eisenhower, 20 August 1955, 1955_08_19.pdf

29 1st Air Division (Meteorological Survey) Strategic Air Command. Final Report Project 119L, Top Secret. CIA-RDP89B00708R000500040001-0: 12.

30 Mike Rogers, interview with author,12 December 2019.

31 'R.A.F. Station Re-Opened at Evanton', Ross-*shire Journal*, 8 August 1955; also, 'Evanton to be "Balloon" Base – High Altitude Research', *North Star*, 13 August 1955.

32 'Air Force Met. Station for Evanton', *Inverness Courier*, 13 August 1955; 'R.A.F. Station Re-Opened at Evanton', *Ross-shire Journal*, 8 August 1955; also, 'Evanton to be 'Balloon' Base'.

33 'The GENETRIX program at Evanton', Stratocat, accessed 19 November 2018, stratocat.com.ar/bases/82e.htm.

34 1st Air Division (Meteorological Survey) Strategic Air Command. Final Report Project 119L, 20.

35 '1955, Project GENETRIX Assorted Sources', Giebelstadt, West Germany, accessed 11 October 2018, c-and-e-museum.org/Pinetreeline/Giebelstadt.

36 David Fraser, interview with author 6 January 2019.

37 Ken Munro, interview with author 5 January 2020.

38 1st Air Division (Meteorological Survey) Strategic Air Command. Final Report Project 119L, 20–21.

39 David Hambling, 'Not just pie in the sky', *The Guardian*, 10 January 2002, theguardian.com/science/2002.

40 1st Air Division (Meteorological Survey) Strategic Air Command. Final Report Project 119L, 114, 116.

41 1st Air Division (Meteorological Survey) Strategic Air Command. Final Report Project 119L, 155, 157.

42 'Fairchild C-119 Boxcar, Background Information', accessed 4 January 2020, ruuedleeuw.org.com/c119-info.

43 'Fairchild C-119 Boxcar'.

44 'Fairchild C-119 Boxcar'.

45 Special Photo Intelligence Report No. 79, Genetrix Photography, USSR; Originator of Requirement ACSI ID 15-230; Sanitized Copy Approved for Release 2014/01/07 CIA – RDP81B00006R0001000 10001-4 https://www.cia.gov/readingroom/docs/CIA-RDP81B00006R000100010001-4.pdf [accessed 29May 2021].

46 'The GENETRIX program at Evanton', Stratocat, accessed 19 November 2018, stratocat.com.ar/bases/82e.htm.

47 'GRANDSON / GRAYBACK / GENETRIX / ASH CAN / MELTING POT'.

48 Russianwarrior.com. 15 November 2020.

49 Pedlow and Welzenbach. *The Central Intelligence Agency and Overhead Reconnaissance* 169.

50 Welzenbach, 'Observation Balloons and Reconnaissance Satellites', 21–28.

51 Memorandum of Conference with President Eisenhower, Washington, December 27, 1955, The Foreign Relations

of the United States, 1950–1955, The Intelligence Community, 1950–1955, United States Government Printing Office Washington DC, 2007; Folio 249.

Cabell was forced to resign as Deputy Director by President Kennedy on 31 January 1962, following the failure of the Bay of Pigs Invasion. Cabell's brother, Earle Cabell, was Mayor of Dallas when Kennedy visited that city and was assassinated on 22 November 1963.

52 1st Air Division (Meteorological Survey) Strategic Air Command. Final Report Project 119L, 96, 169.

53 'Fairchild C-119 Boxcar', also, 1st Air Division (Meteorological Survey) Strategic Air Command. Final Report Project 119L, 21.

54 '1955, Project GENETRIX Assorted Sources'.

55 Welzenbach, 'Observation Balloons and Reconnaissance Satellites', 24.

56 Pedlow and Welzenbach. *The Central Intelligence Agency and Overhead Reconnaissance*, 86.

57 Gildenberg, 'The Cold War's Classified Skyhook Program: A Participant's Revelations', 38–42;

58 Pedlow and Welzenbach. *The Central Intelligence Agency and Overhead Reconnaissance*, 87.

59 Pedlow and Welzenbach. *The Central Intelligence Agency and Overhead Reconnaissance*, 87.

60 Siddiqi, Asif A. Beyond Earth: A Chronicle of Dep Space Exploration, 1958–2016, The NASA history series (second ed.) (Washington, DC: NASA History Program Office, 2018) 15–16.

61 'The GENETRIX program at Evanton', Stratocat.com, accessed 19 November 2018, stratocat.com.ar/bases/82e. htm. Also, 1st Air Division (Meteorological Survey) Strategic Air Command. Final Report Project 119L, 207.

62 'U.S.A.F At Evanton', *Highland News*, 14 April 1956; also, 1st Air Division (Meteorological Survey) Strategic Air Command. Final Report Project 119L, 120.

63 Welzenbach, 'Observation Balloons and Reconnaissance Satellites', 23; 1st Air Division (Meteorological Survey) Strategic Air Command. Final Report Project 119L, 308. Dollar worth was calculated using usinflationcalculator.com.

64 Photographic Intelligence memorandum, Genetrix Photography, GP/I–163, 12 April 1956, Central Intelligence Agency Office of Research and Reports; https://www.cia.gov/library/readingroom/document/cia-rdp-78t05694a000200560004-2 ; [accessed 3 May 2020]; also, 1st Air Division (Meteorological Survey) Strategic Air Command. Final Report Project 119L, 179.

65 'What is this at Evanton?' Aircrew Forums, *Military Aviation*, accessed 14 November 2020, https://www.pprune. org/archive/index.php/t-378028.html.

66 Frank Card, *Whensoever: 50 Years of the RAF Mountain Rescue Service 1943–1993* (Glasgow: Ernest Press, 1993).

67 Steven McKenzie, 'RAF leader sought evidence of Highland Sputnik crash', BBC Scotland, Highlands and Islands report, 18 July 2012.

68 McKenzie, 'RAF leader sought evidence of Highland Sputnik crash'.

69 Dan Doyle, 'Cold War Spy Flights Uncovered', *The Scotsman*, Tuesday, 24 June 1977, 3; also, Keith Bryers, interview with author 15 March 2020.

70 Doyle, 'Cold War Spy Flights Uncovered', 3.

71 Polyethylene, Wikipedia, accessed 21 November 2020, Wikipedia.org/wiki/Polyethylene.

72 Simon Duke. *U.S. Defence Bases in the United Kingdom: A Matter for Joint Decision?* (Basingstoke: Macmillan, 1987), 1–4, 19–20.

73 'NATO Exercises: Mainbrace', *Flight* magazine, 26 September 1952, 404-06; also, B.C. Laite, *Maritime Air Operations: Brassey's Air Power: Aircraft, Weapons Systems and Technology Series Volume 11* (London: Brassey's, 1991), 30.

74 Baylis, Anglo-American Defence Relations, 40–1, 78. Reynolds, A Special Relationship?, 1–20.

75 Appendix to Frank C. Nash's White House report on U.S. Overseas Military Bases, Country Studies: Great Britain. Miscellaneous, 1 November 1957. Reproduced in Declassified Documents Reference System. Document Number: CK3100288057. [accessed 25 June 2006].

76 Lavery, Brian 'The British Government and the American Polaris Base in the Clyde', *Journal for Maritime Research*, September 2001.

77 Lavery, 'The British Government and the American Polaris Base in the Clyde'.

78 State memorandum from Under Secretary for Political Affairs, to The Secretary of State, 27 July 1980, Top Secret, EUR: I White/vh, NACP 741.56311/7-2760; also, From State, Top Secret, to Embassy London, 2621, 27 October 1960, 'Dear Harold, I am delighted that agreement has been reached on the project for berthing facilities for our Polaris tender in the Clyde area'. Also, Walter Wagoner, 'Britain will get US Polaris base', *New York Times*, 18 October 1960, 11.

79 Author's personal experience.

80   Foreign Service Telegram from Amconsul Glasgow to Department of State, Subject: The Polaris Submarine Depot in the West of Scotland, 10 November 1960, Official Use Only, NACP 741.56311/11- 1060.

81   The author was one of the crowd; also, 'Remember when .... Alexei Kosygin visits Scotland, 1967', *The Herald*, 19 January 2021.

82   '1958 US–UK Mutual Defence Agreement', accessed 4 January 2019, https://en.wikipedia.org/wiki/1958_US–UK_Mutual_Defence_Agreement.

83   Appendix to Frank C. Nash's White House report on U.S. Overseas Military Bases, Country Studies: Great Britain.

84   Lavery, 'The British Government and the American Polaris Base in the Clyde'. '

85   DD12/3077, Folio 54; Project Lamachus; On arrival arrangements. NAS 21 November 2019.

86   Mackay, *Scotland the Brave?* 67.

87   'The Glesca Eskimos' (T.S. Law / Morris Blythman / Jim McLean).

88   Lavery, *The British Government and the American Polaris Base in the Clyde*; also, Wyman H. Packard USN (Retired), *A Century of US Naval Intelligence*, A joint publication of the Office of Naval Intelligence and the Naval Historical Center, Department of the Navy: Washington, 1996.

89   The briefings were drawn up by DIO-3ND special agent Martin Randisi – see Packard, *A Century of US Naval Intelligence*.

90   Andrene Messersmith, *The American Years: Dunoon and the U.S. Navy* (Glendaruel: Argyll Publishing, 2003), 29.

91   Ron Gumbert, interview with author 3 March 2020; Messersmith, *The American Years*, 90.

92   Brian Wilson, interview with author 28 July 2020.

93   Messersmith, *The American Years*, 58.

94   Arthur Clark Bivens, *Of Nukes and Nose Cones* (Baltimore MD: Gateway Press, 1996), viii.

95   Norman Polmar, 'The Polaris: A Revolutionary Missile System and Concept', More Bang for the Buck: U.S. Nuclear Strategy and Missile Development 1945–1965, Colloquium on Contemporary History, 12 January 1994 No. 9, history.navy.mil/research/library/online-reading-room; also, Robert Gardiner, Stephen Chumbley, *Conway's All the World's Fighting Ships 1947–1995* (London: Conway Maritime Press, 1995), 352–353, 549, 553–554.

96   Bryan Ranft and Geffrey Till, *The Sea in Soviet Strategy*, Second Edition (Basingstoke: Macmillan, 1989), 205–11.

97   Hyman George Rickover," *Naval History and Heritage Command*, accessed 18 November 2019, History.navy.mil.

98   [5]Edward H. Mortimer, *Experiencing War: Submarines, The Silent Service*, Library of Congress interview, accessed 1 April 2020, www.loc.gov/vets/stories/ex-war-submarines.html; also Norman Polmar and Thomas B. Allen. *Rickover: Father of the Nuclear Navy.* (Lincoln NE: Potomac Books Inc, 2007.)

99   'Ronald P.C. Waller', *Experiencing War: Stories from the Veterans' History Project*, accessed 3 February 2020, memory.loc.gov/diglib.

100 Peter Pringle and William Arkin. *SIOP: The Secret U.S. Plan for Nuclear War.* (Toronto: W.W. Norton & Co, 1983) 173; also, D. Ball, 'U.S. Strategic Forces: How Would They Be Used?' *International Security*. The MIT Press. 7 (3) (Winter 1982–1983): 31–60.

101 Bivens, *Of Nukes and Nose Cones*, 104; Pringle and Arkin, *SIOP: The Secret U.S. Plan for Nuclear War*, 154, 161.

102 Pringle and Arkin, *SIOP: The Secret U.S. Plan for Nuclear War*, 157–160.

103 DEFCON DEFense CONdition', Federation of American Scientists, accessed 26 November 2019, https://fas.org/nuke/guide/usa/c3i/defcon.htm.

104 Bivens, *Of Nukes and Nose Cones*, 118.

105 Pringle and Arkin, SIOP: *The Secret U.S. Plan for Nuclear War*, 160.

106 Mike Giambattista, interview with author 31 October 2019, also, Waller, 'Experiencing War'.

107 Bivens, *Of Nukes and Nose Cones*, 51.

108 Bivens, *Of Nukes and Nose Cones*, ix; Bud Lewis, interview with author 10 January 2020.

109 'Submarine Training School', *My Hitch, My Boats* (1960–1968), accessed 16 April 2021, quietwarriors.wordpress.com.

110 'Submarine Training School', also Giambattista.

111 Giambattista; also Dr Mark N. Bing & CDR Eisenberg, Psychological Screening of Submariners: The Development & Validation of the Submarine Attrition Risk Scale (SARS), Naval Submarine Medical Research Laboratory Submarine Base New London, annex.ipacweb.org/library/conf/03/bing.pdf; and Benjamin B. Weybrew and Ernest M. Noddin, The Mental Health of Nuclear Submariners in the United States Navy, NSMRL Report No. 851, Naval Medical Research &Development Command, National Naval Medical Center Bethesda, Maryland, 31 March 1979.

112 Giambattista; Bivens, *Of Nukes and Nose Cones*, 64.

113 John Everson, interview with author 11 November 2019.

114 Lacey; also, 'Nuclear Power School', accessed 4 February 2020, https://en.wikipedia.org/wiki/Nuclear_Power_School; 'Naval Sea Systems Command', accessed 4 February 2020, https://www.navsea.navy.mil/Home/NNPTC/powerschool.aspx

115 Aaron Amick, 'Nukes, Nubs and Coners: The Unique Social Hierarchy Aboard a Nuclear Submarine', The Drive, accessed 30 March 2020, https://www.thedrive.com/the-war-zone/34104/nukes-nubs-and-coners-the-unique-social-hierarchy-aboard-a-nuclear-submarine.

116 'Submarine Training School', also Giambattista, interview.

117 Lewis, interview.

118 Lewis, interview.

119 Amick, 'Nukes, Nubs and Coners'.

120 John Everson, interview with author, 11 November 2019.

121 Giambattista, interview; also, Lewis, interview, and Lacey interview.

122 Giambattista, interview and 'Submarine Warfare insignia: United States, 4.2–4.6', Submarine Warfare Insignia, accessed 24 June 2019, https://en.wikipedia.org/wiki/.

123 Giambattista, interview.

124 Philip Giambri, interview with author 1 September 2019.

125 Trevor Royle, *Facing the Bear: Scotland and the Cold War* (Edinburgh: Birlinn, 2019), 65.

126 Giambattista, interview.

127 Bivens, *Of Nukes and Nose Cones*, 40.

128 'Data Sheet 5: Submarine Missile Test Firings 1960 to 1991, USCS/DS/5', Universal Ship Cancellation Society, 27 August 2020, http://www.uscs.org/wp-content/uploads/2012/04/DS05_Sumarine-Missile-Firings.pdf.

129 'Submarine Weapons: Ballistic Missiles', Fast Attacks and Boomers, Submarines in the Cold War, The National Museum of American History, 14 June 2020, https://americanhistory.si.edu/subs/weapons/ballistic/nuclear_test.html.

130 Bivens, *Of Nukes and Nose Cones*, 42–4.

131 Mackay, *Scotland the Brave?* 159; Bivens, *Of Nukes and Nose Cones*, 43–4.

132 SSBN619.com.

133 SSBN657.com.

134 Bivens, *Of Nukes and Nose Cones*, 42.

135 SSBN657.com.

136 SSBN657.com.

137 Giambattista, interview.

138 Boyne, interview.

139 Giambattista, interview; Bivens, *Of Nukes and Nose Cones*, 51.

140 Giambattista, interview.

141 Naval Warfare Publications library (NWPL) is the group of communications and operational publications designated as part of the publication allowance for the command. These publications contain required procedures, signals, and other information of an operational or mission-essential nature.

142 Bivens, *Of Nukes and Nose Cones*, 40.

143 Arkin and Handler, 'Naval Accidents 1945–1988', 49, 51.

144 Peter Hennessy and James Jinks, *The Silent Deep: The Royal Navy Submarine Service since 1945* (London: Allen and Lane, 2015), 352.

145 'Crew Rotation in the Navy: The Long-Term Effect on Forward Presence', CBO Paper October 2007, accessed 11 July 2020, http://www.cbo.gov/ftpdocs/87xx/doc8771/10-31-Navy.pdf.

146 Bivens, *Of Nukes and Nose Cones*, 116.

147 'USS Nathanael Greene SSBN-636', Navysite, accessed 16 October 2020, navysite.de; Arkin and Handler, 'Naval Accidents 1945–1988', 66–67.

148 Arkin and Handler, 'Naval Accidents 1945–1988', 69.

149 Waller, *Experiencing War*.

150 Norman Polmar, 'The Polaris: A Revolutionary Missile System and Concept: More Bang for the Buck: U.S. Nuclear Strategy and Missile Development 1945–1965', Colloquium on Contemporary History January 12, 1994, No. 9, history.navy.mil/research/library; Gumbert, interview; also, All Hands June 1981.

151 *All Hands* June 1981.

152 'Why does it take so long to restart a nuclear power plant?' Engineering Beta, 11 November 2020, https://engineering.stackexchange.com/questions/7394/.

153 Mike Masishin, interview with author 28 August 2019; also, Amick, 'Nukes, Nubs and Coners'.

154 Waller, 'Submarine Frequently Asked Questions, Chief of Naval Operations Submarine Warfare 'Division'' accessed 22 May 2021, https://web.archive.org/web/20150420232753/http://www.navy.mil/navydata/cno/n87/faq.html.

155 Pringle and Arkin, *SIOP: The Secret U.S. Plan for Nuclear War*, 161.

156 Mortimer, *Experiencing War*.

157 Pringle and Arkin, SIOP: *The Secret U.S. Plan for Nuclear War*, 157.

158 Pringle and Arkin, SIOP: *The Secret U.S. Plan for Nuclear War*, 158.

159 Gumbert, interview.

160 Paul Dent, Tupolev Tu-142MR: Inside Soviet Union's Tacamo, Nuclear Companion, nuclearcompanion.com/Tupolev-tu-142, 17 October 2020.

161 Adam Scott, interview with author 1 September 2019; Ar Bivens, *Of Nukes and Nose Cones*, 53–54.

162 Bivens, *Of Nukes and Nose Cones*, 53–54; Pringle and Arkin, SIOP: The Secret U.S. Plan for Nuclear War, 160.

163 Mackay, *Scotland the Brave?* 115.

164 Nautilus (SSN-571) 1954–1980, accessed 3 February 2019, Naval History and Heritage Command, history.navy.mil/content/history/nhhc/research.

165 Mackay, *Scotland the Brave?* 122.

166 David Ebbs, interview with author 6 November 2019; also, 'Archerfish SSN-311', Navy History, accessed 19 December 2019, www.navyhistory.com/Submarine/Archerfish.htm.

167 Giambattista, interview. and Amick, 'Nukes, Nubs and Coners'.

168 Peter Boyne, interview with author 29 September 2019; also, Giambattista, interview.

169 Boyne, interview; Giambattista, interview.

170 Fred Ver Planck, interview with author 14 November 2019; also Addendum to [Briefing Paper] HAG/CP-2. [May 1964?] 1 p. CONFIDENTIAL. Declassified May 2, 1979. Johnson Library, NSF, International Meetings and Travel, NATO Ministerial Meeting, The Hague, May 12–14, 1964. Paper. DEPARTMENT OF STATE. CONFIDENTIAL. Date Declassified: May 02, 1979. Sanitized. Incomplete. 2 page(s).

171 Mackay, *Scotland the Brave?* 122.

172 https://www.forgottenairfields.com/airfield-raf-scatsta-and-raf-sullum-voe-867.html.

173 Mackay, *Scotland the Brave?* 122; also USCG Commandant's Bulletin, 52–80, 1980; 10–11.

174 Mackay, *Scotland the Brave?* 122; also, 'LORAN Stations', USCG History, accessed 18 August 2019, http://www.uscg.mil/hq/g-cp/history/STATIONS/LORAN.

175 'LORAN Station Mangersta', accessed 3 July 2019, LORAN-history. info: 'LORAN Station Garth's Ness', accessed 3 July 2019, LORAN-history.info; Finlay J. Mcleod, interview with author 18 November 2019.

176 Van Der Planck, interview.

177 Gordon Brewer, 'Target Shetland?' *The Shetland Times*, Friday, 17 April 1981; p. 5; Rodney Pinder, 'Bleak Base in Scotland Appeals to Coast Guardsmen', *Sunday Call Chronicle*, Allentown, PA, 10 June 1973.

178 Boyne, interview; also, [Defense] Omega Navigation System [budget, FY 1967: because LORAN A, LORAN C, and the Satellite Navigation system satisfy the needs of all users, the Omega system should be continued at a low funding level and not be made operational]. Memorandum. [1965?] 2 p. CONFIDENTIAL. Declassified Mar. 18, 1977. Johnson Library, NSF, Agencies, DOD, FY 1967 Budget Book. Memorandum. DEPARTMENT OF DEFENSE. CONFIDENTIAL. Date Declassified: Mar 18, 1977. Sanitized. Incomplete. 2 page(s).

179 Edward E. Mathus, Facebook LORAN.org.

180 Charles Mac MacLean, Facebook LORAN.org.

181 Dietz, interview.

182 Bill Broome, interview with author 3 February 2020.

183 Facebook LORAN.org.

184 Larry Oliszewski, interview with author 2 February 2020.

185 Alex McMahan, interview with author 6 September 2019.

186 Teri Sanders, interview with author,12 March 2020.

187 Chris Carlson, interview with author 13 November 13, 2019.

188 Facebook LORAN.org.

189 Broome, interview; Dietz, interview. Also, 'RAF Scatsta and RAF Sullom Voe', 28 May 2020, https://www.forgotte-nairfields.com/airfield-raf-scatsta-and-raf-sullom-voe-867.html.

190 Amick, 'Nukes, Nubs and Coners'.

191 Giambri; also, Viktoria Tkaczyk, Mara Mills, Alexandra Hui (eds), *Testing Hearing: The Making of Modern Aurality* (OUP USA: 2020).

192 Hervey, *Submarines*: Brassey's Sea Power, 190; also, Arkin and Handler, 'Naval Accidents 1945–1988,'44.

193 Hervey, *Submarines*: Brassey's Sea Power, 61.

194 Gumbert, interview; Giambattista, interview; Ulmer, interview.

195 Archive: 'Portavogie trawler dragged at sea in 1987', BBC News Northern Ireland, 16 April 2015.

196 Matthew Weaver, 'Scottish cold war nuclear submarine collision kept secret for 43 years', *The Guardian*, Wed 25 Jan 2017.

197 'Cold War Catastrophe', *The Sun*, 25 January 2017; also, Hans Kristensen, 'Declassified: US Nuclear Weapons at Sea', Federation of American Scientists, 3 February 2016, accessed 19 October 2019, https://www.fas.org/blogs/security.

198 USSJamesmadison627.com; and Marek Benda, Avneesh Chandra, Signe Janoska-Bedi, Jamey Kane & Jonny Vannucci, 'Silent Dangers: Assessing the Threat of Nuclear Submarines', Workshop in International Public Affairs Spring 2019, Robert M. La Follette School of Public Affairs, University of Wisconsin – Madison, 12, 21, 26, www.lafollette.wisc.edu/outreach-public-service.

199 USS JAMES MADISON SSBN 627 – TRIBUTE TO A FOUNDING FATHER, The Lean Submariner, 26 April 2019.

200 USSJamesmadison627.com.

201 http://www.chinfo.navy.mil/navpalib/cno/n87/usw/issue_27/asw2.html#16; also, http://www.decklog.com/ssbn-601.asp.

202 Arkin and Handler, 'Naval Accidents 1945–1988', 57.

203 Amick, 'Nukes, Nubs and Coners'.

204 Giambattista, interview; Gumbert, interview;

205 Thomas Weeks, interview with author, 11 December 2019.

206 Jim Craig, interview with author 24 August 2019.

207 Amick, 'Nukes, Nubs and Coners'.

208 Craig, interview.

209 Arkin and Handler, 'Naval Accidents 1945–1988', 9, 11.

210 Trevor Royle, *Facing the Bear: Scotland and the Cold War*, (Edinburgh: Birlinn, 2019).

211 Joel I. Holwitt, 'Sub vs. Sub: ASW Lessons from the Cold War', US Naval Institute, Proceedings, Vol. 145/10/1,400, October 2019, usni.org/magazines/proceedings/2019/October; Zoltan Barany, Democratic Breakdown and the Decline of the Russian Military (Princeton and Oxford: Princeton University Press, 2007), 33–35.

212 Arkin and Handler, 'Naval Accidents 1945–1988', 47, 53, 55, 56, 59, 69.

213 Bivens, *Of Nukes and Nose Cones*, 45; USS *Theodore Roosevelt* II (SSBN-600), Naval History and Heritage Command, accessed 14 June 2019, history.navy.mil/content/history/nhhc/research.

214 Policy paper: Dreadnought submarine programme: factsheet; Updated 19 February 2018, at gov.uk/government/publications/successor accessed 10 November 2020; also, U.S. Navy Active Ship Force Levels, U.S. Naval History and Heritage Command, accessed 14 December 2020, history.navy.mil/research/histories; also, Arkin and Handler, 'Naval Accidents 1945–1988', 39.

215 Giambattista, interview; Ulmer, interview; Gumbert, interview.

216 E. Foster-Simeon, *All Hands*, Magazine of the U.S. Navy, December 1985, Number 825; also, Giambattista, interview.

217 DD12/3079, 1164/0.700/1; Lamachus Progress Report; 19 November 1960. NAS 21 November 2019.

218 Fisheries Research Services Internal Report No 08/04, AN ENVIRONMENTAL ASSESSMENT OF ORGANIC CONTAMINANTS IN THE FIRTH OF CLYDE, Lynda Webster, Lesley Phillips, Marie Russell, Eric Dalgarno and Colin Moffat, October 2004.

219 AFDB: (Navy) Auxiliary Floating Dock Big; 29 April 1961, the *Glasgow Herald*: Saturday, 29 April 1961: Dry Dock for the Loch Trans-Atlantic Tow: Jacksonville, Florida, Friday, and JAX Air News (Jacksonville, Florida), 4 May 1961.

220 AFDB-7 *Los Alamos* Holy Loch Scotland 'In the Beginning', The Lean Submariner, accessed 14 October 2019, theleansubmariner.com/2014/04/04/afdb.

221 James Brandon, interview with author 11 November 2019.

222 Munier, Robert S.C. and Botwinick, Virginia J., ADA167192, AFDB-7 *Los Alamos* mooring Overhaul Holy Loch, TRACOR MARINE PORT EVERGLADES FL OCEAN TECHNOLOGY DIV, Report Date 1984-03-26.

223 E. Foster-Simeon, *All Hands*, Magazine of the U.S. Navy, December 1985, Number 825.

224 E. Foster-Simeon, *All Hands*.

225 Brandon, interview.

226 Alfred H. Singleman Jr, USS *Francis Scott Key*, Aug. 69–Mar. 75.

227 Mike Robertson, USS *Francis Scott Key*, Aug. 69–Mar. 75.

228 Martin Hastings, interview with author, 30 November 2019.

229 The Scottish American History Club Newsletter April 2004, chicagoscots.net, accessed 3 February 2021; also, spaceflight.nasa.gov/shittle/archives, accessed 4 February 2020]; LAUREL BLAIR SALTON CLARK, M.D. (CAPTAIN, USN) NASA ASTRONAUT (DECEASED) Biographical Data, Lyndon B. Johnson Space Center NASA, accessed 3 February 2020, https://www.nasa.gov/sites/default/files/atoms/files/clark_laurel.pdf; 'Columbia astronaut's Scots link', BBC News, 3 February, 2003, accessed 3 February 2020, http://news.bbc.co.uk/1/hi/scotland/2719973.stml.

230 Ray Conner, interview with author 23 August 2019.

231 Conner, interview.

232 Martin Hastings, interview with author, 30 November 2019, online.

233 Scott, interview.

234 Charlie Witherow, interview with author, 12 September 2019.

235 Author's personal experience.

236 Frank Murray, interview with author, 5 October 2019.

237 Nat O'Dell, interview with author, 3 September 2019.

238 Paul Davis, interview with author, 17 February 2020.

239 Anne Donnelly, interview with author, 5 September 2019

240 AFDB-7 *Los Alamos* Holy Loch Scotland 'In the Beginning', The Lean Submariner, accessed 14 October 2019, theleansubmariner.com/2014/04/04/afdb.

241 Bernie Gantt, interview with author 22 August 2019.

242 AFDB-7 *Los Alamos* Holy Loch Scotland 'In the Beginning', The Lean Submariner, accessed 14 October 2019, theleansubmariner.com/2014/04/04/afdb.

243 AFDB-7 *Los Alamos* Holy Loch Scotland 'In the Beginning', The Lean Submariner, accessed 14 October 2019, theleansubmariner.com/2014/04/04/afdb.

244 AFDB-7 *Los Alamos* Holy Loch Scotland 'In the Beginning', The Lean Submariner, accessed 14 October 2019, theleansubmariner.com/2014/04/04/afdb.

245 Greggery Kunkle, interview with author, 27 February 2020.

246 Arkin and Handler, 'Naval Accidents 1945–1988', 29.

247 Greg Kent, interview with author, 29 October 2019.

248 Tom Courtien, RUSS Christie and John Linville 'Thanksgiving 1970 – Fire on the *Canopus* SSBN657', accessed 27 May 2020, http://www.ssbn657.com/Sea%20Stories/sea-*Canopus*fire.htm.

249 '2 Prisoners and Guard Died in Fire on Polaris Tender', *New York Times*, 30 November 1970, 19.

250 Winds Batter Scotland; Toll Is 20 -- Glasgow Hard Hit -- Snow Falls in Mideast Storms Lash Europe, Mideast; Scotland Hard Hit', *New York Times*, 16 January 1968.

251 Martin Hastings, interview with author, 30 November 2019.

252 AFDB-7 *Los Alamos* Holy Loch Scotland 'In the Beginning', The Lean Submariner, theleansubmariner.com/2014/04/04/afdb, accessed 14 October 2019.

253 Jack McNeelly, interview with author, 4 August 2019.

254 Kent, interview.

255 Arkin and Handler, 'Naval Accidents 1945–1988', 62.

256 B.S. Miller, D.J. Pirie, C.J. Redshaw, An Assessment of the Contamination and Toxicity of Marine Sediments in the Holy Loch, Scotland, Marine Pollution Bulletin, Volume 40, Issue 1, 2000, 22–35, https://doi.org/10.1016/S0025-326X(99)00190-3. (https://www.sciencedirect.com/science/article/pii/S0025326X99001903)

257 Arkin and Handler, 'Naval Accidents 1945–1988', 66.

258 'Radioactive waste was dumped in Holy Loch, says ex-Polaris captain', *Herald*, 14th January 1989.

259 Fisheries Research Services Internal Report No 08/04, AN ENVIRONMENTAL ASSESSMENT OF ORGANIC CONTAMINANTS IN THE FIRTH OF CLYDE, Lynda Webster, Lesley Phillips, Marie Russell, Eric Dalgarno and Colin Moffat, October 2004

260 Rob Edwards, 'Cold War waste fouls the Clyde', *New Scientist*, 8 March 1997.

261 Memorandum from Vice Chief of Naval Operations to Commander-in-Chief US Fleet and Chief of Naval Operations, Subject: The continuation and development of Communications Intelligence, Top Secret Ultra, Op-20-4-em (23 August 1945), Serial 0005020, (SC) A6-2/A8, NSA Declassified DOCID 3978331.

262 Stephane Lefebvre, 'The Difficulties and Dilemmas of International Intelligence Cooperation', *International Journal of Intelligence and CounterIntelligence,* 16 (2003): 527–542; Memorandum from General Marshall to Admiral King, 18 August 1945, Subject: Signals Intelligence, Top Secret Ultra, NSA Declassified DOCID 3978305.

263 Jordan Chittley and Kevin Newman, 'Canada's role in secret intelligence alliance Five Eyes', CTV News [accessed 17 January 2021]; also Newly Released GCHQ files: UKUSA Agreement, The National Archives, nationalarchives. gov.uk/ukusa [accessed 4 November 2019].

264 Mackay, *Scotland the Brave?* 29.

265 Matthew M. Aid, *The Secret Sentry: The Untold History of the National Security Agency* (London: Bloomsbury Press, 2010), 43–46.

266 Christopher Andrew, Foreword in *Secrets of Signals Intelligence in the Cold War and Beyond*, ed. Mathew M. Aid and Cees Wiebes (London: Frank Cass Publishers, 2001); Richard J. Aldrich, 'GCHQ and SIGINT in the Early Cold War 1945–70', in *Secrets of Signals Intelligence in the Cold War and Beyond*, ed. Mathew M. Aid and Cees Wiebes (London: Frank Cass Publishers, 2001), 10.

267 Mathew M. Aid and Cees Wiebes, 'The Importance of Signals Intelligence in the Cold War', *Journal of Intelligence and National Security*, Vol 16, No 1 (2001): 7; Presidential Memorandum to Secretary of State, Secretary of War, Secretary of the Navy, Attorney General, Joint Chiefs of Staff, Director of the Budget, Director of the Office of War Information, 28 August 1945, DOCID 3984134;

268 Aid and Wiebes, Conclusion, in *Secrets of Signals Intelligence*, 316–9.

269 Andrew, Foreword, 4–21.

270 Thomas R. Johnson, *American Cryptology during the Cold War, 1945–1989: Book III: Retrenchment and Reform, 1972–1980* (National Security Agency: Center for Cryptological History, 1998), 353–354, 486.

271 Christopher Andrew & Oleg Gordievsky, *KGB: The Inside Story of Its Foreign Operations from Lenin to Gorbachev* (London: Hodder & Stoughton, 1990), 394, 592.

272 Thomas R. Johnson, *American Cryptology during the Cold War, 1945–1989: Book III: Retrenchment and Reform, 1972–1980*, 254.

273 US Air Force, Memorandum, Ground Intercept of Non-Communications Signals, 11 March, 1952, Top Secret, NARA. Brill, NLS.

274 Trevor Royle, *Facing the Bear: Scotland and the Cold War* (Edinburgh: Birlinn, 2019), 49.

275 Martyn Chorlton, *Scottish Airfields in the Second World War: The Lothians.* (Newbury: Countryside Books; 2008); 'Kirknewton Airfield', Canmore. Retrieved 19 November 2017; U.S. Air Force, Report, No. 1 (Top Secret) Limited Distribution Supplement to the Daily Staff Digest, May 6, 1952, Top Secret, NARA FOIA.

276 RAF STATION KIRKNEWTON, SCOTLAND and the UNITED STATES AIR FORCE (1952–1966), 4 March 2019, rafkirknewton.com.

277 6952nd Electronic Security Squadron, USAF Unit History, 26 October 2019, usafunithistory.com/PDF/6000.

278 'Condensed History of the 37th Radio Squadron, Mobile, RAF Station Kirknewton, Midlothian Scotland', Facebook RAF Kirknewton, 21 October 2019; also, Nicol McBain, interview with author 22 October 2019.

279 RAF Kirknewton, Secret Scotland, 9 September 2019, secretscotland.org.uk/index/php; also, George Montague, interview with author 9 September 2019; McBain, interview.

280 6952nd ELECTRONIC SECURITY SQUADRON', and Montague, interview.

281 Montague, interview.

282 Aldrich, GCHQ and SIGINT in the early Cold War 1945–70, 80–2.

283 Facebook RAF Kirknewton, 'Condensed History of the 37th Radio Squadron, Mobile, RAF Station Kirknewton, Midlothian Scotland'.

284 McBain, interview.

285 RAF Kirknewton.com.

286 James Bamford, *The Puzzle Palace: A Report on America's Most Secret Agency* (Boston: Houghton Mifflin. 1982).

287 'Signals Intelligence', NSA/CSS, 10 August 2019, https://www.nsa.gov/what-we-do/signals-intelligence/.

288 Lee Hendley, interview with author 21 October 2019.

289 McBain, interview.

290 Aldrich, GCHQ and SIGINT in the early Cold War 1945–70, 80–2.

291 McBain, interview.

292 Montague, interview.

293 McBain, interview.

294 Hendley, interview.

295 Hendley, interview.

296 'Viva USAFSS', accessed 19 March 2019, http://vivausafss.org/lorentzen.htm.

297 Duncan Campbell, 'Inside Echelon: The history, structure and function of the global surveillance system known as Echelon', 25.07.2000, accessed 16 August 2017, http://www.heise.de/tp; Royle, *Facing the Bear: Scotland and the Cold War*, 50; and James Bamford, *The Puzzle Palace: A Report on America's Most Secret Agency* (Boston: Houghton Mifflin. 1982), 210.

298 Campbell, 'Inside Echelon'.

299 Duncan Campbell, *The Unsinkable Aircraft Carrier* (London: Michael Joseph Ltd, 1984), 154, 160–1. Robert Jackson, *Strike Force: The USAF in Britain since 1945* (London: Robson Books, 1986), 173: West, Nigel, GCHQ: *The Secret Wireless War 1900–86* (London: Weidenfeld & Nicolson, 1986) 249, 253.

300 'Hotline established between Washington and Moscow', History.com, accessed 19 November 2019, www.history.com; 'If these walls could talk', Whitehouse.blogs.cnn, accessed 23 March 2020, www.whitehouse.blogs.cnn.com.

301 'The Hotline', Crypto Museum, 17 May 2020, cryptomuseum.com.

302 Philip C. Shackelford, *On the Wings of the Wind: the U.S. Air Force Security Service and its Impact on Signals Intelligence in the Cold War* (thesis, Kent State University Honors College May, 2014.

303 McBain, interview.

304 History, 'Hotline established'; Whitehouse, 'If these walls'; 'RAF Kirknewton', Secret wiki Scotland, 23 September 2019, www.secretscotland.org.

305 Shackelford, *On the Wings of the Wind*.

306 Shackelford, *On the Wings of the Wind*.

307 John J. Moore, interview with author, 16 February 2020.

308 'Viva USAFSS', accessed 19 March 2019, http://vivausafss.org/lorentzen.htm.

309 Josh McInally, interview with author, 24 November 2019.

310 James S Hill, interview with author, 23 September 2019.

311 'Hawklaw', Secret Scotland, 31 July 2019, secretscotland.org.uk; McBain, interview.

312 Shackelford, *On the Wings of the Wind*.

313 Shackelford, *On the Wings of the Wind*.

314 McBain, interview.

315 Mackay, *Scotland the Brave?* 29.

316 '6952nd Electronic Security Squadron'.

317 Kenneth Roy and T.L. Hardie, *The Kirknewton Story* (Kirknewton Story Committee: David Watt & Sons, Dunfermline, 1974), 46.

318 'Handwritten letter from David F. Christiansen', NSA 24 October 1978, accessed 24 October 2019, www.nsa.gov/Portals/70/documents; 'Memorandum for the record, Subject: 8 November Meeting with Mr Blakey', NSA 10 November 1978, accessed 24 October 2019, www.nsa.gov/Portals/70/documents; 'Memorandum for the record, House Assassinations Committee Inquiry, 21 November 1978', NSA, accessed 24 October 2019, www.nsa.gov/Portals/70/documents.

319 'Memorandum for the record, House Assassinations Committee Inquiry, 21 November 1978', NSA, accessed 24 October 2019, www.nsa.gov/Portals/70/documents.

320 Memorandum for the Special Assistant to the Secretary and Deputy Secretary of Defense, D1/LAO-047M-78, 21 November 1978', NSA, accessed 24 October 2019, www.nsa.gov/Portals/70/documents; also, 'Memorandum for the Record, 13 December 1978', NSA, accessed 24 October 2019, www.nsa.gov/Portals/70/documents.

321 'Display: SSU 1/2 1976-0383C', NASA Space Science Data: Coordinated Archive, 14 May 2020, https://nssdc.gsfc.nasa.gov.

322 Mackay, *Scotland the Brave?* 43; 'Display: SSU ½ 1976-0383C'.

323 'Edzell, the Beginning', *Edzell Special*, 1 August 1998, Cryptolog, US Naval Cryptologic Veterans Association, 3.

324 DOD, Report, [extract] Status of United States Military Programs as of 30 June 1960, December 10, 1960, Top Secret, DDEL, Brill.com; Mathew M Aid, 'The National Security Agency and the Cold War', Journal of Intelligence and National Security 16, No 1 (2001): 46: Richard J. Aldrich, 'GCHQ and SIGINT in early Cold War, 1945–70', Journal of Intelligence and National Security 16, No 1 (2001): 91.

325 Cryptolog, 2.

326 Montague, interview.

327 'Maintenance Manual for Antenna Groups OA-3867(XN-1)/FRD-10(V) and OA-3967/FRD-10(V), 1972' 10 January 2020, navy-radio.com; Dan Ruzicka, 'HABS No. HI-522-B Report, 10 January 2020, Historic American Buildings Survey.

328 Mackay, *Scotland the Brave?* 40.

329 Mackay, *Scotland the Brave?* 43; 'Display: SSU ½ 1976-0383C'. Also, Mackay, *Scotland the Brave?* 41.

330 'Ban the Bomb', Scottish CND, 19 December 2019, www.banthebomb.org/militaryscotland; 'NAVSECGRU Navy Security Group Activity Adak', Federation of American Scientists, 19 December 2019, fas.org/irp/agency/navsecgru/adak; Dwayne A. Day, 'Above the clouds: the White Cloud ocean surveillance satellites', The Space Review 13 April 2009, accessed 6 January 2020, thespacereview.com/article/1351/1; 'NOSS Double and Triple Satellite Formations, Naval Ocean Surveillance System', Satobs, 8 December 2019, satobs.org/noss; Also, Major A. Andronov, The U.S. Navy's 'White Cloud' Spaceborne ELINT System, (Kosmicheskaya Sistema Radiotekhnicheskoy Razvedki VMS SShA 'Uayt Klaud'), translated by Allen Thomson, Foreign Military Review No.7 (1993): 57–60, Surveillance, Federation of American Scientists, accessed 2 February 2006, fas.org; and Memo from Mrs HD Harrison MOD to Miss Nicol SDD, 28th May 1964, AF/A1629/64/S.13d (Air), … technical site at Inverbervie, NRS.

331 Department of the Navy Naval Security Group Command Headquarters, NSGINST 5450.53A, Ser G142/133?/7272, 3 Dec 1979. From: Commander Naval Security Group Command. Subj: Mission and Functions of US Naval Security Group Detachment, London England/ US Naval Current Support Group, US Naval forces Europe, U.S. Navy Historical Center [accessed 14 December 2005].

332 Mackay, *Scotland the Brave?* 112. Also, Paolo E. Coletta and Jack Bauer, United States Navy and Marine Corps Bases, Overseas (Westport Connecticut and London: Greenwood Press, 1985).

333 Dale Reemett, interview with author, 22 August 2019.

334 Parsch, Andreas (2005). 'Code Names for U.S. Military Projects and Operations', 15 February 2020, designation-systems.net; also, Jack Jackson, interview with author, 12 November 2019; Coletta and Bauer.

335 TSgt Tom Grayson, Elephant Cage Maintenance Essential, *Wingsprad Magazine*, 31 October 1969.

336 Eric Mercato, interview with author 23 August 2019.

337 Joe Mazzafro, interview with author 9 September 2019.

338 Cryptolog, 8.

339 Cryptolog, 19; and Mazzafro, interview.

340 Memorandum of Understanding covering administrative responsibilities for Royal Air Force Edzell, Royal Air Force Inverbervie and Royal Air Force Kinnaber whilst in occupation by the United States Navy, CINCUS-NAVEURINST 005711.1A CH-9, Confidential. 3 May 2019, apps.dtic.mil.

341 Malcolm Campbell, interview with author 2 November 2019.

342 Facebook, NSGA Edzell Scotland.

343 Arne Simonsen, interview with author 20 December 2019; Mercato, interview.

344 Campbell, interview.

345 Dan Flanagan, interview with author 25 September 2019.

346 'Wullenweber Antenna', Navy CT History, 16 January 2019, navycthistory.com/WullenweberArticle.

347 Jim Louis Parham, interview with author 26 April 2020.

348 Keith Collie, interview with author 3 October 2019.

349 Mac McInness, interview with author 26 August 2019, and Willie Hogg, interview with author 24 August 2019.

350 Reemett, interview.

351 Louise Glen, interview with author 1 December 2019.

352 Collie, interview.

353 Christine Pine, interview by author 27 August 2019.

354 Pine, interview.

355 Hogg, interview.

356 William Calderwood, interview with author 18 March 2021. Dwayne A. Day, 'A flower in the polar sky: the POPPY signals intelligence satellite and ocean surveillance', The Space Review, 28 April 2008, accessed 16 February 2020, www.thespacereview.com/article/1115/1; also, Joseph F. Bouchard, 'Guarding the Cold War Ramparts: The U.S. Navy's Role in Continental Air Defense', Naval War College Review, Summer 1999, accessed 18 August 2019, fas.org; and Jeffrey T. Richelson, 'Specialist Describes US Recon Stats', at CIA Electronic Reading Room, accessed 19 August 2019, www.cia.gov/readingroom/docs.

357 Malcolm Spaven, *Fortress Scotland: A Guide to the Military Presence* (London: Pluto Press/Scottish CND, 1983).
358 Coletta and Bauer, United States Navy and Marine Corps Bases, Overseas, 1985, 105.
359 Andronov, 'The U.S. Navy's 'White Cloud' Spaceborne ELINT System'.
360 Reemett, interview.
361 Mackay, *Scotland the Brave?* 42.
362 Campbell, interview.
363 Marion Summers, interview with author 1 December 2018. Further information on Black Projects can be examined at en.wikipedia.org/wiki/ECHELON.
364 Mercato, interview.
365 Grier, interview.
366 McInness, interview.
367 Bill Carpenter, interview with author 3 October 2019.
368 Morton, interview.
369 Flanagan, interview.
370 Simonsen, interview.
371 Morton, interview.
372 Reemett, interview.
373 Jimmy Grier, interview with author 22 October 2019.
374 Hogg, interview; and McInness, interview.
375 Morton, interview.
376 Morton, interview.
377 Flanagan, interview.
378 Bouchard, 'Guarding the Cold War Ramparts'.
379 Morton, interview.
380 Hogg, interview.
381 Hogg, interview.
382 McInness, interview.
383 Facebook, NSGA Edzell, Scotland.
384 Flanagan, interview.
385 McInness, interview; also, 'Classic Owl', Sensor Reach, 19 November 2020, globalsecurity.org.
386 D.A. Romanov, *Fire at Sea: The Tragedy of the Soviet Submarine Komsomolets*, ed. K.J. Moore, trans. by Jonathan E. Acus (Washington: Potomac Books, Inc., 2006), 183; see also: Hennessy and Jinks, *The Silent Deep*, 8–9, 384, 589–90.
387 Reemett, interview.
388 Simonsen, interview.
389 Mercato, interview.
390 Henry George, interview with author 12 October 2019.
391 Grier, interview.
392 DD12/2847, Folio 142; formal clearance for Inverbervie Tower and Buildings: 21 June 1968, NRS; NAS 21 November 2019. Also, Andronov, 'The U.S. Navy's 'White Cloud' Spaceborne ELINT System'. Also, Aerial view of 17th Surveillance Squadron facilities at RAF Edzell, Scotland; National Archives Identifier: 6500391 Local Identifier: 330-CFD-DF-ST-98-05012.jpeg; Creators: Department of Defense. Department of the Navy. Naval Imaging Command. 1988-ca. 1993; Department of Defense. Defense Audiovisual Agency. 6/21/1979–9/30/1985; Department of Defense. American Forces Information Service. Defense Visual Information Center. 1994–1997.
393 Jackson, interview.
394 Jackson, interview.
395 Flanagan, interview.
396 McInness, interview.
397 'NIE Capability of Soviet General Purpose Forces', CIA Released Documents, faqs.org, 3 May 2019.
398 Carpenter, interview.
399 Carpenter, interview.
400 Hogg, interview.
401 Campbell, p.170.

402 'RAF Edzell', Secret Scotland, accessed 4 February 2018, www.secretscotland.org.uk.

403 Collie, interview.

404 Bryers, 'Scotland's wartime airfields: Conflict and legacy', 45–65; also Edward Knox, interview with author, 2 November 2018.

405 A former senior NSG officer, interview with author 24 November 2019.

406 Jim Barnett, interview with author 19 November 2019.

407 Upgrade at Edzell, Scotland costing $1.4M. Hearings Before and Special Reports Made by Committee on Armed Services of the House of Representatives on Subjects Affecting the Naval and Military Establishments; Author(s) United States. Congress. House. Committee on Armed Services, Publisher U.S. G.P.O. p. 36, Brill.com. Also, DECL: OADR. 218. The U.S. embassy in Great Britain is notified that Kenneth Degraffenreid, Special Assistant to the President for National Security Affairs, will be on an official visit to London, England, and Edzell, Scotland from 9/6-9/11/84. Cable. White House. CONFIDENTIAL. Issue Date: Sep 5, 1984. Reproduced in Declassified Documents Reference System. Document Number: CK3100546789/ 90.

408 Cryptolog, 15.

409 Duke, U.S. Defence Bases in the United Kingdom, 148.

410 Mackay, *Scotland the Brave?* 103.

411 *The Times*, 27 July 1961.

412 Nick McCamley, *Cold War Secret Nuclear Bunker: The Passive Defence of the Western World during the Cold War* (Barnsley: Pen and Sword, 2013). 37.

413 State memo from EUR William R Tyler to The Secretary, Secret, 21 July 1961. Subject: Circular 175: Request for authorisation to Negotiate and Conclude an agreement Concerning Certain Facilities for U.S. Navy in the United Kingdom. (Thurso, Rosyth Clyde – DERs) 711.56341/7-1961. NARA 13 SEP 2006.

414 DOCID 3178942, SECRET, Department of Defense Directive, Defense Special Missile and Astronautics Center (Defense? SMAC), 27 April 1964; 'The NSA component will continue to task and technically control those missile and special intelligence collection activities … and will additionally task and technically control the intercept and processing activities of all DoD components. Also, Folio 5; HO/NDS/THS memo; J Kerr to Mr Fotheringham, 2 July 1968. 'Mr Carmichael UKAEA told me that they have had requests for the lease of 30 of their houses (8 by the Royal Navy, 10 by the U.S. Navy, 6 by GCHQ and 6 by DAFS). NRS 21 November 2019.

415 Duke, U.S. Defence Bases in the United Kingdom, 148.

416 Morton, interview.

417 'Scotland: Duty in Thurso', *All Hands*, February 1972.

418 Mackay, *Scotland the Brave?* 66.

419 Mackay, *Scotland the Brave?* 129.

420 Steve Cady, interview with author 14 October 2019.

421 Cady, interview.

422 Ross Buscemi, interview with author 10 October 2019.

423 Cady, interview.

424 Facebook: NAVCOMMSTA THURSO SCOTLAND UK.

425 Kathleen Scollan, interview with author 12 January 2020.

426 Facebook: NAVCOMMSTA THURSO SCOTLAND UK.

427 Facebook: NAVCOMMSTA THURSO SCOTLAND UK.

428 Wally Nerring, interview with author 10 October 2019.

429 Cady, interview.

430 Facebook: NAVCOMMSTA THURSO SCOTLAND UK.

431 Scottish Office memo to GS Murray and Muir Russell (SEDD?), Secret, 31 July 1975, Subject: US Naval Communications expansion near Thurso. NAS. SEP4/2692.

432 Tom McKeown, interview with author 11 November 2019.

433 Dennis Kolodziej, interview with author 9 October 2019.

434 Giambattista, interview.

435 Spaven, *Fortress Scotland*, 71–5.

436 THE HIGHLAND COUNCIL, PLANNING, DEVELOPMENT, EUROPE AND TOURISM COMMITTEE – 15th May 2006; also WIT Transactions on The Built Environment, Vol 143, © 2014 WIT Press www.witpress.com, ISSN 1743-3509 (on-line); also doi:10.2495/DSHF140281 and Defense Communications Engineering Center

Technical Report No. 7-83, Performance Analysis of Digital LOS Link Mormond Hill-Latheron, UK (M0672), September 1983. Also Chief Johnny Moore, interview with author, November, 25, 2019.

437 Ed Martin, interview with author 25 May 2020.

438 Moore, interview.

439 Kevin McCoy, interview with author 26 November 2019.

440 Joe Coia, interview with author, October 10, 2019.

441 Stan Ogrodnik, interview with author 3 August 2020.

442 Michael R. Ellis, interview with author 24 January 2020.

443 Ellis, interview.

444 Steve Cady, interview.

445 Mark Bubs Whitten, interview with author 14 October 2019.

446 Wyllie Northcutt, interview with author 9 October 2019.

447 George McKenzie, interview with author, 27 March 2006; and Cady, interview.

448 Craig Capaldi, interview with author 10 October 2019.

449 Barnett, interview.

450 Ellis, interview.

451 Sarah Murphy, interview with author 6 January 2020.

452 Nerring, interview.

453 Patrick Derham, interview with author 10 October 2019.

454 Facebook, NAVCOMMSTA THURSO SCOTLAND UK.

455 Facebook, NAVCOMMSTA THURSO SCOTLAND UK.

456 Facebook, NAVCOMMSTA THURSO SCOTLAND UK.

457 'How a Soviet nuclear blast would have wiped out Caithness', *John o' Groats Journal & Caithness Courier*, 17 November 2019; and Royle, *Facing the Bear: Scotland and the Cold War*, 97.

458 ANNEX A TO COS 1311/2/5/72, Probable Nuclear Targets in the United Kingdom Assumption for Planning, Holy Loch, Thurso, 2 May 1972, Top Secret. Also, ANNEX B TO COS 1311/2/5/72. The National Archives.

459 Duke, *United States Military Forces and Installations in Europe*, 181–188: also NARA, RG 218: JCS Message from CINCLANT to CNO, Navy Department, 2 April 1956.

460 Christopher Bluth, *Soviet Strategic Arms Policy before SALT* (Cambridge. Cambridge University Press, 1992), 194–5; and Robert C. Manke, NUWC-NPT Technical Report 11,890; 12 August 2008: Overview of U.S. Navy Antisubmarine Warfare (ASW) Organization During the Cold War Era, Office of the Director of Undersea Warfare, Naval Undersea Warfare Center Division Newport, Rhode Island, 9, 14 November 2020, https://apps.dtic.mil/sti/pdfs/ADA487974.pdf.

461 Ranft and Geoffrey Till, *The Sea in Soviet Strategy*, Second Edition.132.

462 Stanley J. Grabowski Jr., 'A Comparative Analysis of Land-Based Antisubmarine Warfare Operations in the Atlantic: U.S. Army During World War II and the U.S. Navy During the Cold War', Dissertation, Army Command and General Staff Coll Fort Leavenworth KS, 1998.

463 Joel I. Holwitt, 'U.S. Navy, Sub vs. Sub: ASW Lessons from the Cold War', US Naval Institute, Proceedings, Vol. 145/10/1,400, (October 2019), 29 November 2020, https://www.usni.org/magazines/proceedings/2019/october/sub-vs-sub-asw-lessons-cold-war. Also, J. Kneece, Family Treason – The Walker Spy Case (Stein and Day, New York, 1986); also M. Chinworth, 'Strategic Trade Management: The Toshiba Machine Co Case-A View 25 Years Later', *Kokusai Anzenhosho (Journal of International Security)* 32(2) (2004): 17–37; and 'A Bizarre Deal Diverts Vital Tools to Russians', *New York Times*, nytimes.com, 20 January 2020.

464 Holwitt, 'U.S. Navy, Sub vs. Sub: ASW Lessons from the Cold War'.

465 Holwitt, 'U.S. Navy, Sub vs. Sub: ASW Lessons from the Cold War'.

466 Robert C. Manke , 'Overview of U.S. Navy Antisubmarine Warfare (ASW) Organization During the Cold War Era', 12, NUWC-NPT Technical Report 11,890, 12 August 2008: Office of the Director of Undersea Warfare, Naval Undersea Warfare Center Division Newport, Rhode Island, 14 November 2020, https://apps.dtic.mil/sti/pdfs/ADA487974.

467 'The SOund SUrveillance System (SOSUS) provides deep-water long-range detection capability', Federation of American Scientists, 20 June 2006, fas.org: SIPRI Yearbook of World Armaments and Disarmaments 1969/70 (Stockholm: Almqvist & Wiksell, 1970), 317–9: 'Integrated Undersea Surveillance System (IUSS)', Federation of American Scientists, 12 July 2006, fas.org.

468 Don Staunton, 'Looking Back at the Cold War and P-3C Anti-Submarine Warfare (ASW) 40 Years Ago', 37,

Semantic Scholar, 4 October 2020, semanticscholar.org/paper; Mackay, *Scotland the Brave?* 85; also, Collie, interview.

469 Staunton, 'Looking Back at the Cold War and P-3C Anti-Submarine Warfare (ASW) 40 Years Ago', 36–37.

470 L.J. Goldstein and Y.M. Zhukov, 'A Tale of Two Fleets – A Russian Perspective on the 1973 Naval Standoff in the Mediterranean', Naval War College Review (2004); 'Carrier Division 16, Report of ASW Barrier Operations During the Cuban Missile Crisis by Group Built around Randolph, 14 December 1962', *Submarines of October*, National Security Archive Electronic Briefing Book No. 75 (31 Oct 2002), 14 August 2020, gwu.edu; J. Robinson-Leon and W. Burr, 'Chronology of Submarine Contact During the Cuban Missile Crisis', *The Submarines of October*, National Security Archive Electronic Briefing Book No. 75 (31 Oct 2002), 14 August 2020, gwu.edu; P.J. Haney, 'Soccer Fields and Submarines in Cuba', *Naval War College Review*, Vol. L, No. 4 (Autumn 1997); also Letter from CINCLANT, Subject: CINCLANT Historical Account of the Cuban Crisis (U), 29 April 1963, Serial 000119/JO9H, DNSA, [accessed 14 July 2006].

471 Major NATO naval exercises will be held in the Northern Atlantic. Report. DEPARTMENT OF DEFENSE. SECRET. Issue Date: Sep 22, 1964. Reproduced in Declassified Documents Reference System. Document Number: CK3100165870, [accessed 6 December 2005].

472 SIPRI Yearbook 1974, 309–14; also, S. Sontag and C. Drew, *Blind Man's Bluff – The Untold Story of American Submarine Espionage* (Public Affairs, New York, 1998); also Michael D. Roberts, *Dictionary of American Naval Aviation Squadrons*, Volume 2, Chapter 3 Patrol Squadron (VP) Histories (2nd VP-29 to 1st VP-40). (Washington, D.C.: Naval Historical Center, Department of the Navy, 2000), 200–3. 'Nuclear Depth Charges: New Weapons for Coastal Command', *Glasgow Herald*, 2 April 1962; Keith Grint, *Leadership: Limits and Possibilities* (London: Macmillan International Higher Education, 2005), 43.

473 Bouchard, 'Guarding the Cold War Ramparts'. Also, Staunton, 'Looking Back at the Cold War and P-3C Anti-Submarine Warfare (ASW) 40 Years Ago', 34.

474 Staunton, 'Looking Back at the Cold War and P-3C Anti-Submarine Warfare (ASW) 40 Years Ago', 38.

475 Bouchard, 'Guarding the Cold War Ramparts'.

476 Tyler Rogoway, 'Confessions Of A U.S. Navy P-3 Orion Maritime Patrol Pilot'. Jalopnik, 7 February 2014, accessed 3 June 2020, https://foxtrotalpha.jalopnik.com/confessions-of-a-pilot-behind-the-us-navys-airborne-sub-1598415741.

477 Staunton, 'Looking Back at the Cold War and P-3C Anti-Submarine Warfare (ASW) 40 Years Ago', 40.

478 Staunton, 'Looking Back at the Cold War and P-3C Anti-Submarine Warfare (ASW) 40 Years Ago', 31.

479 Grabowski, 'A Comparative Analysis of Land-Based Antisubmarine Warfare Operations in the Atlantic', 12; also, 'Man with a Mission', *All Hands*, April 1980.

480 Rogoway, 'Confessions'.

481 'Man with a Mission', *All Hands*, April 1980.

482 Bouchard, 'Guarding the Cold War Ramparts'. Also telegram from Dean Rusk, Secretary of State to American Embassy, London, Top Secret, 9 June 1961, Embtel 3479, Joint State-Defense Message. 711.56341/7-1961. NARA 13 SEP 2006; also, Arkin and Handler, 'Naval Accidents 1945–1988', 46.

483 Bouchard, 'Guarding the Cold War Ramparts'.

484 Hansard, HC Deb 23 November 1999 vol 339 cc590–8.

485 Mackay, *Scotland the Brave?* 93, 119, 120.

486 'E-4B', U.S. Air Force, accessed 4 October 2020, https://www.af.mil/About-Us/Fact-Sheets/Display/Article/104503/e-4b/; 'Doomsday Jets Increase in Cost', Spartanburg Herald-Journal. Associated Press. 5 November 1973, https://news.google.com/newspapers; and 'History of the Post Attack Command and Control System (PACCS)', SAC Airborne Command Control Association, accessed 10 April 2021, https://sac-acca.com.

487 Mackay, *Scotland the Brave?* 136.

488 '2 ACCS: 2nd Airborne Command and Control Squadron', Post Attack Command & Control System (PACCS), accessed 8 March 2021, https://2accs.com/?page_id=456.

489 Mackay, *Scotland the Brave?* 122.

490 'Old Tacamo', Tacamo: Our Props Never Stop, accessed 20 March 2020, www.vaq34.com/oldtacamo.

491 Chico Buffone, interview with author 19 March 2020.

492 R. Aldridge, *First Strike! The Pentagon's Strategy for Nuclear War* (Boston, MA: South End Press, 1983).

493 The Great Soviet Encyclopaedia, 1979 (Moscow: Sovetskaya Entsikilopediya, 1979).

494 Mackay, *Scotland the Brave?* 119, 120.

495 Memo from Mrs HD Harrison MOD to Miss Nicol SDD, 28th May 1964, AF/A1629/64/S.13d (Air), … technical site at Inverbervie, NRS.; also, DD12/2847, Folio 142; formal clearance for Inverbervie Tower and Buildings: 21 June 1968, NRS; NAS 21 November 2019.

496 Mackay, *Scotland the Brave?* 131.

497 Defense Communications Engineering Center Technical Report No. 7-83, Performance Analysis of Digital LOS Link Mormond Hill-Latheron, UK (M0672), September 1983; Mackay, *Scotland the Brave?* 130.

498 Morton, interview; Campbell, *The Unsinkable Aircraft Carrier.*

499 Mackay, *Scotland the Brave?* 130.

500 Mackay, *Scotland the Brave?* 131; also, personal experience of the author.

501 'Ballistic Missile Early Wa rning System', Wikipedia, accessed 18 May 2020, https://en.wikipedia.org/wiki/Ballistic_Missile_Early_Warning_System#Background.

502 Mackay, *Scotland the Brave?* 128.

503 'North Atlantic Radio System', Wikipedia, accessed 27 May 2018, https://en.wikipedia.org/; Aldridge, First Strike!;and 'About the NARS Sites: Mormond Hill/44', accessed 16 December 2019, www.northatlanticradiosystem.com.

504 Royle, *Facing the Bear: Scotland and the Cold War*, 3.

505 Memorandum, Hansen to Director of Operations, Resumption of ECM Flights in the Baltic Sea, 26 October 1951, Top Secret, Brill, NLS.

506 'Project Robin', Spyflight, 24 November 2019, https://spyflight.co.uk/operations/#Project_Robin; also Foreign Relations of the United States, Volume X July – September 1960 : The RB-47 Airplane Incident – Editorial Note; and Richard J. Aldrich, The Hidden Hand: Britain, America and Cold War Secret Intelligence (London: John Murray, 2001), 537.

507 Doug Gordon, *USAF Tactical Reconnaissance in the Cold War* (Barnsley: Leo Cooper, 2005), 75.

508 Aldrich, *The Hidden Hand*, 539, and Jackson, *Strike Force*, 66–7.

509 Jackson, *Strike Force*, 71.

510 Jackson, *Strike Force*, 147, and Royle, *Facing the Bear: Scotland and the Cold War*, 52.

511 Peter Berry, *Prestwick Airport and Scottish Aviation* (Stroud: Tempus, 2005), 88.

512 Berry, Prestwick Airport, 9, 103. 'Reliability', Glasgow Prestwick Airport, 24 November 2019, glasgowprestwick.com; Jackson, *Strike Force*, 31–2, 43, 177; also John Watson, interview with author 15 December 2019;

513 'Prestwick', Airfields of Britain Conservation Trust, 8 May 2020, https://www.abct.org.uk/airfields/airfield-finder/prestwick/; and 'Military Air Transport Service', 21 November 2019, wikipedia.org/wiki.

514 Peter Berry, *Prestwick Airport and Scottish Aviation* (Stroud: Tempus, 2005), 10, 74, 76, 109, 122.

515 'First helicopter flight across the Atlantic by 2 Sikorsky H19's of the USAF in 1952', Scran 15 June 2021, scran.ac.uk. 'First Helicopter Crossing of the Atlantic Ocean', *Ohio History Central*, 2 August 2021, ohiohistorycentral.org.

516 Robert F. Dorr, 'Manifestly Multirole' Sikorsky's H-19 series, in *Air International,* April 1992.

517 'Rotors over the Atlantic', *Flight 15*, August 1962 edition; also, 'H-19A Trans Atlantic Flight', USAF Rotorheads, 6 February 2021, rotorheadsos.us.

518 *Scottish Daily Mail*, 3 March 1960.

519 Coletta and Bauer, United States Navy and Marine Corps Bases, Overseas, 1985, 278–80: Berry, Prestwick Airport, 83; also 67th Special Operations Squadron (SOS), Global Security, 4 November 2019, www.globalsecirity.org; Glasgow Prestwick Airport, Glasgow Prestwick, 30 January 2019, glasgowprestwick.com.

520 Berry, *Prestwick Airport*, 83.

521 Project Magnet (USN), Wikipedia; Berry, *Prestwick Airport*, 96, photo 15.

522 '1370PMG', Aerial Survey and Photomapping History, 16 June 2021, 1370th.org; Berry, *Prestwick Airport*, 79.

523 US Embassy telegram 339 to Royal Norwegian Ministry for Foreign Affairs, Oslo, 27 April, 1953, Al Walcker, Aerial Survey and Photomapping History,18 July 2021, 1370th.org; also, Final Report, Project 53-AFS-1, Phase 1, 1 October 1953, 1370th Photomapping Group History 1955–1958, 16 June 2021, and Station Description, Project 53-AFS-1, 1370th Photomapping Group History 1955–1958, 16 June 2021, 1370th.org/55srw/AW/AW.html; also, Al Walcker, at same, 13, 14, 15, AERIAL Surveyors Revise the World's Geography; Boeing B-50 Superfortress, Wiki.

524 Project Magnet (USN), Wikipedia.

525 State of the Union Address, 30 January 1961, John F. Kennedy Presidential Library and Museum, 4 March 2020, www.jfklibrary.org.

526 Allen R. Schollin, 'BIG LIFT BOON, BOONDOGGLE OR BUST?' *Air Force Magazine*, December 1963. 35.

527 Berry, *Prestwick Airport*, 82, 98, 113.

528 Berry, *Prestwick Airport*, 83.

529 Berry, *Prestwick Airport and Scottish Aviation*, 76.

530 NRL Memorandum Report 1422: A Proposal for an Operational HF Radar, F.M. Gager, R.C. Guthrie, J.M. Headrick, I.H. Page and E.N. Zettle, Radar Division, 10 May 1963. US Naval Research Laboratory, Washington DC.

531 Prestwick, Airfields of Britain Conservation Trust, at https://www.abct.org.uk/airfields/airfield-finder/prestwick/ [accessed 8 May 2020].

532 David L. Haulman, 'Operation New Tape', in *Short War: Major USAF Contingency Operations 1947–1997*, ed. A. Timothy Warnock (Maxwell AFB: Air University Press, 2000) 23, 24.

533 Mackay, *Scotland the Brave?* 35.

534 CIA, OXCART Reconnaissance of Tallinn Sites, 1967, Top Secret Oxcart, at CIA Electronic FOIA Reading Room, Document No. 0001471955, 6 May 2019, www.foia.cia.gov; also, Draft Memorandum, unknown to SA/PC/DCI – Mr. Bissell, Aerial Reconnaissance of the USSR, 15 May 1954, Top Secret. Brill, NLS.

535 Pedlow and Welzenbach. *The Central Intelligence Agency and Overhead Reconnaissance: The U-2 and OXCART Programs, 1954–1974*, 51, 91, 207.

536 US Air Force Memorandum, Summary of USAFE Ferret 52–8, 29 September 1952, Top Secret, NARA; Collection US Intelligence on Europe, 1945–1995. Brill.com.

537 67 Special Operations Squadron (AFSOC), Air Force Historical Research Agency, afhra.af.mil, 19 June 2021; also, Bob Broff, interview with author, 3 August 2021.

538 Broff, interview.

539 History of the USNS *Maurice Rose*, justinmuseum.com 14 May 2021.

540 Helis.com.

541 Usafunithistory.com.

542 Berry, *Prestwick Airport*, 75.

543 Broff interview.

544 'N.A.T.O Airbase in Kintyre', *Glasgow Herald*, 28 April 1959; 'Fleet Air Arm Naval Air Stations RNAS – Machrihanish', Fleet Air Officers Association, 17 June 2018, fleetairarmoa.org; also, 'History', Machrihanish Airbase Community Company, 22 November 2020, Machrihanish.org/history; 'Machrihanish Airfield', Canmore, 18 May 2020, Canmore.org.uk.

545 NAS, DD12/3064=P/SLR/10/AL/18/1, Urgent Telex from Ronayne, Admiralty, to Gillett, Room 505, Subject: Machrihanish-Brief for Lord Forces' Visit to Campbeltown on 4 May 1959, dated 30 April 1959. Also, ANNEX A TO COS 1311/2/5/72, Probable Nuclear Targets in the United Kingdom Assumption for Planning, Holy Loch, Thurso, 2 May 1972, Top Secret. Also ANNEX B TO COS 1311/2/5/72, The National Archives.

546 Author personal experience – lived in Campbeltown 2005–06.

547 'Campbeltown OFD Site', The Oil and Pipelines Agency, 22 October 2020, www.gov.uk/government/organisations; 'Machrihanish Airfield', Canmore, 18 May 2020, Canmore.org.uk.

548 Duke, Simon, US Defence Bases in the United Kingdom, 148–149.

549 'N.A.T.O Airbase in Kintyre', *Glasgow Herald*, 28 April 1959.

550 History of the Custody and Development of Nuclear Weapons (U), July 1945 through September 1977, Prepared by Office of the Assistant to the Secretary of Defense (Atomic Energy) February 1978, 59.

551 Ken Black, interview with author 19 October 2020.

552 Tom Hillman, interview with author 28 November 2019.

553 Mackay, *Scotland the Brave?* 138., Campbell, *The Unsinkable Aircraft Carrier*; also 'The Oil and Pipelines Agency', at gov.uk, 10 February 2021, www.gov.uk/government/organisations.

554 'Machrihanish Airfield, Technical Site and United States Navy Nswu 2 Seals Training Establishment', at Canmore, 18 May 2020, conmore,org.uk; also, Jim Madison, interview with author 11 December 2019.

555 'Machrihanish Airfield, Technical Site And United States Navy Nswu 2 Seals Training Establishment', at Canmore, 18 May 2020, canmore,org.uk; also, Jim Madison, interview with author 11 December 2019.

556 Author's personal experience.

557 'Helocast', at Helocast, Wikipedia, 28 June 2020, https://en.wikipwia.orh/wiki/helocast; Madison interview.

558 Fulton Recovery System, Special Forces History at https://www.specialforceshistory.info/terms/fulton-recovery-system.html [accessed 19 January 2021].

559 RAF Machrihanish.

560 DM (frmr RNAD) Glen Douglas, Wikimapia, 4 December 2020, wikimapia.org/324948; Secret Scotland Glen Douglas Munitions Depot, 10 December 2020, secretscotland.org.uk/index.php/Secrets/GlenDouglasMunitions-

Depot.

561 NAS, AF79/70, Letter from Graham-Campbell, Forestry Commission Scotland, to J. Walker, Department of Agriculture for Scotland, Subject: Craggan Farm (part) Glen Douglas, Dunbartonshire, 8 May 1956, 108680/L/SLR/ AD/GD/S, 229/25, Unclassified: Letter from Ian Orr-Ewing MP, Civil Lord of the Admiralty, to Gilmour Leburn MP, Department of Agriculture, 2 December 1959; letter from Gilmour Leburn MP, Department of Agriculture, to Ian Orr-Ewing MP, Civil Lord of the Admiralty, 15 December 1959.

562 Facebook; U.S. Navy Minemen.

563 Ron Swart, interview with author, 21 April 2020.

564 CNO (OP-374). OPNAVNOTE 5400, Ser 515/OU603911, 21 February 1990, MOMAG DET TWO (2) Machrihanish, UK; MOMAG DET FOUR (4) Glen Douglas, UK. 176, 15 March 2020, apps.dtic.mil.

565 Facebook; U.S. Navy Minemen.

566 Facebook; U.S. Navy Minemen.

567 George Bellairs, interview with author 17 July 2019.

568 Swart, interview.

569 Facebook, hartshorn.us/Navy.

570 Swart, interview.

571 Grant Hoefer, interview with author 6 May 2020; also, CNO (OP-374). OPNAVNOTE 5400, Ser 515/OU603911, 21 February 1990, MOMAG DET TWO (2) Machrihanish, UK; MOMAG DET FOUR (4) Glen Douglas, UK. 176, 15 March 2020, apps.dtic.mil.

572 Murray, interview.

573 Hogg.

574 Gan Starling, interview with author 11 December 2019.

575 Facebook, RAF Machrihanish.

576 Derek Gillies, interview with author 16 November 2019.

577 'RAF Machrihanish Aurora Spyplane,' Above Top Secret, accessed 23 June 2019, http://www.abovetopsecret.com/.

578 'RAF Machrihanish Aurora Spyplane'.

579 'Runway', Discover Space UK, accessed 16 February 2021, http://www.discoverspaceuk.com/runway.php.

580 ANNEX A TO COS 1311/2/5/72, Probable Nuclear Targets in the United Kingdom Assumption for Planning, Holy Loch, Thurso, 2 May 1972, Top Secret. Also ANNEX B TO COS 1311/2/5/72, The National Archives.

581 Soviet Military Power (Washington DC: US Government Printing Office, 1981) 90.

582 Cold War Intelligence, advisor: M.M. Aid, Leiden and Boston: Brill, 2013 http://primarysources.brillonline.com/browse/cold-war-intelligence ; also Matthew M. Aid, The Soviet Target: the U.S. Intelligence Community Versus the USSR: 1945–1991 (Washington, D.C., August 2012).

583 Robert W. Pringle, Historical dictionary of Russian and Soviet Intelligence. (Lanham MD: Rowman & Littlefield, 2015).

584 PREM 11/4721, TOP SECRET, Minute from Sir Burke Trend to Prime Minister, 17 March 1964; also PREM 11/4721, Top Secret, Memo from Prime Minister to Cabinet Office, 24 March 1964, The National Archives.

585 Andrew and Gordievsky, KGB: The Inside Story, 512; and NIE Capability of Soviet General Purpose Forces, National Intelligence Estimate Number 11.14.65, 21 October 1965, Top Secret.

586 'Cold War Warriors', Emmitsburg News-Journal, 19 July 2020, Emmitsburg.net/archive_list.

587 Mike Archbold, interview with author 13 November 2020; also Ullapool Harbour Trust; and 'Exhibition recalls the klondykers' invasion', Hebrides News, 29 May 2015; and John MacKaig, interview with author, 10 December 2019.

588 National Photographic Interpretation Center: Imagery Analysis Report, Soviet Primorye-Class Intelligence Collection Ships (S), SECRET, Z-14096/84, IAR 0045/84, December 1984, CIA.

589 'Caps of Soviet Civilian Maritime Fleets', Under the Red Star, 21 March 2020; undertheredstar.com/nonmvdmarine.htm.

590 Fishingboatheritage.co.uk.

591 MacKaig, interview.

592 Archbold, interview.

593 Confirmed by personal experience of the author.

594 Alan Judd, interview with author 27 May 2020.

595 Judd, interview.

596 Viktor Suvorov, Aquarium: The Career and Defection of a Soviet Military Spy (London: Hamish Hamilton, 1985)

and *Spetsnaz: The Story Behind the Soviet SAS* (London: Hamish Hamilton, 1987).

597 Soviet Military Power (Washington DC: US Government Printing Office, 1981) 93.

598 Ian Bruce, 'Scots bases were prime targets for sabotage Spetsnaz forces set to strike at Clyde', *The Herald*, 14th September 1999.

599 Judd, interview. Douglas H. Wise, interview with author 22 April 2019.

600 Author's personal experience, and Bruce, 'Scots bases'.

601 Andrew and Gordievsky, *KGB: The Inside Story*, 532.

602 Andrew and Gordievsky, *KGB: The Inside Story*, 473/4.

603 Nick Anning and John Sweeney, 'Found: gaping hole that sank the Gaul', *The Guardian* 7 Feb 1999; David Pallister, 'MI6 link to sunken trawler revealed', *The Guardian*, 30 Sep 2000.

604 'US Base for North Scotland; Another Link in DEW Line', *Glasgow Herald*, 27 July 1961.

605 Aid and Wiebes, 'Conclusion', in *Secrets of Signals Intelligence*, 316–9.

606 Andrew and Mitrokhin, *The Mitrokhin Archive*, 268; also John Prados, 'The Navy's Biggest Betrayal', *Naval History Magazine*, June 2010.

607 Andrew and Mitrokhin, The Mitrokhin Archive, 268; also, John Prados, 'The Navy's Biggest Betrayal', *Naval History Magazine*, Volume 24, Number 3, June 2010, https://www.usni.org/magazines/naval-history-magazine/2010/june/navys-biggest-betrayal.

608 Bill Studeman, interview with author 1 September 2020.

609 Stephen Engelberg, 'U.S. Officials fear spy ring in Navy pierced radio link', *New York Times*, 14 July 1985, Section 1, Page 1; George C. Wilson, John Mintz etc, 'Spy Ring Damage Called "Serious," Not "Disastrous." ' *Washington Post*, 7 June, 1985.

610 Richard J. Aldrich, *GCHQ: An Uncensored Story of Britain's Most Secret Intelligence Agency* (London: Harper Press, 2010), 377.

611 Soviet Military Power (Washington DC: US Government Printing Office, 1981) 93.

612 'Mick McGahey (1963 STUC speech opposing Polaris)', Scotland's Greatest Speeches, *The Scotsman*, 24 October 2011.

613 *The Guardian* (1959–2003); London (UK). 24 June 1967: 3.

614 'Seven years for "little fish" spy', *The Guardian*, 24 June 1967: 'McAffer says he spied for Britain and US', *Glasgow Herald*, 6 September 1967. p. 7 and 'Sailor convicted in security case', *The Bulletin*. Bend, Oregon. 26 August 1967. p. 5.

615 Martin Hastings, interview with author, 30 November, 2019.

616 Jim Findlay, interview with author 21 November 2020.

617 Hennessy and Jinks, *The Silent Deep*, 342–344.

618 Andrew and Gordievsky, *KGB: The Inside Story*, 442.

619 Memorandum for the Secretary of the Navy; Subj: Navy Participation in increase program of SIGINT for CUBA (S); Top Secret DINAR, Cuban Missile Crisis Document Archive 1962, NSA Declassified Documents at https://www.nsa.gov/Portals/70/documents/news-features/declassified-documents/cuban-missile-crisis/19_july_memo_sec_nav.pdf [accessed 4 June 2020]; and Robert M. Beer, 'The U.S. Navy and the Cuban Missile Crisis', United States Naval Academy, Annapolis: 22 May 1990, U.S. N.A. -TSFR; 165 (1990), 177.

620 Beer, *The U.S. Navy and the Cuban Missile Crisis*, 42.

621 Signal from DIRNSA to USAFSS, CUBASA, DIRNAVSECGRU, 5 October 1962, TOP SECRET DINAR.

622 Beer, *The U.S. Navy and the Cuban Missile Crisis*, 38–9.

623 Beer, *The U.S. Navy and the Cuban Missile Crisis*, 177, and 'Thirteen Days? The Navy Security Group in the Cuban Missile Crisis', Station Hypo, accessed 14 March 2020, stationhypo.com.

624 Thomas R. Johnson, *American Cryptology during the Cold War, 1945–1989: Book II: Centralization Wins, 1960–1972* (National Security Agency: Center for Cryptological History, 1995), Top Secret Umbra, Excised copy.

625 *The Cuban Missile Crisis, 1962: Selected Foreign Policy Documents from the Administration of John F. Kennedy, January 1961 to November 1962* (London: The Stationery Office, 2001), pp. 62–3.

626 Johnson, *American Cryptology during the Cold War, 1945–1989: Book II: Centralization Wins, 1960–1972*, 331.

627 DTIC ADA 227065, The U.S. Navy and the Cuban Missile Crisis, A Scholar Trident Project Report No. 165 (US Naval Academy Annapolis, MD, 1990); The Cuban Missile Crisis, 1962, Selected Foreign Policy Documents, 82.

628 Steven Cashmore, David Bews, *Dounreay – The Cold War Connection* (1999), at Highland Archives; https://www.caithnessarchives.org.uk/dounreay/coldwar2.htm ; accessed 15 October 2019.

629 Johnson, *American Cryptology during the Cold War, 1945–1989: Book II: Centralization Wins, 1960–1972*, 331.

630 Douglas H. Wise interview.

631 Robert Lynn Wortmann and George T. Fraser, *History of Canadian Signals Intelligence and Direction Finding* (Ottawa ON: Nanlyn, 2005), and Beer, *The U.S. Navy and the Cuban Missile Crisis*, 42.

632 Bouchard, 'Guarding the Cold War Ramparts', 59. Also, 'CINCLANT Historical Account of Cuban Crisis 1962', 29 April 1963, Commander in Chief Atlantic, Operational Archives, Naval Historical Center.

633 Arthur Grant, interview with author 15 May 2015.

634 ADA 227065, A Trident Scholar Project Report, No 165, the U.S. Navy and the Cuban Missile Crisis, United States Naval Academy, Annapolis, Maryland, 22 May 1990.

635 Mortimer, *Experiencing War*.

636 Beer, The U.S. Navy and the Cuban Missile Crisis, 148. Also, ADA 227065, A Trident Scholar Project Report, No 165.

637 Mackay, *Scotland the Brave?* 55.

638 'Kenneth P. O'Donnell Biography', John F. Kennedy Presidential Library & Museum, 16 October 2020, jfklibrary. org; also, David Talbot, Brothers: *The Hidden History of the Kennedy Years* (New York: Simon & Schuster, 2007), 293; also, 'White House Chief of Staff', Wikipedia, 3 October 2020, en.wikipedia.org/wiki/White_House_Chief_ of_Staff.

639 Department of State Intelligence Note; from Roger Hilsman to The Secretary; Moscow Pushes Drive for Air Links to Havana, 17 October 1962, Confidential.

640 'NSA Briefing Book 749', published 17 Mar 2021, nsarchive.gwu.edu/briefing-book, accessed 8 April 2021.

641 The Cuban Missile Crisis, 1962, Selected Foreign Policy Documents, 221.

642 Johnson, *American Cryptology during the Cold War, 1945–1989: Book II: Centralization Wins, 1960–1972*.

643 'Oral History: Linda & Gerry Pursley, Holy Loch Naval Base, Argyll & Bute U.S. Navy', interview with SCRAN, 19 June 2020.

644 'Navy in Holy Loch', *The Herald*, 21 August 2019; 'Phoney war and peace', *The Herald*, 30th November 2019.

645 Pursley, SCRAN interview.

646 Facebook, 'Navy in Holy Loch', George Klein 21 August 2019.

647 'Oral History: Joseph Schmidt, Holy Loch Naval Base, U.S. Navy Dunoon resident', interview with SCRAN, 19 June 2020.

648 'Caps of Soviet Civilian Maritime Fleets'.

649 Facebook, Navy in Holy Loch.

650 'Lizzie Lamb: From One Heilan' Lassie to Another!' at https://lizzielamb.co.uk/2017/03/04/ from-one-heilan-las-sie-to-another/#comment-7831, accessed 3 December 2020.

651 Author's personal experience.

652 Memorandum, Top Secret, NSA, 28 November 1962; at https://www.nsa.gov/Portals/70/documents/news-fea-tures/declassified-documents/cuban-missile-crisis/11_december_cover_letter.pdf [accessed 3 March 2020].

653 Memorandum from Malinovsky and Zakharov to Khrushchev on deployment of Soviet Forces to Cuba, 24 May 1962, Top Secret, https://nsarchive2.gwu.edu/NSAEBB/NSAEBB449/docs, accessed 12 May 2020.

654 'U.S. Navy at War 1941–1945: Official Reports by Fleet Admiral Ernest J. King, USN', 2, 78, 89, 216–217; www. ibiblio.org, accessed 24 June 2021:also, Spartacus Educational, www.spartacus-educational.com, accessed 24 June 2021.

655 Royle, *Facing the Bear: Scotland and the Cold War*, 142.

656 Soviet Military Power (Washington DC: US Government Printing Office, 1981) 91.

657 United States Navy. 'Navy Fact File: Extremely Low Frequency Transmitter Site Clam Lake, Wisconsin', fas.org [accessed 28 November 2020].

658 Courtien, Christie and Linville.